THE

CANCER
RECOVERY
EATING
PLAN

⁊ࡉ

THE RIGHT FOODS TO HELP
FUEL YOUR RECOVERY

Daniel W. Nixon, M.D.
with Jane A. Zanca

Produced by Alison Brown Cerier
Book Development, Inc.

To Gayle Nixon, RN,
and
to the late Dr. Bill Quillian
—D.W.N.

To Amanda and Jesse
—J.A.Z.

This book cannot and must not replace hands-on medical care or the specific advice of your doctor. Use it instead to help you ask the right questions, make the right choices, and work more closely with your doctor and the other members of your health-care team.

Copyright © 1994 by Daniel W. Nixon, M.D., and Alison Brown Cerier Book Development, Inc.

All rights reserved under International and Pan-American Copyright Conventions. Published in the United States by Times Books, a division of Random House, Inc., New York, and simultaneously in Canada by Random House of Canada Limited, Toronto.

Library of Congress Cataloging-in-Publication Data

Nixon, Daniel W.
    The cancer recovery eating plan / Daniel Nixon, with Jane A. Zanca.—1st ed.
            p.   cm.
        ISBN 0-8129-1983-1
        1. Cancer—Diet therapy.   2. Cancer—Nutritional aspects.
    I. Zanca, Jane A.   II. Title.
    RC271.D52N55   1994
    616.99'40654—dc20   94-911

Produced by Alison Brown Cerier Book Development, Inc.
Book design by Chris Welch
Manufactured in the United States of America

9 8 7 6 5 4 3 2
First Edition

FOREWORD

છે

One of the most revolutionary and promising fields of research is that of chemoprevention: the use of micro- or macronutrients, often found in foods, that can prevent, stop, or retard the process of cancer development. Today, the National Cancer Institute has almost forty studies in the area of nutrition that involve fiber, fat, micronutrients, and vitamins. In 1993, over forty abstracts on cancer/nutrition research were sent to the American Association for Cancer Research. These studies are giving us critical information on the substances we may need to add to or eliminate from our diets to help battle cancer.

Every year over 1 million Americans are diagnosed with cancer (excluding skin cancer and in situ cervical cancer) and 500,000 Americans die from it. We now know that the cause of more than 70 percent of malignancies may be in some way related to what we eat; this is true of lung cancer in nonsmokers as well as colon cancer. Every year more evidence accumulates revealing that what we eat has a tremendous influence on whether we will develop cancer. And while the link between diet and cancer is more obvious when we're talking about prevention—preventing cancer in the first place should always be our primary goal—a new body of evidence is emerging showing that what we eat can even have a substantial impact on our ability to fight cancer once it has already developed.

This is a tremendously exciting field of scientific inquiry. While preliminary results are strongly suggestive, it will be years—perhaps even decades—before we have the definitive answers about the cancer/nutrition relationship. Why has it taken the medical community so long to appreciate the connection between diet and cancer? I believe there are several reasons. First, as a nation we tend to focus first on technology. Early in the history of our fight against cancer, in the absence of information on the etiology of cancer, researchers put most of their efforts into developing more effective treatments for battling cancer. Second, perhaps by our very human nature we have been a bit reluctant to investigate the nutrition/cancer connection; admitting that there is a strong relationship between what we eat and whether we get sick means admitting that we may have played a significant role in creating our own illness—not a comforting thought. Also, nutritional sciences have often been considered "soft sciences." Finally, most doctors are regrettably undereducated about the connection between what we eat and our health. Most medical students receive little or no training in nutrition, despite the fact that seven of the top ten causes of death in the United States are related to what we eat. Most doctors, therefore, don't spend time teaching their patients how to eat healthfully—nor does our current health insurance structure reimburse them for doing so. The rising incidence of cancers that may be diet-related indicates that we are all paying the price for this shortsightedness. It is my hope that this new body of research will encourage the medical community to refocus its efforts on nutrition as a key tool in prevention and treatment.

My own experience in cancer research has given me a privileged perspective on the evolution of our understanding of the connection between diet and cancer. When I became Director of the National Cancer Institute in 1980, our focus on the applied sciences was still very much on developing more potent methods of chemotherapy and radiotherapy with fewer side effects. Our major investment was in the science of molecular biology, feeling then as we do now that understanding the causes of cancer at the molecular level was even more important to intelligent prevention than to effective treatment. Promising studies indicating that certain foods and substances in foods were effective in preventing and even halting the progress of cancer suggested a new focus for research.

In 1983, my staff and I started the Division of Cancer Prevention and Control (DCPC) at NCI, whose goal was to develop cancer prevention programs including new efforts in chemoprevention. From 1987 to 1989, Dan Nixon worked with me at NCI. I was very proud to be able to support Dr. Nixon as he supervised the Cancer Prevention Research Program of the DCPC. This included development of the Cancer Nutrition Laboratory, which studied the mechanisms of cancer prevention in animals and *in vitro,* the Chemoprevention Branch, the Diet and Nutrition Branch, and the Cancer Prevention Studies Branch. I was particularly impressed with Dr. Nixon's groundbreaking work in overseeing extensive trials in Finnish and Chinese populations—studies that have given us extremely valuable data on the cancer-nutrition link. (Many people don't realize that NCI is an international institute that supports research all over the world.)

I think the next decade will bring exciting new information that will help us use nutrition as an increasingly effective tool in combatting cancer. The investment the NCI made in molecular biology has paid off handsomely. We are now able to define precise genetic lesions that put people at risk for getting specific cancers. There is a certain urgency in this. We need more information and need it rapidly on how to help these people avoid cancer. These kinds of data can only come from a substantial investment in large-scale clinical trials that are expensive to conduct. As we identify those high-risk groups, we need to develop and test specific preventive strategies to help minimize that risk. Changing the way those individuals eat could be a large part of that preventive strategy.

As we wait for the results of studies in progress, readers will be able to learn about the state of the art in this book. In this essential reference, Dan Nixon clarifies what we know and do not know about the relationship of food and cancer. He describes the emerging body of research that supports his recommendations of specific diets for specific types of cancer, and offers readers a responsible, sensible plan of action to help them work more effectively with their health-care team to fight cancer—and perhaps prevent a recurrence. It is essential that people with cancer understand that nutrition can be an important adjunct to cancer treatment.

Louis Pasteur stated, "Science and its applications are so closely intertwined that they can be likened to a tree and the fruit it bears." Today the fruits of our research are the astonishing advances in cancer prevention and treatment over the last decade.

One of the most important messages of this book is that there is important work you, as someone with cancer, can do to help speed your recovery. I hope this book will make you a more active participant in your health-care team and wish you all the best for a healthy future.

—Vincent T. DeVita, Jr., M.D., *director, Yale Cancer Center, New Haven, Connecticut; former director, National Cancer Institute*

ACKNOWLEDGMENTS

&

Many individuals have contributed their experience, ideas, and energies to the creation of this book.

First, I wish to thank my wife, Gayle Nixon, R.N., for her invaluable help with the entire manuscript, and particularly the sections on dietary modifications, shopping, food selection and the menus. Chapters 9 and 10 (the "how-to" chapters) are based on her experience.

Jane A. Zanca helped greatly with the process of translating complicated medical information into a form that everyone can understand.

Chef Mark Erickson developed wonderful recipes for you to enjoy. His culinary creativity turned nutritional requirements into great food.

Several health professionals and nutritionists have helped with the book. Dr. Ann Foltz contributed most of the suggestions in the chapter "Solving Nutrition Problems and Improving Well-being During Treatment." Mary Hitchings, M.S., R.D., and Dorothy Slater, M.S., R.D., created the recipes in that chapter and shared their nutritional expertise. Cindy Painter analyzed most of the recipes and menus.

Dr. Bill Quillian contributed to several parts of this book, particularly those concerning psychological aspects, and also to the chapter about exercise. His recent untimely death took away a very special physician and friend.

Jane Chandler read and critiqued the breast cancer chapter. Chika Oraka, R.D., gave helpful suggestions as did Margaret Fowler, R.D., and Catharine Kearns, R.D. Billie Parker and Mary Jo Bumpers were also very helpful.

A large number of friends prepared and tasted the recipes in the book and made helpful modifications, including Shirley Ballou; Bill and C. T. Biggers; Betty and Karen Calloway; Boyd and Daphne Eaton; Hilton, Beth, Margaret, and Peggy Fuller; Bob, Kevin, and Grey Irwin; Virginia M. Kincaid; Tom and Jo Koch; Clay and Barbara Moore; Mary Ann Nall; Lanny and Kristen Nixon; Marvin Alan Nixon; Laura and Ray Patterson; Pargen and Lauralee Robertson; Jeanne Frazier; Betty Robinson; members of the Druid Hills Garden Club; and members of the New York State Breast Cancer Dietary Intervention Project Steering Committee. Theresa Jones and Janette Benson cooked many of the recipes for several complete dinners. Karen Kuehl, M.D., Ken Resnikow, Ph.D., and the Kelloggs' Kids Cholesterol Club provided expertise and ideas about dietary modification.

Finally, I owe special thanks to my patients, who have taught me, and continue to teach me, a great deal about recovery from cancer.

CONTENTS

❧

PART 1

CANCER AND NUTRITION

1

FUELING
YOUR RECOVERY

੨ৡ

All I maintain is that on this earth there are pestilences and there are
victims, and it's up to us, so far as possible, not to join forces with
the pestilences.

Albert Camus, *The Plague*

Cancer is clearly one of the major pestilences of all time.
Over 500,000 Americans die from cancer every year. Fortunately, cancer research has begun to decipher some of
the mysteries of malignant diseases, which have baffled physicians
for centuries. We now understand that cancer develops over a period
of time; it does not just suddenly appear. We also know that diet
can play a role not only in the development of certain cancers, but
also in the growth and progression of cancers after they have developed. This is why the quotation above from Camus is so pertinent.
If research indicates that certain dietary habits may help cancer to
develop and grow, we don't have to join forces with the cancer and
continue to eat that way.

People have known for a long time that good nutrition is vital to
health. There's even an old saying about it: "You are what you eat."
There has been lore about food and herbal cures since ancient times.
The wild yam, for example, is sometimes called pleurisy root or
rheumatism root for its purported healing properties. The early use
of foods as medicine was based on simple observations made over
generations: you lived or felt better, or you got sick or even died,
after eating a particular food or herb.

Fortunately, we are more systematic and scientific in our approach to nutrition now. We have the ability to conduct biochemical analyses and to study how various components of food and combinations of foods relate to health. New discoveries are being made almost faster than we can absorb them and analyze their significance. Such scientific findings have revitalized and expanded our concepts about nutrition.

In the last decade, we have learned much about the links between nutrition and health. Discoveries about the relationships between cholesterol, saturated fat, and heart disease; between calcium and osteoporosis; and between salt and hypertension have changed the way all of us, not just scientists, think about food.

With nutritional awareness so high, if you are a person with cancer you have probably wondered whether there are links between nutrition and *your* recovery and continued health. If you have had a feeling that nutrition is an important concern for you, you are absolutely right. Nutrition is indeed linked to cancer in many ways. Reshaping your diet is one of the most important ways you can join your health-care team as an active participant in fighting relapse of your disease, improving your chances of remission, and nurturing your well-being.

This book is about the ways nutrition can help you build a sound defense against the occurrence or recurrence of cancer. (There is a difference between being at risk for cancer and actually having the disease, and in this book I will take care to distinguish between the two.) It will help you support your recovery during treatment and help you choose the right diet for the years to come.

You can also help yourself during times when therapy makes it difficult to eat or difficult to avoid overeating. If you are in therapy, you may feel tired, overwhelmed, or finicky. You may have diarrhea, cramps, or a very sore mouth. Mealtime may seem more a battle than a pleasant and fulfilling routine. The right nutrition and eating tips can increase your comfort as well as support your treatment during this time. (Chapter 8, "Solving Nutrition Problems and Improving Well-being During Treatment," covers this important area.)

But the focus in this book will be on the long term—starting an eating plan that will be enjoyable and sustainable for years to come.

I also want you to understand clearly why the nutritional recommendations I make are important for you.

The information in this book may well be new to you. It may also be new to your doctor. When I graduated from medical school in 1969, my fellow graduates and I had received little or no training in nutrition. Not much was known at that time about the complex relationships between food and chronic diseases such as osteoporosis and heart disease, and virtually nothing was known about the important relationships between nutrition and cancer. Until very recently, nutrition has remained on the back burner in many medical schools.

So when I acquired an interest in the nutritional problems of persons with cancer and in the ways that food might be related to cancer cause and prevention, I was embarking on an adventure. I first became interested in the topic during my medical oncology training at the Massachusetts General Hospital in Boston. By the time I became a faculty member at Emory University in Atlanta, I was thoroughly intrigued by it.

Emory had a clinical research unit with inpatient and outpatient facilities, a specially equipped kitchen, and a supporting laboratory. Dan Rudman, Steve Heymsfield, Glynda Gerron, and other members of the research team in this unit had developed sophisticated ways of measuring the nutritional status of patients and how their bodies were using the food they consumed, that is, their metabolism. For the next twelve years, I conducted and participated in research studies in this unit. We explored the relationships between food, nutrition, and cancer, and I continued this work when I became Associate Director, Cancer Prevention Research Program of the National Cancer Institute and later vice president for professional education of the American Cancer Society.

At present, I am Folk Professor of Experimental Oncology at the Medical University of South Carolina and Director of Cancer Prevention and Control at the Hollings Cancer Center of the Medical University of South Carolina. My research includes continued study of nutritional theories and how they work out in practice. My work in nutrition has taken me all over the world to Australia, South America, Europe, Africa, and elsewhere.

The facts and stories in this book are from the work in which I have been personally involved, as well as from other important scientific research. I will be very careful about how I explain these research findings to you, because in some cases the results are very strong and very encouraging, but not yet definitive. Yet they are the best we have today, and they can help you make the nutritional choices you need to make now. And as new developments occur, with your new knowledge of cancer and nutrition you will be better able to understand them and put them to work for you.

Many persons with cancer have already put nutrition to work for them in fighting cancer. Consider the story of Theresa Pine. Theresa had been overweight for many years when, at age fifty, she found a lump in her left breast. Theresa was terrified at the prospect of breast cancer, and her fear was heightened by her concern for her family. She made up her mind to get prompt attention, but the first step—calling for an appointment with her physician—felt like stepping off a cliff.

Her doctor also felt the lump and ordered a mammogram, which showed a suspicious lesion. A biopsy confirmed that the lump was malignant, but because Theresa had acted promptly, the cancer had not spread. The tumor was removed by lumpectomy, and a pathology examination confirmed that the disease was still local. Theresa began a course of radiation, and her oncologist recommended adjuvant chemotherapy to help prevent recurrence of the cancer. He also suggested that she enter a new diet project designed to decrease total fat-calorie intake, to see if this would support her recovery. He explained that she would be randomly assigned to one of two groups of patients. One group was taught to limit their intake of fats to 20 percent of the total calories each day, and the other group received no nutritional counseling. Theresa was assigned to the low-fat group.

As most people are, Theresa was surprised that such ordinary and simple measures might have an impact on cancer, but she decided to give it a try. With the same zest that she had always put into the care of her family, she worked hard to learn the techniques of low-fat food shopping and cooking.

Theresa's nutritional counselor analyzed the ways she had been eating. Theresa knew that a sudden, total change in diet would be very difficult, so she was greatly relieved when the counselor prescribed a gradual change over several weeks.

During that time, Theresa attended teaching sessions to help her meet the goals set for her by the project director and began introducing tasty, low-fat recipes into her family's meals. Of course, there were setbacks. There were times when Theresa wanted a snack to "settle her stomach," but she learned to choose low-fat foods rather than fatty ones on these occasions.

Over three weeks, Theresa reached her prescribed fat-intake goal. Though she continued radiation therapy and chemotherapy, she had only mild side effects and was able to begin a program of walking thirty minutes, three times a week, as recommended by her physician. Theresa explained to her teenagers and husband that these walks would help her get better and assigned each family member one day a week to "remind Mom to take her walk and make sure she walks the whole thirty minutes." Not only did this give her time alone with a family member once a week, it gave the family a sense of helping with her recovery.

As a person who had tried to lose weight many times, Theresa was amazed to see that, over the next three months, her weight slowly dropped to the level recommended for her height. The chemotherapy continued for six months. She continued the low-fat eating pattern, not just for herself, but for her husband and children as well, and maintained her new, lower weight.

After five years, Theresa was free of disease, and her physician said that he was very optimistic about her future—something that was possible, in large measure, because Theresa had found the courage to make that first "jump off the cliff." I've often wondered if she realized that her family was her parachute. They all had grown and changed dramatically in her five years of recovery, and Theresa had been there to enjoy every moment of it.

Of course, many persons with cancer are not as fortunate as Theresa was, but I have learned important lessons—about science and about life—from each one I have known. So sometimes, to make a point, I will tell the story of someone whose life was improved by nutrition, though recovery was not possible. Keep in mind that much of the initial work of studying the link between nutrition and cancer has been conducted with persons with advanced disease. By observing their progress and problems, I took on the medical and scientific challenges of diet and cancer, but I hope to share with you, through their stories, the part that their own courage, persistence, resilience, and creativity played in the fight against cancer.

Because there is still so much more to be learned about nutrition and cancer, there are some things I would like to be able to suggest, but can't. For example, I wish I could say that *eating* or *not eating* a certain food or that a certain diet will cure a particular cancer, or even make advanced disease better. Unfortunately, there is no scientific evidence at this time to support that statement, and anyone who suggests to you that there is should be regarded with grave suspicion. In fact, I will discuss more fully, in chapter 3, "Making Sound Decisions about Alternative Nutritional Approaches," some of the dietary "cures" and fads that have made more dollars for their proponents than sense for their users. Also, unfortunately, far-advanced cancer frequently cannot be helped by any treatment, and nutrition's role becomes that of improving comfort. Even so, the eating plan in this book is designed to *support* your treatment, whether it is surgery, radiation, chemotherapy, or palliative care.

What I can tell you is that, though we haven't reached our destination, we are well on our way to understanding the mechanisms of nutritional influences on cancer. After many decades of laboratory research and clinical experience with the nutritional problems of persons with cancer, we are poised on the threshold of understanding the complex role of diet as a modulator of cancer growth. And I can say with certainty that diet and nutrition are important in all stages of cancer and in cancer prevention as well.

CANCER AND NUTRITION AT THE CELLULAR LEVEL

From the simplest, single-celled plants and animals to human beings with highly specialized and complex interrelated systems, every living thing's first and foremost challenge is nutrition. Energy and nutrients are necessary for all functions of cellular growth, development, and replication. Without nutrition, the organism will starve.

With improper nutrition, the organism may live, but it will become weak, may suffer irreversible damage that will affect its ability to perform crucial functions, can become more vulnerable to infections, and ultimately, may die. So the proper balance of nutrients is as essential to survival as having enough nutrients.

We think of cancer as a disease, but it is important to keep in mind that *cancer is made up of living cells.* The difference between normal living cells and cancer cells is that *the growth and reproduction of cancer cells are out of control.* Evidence indicates that cancer begins as an event or series of events, called initiation, in the genetic makeup of a single cell. It then takes time for a malignant mass to develop, during which one or more tumor "promotion" steps have occurred. When a person first feels a malignant breast lump, for example, the tumor development process has been going on for a long time—years, or even decades. The role of diet in cancer is most likely that it stimulates cells with genes that have already been altered to grow into a tumor. In other words, poor diet is most likely a promoter of cancer, not an initiator.

Here is a theoretical example of how this might work. Imagine a single, normal breast cell being damaged early in a woman's life. Such damage can occur from a genetic "mistake"—spontaneous mutation—or perhaps from exposure to a cancer-causing chemical. When this damaged cell divides to form new cells, it could pass on its damaged genetic material to the new cells. This could happen very slowly at first, so a tumor would not be formed immediately. Over time, however, a diet high in fat content could provide sufficient energy, plus certain fatty acids that promote tumor growth, plus certain changes in the hormonal environment—all of which would provide a more inviting place for tumors to develop and grow. Theoretically, before long, this combination of factors would result in a tumor mass where once there was a single normal cell.

As you can see, this is a process that is drawn out over a long period of time. In fact, it appears that, for many cancers, it takes many years between the damaging event and the emergence of cancer. This particular feature of cancer development convinces me that nutritional changes may benefit the person who already has cancer, the person recuperating from cancer, and persons who are at risk for cancer. We may not be able to do much about the original damage to a cell's genetic makeup, but we can decrease tumor-cell-promoting activity—by decreasing dietary fat, for example.

There is a saying espoused by people who are concerned about the environment: We all live downstream. In terms of cancer, this is very true. The types of agents we are exposed to may differ from region to region, culture to culture, or family to family, but we are all exposed to things that damage genes. So it may be that all of us develop cancer cells from time to time. Only some of us, however, have the necessary promoting influences to make the damaged cells grow and spread.

If this is so, the preventive approach will take on even greater significance in the future. It may be that, instead of treating existing cancers, we will eventually be able to turn the tide to prevent cancer before it is promoted. Based on what we already know, cancer prevention will have a great deal to do with proper diet. It's a theory that makes very good sense, because cancer needs nutrients, just as plants, amoebae, and human beings do. What we need to know more about is which foods encourage the process of cancer development and growth and which foods can prevent it. Several clinical trials now in progress will help answer these questions (scientific studies in which subjects with cancer undergo a dietary change and their progress is followed to see what effect occurs).

GOOD NUTRITION FOR PEOPLE WITH CANCER MEANS MORE THAN JUST PREVENTING WEIGHT LOSS

Because cancer cells grow and multiply out of control, they are constantly seeking more nourishment. Cancer cells are voracious users of energy. One of the ways that cancer cells kill normal, healthy cells is by depriving them of needed nutrition. In the competition between cancer cells and host (normal) cells, the cancer cells have the potential to take over and use up nourishment and energy for their own purposes. This appears to be why, in many cases of advanced cancer, a person suffers debilitating loss of weight and strength, even when eating an adequate amount of food. In this condition, called cancer cachexia, the person declines but the cancer thrives. The process of cancer cachexia is only partially understood by scientists, but when it occurs, it is vividly apparent that the cancer cells are dominating essential metabolic processes—the way the body uses food.

Many people who lose weight and strength with cancer believe that if they could only eat enough, they would be able to regain their losses. "Eating more" becomes their nutritional goal, and they're often encouraged to do so by their loved ones.

Ironically, studies suggest that a person with advanced cancer is frequently unable to use these extra nutrients to build muscle and lean tissues, but instead converts them into fat tissue. This stored fat is not of much use to the cancer patient; furthermore, some new dietary evidence indicates that excess fat tissue can create an environment in which certain cancers, such as breast cancer, can thrive.

None of the studies leads to the conclusion that you do not need food during your bout with cancer. To the contrary, you do need to eat; as we shall discuss, the *types* of foods you choose may have an important impact on your future outlook.

An important factor that must be remembered when discussing cancer and nutrition is that the cancer cells have their own needs. With its uncontrolled growth and division of cells, the cancer needs food just as your normal tissues do. Your goal is to eat adequately without feeding the cancer. At the same time, you want to be laying the best possible groundwork for prevention of future cancers. Working for the best nutrition can also help you feel better mentally and emotionally, because you are building an improved health outlook for your future.

USING THIS BOOK

Almost every week, we read of new scientific studies exploring and proving that there are important, complex, and previously unrecognized relationships among nutrition, diet, and cancer. The broad foundation for understanding these relationships is not yet complete, but in some areas, scientists have been able to test in the laboratory their vision of how specific nutrients and diet fit with cancer. Also, using data from around the world, epidemiologists are putting together composite pictures of how eating habits, lifestyle choices, and other factors contribute to cancer incidence and cancer prevention. In academic centers and cancer centers throughout the United States, investigators and people with cancer are working hand in hand, in randomized clinical trials, to find definitive answers to questions about nutrition, cancer treatment, and cancer prevention.

This book provides a broad discussion and explanation of the most up-to-date information available on the proper role of diet and nutrition in cancer treatment and cancer prevention. Specific answers to questions in many areas have not yet been found, yet misinformation and fads abound. In this book, I offer my opinions and advice, based on my interpretations of the best available data, to help you make informed judgments. One of my goals is to help you make sense of confusing and often conflicting nutritional headlines. For example, it has been widely reported recently that there is no link between dietary fat and breast cancer, contradicting other reports that the two are indeed linked. These conflicting opinions are discussed and put into perspective in chapter 4, "For Women with Breast Cancer."

We will start, in the next chapter, by talking about the connection between nutrition and cancer in general. We will look at specific nutrients, as well as other chemicals in foods, that are thought to have either anticancer or cancer-promoting effects. Because in dealing with cancer and nutrition you will have to make many decisions and choices based on much information and "news," chapter 3 will help you make sound decisions about alternative nutritional approaches.

In the next part of the book, we will get more specific, talking about the connection between nutrition and particular types of cancers.

In the last part of the book, you will turn theory into practice. Chapter 8 offers several ways to solve nutritional problems and improve your well-being during treatment. Then, for the long term, chapter 9 will help you move to a healthy new eating plan over a three-month period. Chapter 10 shares very practical information you will need to choose and cook foods healthfully. And finally, in chapter 11 you will learn about the role of exercise in cancer and how to support your recovery and your nutritional efforts with physical activity. The diet plan that is the core of the book isn't exotic, made up of hard-to-find ingredients, or good only for the person with cancer. As you probably know, certain cancers tend to run in families. Thus, one of the important additional benefits of this plan is that it can reduce cancer risk in healthy people, *your* family included. I have also prepared a chapter "For the Doctor" outlining major background areas for the book's conclusions and a listing of available resources for cancer patients.

And last, but not least, I have asked an accomplished chef to develop a collection of recipes that demonstrate how accessible and adaptable healthy eating can be. Chef Mark Erickson is a graduate of the Culinary Institute of America (the "CIA") in Hyde Park, New York, and is an American Culinary Federation Certified Master Chef. In 1985, he was honored as "Crystal Chef" for the highest score in the arduous Master Chef competition—only eight chefs have been so honored. He has been a National Team Member of the U.S. Culinary Team, which won three gold medals in the 1988 Culinary Olympics in Frankfurt, West Germany, and was on the U.S. World Cup Culinary Team that won the 1986 Culinary World Cup in Luxembourg. He was awarded individual gold medals in both the 1980 and 1984 Culinary Olympics in Frankfurt. On one occasion he won awards for his low-fat recipes, even though trimming fat was neither required nor expected. In 1986, he was Faculty Member of the Year at the CIA and until 1990, was CIA's Director of Culinary Education. He is now Executive Chef at the Cherokee Town and Country Club in Atlanta, one of the nation's premier private clubs. Chef Erickson's recipes, based on his vast experience, are so appealing that everyone, not just those dealing with cancer, will find them delightful. His recipes are good for you and for other members of your family, so no one will have to worry about preparing separate meals. Chef Erickson uses small amounts of butter and bacon from time to time to demonstrate that you can eat very well without sacrificing flavor. He skillfully uses spices and herbs to avoid blandness, a chief complaint of many who eat low-fat foods. All his recipes derive approximately 20 percent or less of their calories from fat.

Throughout this book, I'll present information to you in language that you will be able to understand without benefit of a medical or nursing degree.

My hope is that this book will help fill a current gap in cancer care. As I said earlier, many health-care providers, myself included, had little or no nutrition training in medical school. As a result, many oncologists and oncology nurses don't feel qualified to offer nutritional advice unless they have developed a special interest in it, and many are uncertain of how to integrate these new findings into traditional medicine. This book will enable you to work closely with your health-care team, including nutritionists, to mount the strongest possible attack on cancer, and will enable others at risk of cancer to build a realistic and healthful defense against cancer, based on sound scientific information.

I wish you a bright future filled with good health and joyous, healthful, and delicious food.

2

THE CONNECTION BETWEEN CANCER AND DIET

ﾞﾞﾞﾞﾞﾞﾞ

Good nutrition is a jigsaw puzzle that you're going to put together for yourself. You need to know what the pieces are—pieces such as fats and fiber and vitamins—and we'll look at them shortly, one by one.

It has been estimated by two leading researchers in the field of nutrition, Doctors Richard Doll and Richard Peto of Oxford University, that up to 70 percent of cancers may be due to diet. By comparison, the percentage of cancers related to tobacco use has been estimated at about 30 percent.

While the exact percentage is uncertain, there is abundant evidence from population studies ("epidemiological" studies) and from the laboratory to link the development of many types of cancer to nutritional factors. Several organizations, including the American Cancer Society and the National Cancer Institute, have recognized the diet-cancer connection and have issued dietary guidelines to help people reduce their cancer risk.

Other data from the laboratory indicate that certain nutritional factors can influence already existing cancer as well, especially in the early stages.

While diet may play a role in modulating the development, growth, and spread of cancer, it is important to remember that diet most likely does not *cause* cancer by itself. It is the combination of poor diet with genetic, environmental, and other factors that can lead to some cancers.

Likewise, *diet alone is not, by itself, a useful treatment for any existing cancer.* This is especially important to keep in mind when considering alternative methods of cancer treatment. For example, "megadose" vitamin therapies have no proven effects against existing cancer (see chapter 3, "Making Sound Decisions about Alternative Nutritional Approaches").

To sum up, nutrition alone is not the sole cause of any cancer, nor is nutrition alone an effective treatment for any cancer, but *good nutrition working together with other factors can contribute to both cancer-risk reduction and the chances of cancer remission.*

Here are three examples of how nutrition may make a difference:

- *Breast cancer* cells may need certain fatty acids to grow. A low-fat diet deprives the cells of these fatty acids.
- Development of *colon cancer* may be linked to carcinogenic substances that act on the colon lining when waste matter remains in the colon too long. A high-fiber diet speeds the passage of waste through the colon, so that even if carcinogenic substances are present, they are not in prolonged contact with the gut.
- In some cancers healthy cells are transformed by a process called dedifferentiation. Cells that normally would become mature and die become immature and out of control. There is strong evidence that vitamin A, which is present as beta carotene in green and deep yellow vegetables, can interrupt and reverse this dedifferentiation process during its early phases. In fact, studies are testing the potential for this vitamin to reverse developing oral, lung, breast, and cervical cancers.

We'll learn more about these exciting connections, and many others, as we go along.

This chapter will explore the ways that nutrition is related to cancers of all kinds. Some cancers have a close relationship to diet and some don't. Chapter 9, "Three Months to a New Eating Plan," will tell how to apply important general principles in your daily diet.

The guidelines for good nutrition vary among the various types of cancer, but the nature of the relationship between the cancer and nutrition tends to fall into one of three groups. As explained below, there are tumors of "overnutrition," tumors of "undernutrition," and cancers where other factors tend to overwhelm any effect of nutrition. (Some cancers have no known nutritional connection.) We'll look at the way nutrition works overall within each group of cancers, then we'll look at the role of specific macronutrients (for example, fat and fiber) and micronutrients (vitamins, minerals, and trace elements).

TUMORS OF OVERNUTRITION

Some cancers have been linked to a diet too high in fat and "fat calories," i.e., percent of calories from fat. Among these are breast, colon, prostate, pancreatic, and endometrial cancers, and as demonstrated most recently, even lung cancer. Important support for this idea has come from the work of epidemiologists, the researchers (who are often also physicians) who study disease trends in populations. Epidemiologists are able to tell us many things about diseases that could not be ascertained by looking at one patient at a time.

Epidemiologic studies have collected facts on the foods eaten by particular populations and have traced the types of cancers that occur (or do not occur) in these populations. Such studies have found that countries with high fat and calorie intakes and low-fiber intakes have higher rates of certain cancers. These countries are largely the ones where the population eats a "Western" industrialized diet high in meats and dairy products.

Other evidence has come from comparing historical changes in the American diet to changes in cancer rates in this country. In the late nineteenth and early twentieth centuries, cancer rates increased so rapidly in the United States that the situation was properly termed an epidemic (and was so called by writers of the time). The epidemic was not an isolated event; rather, it was related to the development of American civilization, particularly, I believe, to the development of the types of meals served at the American table and, of course, to widespread tobacco use.

By the early twentieth century, industrialization and the development of large-scale agriculture had made food abundant and inexpensive. Contributing to the increase in calories and fat in the diet, ranchers and farmers were producing a lot of well-fattened meat—probably more meat than had ever been routinely consumed by any civilization. At the same time, natural, whole foods were being replaced by refined, processed foods with less fiber.

Unfortunately, people were slow to comprehend the dangers of excess fat and low fiber. In an introduction to the revised edition of the *Moosewood Cookbook* (a classic in vegetarian cookery), author Mollie Katzen gives a telling summary of the typical American diet at mid-century:

My earliest culinary exposure was to simple, largely processed foods. A child of the '50s and '60s, I was raised on Minute Rice, Campbell's soups, Velveeta cheese, and frozen vegetables—the miracle convenience foods of the era. We ate red meat about five nights a week; on the other two we ate chicken or fish. "Salad" meant iceberg lettuce, hothouse tomatoes, and mayonnaise. Cucumbers were sometimes included, but that was already edging toward the exotic.

Most of us are living with the legacy of those years. Today, the average American still eats as much or more fat than a generation ago—37 to 40 percent of all calories, every day.

The epidemic of cancer that occurred early in the United States in this century is being repeated now in other countries. In Japan, where Western lifestyles—including the Western diet—are replacing the traditional very low-fat cuisine, rates of breast cancer and colon cancer are rising dramatically.

Colon cancer has been linked to too little dietary fiber as well as to high dietary fat. If you think about some of the typical high-fat foods—for example, cheeses, fatty meats, oils, ice cream—you may notice that high fat content usually means low fiber content. So, in the case of colon cancer, it's important to ask, is it the high fat that causes the cancer? Or is the low fiber the problem? The answer appears to be that the combination—high fat *and* low fiber—is worse than each would be alone. A possible reason for this is that the high dietary fat may increase the content of certain carcinogenic substances in the gut, at the same time that low fiber slows down the transit time for waste, while possibly decreasing fecal volume and concentrating carcinogens as well.

TUMORS OF UNDERNUTRITION

Denis Burkitt, M.D., who has been called the "father of fiber," proposed in 1971 that certain African populations have little colon cancer because of the high fiber content in their diet. Unfortunately, though people in Third World countries have the advantage of consuming less animal fat and more fiber, their diet is often monotonous and deficient in certain vitamins and minerals. Their cancer patterns are usually different from the patterns in affluent countries. Industrialized countries have more cancers of breast, colon, prostate, and other sites, but poor countries, and also poor populations in the United States, tend to have more squamous cancers—that is, those that occur on the lining or covering of organs—of the upper digestive tract (mouth, throat, esophagus) and cervix, as well as stomach cancer. These can be called tumors of undernutrition, because these cancers are often associated in population studies with lack of certain vitamins, minerals, or other nutrients.

It's important to remember that population patterns do not absolutely prove cause and effect, especially singular cause and effect. For example, nasopharyngeal cancer, which is an upper digestive tract cancer, occurs at a high rate in certain parts of China. It is believed that frequent use of highly salted, smoked foods in that part of the world is an important cause, in addition to undernutrition. Excessive alcohol consumption is another cause of upper digestive tract cancers, but it's impossible to ignore the fact that most persons who overindulge in alcohol also have very poor nutrition habits, and that excess drinking and smoking often go hand in hand. While cervical cancer may be related to undernutrition (and as mentioned earlier, may possibly be reversed in its earliest stages by forms of vitamin A), it is also linked with certain types of human papillomavirus. Very recent studies indicate that this type of virus may cause genetic damage that sets up the potential for cancer to develop, which may then be set off by other factors, such as smoking and/or undernutrition. Remember that we said diet is not the sole cause of cancer.

SOME CANCERS APPEAR UNRELATED TO DIET

Not all cancers appear to be affected by diet. Tobacco and lung cancer are definitively linked, and it may be that the carcinogenic effects of tobacco are so powerful that any dietary influences are impossible to determine. Recent evidence, however, does associate dietary fat and lung cancer in nonsmokers.

The causes of some other cancers—leukemia, lymphoma, and bone tumors, for example—remain unknown, although ionizing radiation and certain viruses that alter immune function, including HIV, the virus that causes AIDS, appear to play a role.

Skin cancer, the most common cancer of all, is strongly related to excessive exposure to sunlight. This includes the deadly type called melanoma, as well a the more common squamous and basal cell (innermost skin cell) skin cancers. Dietary factors have not been strongly related to skin cancer to date, although some data exist that link skin cancer to dietary fat content.

The cancers that have no causative or associative link to diet of which I am aware will *not* be covered in separate chapters later in this book. They are: leukemia, Hodgkin's disease, non-Hodgkin's lymphoma, sarcoma of soft tissue and bone, brain tumors, testicular cancer, melanoma, and a variety of rare tumors. Childhood tumors also fall into this category. I don't think there is enough information to specifically discuss pancreatic, ovarian, and stomach cancer and nutrition at present.

For these cancers, if treatment has been successful, and disease has been eradicated by surgery or is in remission from chemotherapy and/or radiation, a prudent approach is to follow the American Cancer Society and National Cancer Institute dietary guidelines (see the end of this chapter). I know of nothing to suggest any special benefit from more specific dietary changes. If your disease is not in remission and treatment is ongoing, you may benefit from the eating tips in chapter 8.

HOW STRONG IS THE EVIDENCE?

Here is my interpretation of how strong the evidence is at this time that diet can affect premalignant cellular changes that can lead to cancer or cancer in its earlier stages.

Breast cancer	strongly suggestive data
Colon cancer	strongly suggestive data
Squamous cancers of cervix, head, and neck	moderately suggestive data
Prostate cancer	moderately suggestive data
Squamous cancers of lung and skin	some suggestive data
Pancreas cancer	data largely inferential
Ovarian cancer	data largely inferential
Stomach cancer	data largely inferential
Lymphoma, Hodgkin's disease, leukemia	no data or negative data
Sarcoma of soft tissue; bone tumors, melanoma, testicular cancer, others	no data or negative data

CHILDHOOD CANCER

Childhood cancer is not covered by the dietary recommendations in this book. A low-fat diet that is appropriate and beneficial for an adult is not necessarily appropriate for a child with cancer. In fact, there is evidence that a very low-fat diet may impair growth and development in very young preschool children, and cases of failure to thrive have occurred because of overzealous manipulation of a child's diet by parents. Before changing a child's diet, consult your pediatrician or pediatric oncologist.

Also, the lessons we will discuss about the lack of benefit from aggressive feeding in later stages of cancer in adults do not apply to children. Growing children may benefit from enteral—that is, passing through the stomach and disintegrating in the intestines—and parenteral—that is, introduced otherwise than by way of the intestines—feeding during cancer treatment. A skilled nutritional support team is essential in this situation.

CALORIES AND CANCER

Now that we've looked at the big picture of cancer and nutrition, we're ready to start putting the pieces of the puzzle together.

From the foods you eat, your body takes the energy it requires for its routine functions and for physical activity such as walking or running. The amount of energy derived from the foods you eat is measured in calories. When you eat more calories than your body can use, it stores the rest as fat tissue.

Whether riding horseback across the old homestead or driving the station wagon to the local grocery store, a body can only burn up so many calories. Our genes are programmed to handle nutrition in a very thrifty manner, because over eons, evolution favored those humans who had the greatest ability to survive and reproduce on a limited and unreliable food supply of foraged grains, nuts, and plants. When our ancestors ate meat, it was from wild animals. These sources of meat were likely to be lean, because animals had their own problems getting food.

In our civilization, by and large, we consume excess calories. As a result, our bodies are growing taller and fatter. This trend is happening so quickly today that it is evident from generation to generation. More than one grandfather has looked up in amazement at a teenaged grandchild already taller than himself, and wondered if there was a mix-up in the maternity ward.

Unquestionably, there are good things to say about the current American diet. At the turn of the century, the average life expectancy in the United States was about 50 years—not much better than Dr. Benjamin Rush observed in the late 1700s. In 1990, it was 75.4 years, and some of the credit for that dramatic increase goes to the availability and quality of food. Nevertheless, we are becoming an obese nation, and obesity is a problem for many reasons.

In terms of cancer, larger people have more cells, and one problem may be that continued caloric excess drives these cells to divide faster. This is called "metabolic overdrive." The faster the cells are dividing, and the more cells there are, the greater the likelihood that a "mistake" will occur, such as a spontaneous mutation or a carcinogen-induced mutation. Calories, in this sense, can be considered carcinogenic.

CANCER CACHEXIA

Calories are also important in later stages of cancer. One of the frustrating facts about cancer is that the same calories that support the healthy metabolism of a normal cell can be appropriated by malignant cells hungry for energy. This can lead to cancer cachexia, the debilitating loss of weight and strength that often happens in advanced cancer. Even if the person is eating an adequate amount of food, overall health declines but the cancer thrives, vividly illustrating that the cancer cells are dominating the body's metabolic processes.

How these processes are initiated and sustained is still poorly understood; however, what we have learned from a few studies is very important. For one thing, we have learned that forcing even more food upon a person with cancer is not always a good idea. This was clearly demonstrated about a decade ago, when the National Cancer Institute became interested in the relationship between a person with cancer and the illness. I participated at that time as a principal investigator in a series of university-based projects. The first project was simply to do a survey of the nutritional status of hospitalized cancer patients. We were surprised to find that almost all of our patients were undernourished in varying degrees. In other words, cancer cachexia was common, even though many of the people we examined did not *look* as if they had this problem. Many had depleted stores of fat and/or lean body mass (protein), while others were lacking certain vitamins or minerals.

We then set out to determine the mechanisms through which this undernutrition occurred. A popular theory a few years ago was that people with cancer became undernourished because of "hypermetabolism," a state in which the body burns up its stores of energy too quickly. We theorized that, if this were true, appropriate drugs might be given to slow down these processes, much like the use of drugs to treat hyperthyroidism.

To test this theory, we studied patients with advanced colon cancer or lung cancer. We chose these particular cancers because they are often accompanied by severe cachexia. We used an instrument called a whole-body calorimeter that could measure up to 99 percent of all the body heat produced by the person. From these results, the metabolic rate could be precisely determined for each study participant.

We then compared the results in people with colon cancer or lung cancer to results in persons who were similarly undernourished but did not have cancer. We also compared the results in the persons with cancer to results in healthy, well-nourished people. We found that, at rest, the people with cancer were not producing more body heat than normal. They were *not* hypermetabolic, so this process did not adequately explain cancer cachexia.

In another attempt to determine the reason for cancer cachexia, we studied advanced cancer patients undergoing either intravenous or tube feeding. The laboratory was able to measure the amounts of certain important nutrients in the feeding solution, as well as the amounts of the same nutrients leaving via body wastes. Using these measures, it was determined that the people with cancer could not manufacture lean body mass normally, although they could create fat tissue. The weight gain that these persons experienced was only fat and water weight, not muscle and lean tissue.

We realized that even though a person with cancer may be losing weight, eating more food was not the appropriate answer in many cases. We also noted that true cancer cachexia is not related to nausea and loss of appetite from cancer treatment.

An additional study further explored the effect of hyperalimentation—that is, the administration of nutrients by intravenous feeding. This method provides all needed nutrients and is a standard and accepted method of feeding persons who are undernourished for reasons other than cancer. The study, which was conducted in the early 1980s, worked with two groups. In the first, the participants were receiving chemotherapy for advanced colon cancer. Members of this group were given hyperalimentation and, if they felt like eating, were allowed to eat whatever they wanted by mouth as well. The intravenous feeding solution given to this group contained calories, amino acids, vitamins, minerals, and trace elements.

Members of the second group were also receiving chemotherapy for advanced colon cancer. They were not given hyperalimentation, but were allowed to eat whatever they normally ate and felt like eating.

Much to our surprise, the persons who received intravenous feedings did not do nearly as well as those allowed to eat as much or as little as they wanted, without hyperalimentation, nor did they live nearly as long.

After the surprising results of this experiment had been analyzed, it was proposed that perhaps something had been left out of the hyperalimentation solution that was essential to normal metabolism. Even though we didn't know what that something was, it was possible that persons with cancer might do better if they were encouraged to eat increased amounts of normal food.

So, in yet another study, a number of colon and lung cancer patients were divided into three groups. One group was encouraged by nutritionists to eat enough to reach a daily calorie goal. A second group was encouraged to reach the same calorie goal and to add certain minerals to their diet. The third group was simply observed, allowed to eat as much or as little as they wanted. Again, no advantage was seen for group one or group two.

Part of the reason for these results appears to be the finding that the person with cancer is not able to create normal lean body mass from food; that is, food is not converted to normal protein and muscle tissue. Instead, food is converted into fat. In the experiments described above, it was not clear if any of the various nutrient approaches contributed to tumor growth; however, we did not see overt acceleration of tumor growth.

Similar tests in animals have been more definitive, showing that starvation does slow tumor growth and overfeeding does, in some experiments, lead to an increase in tumor growth. These findings provide interesting leads but have not yet been proven to be true in humans.

To summarize, these are the reasons why (contrary to what I and many investigators thought before) simply forcing an increase in food intake is not necessarily a good idea for a person with cancer, even if the person is losing weight:

- The increased nutrition intake may not go toward rebuilding normal tissue.
- The increased intake may fuel the cancer itself.

FAT AND CANCER

Dietary fat provides energy for the body and assists in the metabolism of vitamins A, D, E, and K. The problem with fat is that most of us eat much more than is good for us. Even fruits and vegetables naturally contain some fat. Bread also contains fat. So you really don't have to add fat or eat meat to get enough fat in the diet.

Fat appears to have a dual role in cancer. It may act both as a promoter of cancer and as a modulator of the growth of existing cancer. Breast cancer has been extensively studied in this regard, and some of the findings are covered in depth in the chapter on breast cancer.

One reason fat is linked to cancer goes back to the problem of too many calories. If you've ever tried counting calories to lose weight, you're well aware that those little dabs of butter and dribbles of salad oil are packed with calories. A gram of protein or carbohydrate contains 4 calories, but a gram of fat contains 9 calories.

Because dietary fat is the leading cause of too many calories in the diet, *I do not recommend that people focus on how many calories they are taking in, but rather on reducing fats.* When we turn later to starting your eating plan, we will talk about dietary fat instead of calories, and will check our progress by counting grams of fat, not calories.

In addition to its high caloric content, fat harbors certain fatty acids that, in the laboratory, have been shown to stimulate cancer cell growth. This is explained further in the chapter on breast cancer.

Scientists have debated for decades about the relative importance in cancer of fat alone versus the calories in fat. A low-fat, low-calorie diet can inhibit the development of certain types of tumors and can also slow the growth of established tumors in animals. The reverse is also true; a high-fat, high-calorie diet boosts the development and growth of such tumors in the laboratory. Similarly, a low-fat but high-calorie diet (that is, a diet with a high proportion of calories from carbohydrates) has also been associated with tumor stimulation in animals, but the value of these findings in humans has not been studied.

Interestingly, such studies have also shown that animals not only have fewer tumors when fed a low-calorie diet, but also have a longer life span than animals fed a high-calorie diet. It is almost as if the high-calorie diets drive cellular processes faster, to the point that overall life is shortened. This "metabolic overload" is another way to explain the problems of overnutrition.

Because we don't know yet if the types of fat (saturated, unsaturated, omega-3 fatty acids, and so on) make more or less difference in cancer, current recommendations are to reduce *total* fat to reduce cancer risk. However, you are no doubt aware that studies of the relationship between fat intake and cardiovascular disease have shown that saturated fat, which is primarily found in foods from animal sources, should be avoided. We do not know enough yet about the roles of types of fats in cancer; however, I believe that the link with cardiovascular health is strong enough to recommend limiting your intake of saturated fat as an all-around prudent health measure.

The question you're no doubt asking about dietary fat is: How much fat should I ban in my diet? Several national organizations recommend that you consume 30 percent of daily total calories as fat *or less* to reduce your risk for cancer. I think that for an adult at high risk of cancer, 30 percent is too high and that 20 percent of total calories as fat is closer to an optimal level. My recommendation to combat disease recurrence is 20 percent or less for breast cancer, colon cancer, and prostate cancer, for example.

Several clinical cancer trials are now in process, comparing 15 percent versus 30 percent or more of total calories as fat in breast cancer patients. Most of us eat 37 to 40 percent or more of our calories as fat. Most of this fat comes from animal products; thus, I feel that animal fat is the major problem in our diets. Because of this, most research has targeted animal fat and fat calories.

CHOLESTEROL AND CANCER

A diet high in fats also increases levels of cholesterol in the blood. It's not yet clear what role, if any, cholesterol might play in cancer.

For years, everyone believed they understood very clearly how total serum cholesterol, the amount of this fat-related substance found in the blood, is related to heart disease. Now researchers are saying, "Well, yes, there's a relationship. But there's a lot we have to clarify on this topic, including the roles of the so-called good and bad cholesterols." (It's not just in the field of cancer that the problem of flip-flopping of scientific advice occurs!)

At the same time, researchers are wondering if there is a link between cholesterol and cancer. So far, no definitive, direct link has been found, but there is evidence that farnesyl—a substance that is created as the liver synthesizes cholesterol—may have some role in the earliest stages of cancer development. It appears that farnesyl interacts with oncogenes (the genes through which cancer begins) and the products of these genes, possibly as one of a cascade of biochemical triggers that turn cancer on.

If total dietary fat is reduced, serum cholesterol is likely to fall. If the farnesyl hypothesis mentioned above is true, then less cholesterol synthesis may mean less farnesyl action on oncogene products. This may be another way low-fat diets decrease cancer risk.

Different kinds of fat do play different roles in prevention of cardiovascular disease. Animal fat is the most prevalent source of saturated fat, not only in meat, but also in animal products such as butter, cheese, and whole milk. Saturated fats raise blood cholesterol levels, but unsaturated fat (mono- and polyunsaturated) either has no effect on cholesterol or can actually lower it.

We know that cholesterol is associated with cardiovascular disease, but its relationship with cancer is not certain yet, because research has not progressed to the point where the role of different types of fat can be determined. Thus, the current recommendation for prevention of cancer is to limit *total* fat intake.

FIBER AND CANCER

Dietary fiber is sometimes called "bulk" or "roughage." It is a complex mixture of carbohydrates found in cell walls of plants (fruits, vegetables, legumes, grains, and other). Fiber cannot be broken down by digestive enzymes, so it acts like a water-laden mass that moves along the gut. As such, it aids swift and proper elimination of wastes.

There are two major categories of fiber: water-soluble and water-insoluble. Water-insoluble fiber has been associated with decreased cellular activity and decreased polyp formation in the gut, and thereby is thought to help prevent colon cancer. The water-soluble group (gums, pectin, and others) tends to lower cholesterol levels in the blood. If the farnesyl connection to oncogenes mentioned in the cholesterol section above is proven to be significant, then water-soluble fiber may be important in preventing cancer, because it lowers cholesterol levels. When talking about fiber in this book, we will be referring to *total* dietary fiber—water-soluble and water-insoluble.

Most of our fiber intake comes from vegetables, breads, and fruits. It is not known if the fiber from different plant sources has differing effects in cancer.

How does fiber work against cancer? There are several possible mechanisms. The beneficial laxative effect has been mentioned above. Fiber may also bind with carcinogens in the gut, rendering them harmless. A third benefit is that fiber may alter gut bacteria and acidity so that fewer carcinogens are produced.

In 1987, a panel of nutrition experts recommended that healthy adults consume 20 to 35 grams of fiber per day. More recently, the National Academy of Sciences recommended that adults consume five or more servings of fruits and vegetables daily. Though Americans are starting to eat more fiber-containing foods, the average diet still contains about half of what is recommended—only 12 to 15 grams of fiber daily.

CARBOHYDRATES AND CANCER

Carbohydrates are the common starches and sugars that make up most of the world's foods. Cereals, rice, vegetables, and fruits are major sources, and as discussed above, fiber is a type of carbohydrate.

The body uses carbohydrates mainly for fuel. They play important roles in the metabolism of fats and proteins as well.

A number of studies around the world have shown that high intake of carbohydrate-rich foods, especially vegetables and fruits, has a cancer-protective effect. This may be due to the vitamin and chemopreventive compounds contained in these foods, to the fact that high-carbohydrate diets are high in fiber and low in fat, or to all the factors working together. An increased intake of fruits and vegetables is certainly prudent as a preventive measure for cancer.

It is useful to remember that carbohydrates, as mentioned before, contain 4 calories per gram, while fat contains more than twice as many—9 calories per gram.

SUGAR AND DIABETES

Sugar intake is not directly connected to cancer, but it is important to discuss for a moment its link to another disease, diabetes. Because cancer and diabetes are more common in older persons, they frequently occur together, and if you have both diseases, you have some additional nutritional concerns.

People with diabetes have problems with insulin. Insulin is the superintendent in the factory of digestion. Under normal circumstances, the pancreas responds to a meal by producing insulin. When insulin is on the scene, things move along as they're supposed to: The cells of the body use proteins to build, form, and store fats, and turn glucose into useful energy.

There are two types of diabetes: Type I and Type II. Type I is insulin-dependent diabetes, meaning that persons with this type do not produce sufficient insulin and must rely on supplemental insulin, as well as careful dietary measures, to control their disease. About 10 percent of all persons with diabetes have Type I; juvenile diabetes falls into this category. Type II diabetes is much more common; about 90 percent of persons with diabetes have this type, which is also called "non-insulin-dependent" or "adult onset" diabetes. In adult onset diabetes, the problem is not so much with insulin production, but with the body's response to insulin.

Diabetes, at least in some instances, may have a genetic basis. Beyond that, the causes of diabetes are not known. Eating too much sugar is not a cause, but overeating (anything, including sugar) to the point of obesity contributes, especially in Type II diabetes.

Clearly, controlling one's weight seems to be a good measure to prevent many diseases, including cancer.

When persons with Type II diabetes need to lose weight through diet and exercise, they must be supervised by a physician and a nutritionist. The general nutritional guidelines for diabetes fit well with the anticancer recommendations in this book, but if you are a diabetic, you need to work closely with your health-care team, especially if you are taking insulin or oral hypoglycemic agents. In general, a person with diabetes needs to eat more cereals, vegetables, and fruits, and to limit fat intake. Since many high-sugar foods are also high in fat (cakes and cookies, for example), these should be avoided. A lower fat diet may necessitate adjustment of your diabetic medication dosage. Cancer can elevate blood sugar levels, so the person with both diseases has special concerns.

Cancer and diabetes interrelate in that someone who has cancer cachexia may not respond to insulin as he or she should. In this condition, called "insulin resistance," the body's tissues become malnourished, while needed nutrients filter into the blood, causing blood sugar levels to rise. In chapter 11, "Supporting Cancer Recovery with Exercise and Sexuality," we will talk about the ways that exercise may help overcome insulin resistance.

PROTEIN AND CANCER

Dietary protein provides the body with amino acids, the "building blocks" of the body. Amino acids are major parts of every cell, as well as enzymes and hormones, and of body fluids such as the blood. They are used to repair body tissues and make new tissues. The main sources of protein are meat, fish, dried beans, and dairy products.

It has been difficult to evaluate protein's role in the development of cancer in people because high-protein diets are generally also high in fat and calories and may be low in fiber. Several population studies have found a relationship between high consumption of animal protein (meat and dairy products) and breast cancer. In the laboratory, when breast tumors are induced in animals by carcinogens, feeding the animals more protein led to increased tumors. Some epidemiological studies have also linked animal protein intake to colon cancer, prostate cancer, and endometrial cancer.

Another way protein may be connected to cancer was discussed in the section called "Calories and Cancer." It is thought that a major reason for cancer cachexia might be the interference of the cancer with the body's ability to turn food into lean protein and muscle tissue.

VEGETARIANISM

You may be wondering if it wouldn't be much easier or more healthful to get all your protein from vegetable sources and not worry about animal fat at all, or you may have already made this choice for yourself some time ago.

It is true that you do not need to eat meat for health reasons. You can obtain adequate protein by eating both legumes (beans) and grains, nuts and seeds. (Nuts and seeds are very high in fat, however.) Depending on which mode of vegetarianism you choose, your other protein choices may include nonfat cheese, nonfat milk, yogurt, egg whites or a nonfat egg substitute.

Of the three kinds of vegetarian diets, two of them are not necessarily low in fat, however.

- *Vegans* follow a strict diet that excludes all animal products, including dairy products, extracts of meats (which are used in many commercial products, such as instant soup mixes), and animal fats (lard, which may be an ingredient in many packaged products, including pastries).
- *Lacto-Vegetarians* exclude meat from the diet but include dairy products (milk, cheeses, yogurt); however, they do not eat eggs.
- *Lacto-Ovo-Vegetarians* eat no meat but include dairy products and eggs.

As you can see, the vegan and lacto-vegetarian diets are much more limiting, not only in nutritional choices, but also in the whole approach to purchasing foods and cooking. Many of the commercially prepared products that we rely on so much for our food supply, both at home and in restaurants, are highly likely to contain some of the foods that are not allowed on strict vegan and lacto-vegetarian diets.

A strict vegan has to rely on fresh fruits, vegetables, legumes, nuts, and grains for all of the body's nutritional needs. This diet can easily become deficient in calcium and certain other nutrients. It is also monotonous and extremely challenging to follow.

Lacto-vegetarians and lacto-ovo-vegetarians have a great nutritional advantage over strict vegans, in that they can use dairy products for protein and calcium. One important caution, however, is that care must be taken not to rely too much on cheeses as a substitute for meat, and in fact, many vegetarian cookbooks add cheese to nearly every recipe. Unless you use the new reduced-fat or nonfat cheeses, you can easily be doing more harm than good with this version of vegetarianism, because cheese (as well as other diary products) is naturally very high in fat. If you choose the lacto-ovo-vegetarian, eggs represent a source of hidden fat with high cholesterol content, so again, it would be very important to keep a tally of how many whole eggs you eat so you can control your fat intake (egg whites contain no cholesterol).

If you are used to basing your meals around meat, to become a committed vegetarian you will have to learn new ways of meal planning. In many ways, though, the lessons are the same as those you will be learning anyway as you make your diet more healthful. You will have to stay clear of fast food, because just about everything in fast-food establishments centers on meat, but many fast-food choices cause problems for everyone, vegetarian or not. When dining out, avoid the kinds of restaurants where the only vegetable choices are likely to be some rather tired peas and carrots. Chefs in Chinese, Thai, and Japanese restaurants, as well as some nouvelle cuisine establishments, are very amenable to replacing meat with tofu, or deleting meat from any dish. You may decide to try Indian cuisine, which offers a wide array of vegetarian dishes (many of which are ferociously hot; if you are having problems with mouth sores, skip this suggestion until they are gone).

Being a vegetarian is simpler than it used to be because the theory of "protein combining" has been abandoned. It used to be thought that because vegetables and grains are "incomplete proteins," with no one containing all the nine essential amino acids, a vegetarian had to combine two different vegetable protein sources at the same meal to replace a meat protein. One such combination, for example, was rice and beans. Today, though, we know that these foods do not need to be eaten together. What's important is to eat a *variety* of vegetable protein sources.

I do not recommend the strict vegan diet; it lends itself too well to extremes and to nutritional deficits. While I do not oppose lacto-ovo-vegetarianism or lacto-vegetarianism—you do not have to eat meat to live—I do believe that limiting meat consumption to 6 ounces per day or less has as much anticancer benefit as the total exclusion of meat from the diet and prevents a feeling of deprivation which could hamper compliance. If you're considering this option, you might also weigh how much change you can manage while also dealing with the thousand inconveniences and miseries that cancer entails. For some people, the switch to a vegetarian diet will be uneventful. For others, the transition could be more difficult. If you find it difficult to make major dietary changes and are not already a vegetarian, it might be best to put off this kind of change until you've first integrated the prescriptions for healthy eating that are described in this book. Later, if you wish to become a committed vegetarian, you will be well prepared for doing it in the healthiest way possible, because the methods described in this book will work well with vegetarianism.

There is strong evidence that complete low-fat vegetarianism is the best diet to help prevent—and perhaps even reverse—heart disease. This kind of diet also appears to be beneficial in combatting other diseases.

I do strongly recommend everyone consider at least two meat-free (vegetarian) days a week. This will help a lot to reduce total fat intake and increase fiber intake.

For many people, the right approach to vegetarianism isn't the strict one. Instead of thinking of vegetarianism as an all-or-nothing proposition, think of it as a source of recipes and approaches to ingredients that you can draw on as you make your diet more healthful. Try to become at least a part-time vegetarian, and gradually increase the number of meat-free meals you have each week. If you're making a dish with meat, think of the meat as a condiment rather than as a centerpiece. Lavish as much or more attention on the other ingredients to come up with a dish that's high in flavor, visual appeal, and zest.

I do think vegetarianism suffers from an "image problem"; too many people equate it with bland plates of tofu and sprouts. If this is the image you call to mind, you may be interested to learn that some of the most exciting cooking today is taking place in vegetarian kitchens, and there are more restaurants, prepared foods, and cookbooks than ever catering to this preference. There are also many magazines about vegetarian eating. I urge you to explore the wonderful meat-free dishes that are increasingly common today, as well as the beans and grains now available in every supermarket. Chef Erickson has included numerous meatless recipes for you to enjoy.

VITAMINS AND CANCER

Vitamins—organic compounds from plant and animal sources—are essential to all the body's functions. Just as fiber can be divided into water-soluble and water-insoluble categories, vitamins are also classed according to solubility. The water-soluble vitamins are the B vitamins (such as niacin), vitamin C, and others. These flush out of the body and must be replenished daily. The fat-soluble ones are vitamins A, D, E, and K. They can be stored in the liver and to a lesser extent in fat, the kidneys, and lungs.

It has long been known that vitamins are necessary for good nutrition and good health. The absence of certain vitamins can cause disease; for example, lack of vitamin C can lead to scurvy and lack of vitamin D can cause rickets, a disease in which the bones soften and bow.

Several vitamins are known to be important in cancer, but the exact role of individual vitamins in specific cancers is yet to be determined. A number of clinical trials are in progress to test the use of vitamins (especially the antioxidants, which will be described below) to prevent cancer. The usual approach in these studies is to observe the effects of vitamins on "premalignant" lesions, such as adenomatous colon polyps (a precursor to colon cancer; see chapter 6, "For People with Colorectal Cancer") or a particular type of oral lesion called leukoplakia, which is also known to precede cancer. At present, much attention is focused on vitamin A and synthetic counterparts of vitamin A, as well as vitamins C and E. Early results of these studies are encouraging but not definitive.

Scientists are also exploring ways that vitamins can reduce side effects of cancer therapies. One way vitamins are already used clinically is during chemotherapy with methotrexate for several types of tumors. Large doses of methotrexate can cause toxic side effects, including bone marrow damage and severe mouth sores. These side effects can be greatly decreased by taking a form of folic acid. *Whether you are taking methotrexate or not, do not take folic acid supplements without first consulting your physician.*

Another encouraging, but still experimental, use of a vitamin is for a form of leukemia called promyelocytic leukemia. This type of leukemia is often fatal. Treatment with all-trans-retinoic acid (a form of vitamin A) has resulted in remissions of the disease in some individuals.

ANTIOXIDANTS

Vitamins A, C, and E as well as some other nutrients are known as antioxidants. The "other nutrients" include beta carotene, found in green and yellow vegetables and converted by the body into vitamin A, as well as carotenoids (another vitamin A precursor), selenium, lycopene (found in tomatoes and pink grapefruit), and others.

Antioxidants protect the body from molecules known as free radicals, which are thought to roam the body robbing or "oxidizing" other molecules of essential parts of their molecular structures. That process is thought to damage the body, contributing to a variety of diseases, arthritis, for example. (It's rather like a car rusting out, which is another oxidizing process.) Oxidants are capable of damaging DNA and may, in this way, cause cancer.

Where do free radicals come from? They are by-products of normal metabolic processes and can also occur after exposure to radiation or certain carcinogens—for example, through smoking.

FRUITS AND VEGETABLES HIGH IN BETA CAROTENE

Apricots	Persimmons
Broccoli	Pumpkin
Butternut squash	Spinach
Cantaloupe	Sweet potatoes
Carrots	Swiss chard
Collard greens	Turnip greens
Kale	Winter squash
Mangoes	

Recent, very exciting research shows that vitamins A, C, and E help remove these potentially harmful oxidative compounds from the body before they can harm cells. These vitamins have the ability to inhibit the harmful activity of free radicals and prevent oxidative damage, which is why they are termed antioxidants.

The extent of antioxidants' ability to prevent cancer is not yet clear. Some vitamins and vitamin precursors, including beta carotene, appear to hinder the development of skin cancer and upper digestive tract cancers, as well as cervical cancer in its earliest stages. Clinical trials are in progress with vitamins A and E and derivatives of vitamin A. Early results indicate that in some persons, premalignant oral lesions (leukoplakia) respond favorably to this type of preventive treatment, and new cancers of the head and neck have been reduced in patients cured of an initial cancer.

So, without realizing it, you may be helping your body to prevent cancer each time you serve spinach, squash, and other green leafy vegetables and deep yellow vegetables. Nevertheless, even though antioxidants have been promoted heavily in news reports and through commercial advertising, it is not yet possible to recommend a precise dose for supplements or a combination of antioxidants in cancer management.

Antioxidant properties make beta carotene (and a number of its relatives called carotenoids) important members of the natural family of compounds being investigated as potential preventors of cancer. Chapter 7, "For People with Cancer of the Lung, Head, Neck, Esophagus, Cervix, Bladder, or Skin (Squamous Cancers)," discusses these compounds in relation to prevention of oral cancers. Other specific vitamins are discussed in the various chapters by cancer sites.

Chapter 9, "Three Months to a New Eating Plan," includes a chart of the richest natural food sources of antioxidants, as well as other practical information for including more fruits and vegetables in your diet.

Please note that high doses of vitamin A can be very toxic, causing damage to the brain and skin, along with fatigue, abdominal and bone pain, insomnia, headache, and night sweats. These high doses can also cause fetal defects in pregnant women. Excessive intake of beta carotene does not appear to have significant toxic effects other than yellowing of the skin. Because of the potential side effects, you should not take large doses of vitamin A—or any other vitamin, for that matter—outside of established and well-monitored clinical trials. "More" is not always "better."

MINERALS AND CANCER

Minerals are essential for many vital metabolic processes, including bone production and repair, maintaining fluid in the cells, and transmitting nerve impulses. Among them are calcium, sodium, potassium, magnesium, iron, nickel, copper, zinc, and selenium. Of these, calcium, selenium, iron, zinc, and copper, in varying degrees of precision, have been associated with cancer. There is some evidence that selenium, iron, zinc, and copper may have carcinogenic effects, at least in the laboratory. Any similar effects in humans remain undetermined. On the other hand, there is considerable evidence that calcium may decrease cancer risk, especially for colon cancer (see "Calcium" below).

Certain minerals, especially selenium, have received much attention recently, both as possible causes of cancer and as cancer preventives. Selenium is being evaluated at this time, but no conclusive data shows this trace element to have any role in treatment.

SALT (SODIUM)

There is no known direct connection between sodium and cancer, but there are several reasons for a person with cancer to limit sodium intake. First, regardless of your cancer therapy, excess salt intake is not a good idea. It can aggravate high blood pressure, which increases the risk of heart attack, stroke, and kidney disease. If you are on hormonal therapy, your body may tend to accumulate fluids and your blood pressure may rise. Excess salt can contribute to this. Also, certain chemotherapeutic agents can damage the heart and kidneys; salt and fluid overload may exacerbate such damage.

Your body needs only a tiny amount of salt daily. The recommended daily allowance is 2,400 mg *or less,* but many Americans consume far more than this, either by adding salt at the table or by eating foods with high salt content. A quick survey of food labels in your pantry will probably provide quite a surprise, especially if you look at the sodium contents of canned goods such as soups, soy sauce, and processed meats. Frozen prepared entrees and meals are also often high in sodium, which is why I recommend using these sparingly.

To reduce sodium intake, always read the label on all food goods you purchase. If you increase your consumption of fresh fruit and vegetables as I recommend in this book, and add salt—if you must add it at all—at the table, not during cooking, you will cut salt intake dramatically.

Calcium

Sodium is ubiquitous in our culture's foods, so we tend to get too much of it, even if we delete table salt, but most people, especially women, don't get enough of another mineral, calcium.

Calcium is so necessary in metabolism that when dietary intake is not sufficient, calcium is absorbed from bones to maintain blood levels. If blood levels of calcium fall too low, severe problems with muscle function will result. Since the heart is a muscle, it, too, will be affected.

Chronic loss of calcium from bones causes osteoporosis (thinning of the bones). This condition can be seen on a routine X ray, but it often is discovered only after a fracture has occurred, usually of the hip or wrist. This is a common problem for postmenopausal women, because the loss of estrogen contributes to the rate of bone loss. Osteoporosis also can be caused by large doses of corticosteroid drugs, and by the loss of ovarian function that results from some chemotherapy drugs.

Recent data suggest a possible link between calcium and cancer. Epidemiologic studies have shown that the more milk one drinks, the lower the colon cancer risk, and vice versa. Calcium has been shown in laboratory studies to decrease the cell division activity in colon lining cells; calcium may also bind and inactivate carcinogens in the stool. Clinical trials using calcium are in progress to see if this element has clinically useful cancer prevention activity.

Clearly, it is important for both preventive and therapeutic reasons to get enough calcium in your diet. The U.S. RDA (recommended daily allowance) for calcium is 800 mg per day over age 25 and 1,200 mg per day for those under 25. Some experts think post-menopausal women need more. Common food sources of calcium are milk and other dairy products, asparagus, broccoli, Great Northern and navy beans, okra, spinach, and soybean products (tofu).

You can increase dietary calcium by eating more nonfat dairy products and calcium-containing foods, such as dark green leafy vegetables (turnip and collard greens, kale, broccoli, spinach, etc.) or tofu. These, plus a reasonable consumption of dairy products, will quickly add up to the recommended total. For example, a day's allotment might be gained by consuming:

Skim milk—1 cup	300 mg
Broccoli—1 cup	178 mg
Turnip greens—1 cup	250 mg
Nonfat cheese—2 ounces	400 mg
Nonfat yogurt—1 cup	450 mg
Day's total:	1,578 mg calcium

Dairy products are the most concentrated sources of calcium. If you are unable to tolerate dairy products, or if your doctor says you have or are at risk for osteoporosis, it's important to ask about a calcium supplement. Several over-the-counter forms are available, such as Tums. Recent data indicate that calcium supplements do delay osteoporosis in postmenopausal women. Your doctor can advise about the appropriate dosage for you.

NONNUTRIENTS WITH ANTICANCER EFFECTS

It's enormously attractive to imagine that the entire field of nutrition, with all its complicated features and well-kept secrets, could be reduced to a list of vitamins and minerals. We could all stop worrying about what to fix for dinner, pull up to the drive-in window at the local pharmacy, and order a takeout of multivitamins for supper, a jug of water to wash them down, and some minerals for dessert.

Of course, this is not possible. In her great wisdom, Mother Nature has taken into account how quickly we would be bored with

FOODS THAT CONTAIN CALCIUM

FOOD	CALCIUM (MG)
Skim milk* (½ cup)	150
Nonfat yogurt (1 cup)	450
Tofu, firm (3 ounces)	174
Sardines** (3 ounces)	324
Salmon** (3 ounces)	203
Collard greens (½ cup)	148
Spinach, cooked (½ cup)	122
Spinach, raw (½ cup)	28
Broccoli, boiled (½ cup)	89
Chinese cabbage, boiled (½ cup)	79
Kale, cooked (½ cup)	47
Artichoke (1)	47
White beans (½ cup)	80
Vegetarian baked beans (½ cup)	64
Chickpeas (½ cup)	40
Butter beans (½ cup)	40
Tortilla (1)	42

* Skim milk also contains vitamin D, which aids absorption of calcium
** Canned, packed in water, with bones

night after night of vitamins and minerals for supper, and has instead provided us with a cornucopia of food choices. And it's a good thing, for we are just beginning to identify what all the components in foods are, and what their roles are. Though the science is very young, its findings are truly exciting.

In early 1993, for example, an article in the *Proceedings of the National Academy of Sciences* described the discovery of a compound called genistein. This substance is found in the urine of people who eat a traditional Japanese diet, which emphasizes soybeans (for example, tofu, which is a soybean curd). It is also found in lesser amounts in cruciferous (cabbage family) vegetables. Genistein has the interesting ability to block new blood vessel formation. Since, in order to grow, a cancer must somehow get its own blood supply by causing new blood vessels to form, it may be possible to stop the tumor's growth when it is still very small (1 millimeter or less in diameter) by stopping proliferation of blood vessels. Without angiogenesis (blood vessel proliferation), the tumor cannot get the nutrition it needs to thrive and spread. Several such "antiangiogenesis" compounds are being evaluated; genistein is the first to be isolated from a food. In theory, a diet high in soy products, like miso soup, could be a reason that certain populations such as the Japanese have lower rates of cancer of the breast, prostate, and colon (although other factors most likely play a part, such as fat and fiber content of the diet).

Imagine the possibilities in this finding. With further study, including study of how genistein functions in animals and then in human beings, it may be that by simply emphasizing soybeans and vegetables, an individual could be helping his or her own body cut tumors off at the pass!

A similar, recent finding is that flavonoids, which are contained in soybeans, may play a preventive role in breast cancer. Though this is still theoretical, it appears that flavonoids block receptor sites for the hormones that promote breast cancer.

Consider that some of the most powerful weapons we have against cancer are derived from plants. Vincristine comes from the periwinkle plant. Taxol is derived from the bark of the Pacific yew. Many of the agents that are being studied for their ability to prevent cancer are present in plants. Beta-glycyrrhetenic acid, for example, a flavoring agent in licorice, in some laboratory experiments has strongly inhibited certain cancers.

As you can see, the vitamins in soybeans and vegetables have their own important functions to fulfill, but there are other substances in these foods—and in others as well—that serve other, equally important functions. The National Cancer Institute has determined that more than 1,000 of these chemicals have cancer-preventive (chemopreventive) activity, at least in the laboratory. This explains why it's better to include lots of vegetables, fruits, and grains in your diet than to depend on vitamin tablets to maintain your nutritional status.

The table "The Nonnutrient Anticancer Chemicals in Foods" sums up what is known about some of these substances so far.

SOME NONNUTRIENT ANTICANCER CHEMICALS IN FOODS

* = theoretically prevent normal cells from becoming malignant
** = act in preventing malignant cells from proliferating
*** = could do both

CHEMICAL	POSSIBLE ACTION	SOURCES
Lycopene*	antioxidant	tomatoes
Capsicum*	antioxidant	cayenne pepper
Catechin*, other bioflavonoids**	antimutagen, antioxidant, antiestrogen	green tea, berries, woody plants, other plants and vegetables
Beta-glycyrrhetenic acid***	suppresses metabolism of estrogen into more cancer-stimulating forms; inhibits carcinogens	licorice root
Various indoles***	induce metabolism of estrogen to less cancer-stimulating forms	cruciferous vegetables
Limonene*	stimulate removal of carcinogens by liver	citrus fruits
Various sulfides*	stimulate removal of carcinogens by liver	garlic, onions
Isothiocyanates*	stimulate removal of carcinogens by liver	mustard, radishes
Genistein**	antiangiogenesis	soybeans, cruciferous vegetables
Ellagic acid*	may remove or block carcinogens	grapes, raspberries, other fruit
Monoterpenes*	antioxidant; stimulates removal of carcinogens by liver	carrots, cruciferous vegetables, squash, tomatoes

D. W. Nixon, ed. *Chemoprevention of Cancer.*

Paradoxically, some of these same foods contain chemicals that might be carcinogens. Many of these chemicals are natural pesticides, some of which can be anticarcinogenic or carcinogenic depending on the dose and other experimental conditions. Very large doses usually are the carcinogenic ones.

Since some foods do contain such potentially adverse chemicals, it is wise not to overemphasize any one fruit or vegetable in the diet. Examples of foods with natural pesticides are celery, mushrooms, cruciferous vegetables such as broccoli and cabbage, horseradish, pineapple, apples, carrots, grapes, pears, plums, and potatoes. Most of these are clearly safe and even recommended; the point is to eat a varied diet.

OTHER REASONS PILLS CANNOT SUBSTITUTE FOR FOOD

When your physician or nurse asks you, "What medications are you taking?" do you mention any vitamins that you are using? We seldom think of them as medications, because they can be picked up in the grocery store or pharmacy without a prescription. We also tend to think of them as fairly harmless, even in excess. We give them to our children from infancy. In a practice that should be called "hit or myth," many people "prescribe" vitamins for themselves, taking extra vitamin C for a cold or extra iron when feeling lethargic.

As familiar as vitamins are to us, they can be dangerous if taken in excess. High doses of some vitamins may suppress immunity, and overdosage of vitamin A can damage the skin and other vital organs.

In recent years, large ("mega") doses of vitamins have been widely promoted in the media to prevent or cure a variety of illnesses, though the truth is that *there is no evidence that megadoses of conventional vitamins (that is, the kinds of vitamins you can buy over the counter in a grocery store or pharmacy) are helpful in treatment of any illness, including cancer. In fact, megadoses of vitamins can be toxic, so the decision to use more than a normal dose of vitamins should be made only after consultation with your physician.* See the table below for a rundown of the toxic effects of overdoses of some vitamins and minerals.

My intent in talking about these potential side effects is not to discourage you from using vitamin and mineral supplements, but to urge caution about using them in excessive doses, especially without *first consulting with your physician.*

If you are concerned about getting all the vitamins and minerals you need regularly, you can consider a daily multivitamin and mineral supplement with standard doses. Talk with your physician.

SMOKING AND CANCER

The adverse effects from tobacco will overwhelm any benefit from lifestyle changes. Vitamins and minerals can only do so much to help a body that is being abused by tobacco and other harmful substances contained in tobacco smoke. It's been proven that smokers need larger amounts of certain drugs and other agents (such as vitamin C) to gain the same benefits that a nonsmoker gets from an equivalent dose. On this basis, it's possible that one factor in the development of lung cancer is that smoking disarms some of the body's best defenses. By ruining your sense of smell, smoking can also take much of the pleasure out of meals—yours as well as the dining experience of those around you—and this is particularly important for those who need to make substantial adjustments in their diet.

In chapter 7 we will talk much more about smoking's link to cancer.

The message here, of course, is to *stop smoking* or *don't start,* so that your nutrition and therapy plan will be able to do its work without interference. Your doctor can help you stop—ask for help. The use of nicotine gum and patches can be a useful adjuvant to a supervised

SOME TOXIC EFFECTS OF VITAMIN
OR MINERAL OVERDOSE

Note: This is not a comprehensive list.

VITAMINS

A	Vomiting, brain swelling, fatigue, malaise, lethargy, joint pain, headache, insomnia, night sweats, scaly skin, edema, damage to fetuses
B complex	Rare allergic reactions
C	Nausea, diarrhea, increased blood cholesterol; possible (but not yet proven) mutagenic effects and/or immune system suppression
D	Increased blood calcium levels with heart and kidney damage
E	Fatigue, rash, elevated plasma lipids, liver damage. Caution: May increase the effects of anticoagulant drugs, so may be hazardous if used along with anticoagulants.
Folic Acid	Rare allergic reactions may increase seizures in persons taking antiepileptic drugs

MINERALS

Calcium	Increased blood calcium with potential serious renal (kidney) damage
Copper	Nausea, vomiting, diarrhea and abdominal pain, headache, weakness, anemia, hypertension, coma
Iron	Liver damage, diabetes, increased skin pigment, endocrinopathies, heart failure
Magnesium	In persons with renal insufficiency, may cause weakness and skeletal muscle paralysis
Potassium	Cardiac damage, including cardiac arrest and death
Zinc	Nausea, vomiting, abdominal cramps, diarrhea, fever; possible (but not proven) immune system suppression

smoking-cessation program. The American Cancer Society, the American Heart Association, the American Lung Association, and the National Cancer Institute also have helpful material and programs for you.

CANCER AND ALCOHOL

There is no doubt that alcohol, especially when combined with smoking, is associated with cancer of the head and neck, esophagus, and probably breast and other types. Heavy alcohol consumption should always be avoided. Among other things, it can result in liver cirrhosis, which may be associated with liver cancer. I would recommend avoiding alcohol if you have had or are at risk of squamous cancers of the mouth and digestive tract and breast cancer. And for everyone, I recommend that if you drink, it should be only occasionally and sparingly.

NITRATES AND CANCER

The American Cancer Society recommends that everyone limit consumption of salt-cured, smoked, and nitrate-preserved foods.

During the conventional smoking process, foods such as ham, sausage, bacon, and fish absorb some of the tars arising from incomplete combustion. These tars contain numerous carcinogens that are similar chemically to the carcinogenic tars in tobacco smoke. Foods grilled over charcoal also contain many of these carcinogens.

Inferential evidence suggests that salt-cured or pickled foods may increase the risk of stomach and esophageal cancers. The reasons are not clear.

There is chemical evidence that nitrates and nitrites can enhance carcinogenic nitrosamine formation, both in foods and in our digestive tracts. Nitrates and nitrites are traditional meat preservatives used to protect against botulism (acute food poisoning), and also to improve the color and flavor of meats. There are fewer nitrates and nitrites in prepared meats than there used to be, and the government and food industry are looking for improved methods of meat preservation. Still, you should limit the amount of lunch meats, hot dogs, and bacon containing these substances that you eat.

PUTTING IT ALL TOGETHER

In summary, it's important to remember that nutrition alone is not the sole cause of any cancer, nor is nutrition alone an effective treatment for cancer.

Studies of eating patterns in various countries have suggested that the ideal diet for prevention of cancer appears to be a low-calorie, low-fat, high-fiber diet, with abundant fruits and vegetables, similar to what our remote ancestors ate, with the addition of a proper balance of needed trace elements, vitamins, and minerals.

In coming chapters, we will look at each kind of cancer and the diet guidelines that seem best for it at this time.

FEELING OVERWHELMED BY THE NUTRITIONAL PUZZLE?

The scientific data we've discussed so far is important, but there is another dimension to nutrition that is equally important. Eating food and having meals are some of our most psychologically loaded human experiences. Mealtimes can nourish the soul, as well as the body, by providing an arena for shared time and conversation with family, friends, and coworkers. Mealtimes alone are often the setting for "food for thought," spent in reading, thinking, or observing people and events while eating. Meals alone can also be the loneliest kind of aloneness, especially if the aloneness is not by *choice.*

We celebrate births with food, begin our courtships with a romantic meal out, seal up marriage contracts by inviting everyone we know to a huge spread of food, and are comforted and rebound to life by a meal following the burial of a loved one. Foods and food rituals are a basic element of every culture and an important way that we segment our days and our lives.

The broader role of food and nutrition is the reason why food relief sent to people in famine-ravaged countries has to be *acceptable* as well as nourishing; for example, sending beef to India, where the cow is considered sacred, would be both useless and an insult. If there were a famine in the United States, all but the most adventuresome Americans would be indignant if grubs and grasshoppers—which are delicacies in some countries—were sent to alleviate our hunger.

The factor of *acceptability* is so crucial that it was the subject of one of the most interesting studies I ever had the privilege to conduct. While the American Cancer Society had sensible, well-reasoned, and scientifically sound guidelines for nutrition to prevent cancer, no one really knew how acceptable those guidelines were to the American public. What good were these fine ideas if no one found the foods pleasing? So, we chose a controlled situation—the sailors of two navy ships at sea—to test the guidelines. The sailors on one ship got the typical navy diet. The sailors on the other ship had a choice: navy chow or a daily diet selected and prepared according to the American Cancer Society's guidelines. With follow-up questionnaires, we found that the "guidelines" diet was not only acceptable, it was preferred. Furthermore, many of the sailors who chose the guidelines diet lost some excess weight and had lower body fat levels.

As you deal with your diagnosis of cancer and its treatment, you may find it difficult to settle on what's acceptable to you, and the problem of maintaining proper nutrition may seem overwhelming. This is especially so when you've first learned your diagnosis and have not yet learned to navigate the health-care system and the daily routines that work for you. What is acceptable may change from day to day, perhaps even meal to meal, or you may not feel very interested in eating at all.

If you think of food in its broad context, it's easy to see how disruption of your food routines and customs can be a source of great dismay. This is one of the reasons why "jet lag" can be so devastating. It may be suppertime in San Francisco, but if you body is on Atlanta time, it's close to midnight, and the biological kitchen is shut down for the day. It also explains why dinnertime—traditionally a time of togetherness—is the hardest part of the day for someone who has lost a spouse or significant other. And it explains why mealtime may be very upsetting to you until you are feeling better. You may find that you can keep smiling and be brave in the face of surgery, but the sight of a beautiful family meal—that you want to eat but can't—may reduce you to tears.

There are two things that will help you over this difficult period.

The first is information, and that is the purpose of this book. The more you learn about how the right diet can help you fight the cancer, the more ready and able you will be to put those facts to use—as soon as you feel ready.

The other is time. In some ways, the initial period of diagnosis and starting treatment is the hardest, because you have to go through so many new experiences, most of which are not very appealing. Your household may be greatly disrupted until everyone gains sufficient skills to manage the emotional stress and practical problems associated with cancer. Beginning a new phase of treatment or getting a bad test result may restart the cycle.

I hope that this book will help you reclaim the joys of mealtime. The key is to be gentle with yourself. Push toward new goals when you feel you can; rest when you must, without guilt or apology. And keep in mind that though it may not seem so, this too shall pass.

DIET, NUTRITION, AND CANCER GUIDELINES

These are the American Cancer Society's guidelines for reducing cancer risk in all people. My more specific recommendations are in keeping with these broad ones, which are included for your reference. These recommendations are similar to those made by the National Cancer Institute and other health agencies and organizations.

1. Maintain a desirable body weight.
2. Eat a varied diet.
3. Include a variety of both vegetables and fruits in the daily diet.
4. Eat more high-fiber foods, such as whole-grain cereals, legumes, vegetables, and fruits.
5. Cut down on total fat intake.
6. Limit consumption of alcoholic beverages, if you drink at all.
7. Limit consumption of salt-cured, smoked, and nitrite-preserved foods.

3

MAKING SOUND DECISIONS ABOUT ALTERNATIVE NUTRITIONAL APPROACHES

ॐ

O ne of the most exciting changes taking place in medicine today is that people are playing a greater role in making decisions about their health care. They are educating themselves about their options, through reading books and magazines and through asking their doctors questions.

A desire to take control of one's destiny as much as possible is a very healthy impulse. This is why I strongly urge everyone— persons with cancer and persons without cancer—to learn as much as possible about cancer, its prevention, and its appropriate treatment.

Already, some of my patients have benefitted by taking greater responsibility for their health care. This is no small transition when we take into account how medicine has been viewed as a great mystery, and physicians as the gods of medicine, for many centuries. There will, of course, be problems as physicians and persons with cancer work out these new roles. Whenever I think about this problem, I think of Ann Hendricks, certainly one of the most intelligent, independent, and feisty women I have ever met.

Ms. Hendricks was a serious artist. At some time in her life, she had determined that art would be her primary focus, so at age fifty-one she was unmarried, had no children, and was highly selective about who her friends were and how much time she could spend with them. She was also somewhat distrustful of the "medical establishment," so it must have been especially painful for her to be forced, by a diagnosis of breast cancer, to set aside her work and spend lots of time with doctors, nurses, and pharmacists. She questioned everything and made it clear that she would need full information before acquiescing to any treatment.

Ms. Hendricks first had a lumpectomy and axiliary node dissection, followed by radiation, a course of chemotherapy, and then tamoxifen. Her breast cancer extended to six nodes, but she had no metastases (spreading of the cancer) to other organs.

Treatment can be a very intimidating ordeal, and though Ms. Hendricks was courageous in taking the treatments, she remained unconvinced about some of them. She read widely on breast cancer and nutrition, and followed closely any new developments on these topics. This was, in itself, an excellent approach. Unfortunately, some of what she read and heard was not sound advice or was not fully developed.

One night she heard a report on the national news about possible toxic effects of tamoxifen, such as the potential for second primary tumors (that is, second tumors that develop in an entirely different part of the body from the first). It is true that there is such a risk, but this is a topic that deserves a much larger forum than a television report can offer. Nevertheless, Ms. Hendricks simply stopped taking tamoxifen, much to her physician's dismay. Based on her readings, she devised her own program of megavitamins and purges, both of which have the potential to do great harm to health. And somehow, despite what the purges were doing to her energy levels, Ms. Hendricks took up an exercise program that was excessive. When her physician realized that she was becoming weak and malnourished, he called for help.

When Ann Hendricks came to my office, I was expecting a battle, though I wasn't sure how she could find the strength for one, under the circumstances. She was quite articulate, and what she was asking for did not seem unreasonable. She wanted to take charge, as much as possible, of her own recovery. She wanted her treatments to do as little harm as possible, now and in the future, and she wanted to select treatments that would have a meaningful outcome. More than anything, she wanted to be well enough to get back to her artwork, and she wanted to continue that work for as long as possible, without the threat of recurrence or second primary tumors. She had worked hard to gather a great deal of information, and what she needed from me was help in sorting the chaff from the grain.

So we did the smart thing: We negotiated. I felt that the tamoxifen was an important part of her therapy, and asked if she would consider taking it at a lower dose. She agreed that, with the risk thus lowered, she would try tamoxifen again. She felt that the vitamins might offer some help. I agreed, but not with the megadoses. I explained to her that megadoses of certain vitamins can be toxic and are usually wasteful. So we worked out a regimen of daily vitamins, at sensible and effective levels, and a low-fat, high-fiber diet plan. I think she was very relieved to be rid of the exercise program, which we decided would be quite adequate at forty-five minutes a day of walking, which included a warm-up and cool-down period.

Thanks to the improvement in her nutritional status, the satisfaction of having control over her present therapy and her future destiny, and the elimination of excessive and unnecessary practices, Ms. Hendricks did get back to her art. She remains on her tamoxifen, at work, disease-free, and more feisty than ever. In her battle with cancer and with the medical establishment, she feels as though she won—and she did.

GETTING FRUSTRATED

Like Ms. Hendricks, if you have cancer you probably have lots of questions and frustrations about the disease and its treatment. When you were told by your physician that you have cancer, you were undoubtedly faced with a lot of questions that can't be answered: *How did I get this cancer? Was the water in my rural hometown contaminated? Could it be true that exposure to electromagnetic fields can cause cancer? Have I spent too much time around computers? Could it be some virus that I caught when I was a young and foolish teenager?*

One of your next concerns might be about your treatment and its outcome. For many cancers, the answers are not very satisfactory. It is unfortunate that physicians must so often say, "We are still searching for an adequate method to treat your cancer."

Even if the treatment has good results, the next question to face is whether it will "hold." It seems that a countdown begins the instant treatment ends: Will the cancer come back? As you already know, your physicians may be able to make general predictions, but they are usually careful to avoid absolutes such as, "You will never have to deal with this disease again." More likely, you will be told, "You should do well. It appears that you will be able to put this behind you now . . . but come back for your checkups, without fail."

For people with cancer (as well as for their health-care providers), these unanswerable questions about cancer are extremely difficult and frustrating. That we are surrounded by amazing miracles in modern medicine only adds to the frustration. If we can transplant a heart, reattach a severed limb and make it functional, "see" the body's secrets in great detail with new imaging techniques, why can't we develop a way to prevent or cure cancer? Furthermore, why can't we get the story straight on cancer? One day we are told that apples or fluorescent lights cause cancer; a few months or years later, we hear that they don't.

While this flip-flopping is maddening, it is sign of something good. It is the result of the phenomenal progress in cancer research that is occurring in the closing years of the twentieth century. Concepts that have been held true for centuries are being reexamined in ways that as a medical student I never dreamed possible. Now, instead of studying *cellular* biology, scientists are delving into *molecular* biology, observing, describing, and manipulating the processes at the core of life. I have to plow through a mountain of reading each week to keep up with it all—which brings me to my next point.

Much of the confusion and flip-flopping that occurs in cancer news is the result of hasty or inappropriate reporting. Lest my friends in the press leap on me, I don't think it's fair to blame the problem entirely on reporters. In fact, hasty reporting is sometimes done by scientists, especially when competition in a certain area of study is intense. Another problem is conflicting data or lack of data. The recent controversy over the usefulness of mammograms in women under fifty illustrates the confusion that can occur when different groups with different perspectives look at an issue.

It takes only a pencil and paper or a microphone and camera to put together a brief report on a recent discovery, but it takes an expert (and more often, many experts) to put new discoveries *in perspective.* The deliberations of experts can be painfully slow, but their exacting approach will lead to sound, cautious pronounce- ments, such as, "There may be a relationship between alopecia and heart disease, but this requires further study." Of course, who would buy a newspaper with that headline, especially when the competing newspaper says, "BALDNESS CAUSES HEART ATTACKS"?

What results from these flip-flops and the rise and fall of expec- tations is not amusing. They can be a source of great tension be- tween the person who is ill, the family, and the health-care providers, especially when the illness is cancer.

I believe that this tension and frustration plays a major role in the decision to pursue unconventional or unproven methods of cancer treatment. Some people make the decision when it is clear that traditional methods are failing; others decide as soon as they realize that the cancer diagnosis is real. Some continue traditional, proven treatments along with the unproven methods. Some completely forgo scientifically sound methods to try a remedy that they heard about from a friend, read about in a magazine, or saw on television.

THE DANGERS OF UNPROVEN METHODS

A few years ago, a number of people with cancer were refusing traditional treatments and instead took laetrile, a drug made from apricot pits and other seeds. Though the drug had never been shown to have any value against cancer, it got wide attention in the press and on television. Claims of its efficacy were so persistent that many people accused the government of deliberately interfering with the lives and well-being of people with cancer. Promotion and sale of laetrile were illegal acts; nevertheless, its promoters managed to market it quite successfully.

Among those who were caught up in these events were a number of women who refused surgical removal of breast lumps in favor of trying laetrile. Knowing what we know now about the role of surgery in breast cancer—that in some cases, it is all the treatment that is needed to effect a cure—the decisions made by those women are especially horrifying.

In my own practice, I have seen a number of persons with cancer who delayed medical care to try "self-healing," religious therapies, or other methods. By the time they realized that the alternative method was not working, it often was too late for me to help them. *Some of these people had a chance for cure and lost it.* What is even more tragic is that they had to come to terms with this loss, at a terrible cost in guilt, anger, and recrimination.

Unproven methods can have many costs. Some cost precious time—time that would be better spent tackling the disease with scientifically proven methods. The cost of an unproven method can be life. Some unproven methods cause senseless suffering because they are harsh and directly harmful to health. This is especially true of the purging methods, such as a regimen of coffee enemas, which is touted now and then in different versions. Some of the methods cost a lot of money as well, especially those that can only be taken in another country (usually because they have been banned from the United States, with good reason).

People who use alternative methods are not stupid people, nor are they more likely to be poor or uneducated. A recent American Cancer Society survey showed that affluent, better educated persons were the most likely to seek alternative therapies. Women were slightly more likely than men to use such treatments. According to the survey, 9 percent of persons with cancer used at least one alternative treatment for cancer. Most had also received conventional cancer treatment of some type, which suggests that their motive was to add to standard therapy, not to avoid it.

The survey showed that the most frequently used therapies were "mind" therapies that promise to engage the powers of the mind over the processes of disease. In the American Cancer Society's survey, mind therapies were more popular among men than among women. Other popular methods included diets, which were favored more by women, as well as drugs and other methods.

The American Cancer Society monitors news and reports of unproven methods of cancer treatment, some of which seem to appear and reappear regularly. The methods are reviewed by a committee of experts, and their findings are available to the public on request. In the list of methods, each is ranked "of highest concern," "of high concern," "of concern," or "of concern, but inactive." Laetrile is one that is of highest concern. Other unproven methods described in the list are the "Greek cure," immunoaugmentative therapy, iscador, and hyperoxygenation therapy.

The proponent of the "Greek cure," the nature of which was not revealed, is now deceased. Immunoaugmentative therapy, promoted in the Bahamas, is claimed to enhance the body's resistance to cancer; the injected substance has been found to contain harmful contaminants. Iscador, an extract of mistletoe, has some laboratory interest but is unproven in humans. Hyperoxygenation is based on the anabolic theory of cancer (that cancer cells thrive with decreased oxygen exposure); oxygenating compounds such as hydrogen peroxide are injected to supposedly hinder tumor growth. To find out more about unproven cancer treatments, you can call (800) ACS-2345.

MAKING SOUND DECISIONS IS AN IMPORTANT PART OF YOUR WORK IN FIGHTING CANCER

While the decision to try an unproven method can be a bad one, I think that the source of the decision—a desire to control your own destiny—is actually good. One of your most powerful weapons in the fight against cancer is *accurate and complete information.* If you were planning to buy a new car, whom would you trust most: the salesman or a documentary report that compares the car's performance and cost to other cars, perhaps in *Consumer Reports?* You know that the salesman may be telling you the truth, but on the other hand, he is also thinking about the commission he's going to make. And where did he get *his* information? From the manufacturer, who needs to keep those cars moving off the lot to make room for next year's model. Certainly they're not going to tell you about the little problem that turned up in a few thousand of the transmission systems.

For the same reasons, when choosing a path for the treatment of cancer, look first to your physician. If you are not completely satisfied with his or her response, there are many additional sources of good information on cancer and cancer treatments, and some are as close as your telephone. The American Cancer Society's Cancer Response System is an excellent place to start, at its toll-free number: (800) ACS-2345. The National Cancer Institute also operates a Cancer Information Service, which can be reached at (800) 4-CANCER. Other information sources are listed at the back of this book.

For information on the newest therapies for a particular cancer, including therapies that are in the clinical trials phase, ask your physician to consult the "PDQ'" service ("Physicians' Data Query") of the National Cancer Institute. This service can give your physician information on drugs or methods being tested in clinical trials, some of which may be useful for your cancer. At this stage of study, the drug or method has already been shown to be safe and effective in a small group of human subjects, and now is being tried in a large group.

UNPROVEN NUTRITIONAL THERAPIES

One of the most frequently promoted unconventional therapies is some version of a nutritional therapy. There are several reasons for this. For one thing, a nutritional method is usually cheaper than other methods. It's easier to sell, because the public will feel a lot safer eating bags and bags of grapes or whatever than taking pills or potions from a manufacturer that no one has ever heard of. Also, it's no secret that nutrition and diet *are* clearly important in cancer prevention and treatment. This fact was recognized in the National Cancer Act of 1974, which states: "In carrying out the National Cancer Program, the director of the National Cancer Institute shall collect, analyze, and disseminate information respecting nutrition programs for cancer patients and the relationship between nutrition and cancer, useful in the prevention, diagnosis, and treatment of cancer." The information about cancer and nutrition in the other chapters in this book has been developed in large part from scientific studies arising out of the National Cancer Act.

Unfortunately, since 1974 progress has been painfully slow. It takes time to develop a promising lead from the laboratory into an effective treatment in the clinic. Many nutrition clinical trials are now in progress, but such trials take years to complete. Many of the promoters of unproven nutritional methods borrow just enough information from such scientific trials to make their method sound sensible and workable, either because they actually believe they're right (with no documentation to prove it) or because it will help sell a totally fraudulent product to people who are feeling desperate. They are especially adept at preying on people with lung cancer, colon cancer, or breast cancer, or people whose cancer has advanced beyond the range that can be treated by surgery. The period in which side effects of surgery, radiation, or chemotherapy are at their worst is also a vulnerable time, one in which it seems almost anything would be better than what you're going through at that moment.

I want to review some of the most common unproven nutritional therapies so you'll be aware of the medical consensus on them.

LAETRILE

Laetrile, which I mentioned earlier, is perhaps one of the most widely used unproven methods. This substance, found in apricot pits and certain other seeds, is purported to work by being converted to hydrogen cyanide, which kills cancer cells.

According to proponents laetrile does no harm to normal cells, because normal cells contain a detoxifying enzyme that is not present in large quantities in cancer cells. There is no doubt that laetrile can be converted to cyanide, which is very poisonous. Certain gut bacteria contain beta glucosidase, a substance that promotes such conversion. Unfortunately, for some persons who have taken laetrile this conversion did occur, and they died from cyanide poisoning.

Laetrile has been the subject of a number of court actions. In *Rutherford v. the United States,* individual physicians were given the right to import laetrile. Several states have allowed production of laetrile within their borders, and many clinics in Mexico and elsewhere administer it to cancer patients.

Aside from legal questions, the real question of laetrile is: Does it work? Some time ago, the National Cancer Institute conducted a survey of more than 400,000 physicians and other health-care providers, and asked them to submit information on any patients who had cancer, took laetrile, and appeared to have responded to laetrile. In response, NCI received results on ninety-three persons. Careful review and analysis of the records showed that only six of the ninety-three "responders" had experienced improvement that could accurately be attributed to laetrile. Later, in a clinical trial sponsored by the National Institutes of Health, laetrile showed *no* evidence of significant tumor-killing activity.

DETOXIFICATION THERAPIES

One of the basic beliefs behind many dietary therapies is that toxic, cancer-causing substances accumulate in the body naturally, or through ingestion of processed foods or other foods contaminated with pesticides, preservatives, or other chemicals. The secret, promoters say, is to purge the body of these toxins.

One therapy built around this belief is the Gerson method, a metabolic treatment developed in the 1920s. The method is an extreme "nutritional" approach using vigorous purges, including castor oil by mouth, castor oil enemas, and coffee enemas. The dietary component consists of large amounts of various juices, liver, linseed oil, and vegetables. The inclusion of liver is somewhat perplexing, since liver and other organ meats are sites where some contaminants accumulate in animals. Another irony of the Gerson method is that coffee is given by enema, but drinking coffee is forbidden. The regimen further forbids salt, nuts, drinking water, dairy products, fish, and meat, as well as canned, preserved, refined, or frozen foods.

The proposed goal of the Gerson method is to "detoxify" the body so that "natural" healing can occur. Natural healing is aided— say the Gerson proponents—by enzymes in various juices and calf liver, and by thyroid extract, pancreatic enzyme, iodine, vitamins, and royal jelly (a highly nutritious substance secreted by honeybees and fed to queen bee larvae), which are administered to patients in the Gerson clinics. Some of the Gerson clinics have also added "new improved methods" that have arisen in other camps: laetrile, intravenous solutions of electrolytes and insulin, ozone enemas, and hydrogen peroxide.

A basic tenet of the Gerson method is that to achieve a cure, the person with cancer must adhere strictly to every aspect of the prescribed therapy. The implication, of course, is that if the patient does not obtain a cure from this regimen, it is presumably because of failure to follow the program, not because the program doesn't work.

There is no sound scientific evidence that this or any other "detoxification" therapy has any effect on cancer. Coffee enemas are not known to do anything more than any other enema, which is to flush out the contents of the colon. It is known, however, that the frequent use of enemas can lead to dehydration and chronic malabsorption of fat, fat-soluble vitamins, and calcium. Deaths from dehydration and electrolyte imbalance have occurred following frequent coffee enemas.

Likewise, there is no credible evidence that enzymes in fruits, vegetables, and calf liver have any effect in restoring the function of "poisoned" (that is, cancerous) cells. Such enzymes are by and large destroyed in the process of digestion in the gut and are not absorbed intact. Contrary to what some proponents have claimed, there is no evidence that "detoxification" produces any anticancer "allergic" response.

Macrobiotic Diets

Another frequently cited dietary cancer treatment is the macrobiotic diet. The term comes from the Greek *makros,* meaning long, and *bios,* meaning life; thus, long life or longevity. This combination of diet and philosophy, which became popular about thirty years ago, is a type of vegetarian diet. It was originally known as the Zen macrobiotic diet.

Macrobiotic theory incorporates the oriental concepts of yin and yang. Imbalances of these two forces are believed to lead to disease, so balance must be restored by adding foods with the required yin or yang attributes. In general, the macrobiotic diet features predominantly whole grains, with lesser amounts of vegetables, soups, and beans. Meat, poultry, animal fat, eggs, dairy products, coffee, frozen food, refined sugar, and honey are forbidden (in this, the diet is similar to the Gerson diet described above). Chewing each bite of food 150 or more times creates yang. Ginger and other vegetable-based plasters and compresses are used for pain relief. Some macrobiotic enthusiasts have tried to exist on a diet of brown rice alone, an extreme practice that places anyone, including persons with cancer, at grave risk. As with the Gerson method, promoters of the macrobiotic approach say that the diet must be followed exactly for cure to occur.

A number of health problems have been associated with macrobiotic diets. Prominent among these are growth and development problems in children fed macrobiotic diets. Deficiencies of vitamins and minerals have also been reported. Vegetarian diets clearly can be healthy and nutritionally adequate if planned properly, but care must be taken to ensure intake of adequate amounts of needed nutrients.

Some macrobiotic practitioners—and others in alternative healing as well—teach that a person with cancer is directly responsible for the development of his or her disease. While this may be true for lung cancer in heavy smokers, such a belief can add a heavy emotional burden, especially in cancers that have no known cause.

The most direct harm that comes from macrobiotic and other alternative methods is that the patient may be urged to forsake conventional management and thus may fail to receive effective treatment for cancer.

As I have emphasized elsewhere in this book, *there is no evidence that any dietary manipulation alone will cure cancer.* Extreme dietary practices have no documented validity in cancer treatment. The National Institutes of Health now have an Office of Alternative Medicine to evaluate unproven methods scientifically to determine if any are effective in treating cancer and other diseases.

THE SECRETS OF THE AGES

Many promoters of an unproven method will claim that the method is "an ancient secret, recently rediscovered." Certainly there have been many nutritional treatments tried for cancer over the centuries, some of them strange and bizarre.

Around the sixteenth century, someone originated a cancer "remedy" that is resurrected periodically, even in this century: the grape diet. Why grapes were chosen is not clear. Grapes do contain compounds that have anticancer activity (quercetin and ellagic acid), but this information was clearly not known when the diet first appeared. Advocates of the diet prescribed a diet of only grapes for one to two weeks. They acknowledged that the program might become a bit monotonous: "A loathing for grapes indicates a need for a fast. Skip a few meals." I do not know of any reliable data that supports this theory.

Other unusual methods proposed over the years include products derived from material obtained from the medicine man of a tribe of South American head shrinkers. This substance was highly toxic until the number of plant extracts it contained was reduced from thirty to six. In the early 1950s, a representative of the National

Cancer Institute indicated that some tumor regression had occurred with this material. This could be possible since plants clearly contain very powerful cellular toxins. The National Cancer Institute has a very large investigative program for antineoplastic properties of plant substances, and several useful drugs have come from this work—taxol, for example. Several hundred other plant-derived substances are now being evaluated for their cancer preventive potential.

THE ROLE OF STRESS, ANXIETY, AND EMOTION IN CANCER

The idea that you can prevent or control cancer by dealing with stress, anxiety, and emotion crops up on talk shows, in self-help books, and in testimonials by well-meaning people who have cobbled together various theories from here and there. These theories often suggest that the person with cancer brought the disease on by living too stressful a lifestyle or suppressing his or her emotions, for example. The facts show that the relationship between stress and cancer is far more complex than that.

The idea that people can control their health is found in the earliest medical writings. This quotation from Democritus (about 400 B.C.) bears this out: "They pray to their gods for health; they do not realize that they have control over it themselves. They jeopardize it by their excesses and so their greed makes them traitors to their health."

So the connection between behavior and disease is nothing new, and the belief that controlling behavior, including the emotions, would help cure disease is a reasonable one. We now know that certain behaviors are clearly harmful (smoking, excess drinking, overeating, etc.) and we are beginning to understand the effects of emotions on disease.

A new field of study, psychoneuroimmunology (psychology plus neurology plus immunology), is looking at the possible effects of stress and emotions on physiologic processes, including the immune system. Using highly sophisticated methods to measure immunologic responses, it has become clear that periods of acute stress and anxiety (for example, grief after the loss of a loved one) are associated with reduced function of the boy's immune surveillance mechanisms. This may explain why many people get more cold sores during times of anxiety.

Some researchers think that psychological depression may have the same effect, and in some studies, it has been documented that even mild depression may suppress immune activity. On the other hand, fear and acute stress may increase immune activity by increasing production of some types of white cells, the parts of the blood that fight infections. It appears that, just like people and other animals, immune systems have a mixed response to danger—"fight or flight."

We know that under acute stress the adrenal glands produce adrenaline and other steroids, and these increase alertness, muscle activity, and the number of white cells in circulation. Based on this process, it has been theorized that persons who respond to stress with an "I give up" reaction may be the ones with loss of immune activity. From this, some have further proposed that there is a "cancer-prone personality," and that a person with such a personality is passive and has a helpless and hopeless outlook. Another claim is that this type of personality is associated with a worse outcome after cancer diagnosis. These are highly controversial theories. Does a person feel helpless and hopeless because his or her immune system is depressed? Or does feeling helpless and hopeless cause the immune system to become depressed? Or neither?

I personally have a problem with the idea of a "cancer-prone personality." Throughout my years of treating cancer in people from all walks of life, it never seemed to me to make much difference in outcome whether the original personality was an aggressive "type A" or a more passive type. (I did not do in-depth psychological studies on my patients, however.)

Stress and anxiety do affect the functioning of the body in some ways, but pinning down exactly how is very difficult. We all know what happens to our gastrointestinal tract when we get scared. We also know that a tension headache is the predictable outcome of a three-hour traffic jam. Scientists have been able to document some of the effects of anxiety by observing college students in the anxious period just before exams. Blood tests showed that the students experienced a transient rise in cholesterol levels and reduction of immune function during that period. The obvious question raised by such findings is, what about the other things that go on when one is under stress? What about midnight pizza and donuts, increased use of alcohol or cigarettes, staying up until the crack of dawn, use of caffeine tablets or other over-the-counter or prescription drugs? Could these typical college-student responses to stress play a part in elevated cholesterol levels? Until we know all the answers, it will not be possible to define the relationship between stress and developing cancer, and even then, we will have the greater task of determining what to do about it.

Most studies of immune function have been done in healthy subjects, but a few investigators have looked at immune function in persons with cancer. Their research showed some relationship between passive responses to disease and white cell activity, but overall, the results are inconsistent. Again, we must look at what else is going on. Persons with cancer usually are undergoing cancer therapy, and such therapies can profoundly affect the immune system.

Some researchers have found that people survive cancer longer when they used relaxation and imaging techniques, but we lack the kind of random trials that are needed to prove this. One recent study did demonstrate that women with metastatic breast cancer who participated in support groups lived longer than women with breast cancer who did not participate in such groups. Unfortunately, immune function was not assessed in this study, and the findings were unusual in that survival of both groups, with or without support, was shorter than expected. The reason for this has not been explained.

In one study in which immune activity was measured, a group of persons with melanoma experienced an increase in immune function when they participated in support groups that focused on coping and relaxation skills. One especially important finding was that a certain type of immune cell—natural killer cells—increased their activity. This meant that the body was using its own armament against the melanoma, presumably in response to the improved emotional status of the study participants. As encouraging as these findings are, there were problems with the way the study was carried out. Not the least of the researchers' problems was that the persons in the control group, who did not have a support group intervention, kept dropping out of the study because they wanted to join the support group. While I'm on their side—if you want social support to fight your cancer, go for it!—these switchovers may have biased the study results.

As you can see, there's a lot of work to be done. It will be necessary to examine many of the body's biochemical processes—such as interactions between hormones and the central nervous system—and how these are affected by stress. Next, it will be important to see how these factors relate to DNA damage and cancer-cell formation. In the meantime, I think it is unlikely that therapies aimed at stimulating the body's defenses through psychological means alone are going to have any significant effect on cancer survival. Even the most intense immune stimulation drug therapies in clinical trials have had only limited success to date, and this success is restricted to just a few cancers (in particular, melanoma and kidney cancer). (An exception may be the drug levamisole, which, in colon cancer, may or may not be acting via an immune mechanism—see chapter 5, "For People with Colorectal Cancer.")

It is not yet known whether techniques such as "imaging" the immune system fighting against cancer cells, relaxation tapes, and other mind therapies have any real clinical value. These must be evaluated in well-designed clinical trials. At present, there is little evidence that such approaches can prolong survival in cancer, although it certainly makes sense that there are psychological benefits from actively participating in the fight against one's illness. You should seek whatever psychological support you need in order to cope, not only because if you need it, it will do you good, but also because a support group will give you the opportunity to share what you learn about managing the problems of cancer. An attitude of helplessness can defeat any efforts to help oneself; it is reasonable to expect that support groups will help you follow and complete a defined treatment plan, including a nutritional plan. At the same time, there is absolutely no evidence to support *replacing* conventional treatment with support groups and similar therapies.

IF YOU ARE THINKING ABOUT AN ALTERNATIVE THERAPY

Her are some guidelines and suggestions to consider if you are contemplating an alternative type of therapy for cancer.

1. Discuss it with your oncologist. *Be sure you understand what his or her treatment plan is before you decide to abandon it.* Ask if the alternative treatment can be safely taken along with the conventional treatment. It's likely that mind therapies will be easy to work into your conventional routine. In fact, some hospitals provide relaxation and imaging tapes. Appropriate social and psychological support is always acceptable.

2. Investigate the claims about the alternative treatment that interests you. Insist on facts. Beware of claims that are subjective. You should look for the kind of objective measurements that a scientist would require. In medical studies, the gold standards are *measurements of tumor response rates* (that is, how well the tumors respond to treatment) and *overall survival durations* (how long the treated person lived after treatment). Keep in mind that some people feel better simply because they were treated, even if the treatment was a placebo. This phenomenon is real, and it usually is reported as "improved appetite," "increased energy levels," and "better quality of life." These categories of "improvement" are very hard to measure, and this is why the random, double-blind study technique is so important. By randomly assigning subjects to one or another treatment group and making sure neither the

subject nor the health team knows which treatment is being given (placebo or active agent), several types of problems are avoided. These problems are called "bias" and can cause real complications with interpretation of results.

For the same reasons, be very skeptical about testimonials. It often happens that the person who claims to be "cured" never really had cancer; his or her "diagnosis" (as well as cure) may have come from the promoter of the method, who based the determination on blood test results, urinalysis results, or obscure physical findings. A cancer diagnosis requires a tissue diagnosis from a biopsy, read by a competent pathologist.

3. Remember that effective cancer treatment has side effects, and that a treatment that promises easy results is suspect. Cancer is a serious disorder involving fundamental changes in the basic mechanisms of the cell. Those changes are not going to be reversed by trivial therapies.

If conventional treatment is causing side effects, *don't give up.* Nausea, mouth sores, and other side effects are not permanent. They will get better. If the side effects are unbearable, don't hesitate to ask your physician or nurse for help, and try the recommendations in chapter 8, "Solving Nutrition Problems and Improving Well-being During Treatment."

If someone is offering you a program that sounds too good to be true, it probably is.

LET YOUR PHYSICIAN BE YOUR GUIDE

Do you have trouble asking your physician questions? Do you believe that you shouldn't take up too much of your health-care provider's time? Many people feel this way, in no small measure because physicians are generally very busy and may reflect this in their bedside manner. However, one of your most important jobs as a patient is to keep your physician fully informed of your progress, including any methods you are trying on your own. And one of your physician's most important jobs is to inform you of all of your options, and to help you make sound judgments about such methods. If you are feeling awkward about asking questions, an excellent book to read is *Choices: Realistic Alternatives in Cancer Treatment* by Marion Morra and Eve Potts, which outlines the questions that you should be asking and thinking about.

Another health professional whom you may want to consult is a nutritionist. Most oncologists have a consulting nutritionist on staff, or can recommend one to you. Another source of referrals is the state licensing board, if your state licenses nutritionists. Look for a Registered Dietitian degree, a master's in the Science of Nutrition, or a Ph.D. in Nutrition. Being on a hospital staff stands as a strong recommendation. Beware of storefront nutritionists.

PART 2

SPECIFIC CANCERS AND NUTRITION

4

FOR WOMEN WITH BREAST CANCER

੨ঌ

Then his is story of two women, one of whom got breast cancer. From the day they met in kindergarten, Jeannette Cole and Adina Johnson were best friends. They were born on the same day, November 2, 1945, in the same hospital. They grew up just a block from each other, went to slumber parties together, and often ate meals at each other's homes. Jeannette's mother was famous for her fried chicken, coconut cream pie, and batter-fried vegetables with mayonnaise sauce. Adina's mother cooked more plainly, but Jeannette was amazed to find how many delicious ways beans could be prepared.

When Jeannette had her first period at age eleven, she felt shy and embarrassed about discussing this new experience with everyone except Adina. Each month they wondered when Adina would start having her periods, too. They had a long wait, because Adina didn't begin until age seventeen.

At fifteen, after sharing a first cigarette, the two young girls took a solemn vow that they'd never take up smoking, but Jeannette didn't keep it. Jeannette never admitted this, but Adina knew by the way Jeannette's hair, clothes, and bedroom smelled, and by the flecks of tobacco that fell out of Jeannette's purse.

It was around this time that the two began to see less of each other, partly because Jeannette wanted to spend more time with her friends who smoked, but mostly because Adina's interest in sports meant long after-hours practices. Jeannette joined the Future Secretaries club. Every day, after school, she curled up with a smoke and a Coke and potato chips and the latest rock album and practiced taking down the lyrics in shorthand.

Still, the two young women stayed in touch, and when Jeannette's young aunt—her mother's youngest sister—died of breast cancer, Adina went to the funeral and sat through the service, holding Jeannette's hand and thinking how frightening it was that someone could die at age thirty from cancer.

At high school graduation, Jeannette and Adina found each other in the crowd and hugged and cried, swearing to keep their friendship alive. That fall, armed with the only sports scholarship awarded to a female in the state that year, Adina began studying physical education at the local college.

Jeannette was thrilled when she quickly found a job as a typist in a law firm. Six months later, Adina stood as a bridesmaid in Jeannette's wedding to a construction worker, a handsome young man she'd known from church. The next time the two ran into each other, Adina teased Jeannette about how married life certainly seemed to be agreeing with her, because—though Adina was too polite to come right out and say it—Jeannette certainly was putting on weight. Jeannette replied that it wasn't so much the marriage as it was the job; though she had had several promotions and had an excellent salary, she was still tied to a desk all day, and never got any exercise.

Looking at Jeannette's plump stomach, Adina wondered if Jeannette might be pregnant, but she wasn't. In fact, Jeannette and her husband wanted to get everything in their lives in order before having children, so the first and only child didn't arrive until Jeannette was thirty-two. By that time, the two women had not seen each other for several years, but Jeannette heard through the grapevine that Adina had married in her sophomore year of college, and that she and her husband, a football coach at the local high school, had three children, and that she was continuing to pursue her college degree, one course at a time.

The two friends saw each other only occasionally after this, usually by chance at the grocery store. At one of these encounters, Jeannette said that her mother had recently died of breast cancer. Adina, who had finally gotten her degree and was coaching sports and teaching health in a nearby high school, secretly thanked God that there was no history of breast cancer in her family. "With your family history," Adina told Jeannette, "it might be a good idea for you to check your breasts each month."

The two parted with a hug, but Jeannette wandered off to the meat counter, and by the time she had gotten sausage, a roast, and two chickens for frying, she had forgotten Adina's advice. It didn't come back to her until the summer of 1988, when on a whim, she decided to attend the twenty-fifth reunion of her high school class. She had lost ten pounds—at the expense of an extra six cigarettes a day—to fit into a new dress, and she was anxious for Adina to see her new, slender self. When the evening was half-spent, and Adina hadn't shown up, Jeannette asked at the registration table whether her friend had responded to the reunion invitation. "Oh, I thought you would have known," she was told. "Adina's just gotten out of the hospital. She had surgery for breast cancer. Thank God, they caught it early. She went in for an annual checkup and they found it on a mammogram."

Were you expecting the person with breast cancer to be Jeannette? All the clues seemed to point in that direction. Jeannette had a family history of breast cancer in two relatives, one of whom died of the disease very young; her periods began at a young age; her first childbirth was after age thirty; she ate a high-fat diet; and she was overweight. Also, Jeannette smoked, which is a risk factor for many cancers, though maybe not for breast cancer.

These are very important and valid indicators of who is at risk for breast cancer, but *not every woman who has risk factors for breast cancer will actually get the disease.* If you have breast cancer now, you may be someone who seemed to be doing "everything right."

Remember, though, that the story of Jeannette and Adina stopped at 1988, when both were forty-two years of age. If Jeannette continues on her present path, making poor lifestyle choices, she is at serious risk, not only for getting breast cancer, but also for dying from the disease. Adina's lifelong healthy diet and exercise program, on the other hand, will make it easy for her to support her recovery. And by having regular checkups and a mammogram, she had the benefit of early detection.

Scientists are learning more each day about risk factors and how they apply to individuals. Until we can better pinpoint who is at risk, every woman should be aware of the risk factors and take control of as many of these as she can. Even if you think you are at low risk, the statistics for breast cancer are enough to make every woman pause.

In 1991—a year in which 170,000 women were given a diagnosis of breast cancer—the American Cancer Society announced that the lifetime risk of breast cancer in American woman had risen from 1 in 10 to 1 in 9. This means that by age fifty, a woman's lifetime risk of breast cancer is 1 in 50; by age sixty, that risk rises to 1 in 23. By age seventy, the risk is 1 in 14; by age eighty, it is 1 in 10; and by age eighty-five, it is 1 in 9. (In 1993, the National Cancer Institute announced that the risk is 1 in 8, but this was based on a lifetime of ninety-five years. In deriving the 1 in 9 figures, the American Cancer Society assumed a lifetime of eighty-five years.)

A side note: It's no small matter that Jeannette is also at risk for lung cancer. In 1990, lung cancer became the number-one cause of cancer deaths in women, surpassing breast cancer, which had been number one for nearly fifty years. This statistical turnaround did not reflect a decrease in breast cancer. It is the unfortunate, predictable result of accumulated decades of damage to women's health by tobacco use. While lung cancer deaths now exceed breast cancer deaths, breast cancer mortality holds a strong second place and continues to rise at the rate of about 3 percent per year; in total number of new cases, breast cancer exceeds lung cancer.

Understandably, these figures have been a source of distress and anxiety—even anger—among women. It is important that we do not let the specter of these statistics overshadow the important progress that has been made in recent years. Breast cancer is curable if it is detected early. The reason that breast cancer was usually a death sentence in preceding generations is that we have only learned, in the past few decades, how to detect breast cancer early. The technology we need to detect breast cancer early—mammography—is in place, and it is becoming easier for women to have access to this procedure. Private insurers and Medicare have seen the benefits of early detection, and have increased coverage for the costs of mammography. Better technology and accreditation programs, including the new nationwide Mammography Quality Standards Act, are resulting in better-quality mammograms at lower doses of radiation exposure. At the same time, physicians are learning how to interpret more accurately the findings on mammograms, especially the findings that are not clearly positive or definitively negative.

Perhaps most important is the shift in approach to all cancers, especially breast cancer, in the closing years of the twentieth century. While an aggressive search for cures will continue, there will also be vigorous pursuit of the means to *prevent* cancer, and much of the focus will be on the role of nutrition.

The common thread in these advances is that *each offers some control over your destiny in relation to breast cancer.* You can learn about ways to *prevent* breast cancer, especially new ways of healthy eating and chemoprevention, as new findings accumulate. You can learn about ways to *detect* breast cancer, and how often you should have a mammogram or examine your breasts. If you have breast cancer now, you also have much more control over your destiny than you would have had a generation ago.

The Revolution in Breast Cancer Treatment

It used to be that a woman with suspected breast cancer was whisked into the hospital immediately for a biopsy of the lump under general anesthesia. Before entering the operating room, she was required to sign permission for the surgeon to proceed immediately to mastectomy (removal of the entire breast) if the biopsy showed malignancy.

While its intention was to rid the body of the tumor as quickly as possible, this haste placed a terrible burden on the woman with cancer. She had no time to adjust to the diagnosis, no opportunity to prepare for the treatment, and no sense of control over a difficult and deforming procedure. Under these circumstances, it is little wonder that breast cancer was perceived as something that "struck" women, an event that could not be controlled or overcome.

Fortunately, all this has changed. Radical mastectomy is rarely performed now. Biopsies are usually performed on an outpatient basis, and if the diagnosis is cancer, the woman is informed of her options in face-to-face meetings with members of the health-care team. If she wishes, a woman with breast cancer may request consultation with a woman who has been through the same decision-making process in dealing with the disease. An important step in the treatment—staging—helps determine how far the disease has progressed. As with any cancer, the stage of breast cancer is a vital factor in the number of options a woman has for her future.

If detected early enough, surgery alone may be all that is needed to cure breast cancer. The types of surgery used have been reduced, simplified, and improved. Depending on the stage and extent of disease at diagnosis, the options may include lumpectomy (removal of the tumor only), quadrantectomy (removal of a quarter section of the breast, encompassing the lump), or a mastectomy (removal of the entire breast). To see if the cancer has spread to lymph nodes under the arm, the lymph nodes are also biopsied.

The sooner breast cancer is detected, and the more confined the disease is, the greater are the chances for cure by surgery alone. Once the cancer has spread to the lymph nodes or beyond, however, cure rates fall dramatically. Also, certain types of tumors are known to be associated with a worse course of disease and less favorable outcome, even if they do not spread to the lymph nodes. In both of these situations, it is necessary to use additional, aggressive therapy. This additional therapy is called *adjuvant* therapy (therapy given as an auxiliary to the main treatment in order to enhance its effectiveness).

For breast cancer, the choices for adjuvant therapy are chemotherapy, radiation treatment, hormonal therapy, or a combination of these methods. For each person with breast cancer, the decision about which treatment method is best depends on many factors, including personal preferences.

If you and your physician have agreed to pursue adjuvant chemotherapy or hormonal therapy, there are some facts you need to know.

First, always keep in mind that the treatment is designed to improve your chance for cure. You may experience side effects from your chemotherapy. These may include nausea, vomiting, hair loss, sores in the mouth, and bone marrow suppression with low blood count. These side effects are temporary.

If you have severe nausea and mouth sores, you may lose weight. Surprisingly, if your side effects are less severe, you may actually gain weight—sometimes considerable amounts—possibly from snacking. (Many people take up snacking because keeping food in the stomach reduces nausea.) Also, while undergoing cancer therapy, you may develop aversions to certain foods, even foods that were previously your favorites. Some of these problems have simple remedies. See chapter 8, "Solving Nutrition Problems and Improving Well-being During Treatment."

As soon as possible, you should focus on changing the way you eat and what you eat so that your diet supports your recovery rather than undermines it. Think of this as serious business, because it is. It is an adjuvant treatment in which you, the patient, use dietary changes to reinforce the good work accomplished by surgery, hormonal therapy, chemotherapy, or radiation therapy and to help prevent disease recurrence.

EXCESS BODY FAT AND BREAST CANCER

An important nutritional goal for people with breast cancer is to achieve a healthy amount of total body fat. The primary way to do this is to decrease the amount of fat you eat. Dietary fats are concentrated sources of calories, and those that the body doesn't need are stored as more body fat.

The problem with an excess amount of body fat (a problem that has reached epidemic proportions in the United States) is much greater than not being able to zip into your jeans. Scientific studies indicate that, if you carry too much fat, you are at increased risk for:

• Getting breast cancer
• Having a shorter survival time, if you get breast cancer
• Relapsing from the disease, once you have been treated for breast cancer, whether the disease has spread to the lymph nodes or not
• Dying from breast cancer

In these studies, the greater the percent of body fat, the more pronounced these differences were. For example, in studies of women in the United States and in Holland, which ranks eighth in breast cancer deaths worldwide, overweight was linked to having more extensive disease at diagnosis. As weight went up, the number of lymph nodes under the armpit (axillary nodes) affected by disease increased.

In another study, the American Cancer Society tallied dietary habits and health of thousands of people. The results showed that death rates from cancer, including breast cancer, were much higher among patients who were 40 percent or more above their ideal weight. A study published in 1994 of 735 women with breast cancer on adjuvant chemotherapy showed that, even with such chemotherapy, obesity was an indicator of poor outcome. The risk of relapse for obese patients was 1.33 times that of the nonobese group.

What you weigh is not as important as how much fat is in your body. Women normally have more body fat than men. The percentage of body mass that is fat is measured in several ways. The most common method is for a nutritionist to measure the thickness of a pinch of skin with a skin-fold caliper. For accuracy, several sites must be measured (the back of the arm, the waist, and thigh are commonly measured). A formula is then used to estimate fat percentage. A trained dietitian can measure your body fat accurately with this method. Another method, underwater weighing, is a more sophisticated technique, but is not widely available.

The recommendations in this book for fat grams are based on a medium frame. A dietitian can also assess your body-frame size by elbow or wrist measurements. If you do not fit this category, you should consult with your physician to determine the number of fat grams that are best for you. If you gain weight while you are on therapy or during your recovery, consider asking your doctor for a nutrition consultation.

Why is excess body fat so harmful? Suppose we assume—and this is a genuine possibility—that small tumors form in the breast, nesting there quietly for many years, until something stimulates them to grow. One theory is they are stimulated by this chain of events:

- Excess calories plus decreased exercise leads to extra body fat.
- Increased body fat increases the body's estrogen levels.
- This increased estrogen may stimulate the quiescent breast cancer cells.
- Once the malignant stimulation is established, if unchallenged, the cancer can spread to cause illness and death.

As most of us know, it's very easy for the first step in this process to happen. Eating is the great American pastime. The second greatest is trying to lose the fat that results from all that eating.

Achieving a healthy weight can be a special challenge for people with breast cancer because, as I mentioned above, the treatment itself often causes weight gain. At least ten studies since 1982 have shown that many persons who are on adjuvant hormonal therapy or adjuvant chemotherapy—common treatments for breast cancer— gain weight, up to fifteen pounds or more. These studies also showed that persons who gain substantial amounts of weight during adjuvant treatment have a greater tendency to disease relapse. This was true for both pre- and postmenopausal patients, but was only "statistically significant" in the premenopausal group. This means that the differences in the premenopausal group were great enough to have been unlikely due to chance alone.

Weight gain during therapy can be very upsetting. One of my patients, a woman who had fought weight gain all her life with reasonable success, found that her adjuvant chemotherapy caused queasiness and nausea. These were relieved by nibbling all day and into the night. The nibbling, plus inactivity caused by both the disease and its treatment, resulted in several miseries. Her clothes no longer fit, she felt angry and depressed, and she actually began to miss her clinic appointments. Finally, her husband convinced her to come in. Together, she and I were able to work out a low-fat snack plan that satisfied her need to reduce the nausea and allowed her to lose much of the accumulated fat and to complete her therapy. She was amazed that changing from high-fat cookies and ice cream to vegetables and occasional nonfat pastries could make such a difference.

If you have breast cancer, too much fat in your diet can do at least three bad things:

- Fat is full of calories and calories can stimulate cancer cells to grow. Dietary fat is a very concentrated source of calories (9 calories per gram versus 4 calories per gram of protein and carbohydrate).
- Fat accumulates in the body and fat cells create estrogens, which may stimulate cancer cells to grow.
- Fat contains certain fatty acids that may stimulate cancer cells to grow.

STUDIES OF FAT INTAKE AND BREAST CANCER

There is an enormous body of data on diet and breast cancer, both in the area of primary cancer prevention and in the area of diet as adjuvant therapy for cancer after it has developed. As with any area of study, there are conflicting findings. Recently articles have appeared that cast doubt on the relationship between diet and cancer prevention. The large study that prompted these articles was an analysis of dietary habits of nurses, as determined by a questionnaire. The study found no relationship between fat in the diet and the subsequent development of breast cancer.

Critics of the so-called nurses' study point out three problems. First, there were potential inaccuracies in the dietary questionnaire. Diet questionnaires have problems similar to all questionnaires. All subjects may not be equally conscientious about filling them out, may not remember precisely, and may have a tendency to respond in a way that they think the researchers want. Second, the findings were based on recall of food intake, which is an unreliable method. Third, it is possible that not enough of the nurses had very low fat intake to allow definitive conclusions.

The nurses' study is countered by others that did show a relationship between breast cancer and diet, so the proposed connection is still very much alive as a research issue. The National Institutes of Health recently funded sixteen studies around the country in which researchers will examine the preventive effects of decreased fat intake on breast cancer and other chronic disease rates.

Earlier, we talked about the ways that population studies have given us insights into the ways that diet relates to cancer. This is certainly true of breast cancer and dietary fat. Breast cancer knows no boundaries, national or international. Some women in every country have or will have breast cancer. But some countries have higher rates of breast cancer than others. The death rate from breast cancer is very high in the United States: 22.4 deaths for every 100,000 persons. Surprisingly, even at this high rate, the United States ranks sixteenth in the world for breast cancer deaths. England and Wales rank first, at 29.3 deaths per 100,000. The lowest death rates in the world are in Thailand, where only 1 woman per 100,000 dies of breast cancer.

Scientists have long been puzzled by these differences. Many studies have been conducted to determine what the source of those differences are. Most of the studies have focused on the conditions, events, and practices that are common in a particular population but different from other populations.

Most of these factors are related in some way to diet. For example, early age at first menstruation is a risk factor for breast cancer. But what influences the age at which menstruation first begins? Studies show that diet plays an important part. American girls, who are raised on a high-protein, high-fat diet, begin menstruation at a relatively early age, and there has been a trend for this age to be moved back a little with each generation. In girls from less developed countries, where meat is scarce, menstruation begins at a later age.

One of the most enlightening studies of the role of diet in breast cancer has been a comparison of breast cancer rates in Japanese women versus American women. Breast cancer incidence is very low in Japan. Also, Japanese women who do get breast cancer have a greater chance of surviving the disease than do American women. The advantage Japanese breast cancer patients have is not due to earlier diagnosis, differences in type of breast cancer, or better treatment; rather, it is most likely due to diet. The traditional Japanese diet is very low in fat.

Meat, which is a major source of fat in the U.S. diet, is used sparingly in traditional Japanese cooking. With the emphasis on grains, vegetables, and nonfatty sources of protein, such as bean curd or fish, the traditional Japanese woman consumes only 10 to 12 percent of her diet as fat. By comparison, the average American consumes about 37 to 40 percent of daily calories in fat.

Not surprisingly, when new immigrants to America adopt the high-protein, high-fat, American way of eating, the incidence of certain cancers rises. One of those is breast cancer in the offspring of immigrants.

When scientists are curious about a human health problem, they often begin by looking at how the problem works out in animals, such as rats. The findings in such studies—sometimes called "animal models"—help them to size up the situation and make plans for further studies. It's important to remember, of course, that what is true in animal models is usually, but not always, true for humans. Here are some things that scientists have learned, in recent studies of animals, about dietary fat and breast cancer:

- Dietary fat promotes primary breast cancer in animals (i.e., fat is involved in *producing* the cancer).
- Once primary breast cancer is established in animals, excess dietary fat promotes metastasis, the spread of the disease (i.e., fat makes existing cancer *worse*).
- When breast cancer is induced in animals (by injecting them with cancer-causing substances), there are fewer tumors and the tumors are smaller if the animals are kept on a low-fat diet instead of a high-fat diet (i.e., fat reduction *hinders* existing cancers).

- If the diet is switched from low-fat to high-fat, the tumors begin to grow more rapidly.
- If the diet is switched from high fat to low fat, the growth of the tumors slows.
- In induced breast cancer, animals on a low-fat diet live longer than animals on a high-fat diet.

When epidemiologists studied the diet and source of disease in persons with cancer, they found that fat *intake* in humans is related to the *outcome* of breast cancer, as well.

Dietary fat intake has been clearly linked to breast cancer survival in this country and elsewhere. Increased body weight is also associated with shorter survival. Heavier women tend to have more axillary node metastases, and one study has found that high fat intake decreases survival in patients with breast cancer which has spread to distant organs.

A very interesting study from Sweden, published in 1993, found that in women with estrogen-receptor-positive breast tumors, dietary habits at the time of diagnosis were related to prognosis. Specifically, those who relapsed had higher intakes of total fat, saturated fatty acids, and polyunsaturated fatty acids than those who did not relapse. These researchers suggested that dietary intervention might serve as an adjuvant treatment to improve the prognosis of women with breast cancer.

DIETARY FAT AND ESTROGEN

The word *hormone* is derived from the Greek verb, *horman,* which means to rouse or set in motion, and this is essentially what hormones do.

Hormones are control chemicals, and there are many kinds. They are biologic commuters that are secreted in one part of the body, then travel to another part to do their job. They rouse or set in motion behavior, sexuality, blood sugar levels, the internal clock of circadian rhythms, human growth and development, digestion, metabolism, chemical balances, inflammation (which is the body's healing process in action), nerve activity, and many facets of reproduction. Differences in hormonal activity are the core of biologic differences between the sexes. It is the concentration of male sex hormone that determines the development of genitalia as masculine or feminine. And these are just a few of their functions.

As you can imagine, an abnormality of any one of the many hormones can wreak havoc, not only by directly disrupting its target function, but also indirectly, by disrupting the delicate balance of relationships with other hormones. For example, an insufficiency of thyroid-stimulating hormone leads to hypothyroidism (low thyroid function), a condition that can cause lethargy, dry skin, loss of hair, sensitivity to cold, and constipation. Untreated, it can result in irreversible loss of mental abilities. On the other hand, too much thyroid-stimulating hormone causes hyperthyroidism, which is characterized by nervousness, sensitivity to heat, sweating, restlessness, headache, weight loss, and a host of other problems.

Certain hormones play an important role in breast cancer growth and metastasis. Physicians have noted that breast cancer in younger woman (before menopause) is often more aggressive than breast cancer in older women (after menopause). One of the most plausible explanations for this difference is that higher estrogen levels, as premenopausal women have, make the disease worse.

Estrogen is a hormone that promotes female characteristics. It stimulates growth and development of the uterus and vagina, pubic hair, breast development, and some changes in voice quality, and it directs shaping of the pelvis to accommodate pregnancy. Estrogen also triggers the menstrual cycle. So it makes sense that estrogen is at flood stage in younger women, doing its job in relation to the biologic tasks of the younger woman. A related hormone, progesterone, has important functions in pregnancy, including interruption of the high tide of estrogen that occurs at ovulation.

At the climacteric—usually between ages forty and fifty—the ovaries begin to atrophy and the flood of estrogen is reduced to a trickle and then stops. Removal of the ovaries has the same effect.

Some forms of chemotherapy also cause ovarian function to cease. The scarcity or absence of estrogen and progesterone leads to cessation of menstruation, and menopause ensues.

As you probably know, it is possible to replace estrogen by taking oral estrogen, injecting estrogen, or wearing an estrogen patch. At present, we know that short term estrogen replacement therapy after age forty to fifty is relatively safe, and that there is only a very small or nonexistent risk of breast cancer from this type of therapy. Long-term use of estrogen therapy is another matter. Studies show that using estrogen replacement therapy for more than fifteen years does carry a modest increase in risk of breast cancer. So for a younger woman with breast cancer, the decision to use estrogen replacement therapy must be carefully weighed by both doctor and patient, considering both risks and benefits.

Another area of concern is the use of progesterone with estrogen replacement therapy. This combined regimen has been recommended as a method superior to estrogen alone, because estrogen alone has been linked to endometrial (uterine) cancer. However, there is new concern that estrogen plus progesterone may increase risk of developing breast cancer. Until this is all sorted out in extensive clinical studies, this is an area of concern that you and your physician should discuss.

Estrogen has an interesting relationship with body fat. During puberty, estrogen initiates redistribution of body fat, remolding the straight-as-a-stick lines of a little girl into a soft and rounded adolescent. The more body fat, the more estrogen is stimulated.

Similarly, an adult woman carrying too much body fat will be producing more estrogen than others. Taking in too many calories and too much dietary fat results in more fat tissue in the body—unless exercise is increased to burn off the fat—and this in turn promotes the synthesis of estrogen.

If you contemplate the effects of estrogen mentioned thus far, you will notice that all of those functions are related to stimulation of growth of cells. And this is one of the problems with estrogen. A high level of estrogen is a tremendous stimulus to growth of cells, including certain cancer cells.

This may be why early age at first menstrual period is a known risk factor for breast cancer. Estrogen levels fluctuate during the menstrual cycle each month; at their peak, ovulation occurs. Ironically, the longer a woman has been exposed to this normal, healthy cycle of estrogen peaks, the greater her chances of breast cancer. Studies have shown that women who started menstruation at age twelve or earlier have a greater risk of developing breast cancer than women whose periods began after age thirteen. As explained previously, the high nutrient intake in industrial countries is pushing back the age at which girls begin their periods, thus lengthening the total time of exposure to estrogen.

Estrogen's power to stimulate cells may be the reason why giving birth at a late age or never having children is a risk factor for breast cancer. When conception occurs, progesterone takes over, suppresses estrogen production, and interrupts the monthly cycle. Thus, one of the natural outcomes of pregnancy is to prevent too much estrogen over too long a period of time.

The longer pregnancy is delayed, the more cycles of estrogen peaks are experienced, thereby lengthening the total duration of estrogen exposure. Present-day Western culture is probably the first civilization to delay pregnancy into the late twenties, the early thirties, and even the late thirties. We've suddenly changed a biological system that has been operating for thousands of years. The system relied on frequent pregnancies beginning at a young age. (Of course, the system was not perfect. Pregnancy at a young age has its own risks.) This is not to suggest that we should turn around the direction of our civilization; however, we should be aware that it will be some time before human biology has adapted to this change. Based on existing evidence, it appears that one of the consequences of delayed pregnancies may be increased rates of breast cancer. We know that a woman who has never been pregnant is at increased risk of breast cancer, and that having the first child before age nineteen cuts the risk in half, compared to the risk of women who have never had children. Why? Because there is one key flaw in the normal, healthy cycle of menstruation and estrogen fluctuations, and that is that breast tissues are still very actively proliferating and developing in the adolescent and early adult years. Long-term estrogen stimulation of the breast cells at this time was not part of Mother Nature's plan.

We know that excess calories alone may influence breast cancer growth and metastasis by stimulating cell growth in general. Excess food intake may provide three things needed for the development of tumors: (1) an adequate energy supply; (2) the specific nutrients required for cell growth (for example, building-block nutrients such as amino acids); and (3) increased fat, which stimulates increased levels of estrogen, which in turn stokes the fires of cell development.

Besides playing a role at the beginning of the cancer, it is possible that hormones influence cancer later in the history of the disease, causing it to grow and metastasize. Among the possible mechanisms being studied are steroid hormone levels, cell membrane structure and function, synthesis of prostaglandins (which have multiple functions in immune system regulation), and immune function itself.

Based on these facts and speculations, it is clear that decreasing the number of calories and the amount of fat eaten should have a positive, preventive effect against breast cancer, by preventing excess energy that would fuel cellular proliferation *and* by keeping estrogen levels in check. The latter is essentially the same goal as tamoxifen treatment—thus, the proper diet could boost the desired effects of chemotherapy using tamoxifen. One of the tasks of research is to now prove these theories in clinical trials.

Increasing fiber-containing foods in the diet can also change hormone levels favorably. Lignin, a form of fiber, has antiestrogen effects in the body, just as tamoxifen does.

The idea of reducing weight as an adjunctive treatment for breast cancer—based on the fact that lower weight means lower estrogen levels, and therefore decreased risk of breast cancer recurrence—is not new. It was proposed more than a decade ago and has since been raised as a plausible measure in breast cancer treatment by several research groups.

In considering the role of hormones, it's important to keep in mind that some of the effects of diet on cancer cells are additive— that is, changes may occur in a domino effect, with each new change spurred on by the one that preceded it. This is why it's important to focus on dietary patterns—such as the overall tendency to a high-fat diet—rather than focusing on single factors, such as potato chips or vitamin C.

AN EATING PLAN FOR WOMEN
WITH BREAST CANCER

Most of the data on dietary fat and breast cancer has been collected on postmenopausal women—in part because most cases of breast cancer are in this age group. So the following recommendations, with one exception, pertain to you if you are postmenopausal. Regardless of your menopausal stage, however, you should get your physician's permission before changing your diet.

The bedrock of the eating pattern is this: Reduce fat intake to no more than 20 percent of total calories by following the guidelines in chapter 9. Breast cancer, among all cancers, has the closest scientific link with dietary fat, and as I explained earlier, dietary fat has several clearly adverse effects on you if you have breast cancer.

I cannot say that fat reduction will help if your disease is metastatic, and especially if it is progressing despite other therapy. It is most likely that reduction of fat will help in earlier disease, especially if you are being given adjuvant chemotherapy and hormonal therapy. As I stated earlier, diet is an aid in treatment, not a treatment alone.

Recent data indicate that dietary fiber may inhibit breast cancer, perhaps by changing the gut absorption of hormonal factors. Thus, I think it is prudent to increase your fiber intake to 25 grams per day or more. See chapter 9 for more specific guidelines.

Whether or not you have reached menopause, weight gain during treatment is thought to be harmful. Eating a low-fat diet, with emphasis on low-fat snacks, can be helpful here. If you are trying your best to eat less fat but your body fat persists, you should consider a walking program with your doctor's okay.

Recommendations for
Breast Cancer (if you are postmenopausal or have completed adjuvant treatment or premenopausal and on adjuvant treatment and are gaining weight)

BASIC PLAN

1. Decrease fat consumption to no more than 20 percent of daily calories.

2. Increase fiber intake to 25 grams per day or more.

RATIONALE

Cutting fat intake can contribute to an environment unfriendly to breast cancer, by decreasing calories (which provide energy for tumors to grow), decreasing tumor-stimulating fatty acids, and decreasing circulating estrogen levels. Decreased estrogen levels from a low-fat diet may be an antiestrogen strategy like tamoxifen. The relationship between fiber and breast cancer is unclear, but a mechanism may be that high fiber intake reduces estrogen levels by changing the way food is absorbed in the gut.

SPECIFIC FOODS AND NUTRIENTS YOU SHOULD STRESS IN YOUR DIET

Foods that contain beta carotene. These fruits and vegetables are also low in fat. They are usually high in fiber and are also high in other chemopreventive compounds. Studies suggest that certain forms of vitamin A may prevent second primary tumors in breast cancer—this is being evaluated in studies in Italy.

ADDITIONAL COMMENTS

Achieving a diet with no more than 20 percent of calories from fat is an ambitious goal and you will almost certainly have occasional lapses. Don't waste time feeling guilty—just get back on the program and keep going. If you are premenopausal and start to gain weight, consider a nutritional consultation. Exercise and controlling your fat intake should help reduce this gain. (See chapter 11, "Supporting Cancer Recovery with Exercise and Sexuality.")

There is some information that increased fat intake decreases survival in metastatic breast cancer; whether decreased fat intake improves survival in this situation is not known and requires investigation.

The chart on page 96 shows the approximate daily amount of fat grams for a 20 percent fat diet according to height. See Part III for instructions about reaching a 20 percent fat from calories diet.

APPROXIMATE DAILY FAT GRAMS FOR
20 PERCENT CALORIES FROM FAT

HEIGHT (NO SHOES)	FAT GRAMS OVER AGE 50*	FAT GRAMS UNDER AGE 50
WOMEN		
5'0"	25	28
5'1"	26	29
5'2"	27	30
5'3"	28	31
5'4"	29	32
5'5"	30	33
5'6"	31	34
5'7"	32	35
5'8"	33	36
5'9"	34	37
5'10"	35	38
5'11"	36	39
6'0"	37	40

* These fat gram amounts are calculated on basal levels of calories needed for ideal body weight at a particular height for adults of medium frame. If you are very active and have reached your daily fat gram goal but are still hungry, eat fruits, vegetables, and nonfat snacks, not more fat.

5

FOR PEOPLE WITH COLORECTAL CANCER

ं

Joe Harris already had a lot on his mind. And then his doctor told him he had colorectal cancer.

Joe's job in a busy accounting firm kept his nerves in knots. In all his fantasies about being forty-five years old, he had always pictured himself kicking off his shoes, getting settled into a deck chair, and surveying his small suburban estate.

He did own a nice home that was ample evidence of the years of diligent hard work that he'd put into his career, but it seemed he could never get out of his office. There was never time for that delicious moment of admiration. Every weekend, the lawn needed a manicure, the concrete needed patching, or the garage needed another once-over.

Joe's wife, Kathy, complained that he should slow down, that he was ruining his health by never taking a long weekend, never sitting down to a decent meal. In fact, meals had become a big issue between them. Kathy was tired of cooking a nice supper, then eating alone. Joe worked late often, and when he did, supper was a fast-food meal of hamburgers, french fries, and a chocolate shake.

Every time Kathy mentioned his work schedule, Joe's stomach started churning. That's what sent him to the doctor: the churning. He thought he was getting an ulcer. And he figured that, while he was there, he'd ask the doctor to recommend something new for his constipation, which no longer responded to over-the-counter laxatives.

The doctor listened to Joe's complaints. He asked Joe about his parents' health, and Joe mentioned that his father had died of colorectal cancer. The doctor told Joe to come back in two days for a sigmoidoscopy, an examination of the rectum and lower colon using a flexible device that would be inserted through the rectum. Joe said, "I'll think about it."

His physician replied, "Think about it all you want, but be here in two days. You need this test."

When the procedure was completed and the results were back, the physician informed Joe that he had colon cancer. Joe's first thought was, "I'm too young to have cancer."

Fortunately, through his physician's careful attention to Joe's history and symptoms, and insistence on the sigmoidoscopy, Joe's cancer was caught early.

Many are not so fortunate. Cancer of the colon and rectum is a significant cause of death in the United States. More than 50,000 people die yearly in this country from the disease. Many could have been spared by early detection and prompt treatment. In the early stages, surgical removal of the cancer can cure the disease. Once the disease progresses, the chance of cure is not so great because radiation and chemotherapy do not have much impact.

The fact that Joe's father had colorectal cancer was a key clue for Joe's physician. This meant that Joe was at increased risk for colorectal cancer. A family history of adenomatous polyps, a type of growth in the colon that has a strong tendency to transform to cancer, is another risk factor, as is a personal history of polyps or chronic inflammatory bowel disease.

Joe had no choice in his genetic inheritance, but he was innocently making some lifestyle choices that greatly increased his risk of colorectal cancer. His *high-fat, low-fiber* diet was a serious problem, so one of the most important tasks of his recovery was to rethink his nutrition choices.

On the other hand, I have to give Joe credit where credit is due: He did get himself to the doctor, and he agreed to a digital rectal examination and a flexible sigmoidoscopy examination. These were steps to early detection; possibly, the sigmoidoscopy was the most important. When I was in medical school in the 1960s, it was a fact that most colorectal cancers could be detected by digital rectal examination. We don't know why, but this has changed; in recent years, the disease is more commonly found higher in the colon, where it cannot be felt by digital rectal examination. So the sigmoidoscopy has become a more important test.

Because early detection plays such an important part in survival of colorectal cancer, the National Cancer Institute and American Cancer Society recommend that men and women over the age of forty have a digital rectal examination every year; after age fifty, everyone should have a test for blood in the stool (fecal occult blood test) every year and sigmoidoscopy every three to five years, according to what your physician recommends. You may have read about the controversy over the usefulness of the fecal occult blood test. It is true that this test is not 100 percent reliable. It has a high level of false negative and false positive findings. This is why it is recommended in the context of other examinations, all of which would be carried out in conjunction with an opportunity for you and your physician to discuss any problems that are cause for suspicion. Since major health organizations like the National Cancer Institute and the American Cancer Society continuously review new findings, its guidelines are subject to change. But for now, the fecal occult blood test is still recommended, and recent data shows that its routine use does save lives.

The guidelines just described are for persons who do not already have symptoms. A person with symptoms of rectal bleeding or a change in bowel habits should see a physician promptly, and the physician may recommend a more extensive evaluation, perhaps including a barium enema (an X ray of the colon taken after instilling an enema of radio-opaque barium) or colonoscopy (examination of the entire colon). This is especially true if you have a history of abnormalities, such as colon polyps.

A polyp is a small, benign growth or protrusion of tissue. Not all polyps are alike. Benign hyperplastic polyps, for example, are harmless. These do not have to be removed and are no cause for worry. Adenomatous polyps are also benign when they first appear, but they are known to be a precursor to cancer; that is, they can and often do "transform" or change into cancer.

There's an old saying that sometimes it's best to nip things in the bud. An important recent study showed that removal of such polyps by colonoscopy did reduce the rate of colon cancer over time. I believe that it's quite probable that primary prevention of adenomatous colon polyps would also nip colon cancer in the bud. To test this idea, I am conducting an American Cancer Society study through its Virginia Division staff and volunteers, to determine if a daily supplement of high-fiber cereal in the diet will prevent new adenomatous polyps from forming in persons who have such polyps. In this study, after the polyps have been surgically removed, people are assigned at random to one of two groups. One group eats a normal diet, with the addition of a very high-fiber cereal (insoluble wheat fiber). The other group also has a normal diet, with the addition of a cereal that is not high in fiber ("placebo"). We will be following the progress of the study participants for several years, keeping track of how many do or do not develop new adenomatous polyps, and if new polyps develop, how extensive they are at the time they are found and removed. The final data analysis should tell us if fiber really does prevent colon cancer, since adenomatous polyps are colon cancer precursors.

Several laboratories around the country are closing in on the genetic changes that lead to colon cancer. It appears that several genes must be altered to create an invasive colon cancer and that it takes a considerable amount of time for all these alterations to occur. Studies are now being conducted to determine how fat, fiber, and other dietary considerations are involved in the process.

It has often been said that the secrets of cancer lie in genetics. Over the last quarter century, studies have found more and more evidence to support this statement, but in May 1993, the world of science was rocked by a series of findings from a group of researchers in Helsinki, an American team, led by Dr. Bert Vogelstein, one of the most accomplished investigators in the field of colon cancer research in the world, and from Dr. Stephen J. Thibodeau and his coworkers at the Mayo Clinic in Rochester, Minnesota.

What these researchers found was not only a new cancer gene, but one that behaved completely differently from all the cancer genes that had previously been identified.

In recent decades, scientists had observed again and again that cancer begins when cancer genes remove the normal "brakes" on cell division. The result is wild growth of new cells, and thus the formation of tumors.

The 1993 research findings were that a gene located in chromosome 2 allows mutations to occur in cells. Given enough time, these mutations could accumulate, predisposing the carrier to cancer. In fact, the researchers believe that this explains why cancer usually develops after age forty, instead of at a younger age.

The gene is carried by 1 in 200 people, and in 65 percent of these people, colon cancer develops. The gene does not account for *all* colon cancers, only about 13 percent, but 90 to 100 percent of people with the gene will get some type of cancer—including cancers of the uterus, ovary, stomach, small intestine, gallbladder, urethra, pancreas, or kidney. Uterine cancer is the second most frequent type that occurs.

Unfortunately, it is not yet possible to test everyone for this gene—but imagine the possibilities this finding holds for the future! People who are known to have the cancer gene will know that they *must* have regular checkups for cancer, so that it will be caught at its earliest stages and then *cured*. Equally exciting, this new understanding of how cancer "happens" holds much promise for new approaches to prevention and treatment.

TREATMENT OF COLORECTAL CANCER

Joe, whose story opened our chapter, was fortunate not only in his early detection, but in his treatment as well. All of the detectable disease in the colon and the adjacent lymph nodes was removed surgically, and then Joe was treated with 5-fluorouracil (5-FU) and levamisole.

Until 1989, the drug 5-FU had been used alone for many years in persons with advanced colorectal cancer, but the results were generally poor. Some researchers tried combining 5-FU with other chemotherapy agents, which improved survival a little but caused toxic side effects. Finally, in 1989, the National Cancer Institute announced that a combination of 5-FU with levamisole produced better results in persons with Dukes' C colon cancer, which is the type of colorectal cancer that Joe Harris had.

Levamisole is a curious drug. It has been used by veterinarians for years to kill parasites in animals. Somewhere along the way, it was discovered that levamisole stimulates the immune system, which is probably one of the ways it works against colorectal tumors when combined with 5-FU. The rest of its antitumor action is not well understood. (You may remember the name levamisole because of a recent controversy about the cost of the drug—when used to react parasites in sheep, it costs only pennies per dose, but the same drug sold for anticancer therapy in humans is much more expensive.)

When colon cancer has spread to the lymph nodes, the combination of 5-FU and levamisole increased the survival rate by about 30 percent. The side effects of this combination include nausea, vomiting, mouth soreness, and diarrhea (see chapter 8, "Solving Nutrition Problems and Improving Well-being During Treatment," for help in overcoming these).

Whether a high-fiber diet will boost the effects of 5-FU and levamisole therapy remains to be seen, but I feel certain that the two approaches will not be in conflict.

In more advanced stages of colon cancer, 5-FU alone is usually given, but this is helpful to about one in five persons, and then not for very long. Combinations of drugs have not been any more successful. In Dukes' A and B cancer (earlier stages then C), surgery alone is the usual treatment.

NUTRITION AND COLORECTAL CANCER

Despite the promise of 5-FU and levamisole in the treatment of colorectal cancer, the disease remains a major problem. The poor results of radiation or chemotherapy have forced scientists to think about a different approach to this disease, and especially about prevention. Analysis of statistics has shown that diet plays a significant role in colorectal cancer, so several laboratories are developing and testing synthetic "chemopreventive agents"—a big name for substances, such as calcium, that are derived from foods—but few of these are ready for large-scale clinical tests in humans.

Three food components that are most often associated with colorectal cancer are fiber, fat, and calcium. Studies have shown that in countries that have a high-fat, low-fiber diet (like Joe's donut and coffee in the morning, pizza at lunch, hamburger/fries/shake at night, and slice of cake before bedtime) the rate of colorectal cancer is higher than in countries where people eat lots of fiber and not much fat. Another intriguing piece of evidence comes from studies of immigrants to the United States. When immigrants from a country that has a high-fiber, low-fat diet (Japan, for example) adopt the typical low-fiber, high-fat American diet, their risk of colorectal cancer rises and, over time, matches the risk that a lifelong American citizen faces. Remember that the same increased risk occurs for breast cancer in certain immigrant groups.

FIBER

No one is certain why high-fiber foods are helpful in reducing colon cancer risk but it's possible to make some educated guesses. Over twenty years ago, Dr. Denis Burkitt, an Irish surgeon and Presbyterian missionary to Africa, championed the idea that high dietary fiber intake was protective against colon cancer. He proposed that dietary fiber might inhibit large bowel cancer by hurrying food along through the gut and helping to increase the bulk of stool. As explained in chapter 2, "The Connection Between Cancer and Diet," this prevents naturally occurring carcinogens in stool from staying in contact with the colon for long. New studies are confirming that theory. More recent information indicates that fiber helps in other ways, too. It binds with substances in the gut that could become a source of cancer, modifying or neutralizing them so that they can do no harm. (See chapter 2 for possible reasons for fiber's effects.)

DIETARY FAT

Fat has also been a suspect in colorectal cancer for decades. The primary sources of dietary fat in this country are dairy products and high-fat meat. This is one reason scientists have frequently connected meat consumption with colorectal cancer. The problem seems to be not so much the meat as the fat, which is present to some extent in even the leanest cuts. (Some scientists believe that animal protein is also involved in colon cancer.)

Also, a diet high in fat is a diet high in calories, and a diet high in calories causes larger body size, which in turn can raise cancer risk. This may sound simplistic, but it's plausible that the more body cells you have, the more chances you have of cell transformation to cancer.

Another way that fat contributes to cancer is that fat may increase production of bile acids. These can be converted to toxic "secondary" bile acids in the colon wall, stimulate cell division, and promote tumors.

A diet high in fats also increases cholesterol in the blood. Cholesterol may play a role in colon cancer, but what that role is remains controversial. Very low blood levels of cholesterol have been associated with colon cancer, but the reasons for this are not clear. Some investigators argue that the disease lowers the cholesterol levels as part of cancer cachexia (see chapter 2). In other words, they think low cholesterol doesn't cause the disease, but rather that cancer causes the low cholesterol. It is known that certain bile acids, which are strong promoters of tumors in animals, arise from the body's metabolism of cholesterol. It may be that persons with low cholesterol are more efficient at converting cholesterol to these bile acids, which then enter the gut and promote tumor formation. If this is true, diet and exercise might be engaged to lower blood cholesterol, thus decreasing bile acid formation and preventing cancer.

One recently revealed clue to a possible link between cholesterol and cancer is that a substance called farnesyl, which is produced as the liver synthesizes cholesterol, interacts with certain genes, perhaps in the earliest stages of a developing cancer. The genes affected by farnesyl are the so-called oncogenes, which initiate the transformation of a cell into cancer. Presumably, then, the higher the cholesterol level goes, the more farnesyl is produced, and the more oncogenes and their products are enabled to initiate cancer.

CALCIUM

Epidemiologic studies show that high dietary levels of calcium tend to be associated with lower risk of colorectal cancer. In the laboratory, calcium can counteract the harmful effects of toxic bile acids and may decrease the excessive proliferation of colon lining cells thought to be a precursor to colon cancer.

ALLIUM VEGETABLES

We smile to think of the old superstition that a garlic clove worn around the neck will keep the devil away. Now it seems there may be a scientific truth buried in the superstition, especially if the devil is cancer. Several epidemiologic studies have shown that certain populations in China and Italy with a high consumption of garlic and its relatives in the allium genus, such as onions and leeks, have a reduced risk of gastrointestinal cancers. Biochemical analyses and animal studies have established that some of the sulfur chemicals in these vegetables—the same chemicals that produce their distinctive taste and smell—are potent inhibitors of cancer.

Including these vegetables in your daily diet would be a prudent part of an overall anticancer nutritional program. If you don't like the pungency of garlic, or it upsets your stomach, here's a wonderful way to enjoy garlic without consequences and without having to chop: When making homemade soup, stew, or beans, add several cloves of garlic, rinsed and unpeeled, to the pot, early in the cooking sequence. When ready to serve, fish out the whole cloves and put them on a saucer. Using a knife, smooth the softened garlic out of its peel. Discard the peel. Spread the garlic—which is now very mild tasting and creamy—on toast (with some nonfat margarine, if you wish), or return it to the pot and stir into the soup, stew, or beans.

FOODS THAT BOOST IMMUNITY

Since colorectal cancer is predominantly a disease of older people, and the immune system declines with aging, some investigators have proposed that there may be a connection between cancer and the declining immune system. Recent data show that the decline in immunity with age can be slowed by nutritional interventions. Beta carotene and vitamin E are important immune boosters, and vitamin C may play a role as well.

Fortunately, you can easily boost the intake of vitamin-rich foods as part of a high-fiber, low-fat diet. Vegetables and fruits and fortified cereals are high in fiber and vitamins *and* low in fat—a very convenient combination!

The one exception is that it may be impossible to get enough vitamin E when you are following a low-fat plan, because this vitamin is found in oils and fatty foods. For this reason, you should ask your physician about a multivitamin supplement that contains vitamin E, or a vitamin E supplement by itself.

Remember that very high doses of some other substances—zinc, vitamin A (not beta carotene), and selenium, for example—can suppress immunity. The old saying, "If a little is good, a lot must be better," does not apply here.

An Eating Plan for People with Early Colorectal Cancer or Adenomatous Polyps

I believe that a high-fiber, low-fat diet is an important preventive measure if you have a history of premalignant adenomatous colon polyps, inflammatory bowel disease, or a family history of colon cancer. An extra benefit may come by increasing foods that contain calcium (see page 43 for a list of calcium-containing foods). *Consult with your doctor before taking calcium supplements or any dietary supplements.* It is also a good idea to increase your consumption of the garlic-family vegetables and foods rich in beta carotene (see page 38 for a list of beta-carotene-rich foods).

The same data that support this suggestion can be taken as evidence that a similar diet might help defend against second primary cancers and possibly disease recurrence if you have had early colorectal cancer removed surgically. In other words, if you have had complete surgical removal of a colorectal cancer, or if you are receiving 5-FU and levamisole as adjuvant treatment of colon cancer that has extended to adjacent lymph nodes, it is prudent to adopt a high-fiber, low-fat diet that includes high-calcium foods. Note the word *prudent.* As yet, there are no results from clinical trials to prove this recommendation, but there is much evidence from other types of studies to support it. Dietary fiber has been shown to reduce the size and number of adenomatous polyps in people with familial adenomatous polyposis, and many epidemiologic studies show the preventive effect of fiber in colorectal cancer. Thus, I emphasize fiber first in the eating plan, but low fat comes in a close second. The role of calcium is supported by less data, but more is coming from studies in progress.

To date, researchers have had to be concerned with the "big picture" of what effects these dietary factors have. They have not yet been able to refine their findings to the point where a specific amount of fiber, calcium, or fat can be designated as the ideal measure. Nevertheless, I think that a reasonable goal is 30 to 35 grams of fiber a day, and a fat intake restricted to no more than 20 percent of calories or less. Calcium-rich foods that are also low in fat and that therefore should be emphasized in your diet are listed on page 43.

These observations are especially important for people with a family history of adenomatous polyps or colon cancer, or who have had such polyps or previous surgery for colon cancer. They may have higher colonic cell proliferation rates. In those with prior colon cancer, second colon tumors can and do develop. Be sure to discuss any plans to increase dietary fiber with your doctor and be sure he or she agrees; there may be abdominal symptoms that he or she will need to be aware of.

T HE C HANGES J OE M ADE

By now, you can see why Joe's diet—which is typical of so many Americans—was such a problem. His mind-set was, "I don't have time to eat well." Not eating well cost him in every way. Lack of fiber caused constant constipation. Joe paid a lot of money for over-the-counter laxatives to relieve this problem and overuse of laxatives made the constipation worse. The constipation made him lethargic, which is one of the reasons why every task seemed to require intense effort and longer hours. All of this, plus long hours on the job, conspired to keep Joe from exercising, which meant that he never allowed himself to shed the tensions of his job. This was bad for his heart and bad for his attitude at home.

Like most habits, Joe's diet habits did not develop in a vacuum. He grew up in a time when "health" meant "three square meals a day," with lots of meats and cheeses, and little concern for fat content. Advertising and a competitive work environment gave strong support for poor dietary choices, including fried food, donuts, and fast foods.

Joe had to make changes in his diet, but first he had to see how his diet habits were entangled with his feelings about his job. Like many people who are diagnosed with cancer, Joe found his encounter with this serious disease to be a life-changing event. His recuperation time in the hospital and at home was spent rethinking his priorities. His surgery had made his constipation even worse, so he suddenly got smart and decided to try what the doctor ordered: increased fiber and reduced fat in his diet. (Or at least, that's the way he likes to tell it. The truth is that Kathy took over and laid down the law to him in no uncertain terms.) Between the two of them, they increased his daily fiber intake to 30 to 35 grams and decreased his daily fat intake to 20 grams or less. Over time, they learned to maintain that level by incorporating fresh fruits and vegetables, as well as high-fiber cereal, into their meals.

As soon as he was able, Joe also began to exercise, starting out walking twenty minutes three times a week, then increasing this gradually to forty-five minutes five times a week. He was amazed at how much this relieved his tension and restlessness. He was also astonished to find that rough spots give sidewalks a kind of character, and that tall grass can look quite friendly waving in the wind.

Joe enjoys french fries—prepared according to Chef Erickson's recipe—and he doesn't mind the new nonfat "ice cream." He's learned a lot and made tremendous progress. He still eats out at a lot of fast-food places, but he takes advantage of the salad bars and new low-fat and whole-grain choices that many fast-food chains are now offering. He's experimented with new activities with his co-workers that don't rely on food and overwork, and to Kathy's delight he comes home most nights for dinner.

DIET IN ADVANCED COLORECTAL CANCER

Unfortunately, there is no evidence yet that any type of dietary manipulation helps prolong the life of a person with advanced colorectal cancer; however, dietary measures can provide relief from the rigors of chemotherapy or radiotherapy. Using the tips in chapter 8, "Solving Nutrition Problems and Improving Well-being During Treatment," your ability to eat may be restored, and quality of life greatly improved.

If you have advanced disease, you may already be facing difficult decisions about nutrition. You may be experiencing difficulty taking food by the normal oral route, diarrhea may be depriving you of your strength, or you may be losing weight. There are several options for you and your physician to consider.

One option is to take feedings by a nasogastric tube. This is the option that Nat Wilson reluctantly undertook. At sixty-five, Mr. Wilson would have much preferred to be overseeing the operation of his farm than seeing me for cancer of the colon. He had undergone surgical removal of most of his colon, both to treat the cancer and to correct adhesions that resulted from the surgery (an abnormal condition in which wounded tissues literally adhere to one another, causing pain and blockage). He also had adjuvant chemotherapy.

As a result of the colon surgeries, Mr. Wilson suffered constant diarrhea and severe weight loss. We had to act quickly to restore his nutritional status, so I ordered nasogastric tube feedings. The tube was quite a trial for Mr. Wilson. He hated the way he looked when it was in place.

Being a farmer, Mr. Wilson knew a lot about making the best of situations in which Mother Nature held most of the votes. So instead of rejecting the tube altogether, he improvised. He learned to put the tube in at night, so that the feeding solution could infuse slowly, in private. Not only did this improve his strength, it made it possible for Mr. Wilson to live life the way he wanted to. He reinstated the acquaintances and friendships that had been waylaid by his cancer and the treatment.

The colon cancer spread to Mr. Wilson's lungs; nevertheless, because he was able to take nourishment, he was also able to continue with chemotherapy. The treatment shrank the metastatic lung tumors and he did well long enough to resume his work on the farm.

Another way of dealing with nutrition problems in very advanced disease is hyperalimentation, in which all of a person's needed nutrients are given in an intravenous solution. Before using this technique, it's important to discuss all of the options and to make an informed decision about what you hope to accomplish by taking hyperalimentation. In the section about cancer cachexia in chapter

2, "The Connection Between Cancer and Diet," are accounts of various studies that have been done with hyperalimentation. Converting food to normal protein and muscle tissue is a basic task of a healthy body. This task goes on every day to replace tissues that have been damaged or have reached the end of their normal life span. What the studies described in chapter 2 reveal is that the person with cancer frequently is unable to use nutrients appropriately, even if the nutrients are adequately provided. *Instead of creating lean body mass, the person with cancer often converts nutrients into fat, which is not of much use.*

So, while nasogastric tube feedings and hyperalimentation are options, they are not appropriate or useful for every person. In considering the choices for maintaining nutritional status in advanced disease, it's important to get all the facts and discuss all aspects of the decision with your physician, including your preferences and emotional needs as well as your physical needs. Together, you can make an informed decision about what's best for you.

Recommendations for Colorectal Cancer

BASIC PLAN:

1. Increase fiber intake to 30 to 35 grams per day. (See the Fat and Fiber Gram Calculator on page 218.)
2. Decrease fat consumption to no more than 20 percent of daily calories.
3. Select a variety of fruits and vegetables.
4. Emphasize calcium-rich foods (see page 43).
5. Stress beta carotene-rich foods (see page 38).
6. Include allium vegetables (garlic, onions, leeks, etc.).

RATIONALE:

In both experimental and epidemiologic studies, high fiber and low fat have been shown to have strong anti–colon cancer effects. Evidence is emerging that calcium and sulfur-containing compounds in garlic may also have an effect. Those who may benefit are persons with a family history of colon polyps or colon cancer, or a

APPROXIMATE DAILY FAT GRAMS
FOR 20 PERCENT CALORIES FROM FAT

HEIGHT (NO SHOES)	FAT GRAMS OVER AGE 50*	FAT GRAMS UNDER AGE 50
MEN		
5'2"	30	34
5'3"	31	35
5'4"	32	36
5'5"	33	37
5'6"	34	38
5'7"	35	39
5'8"	36	40
5'9"	37	41
5'10"	38	42
5'11"	39	43
6'0"	40	44
6'1"	41	45
6'2"	42	46
WOMEN		
5'0"	25	28
5'1"	26	29
5'2"	27	30
5'3"	28	31
5'4"	29	32
5'5"	30	33
5'6"	31	34
5'7"	32	35
5'8"	33	36
5'9"	34	37
5'10"	35	38
5'11"	36	39
6'0"	37	40

* These fat gram amounts are calculated on basal levels of calories needed for ideal body weight at a particular height for adults of medium frame. If you are very active and have reached your daily fat gram goal but are still hungry, eat fruits, vegetables, and nonfat snacks, not more fat.

personal history of colon polyps. Those who have had colon cancer are at increased risk for second primary cancers of the colon; therefore, it is important to follow the basic plan above to reduce the risk of second colon cancer.

Some chemopreventives are in development, but these are not available yet outside of clinical trials.

See Part III for a three-month way to achieve this basic plan.

ADDITIONAL COMMENTS:

The RDA (recommended daily allowance) for calcium is 800 milligrams for men and women over twenty-five. An 8-ounce glass of skim milk has about 300 milligrams, as does 1 cup of fresh cooked collard greens and 2½ ounces of canned sardines. Some experts recommend 1,200 milligrams of calcium a day for anticancer effect, but this is not yet proven. I recommend at least three glasses of skim milk per day (or 900 milligrams calcium/day) or the equivalent (see page 43). If you consider a calcium supplement, consult your doctor first. When checking the label on a calcium supplement, "elemental calcium" is the important number. Some antacids have about the same amount of calcium as a glass of milk (300 milligrams). (Calcium also helps prevent osteoporosis in post-menopausal women.)

You might consider asking your doctor about a vitamin E supplement, since a low-fat diet may not contain adequate vitamin E, and this vitamin may be an important part of your defense against cancer. Avoid megadoses of any vitamin supplements—some can actually harm the immune system.

Vitamin D supplements are not usually recommended, because they can raise blood calcium too high. You should be getting adequate vitamin D in the fortified skim milk that is part of your daily diet, and from sensible sun exposure, which creates vitamin D in the skin.

6

FOR MEN WITH
PROSTATE CANCER

❧

At first glance, you would think that Tom Pritchett and Ned
Cullen have little in common, other than their age. Both
were born in the same part of North Carolina in 1926, but
even at birth, their paths were on different social tracks. Tom's
parents were white and considered themselves proud but poor. They
struggled to hold together their farm. Their home was spare and
simple but adequate, and when Tom was born, Mr. Pritchett was
proud to take his wife to the hospital for the birth—the first hospital birth in his entire family. The Pritchetts' other three boys had
been born at home, attended by the country doctor.

Ned's parents were black, also scrambling to hold together a
farm, equally proud but considerably poorer than the Pritchetts.
Their house was older, but Mr. Cullen determinedly kept it patched
together. Ned's mother delivered all six of her boys at home, as-
sisted by an ancient, skilled midwife.

Tom finished high school in a neat brick building in town; Ned
walked three miles to the "school for Coloreds," and at the end of
eighth grade, quit to help his father run their farm. Though seg-
regated into two different worlds, Tom and Ned had several things
in common. Both families relied on the Bible for guidance, the earth
for a living, and simple, basic foods, cooked in much the same
manner, for nurture.

In that time, in their moderate-sized town, their paths would rarely, if ever, have joined—except that in 1944, there was a war going on. Both young men enlisted in the army, and both eventually signed on as career soldiers. So they ended up living in similar base housing, traveling to similar locations, and buying food from the same commissaries. They both married young women from back home, and carried their North Carolina cooking traditions with them wherever they went.

In the late 1960s, Tom retired to a new brick ranch house, just up the road from the family's old home. He and his wife bought a recreational vehicle and took to the roads, except in winter, making contact with old friends, and visiting a week each year with each of his brothers. Tom later referred to those early years of retirement as the true golden years. He was still young and vigorous enough to enjoy life, and sufficiently free of financial worry to dabble in a few hobbies to supplement his income.

Around the same time, Ned checked into a hospital with what his mother worried would be "Cullens' disease." It certainly seemed that it was a Cullen family illness—Ned's father had died from it, a male cousin had died from it, and now Ned had it. It seemed to start with too many trips to the john in the middle of the night. Beyond that, the men didn't talk about it much, just got more miserable until it was clear that it wasn't going to go away.

The disease was prostate cancer, and in 1972, diagnosed at age forty-six, Ned already had bone metastases.

Tom was more fortunate; life was one beautiful trip down the highway in the R.V. after another. But in spring of 1990, he developed an embarrassing problem with dribbling urine. At first he thought his urinary tract was blocked, perhaps by a kidney stone, but when the anticipated pain didn't develop, he began to think that perhaps it was BPH (benign prostatic hypertrophy: enlarged prostate)—a condition an older friend had once described. Luckily, he decided to quit diagnosing himself and went to his physician, who determined that Tom, like Ned, had prostate cancer. Though the doctor was very reassuring that Tom was in no imminent danger, Tom didn't ask many questions. He asked the doctor to explain it to his wife, then told his wife to keep it between the two of them. There just wasn't any need, he said, to trouble the kids and relatives with it, and if his round of visits to them were going to be interrupted, well, they'd have to make up some story to account for it.

Fortunately for Tom, he hasn't had to invent a story yet; his disease has barely progressed. But his experience and Ned's are typical in many ways. Though they didn't know it (in fact, no one recognized it until recently), these men grew up in a hotbed for prostate cancer. Compared to all other countries, the United States of America has the highest incidence of prostate cancer, and rates are increasing. American black men have substantially higher rates of prostate cancer, as well as higher mortality rates from the disease, than do white men. And Ned's case was something of a classic: Black men in parts of the Southern United States have the highest rate of prostate cancer in the world.

Who Gets Prostate Cancer?

Ned had many counts against him. In addition to the high incidence of cancer in black men, statistics show that many black men develop prostate cancer at a younger age than do white men. High mortality rates suggest that the type of prostate cancer that occurs in black men may be more aggressive and progress more quickly. Also, it is clear that black men tend to be diagnosed later, largely because of poverty and lack of access to proper screenings and medical care.

Genetic factors may also play a part in prostate cancer; however, even though Ned's family thought of it as Cullens' disease, and a cousin and his own father had died from it, there is a possibility that, with earlier diagnosis and proper care, there could have been a different outcome for Ned. Doctors have enough information to make some generalizations about prostate cancer, but even within a particular ethnic group, there are variations. Some men have been observed to have had cancer that grew slowly or not at all for many years. Others in the same ethnic group have prostate cancers that grow very rapidly. It is very likely that both the characteristics of the tumor itself and the individual resistance of the person who has the cancer play a role in this.

The fact that Ned and Tom were raised on farms may have some relevance. There is evidence that exposure to some of the chemicals used in farming may be associated with increased risk. Some industrial chemicals (for example, those used in the rubber industry) have also been implicated.

Our knowledge of prostate cancer is growing so rapidly that it is hard to keep up with it. For one thing, we are learning that it is an extremely common disease. In fact, next to skin cancer, it is the most common cancer in men. One in 11 men will be diagnosed with it in their lifetime. Many men have it and don't even know they have it. Autopsy studies show that many (in some studies, as many as two thirds of) men die with—but not from—prostate cancer, and that neither they nor their physicians were aware that prostate cancer had developed.

SIMILARITIES TO BREAST CANCER

Prostate cancer has been likened to breast cancer in many ways. Roughly the same number of people die from these diseases each year. Both prostate cancer and breast cancer are related to aging (though they do occur in younger persons, the risk increases with age). When breast cancer occurs in a very young woman, it tends to be more virulent, and the same is true of prostate cancer in young men. In the closing years of the twentieth century, both prostate cancer and breast cancer are considered to be occurring in near-epidemic proportions, and projections are that they may continue to rise dramatically as our population ages. In both breast cancer and prostate cancer, early detection is a vital step in staving off suffering and saving lives.

The causes of the diseases also have similarities. Both have been related to hormonal factors (breast cancer to estrogen, prostate cancer to androgen), *and these hormonal factors are in part related to diet.* Some researchers believe that the diseases can exist quietly in the body for many years, then are triggered by some circumstance, such as diet, an environmental exposure, or some process of aging, perhaps declining immunity or changing hormone levels.

Prostate cancers are usually adenocarcinomas (tumors of glands), as are most breast cancers and colorectal cancers. Interestingly, these three cancers are the ones most closely identified with high-fat, low-fiber diets. Prostate, breast, and colorectal cancers are more common in developed countries. Risk for these three cancers increases when immigrants move from low-risk to high-risk areas. Dietary habits are strongly implicated in these risk patterns, especially diets high in fat.

Some studies link prostate cancer to high consumption of total protein, especially beef products. Limited data from animal studies indicate that protein-depleted diets inhibit the growth of prostate cancer that has been induced in animals. However, the inhibition may result from a lack of calories rather than from a lack of protein. Also from animal studies, investigators have learned that reduced protein and calorie intake may decrease levels of the hormone testosterone or prolactin in the blood.

One other similarity: Until recently, breast and prostate cancers were characterized by a thundering silence. Like Ned and Tom, most men don't want to talk about prostate cancer. The same was once true of breast cancer, though it is hard to believe it when you see how breast cancer is now the focus of articles, books, and daily talk shows. Just as Tom didn't want his family members to know about his diagnosis, just a decade or two ago it was not uncommon for a woman to undergo mastectomy without breathing a word to her own friends and neighbors, and though her husband knew the details, it was sometimes never discussed between the couple.

Recently, Senator Robert Dole and several other senators issued an astonishing challenge to the code of silence by sharing their own diagnoses of prostate cancer. The way that prostate cancer is regarded will never be the same, thanks to their courage.

Senator Dole was diagnosed after he had symptoms of difficulty in urination. He was determined to learn as much as he could about the disease. He was appalled to find that so little attention had been given to potential methods of early diagnosis, and that in fact, it would be about sixteen years before the National Cancer Institute could complete a study of early detection methods. "Half a million men could die by that time," said Senator Dole.

His estimate was very close. Approximately 132,000 men were diagnosed with prostate cancer in 1992, and about 34,000 died of the disease. In black men, mortality from prostate cancer is second only to lung cancer.

POSSIBLE CAUSES OF PROSTATE CANCER

No one knows why this small, walnut-shaped gland at the base of the bladder, just inside the rectum, is so prone to cancer. Its function is to produce a milky liquid that is discharged into the urethra to become part of the seminal fluid.

Most cases of prostate cancer occur after sixty-five. As in Tom Pritchett's case, many cases grow extremely slowly and require only careful monitoring. When the disease occurs at a younger age, as it did for Ned Cullen, it is usually a more virulent form.

Just as breast glandular tissue is affected by estrogen and a variety of other hormones (see chapter 4, "For Women with Breast Cancer"), the prostate gland is affected by the male hormone androgen, as well as other hormones. Although the exact mechanisms remain unclear, when breast and prostate cells become malignant, they often retain some sensitivity to hormones. Clinical experience has shown that either giving hormonal agents—for example, tamoxifen in breast cancer, estrogen in prostate cancer—or doing something to eliminate hormones (oophorectomy—removal of ovaries—in women, orchiectomy—removal of testicles—in men) will shrink breast and prostate cancer, respectively, with a fair amount of success.

It is not known why American black men have the highest rate of prostate cancer in the world; however, a recent study provided intriguing clues to this question, as well as to questions about the roles of hormones and diet in prostate cancer. The study compared the hormone levels and prostate rates of American black men with those of black men of the West Indies. The Americans' rate of prostate cancer was higher. The study also found that the American black men typically ate a high-fat, low-fiber diet, while the West Indian men ate a high-fiber, low-fat diet whose staple is the starchy vegetable called the cassava.

Another intriguing link between prostate cancer and diet is that the disease is uncommon in Asian men, but descendants of Asian immigrants to the United States have an increased risk of prostate cancer, and this has been attributed to adoption of a Western diet that is high in fat and calories and low in fiber (see chapter 4 for a similar link in that disease). Several very interesting autopsy studies have shown that the rate of small prostate cancers is the *same* in American, African, and Japanese men. Nevertheless the rate of *advanced* prostate cancer is much higher in Americans. The high-fat, low-fiber diet of Americans may therefore stimulate "latent" prostate cancer cells to grow. Seventh-Day Adventists, who abstain from meat and consume eggs and cheese sparingly, have a low prostate cancer mortality rate. In the laboratory, human prostate cancer cells (and breast cancer cells) are stimulated by the polyunsaturated fatty acid linoleic acid. Conversely, omega-3 fatty acids in fish oil inhibit prostate cancer and breast cancer cells in the laboratory.

As with breast cancer, the importance of early detection of prostate cancer cannot be overemphasized. In men whose cancer has already spread at diagnosis, only one in five survives for five years. Until recently, the only means of early diagnosis was digital rectal examination, an examination of the rectum and prostate by gloved finger. Unfortunately, many men avoid this test until their symptoms signal an urgent need for attention. Now there is a new diagnostic tool—a blood test called the prostate-specific antigen (PSA) test.

When there are higher-than-normal levels of PSA in the blood, it's highly likely the prostate is being damaged. The problem is—damaged by what? Increased PSA levels can signal the presence of prostate cancer *or* benign prostatic hypertrophy. These are two very different diseases. The first has the potential to metastasize and kill and may require drastic surgery or other therapy. The second can be serious but is not malignant and requires less threatening treatment. For this reason, a PSA test by itself is not a good diagnostic tool. The American Cancer Society has recommended that the PSA be used in conjunction with a digital rectal examination and, if necessary, transrectal ultrasound (TRUS) test. The TRUS is another new development—an ultrasound study that is performed using a rectal probe. The NCI has not yet taken a stance pro or con PSA testing.

In its guidelines for prostate cancer screening, the American Cancer Society recommends that every man over the age of fifty have an annual digital rectal examination and PSA test, plus TRUS if results of either are abnormal. Men who are at high risk, such as African Americans, or any man who has a strong family history of prostate cancer may want to begin this screening earlier.

You may recall that when Tom first developed problems with urination, he thought it might be benign prostatic hypertrophy. This very common condition has much the same symptoms as early prostate cancer, such as weak urine stream, dribbling of urine or difficulty starting urination, and frequent urination, especially at night. Since the prostate gland enlarges in benign prostatic hypertrophy, it takes careful medical evaluation to distinguish between this benign condition and prostate cancer. Prostatitis (infection in the prostate) can also cause similar symptoms, and if the infection spreads to the bladder, there may be blood in the urine, which could also suggest kidney stones. And, like kidney stones, advanced prostate cancer can cause pelvic pain, especially when it spreads to bones. So no one should waste valuable time trying to diagnose these kinds of symptoms on his own, without a doctor. (By the way, benign prostatic hypertrophy does not appear to be directly associated with prostate cancer.)

TREATMENT OF PROSTATE CANCER

As you are aware, when you and your physician make decisions about how to treat your cancer, you must take into account other medical conditions that you have, such as heart disease, stroke, or diabetes.

If your tumor is limited to the prostate, the options may include surgery and radiation therapy. These methods are about equal in their results.

Surgery was once undesirable because it could result in nerve damage that led to impotence. Recent surgical advances have largely overcome this problem. Radiation therapy can cause bone marrow damage, diarrhea, or greater urinary frequency, as well as impotence.

If the cancer is more advanced, radiation therapy or hormonal manipulation (or a combination of both) may be tried. The goal of hormonal manipulation is to decrease male hormone (androgen) levels. There are several ways to accomplish this:

- Bilateral orchiectomy (removal of the testicles)
- Administration of estrogen, to block the body's production of testicular androgen
- Administration of gonadotropin-releasing hormone-like drugs (GRH), to decrease production of testicular androgens

Recently, a new antiandrogen drug (flutamide) plus orchiectomy or GRH agents has given encouraging results.

None of the above methods is very useful if the disease is in a very late stage; instead, it is important to focus on relieving pain and discomfort. One important measure is radiation therapy to painful areas of metastases in the skeleton. Chemotherapy with cytotoxic drugs (i.e., nonhormonal chemotherapy) has also provided pain relief in some men with advanced disease.

As more and more men reach the age at which risk of prostate cancer increases, the question of prevention will gain increasing attention. The National Cancer Institute is sponsoring a clinical trial to see if Proscar (fenasteride), a drug that inhibits androgen production, can prevent prostate cancer. Proscar is usually used to treat benign prostatic hypertrophy. Unfortunately, the results of this study are several years away.

An Eating Plan for People with Prostate Cancer

Despite the strong suspicion of a link between diet and prostate cancer, there have been very few clinical trials to test diet's role in prevention or as an adjunct to treatment of the disease. Nevertheless, it is known that, like colorectal, breast, and other cancers, the more fat in the diet, the greater the chance of developing prostate cancer. There is also a suggestion that low intake of foods containing beta carotene may increase prostate cancer risk. Consult your doctor before making any dietary changes.

These facts have been gleaned from research, but it is not yet certain how they can be applied to improve prevention and treatment of prostate cancer. There is no evidence that megadoses of vitamins, selenium, or other minerals are helpful, and as described in chapter 2, "The Connection Between Cancer and Diet," megadoses can be dangerous.

Until randomized clinical trials of either chemopreventive or nutritional methods are completed, recommendations for dietary changes to prevent prostate cancer are limited. Even with these limitations, the American Cancer Society's dietary recommendations (see chapter 2) are a good place to start. Using those recommendations, you will have the advantage of a diet that offers general cancer-fighting properties and that counters some of the other problems that older men generally face; the high-fiber content will help maintain regularity, and the low-fat content may help to delay or prevent cardiovascular disease.

If your prostate cancer was diagnosed early and the tumor has been completely removed, your chances of cure are high. In this case, the above guidelines are quite appropriate.

If you have had surgery or radiotherapy and there is some doubt that all of the disease has been eradicated, it would be prudent to reduce your fat intake to 20 percent or less and increase your consumption of foods containing beta carotene (see page 38). I would suggest at least six servings or more of fruits and vegetables daily.

If your cancer has metastasized to the bone or elsewhere, changing the types of food you eat is not likely to help much. Chapter 8, "Solving Nutrition Problems and Improving Well-being During Treatment," has information to help you overcome the side effects of treatment in this case.

Recommendations for Prostate Cancer

BASIC PLAN:

1. For cured prostate cancer (early disease, localized to the gland, and the gland is completely removed), follow the NCI/AC nutrition guidelines (see page 53) .

2. For more advanced disease with uncertainty about complete eradication, lower dietary fat to 20 percent or less of total calories and increase foods containing beta carotene. Consider this recommendation if you have a clear family history of prostate cancer. (See the chart on page 125 and Part III.

3. For metastatic cancer, see chapter 8, "Solving Nutrition Problems and Improving Well-being During Treatment."

ADDITIONAL COMMENTS:

Since prostate cancer is a disease that is associated with aging, and the immune system tends to weaken in older persons, you should consider asking your doctor about a multivitamin supplement and a vitamin E supplement. Vitamin E, an antioxidant, may not be present in sufficient quantity in a low-fat diet, because it is primarily found in oils and other fatty foods.

APPROXIMATE DAILY FAT GRAMS
FOR 20 PERCENT CALORIES FROM FAT

HEIGHT (NO SHOES)	FAT GRAMS OVER AGE 50*	FAT GRAMS UNDER AGE 50*
MEN		
5'2"	30	34
5'3"	31	35
5'4"	32	36
5'5"	33	37
5'6"	34	38
5'7"	35	39
5'8"	36	40
5'9"	37	41
5'10"	38	42
5'11"	39	43
6'0"	40	44
6'1"	41	45
6'2"	42	46

* These fat gram amounts are calculated on basal levels of calories needed for ideal body weight at a particular height for adults of medium frame. If you are very active and have reached your daily fat gram goal but are still hungry, eat fruits, vegetables, and nonfat snacks, not more fat.

7

FOR PEOPLE WITH CANCER OF THE LUNG, HEAD, NECK, ESOPHAGUS, CERVIX, BLADDER, OR SKIN (SQUAMOUS CANCERS)

❧

T hese cancers, called the "squamous cell cancers," arise from cells that cover organs and form the lining of tissue surfaces. Most are related to tobacco use; skin cancer is caused by excess sunlight and cervical cancer may be associated with a particular group of viruses. Squamous cell cancers require similar nutritional plans, so we will talk about them together.

EXTERNAL INFLUENCES

The word *squamous,* from the Latin *squama,* means scale (as in fish scales), and refers to the cells that make up the lining or covering layer of organs (for example, the cells that cover the cervix). The other major type of cancer, adenocarcinoma, arises in glandular structures (*aden* or *adeno* in Greek means gland) in the affected organ, such as glands in the breast. Adenocarcinomas are frequently found in the breast, colon, prostate, or other organs that contain lots of glandular tissue.

Because most glands are not directly exposed to the external environment, it is thought that whatever causes these organs to develop cancer (if it is an external cause) most likely reaches the organ through the body's circulatory system. For example, the blood might transport chemical carcinogens, fat, or fatty acids to these areas.

By contrast, squamous cell cancers are subject to both internal and external influences. In the case of lung cancer, squamous cells lining the lungs are exposed to toxins from outside the body, especially tobacco smoke, and at the same time are exposed to tobacco carcinogens absorbed into the bloodstream. Cigarette smoking plays a major role in the development of squamous cell cancers, not only of the lung, but of the head and neck region, esophagus, bladder, and elsewhere. Smoking has even been linked to cancer of the cervix. It is clear that the carcinogens inhaled with smoking can reach distant parts of the body, including the cervix, and can cause genetic damage to these tissues. When this damage is combined with certain other biologic assaults, such as human papillomavirus (HPV) infection in the cervix, the effect often is that a cancer develops.

In recent years, we have learned that the damage caused by cigarette smoking extends much further than previously realized. Smoking is not just a personal decision. A parent's smoking can cause respiratory illness in children and increase the risk that the child will take up smoking in adolescence or adulthood. A pregnant woman who smokes exposes her fetus to the same carcinogens that she is exposed to, and there is documentation that the woman's smoking increases the fetus's risk of low birth weight, which can cause a variety of health and developmental problems. Very recently, a group of researchers also linked the father's smoking to decreased birth weight, though to a lesser degree than when the mother smokes. If one member of a couple smokes, the nonsmoking member is at increased risk of lung cancer because of exposure to secondhand smoke.

Skin cancers are most often associated with radiation damage caused by excess sun exposure; however, there are some studies that have linked skin cancer to tobacco smoke as well. Squamous cell skin cancers have also been linked to radiation exposure other than sunlight and to exposure to certain chemicals, such as arsenic.

Something Missing in the Diet

The squamous cell cancers are alike in another way, too—they are cancers of "undernutrition," the group we talked about in chapter 2, "The Connection Between Cancer and Diet." Unlike breast, colon, and other cancers of overnutrition, which are thought to be most directly linked to too much fat or calories, squamous cell cancers have been linked in population studies to something *missing* from the diet.

In squamous cell cancers, the "something missing" may be certain vitamins—especially A and E. The role of these antioxidant vitamins in cancer is described in chapter 2.

The tumors of undernutrition may result from an absolute dietary deficiency of an essential substance, or from a relative deficiency caused by something like tobacco use. While smokers are not necessarily malnourished in the usual sense, they have a much greater need for antioxidants, because smoking increases the level of oxidants that damage cells. The body needs more antioxidants to try to reverse the process.

Also, there is evidence that smoking interferes with the body's ability to use vitamins. For example, it is known that smokers must have a higher intake of vitamin C to gain the same benefit that this vitamin has on a nonsmoker.

Tobacco has so many negative effects on the body that the U.S. Surgeon General has issued several weighty volumes to describe them. One effect is that tobacco causes cells to behave in a manner that tends toward cancer. One of these behaviors that changes is differentiation, the crucial process that determines a cell's character and function. In cells that are shaping up as cancer cells, some vitamins, including vitamins A and E, can reorient the cell functions to more normal processes, thus interrupting an ominous sequence.

Interestingly, there are parallels between this protective capacity and the function of vitamins in some nutritional deficiency diseases. Vitamin A deficiency causes "metaplasia," a disruption of squamous (lining) cells of the cornea and elsewhere. Laboratory studies with animals have shown that vitamin A protects squamous cell tissues from carcinogens. Others have reported an association between lung cancer and low dietary intake of vitamin A. In other words, certain individuals at high risk might be protected against some squamous cell cancers by manipulation of vitamins.

As we review each of these squamous cell cancers, you will see how the "something missing" plays a role in the development of each one.

LUNG CANCER

Nearly every case of lung cancer is a double tragedy. First, in the majority of cases, the disease is preventable by *not smoking* or not being exposed to secondhand cigarette smoke. Second, it is very difficult to detect lung cancer in its early stages. Symptoms of lung cancer, such as cough, bloody sputum, chest pain, and lung infections, tend to appear late in the course of the disease. Persons who have these symptoms often ignore or deny them, for example, assuming it is "only" smoker's cough. And unlike other routine cancer screens (such as Pap smears and mammograms), screening of people without symptoms for lung cancer by chest X ray has not been a useful cancer control measure, because it would be necessary to screen hundreds of thousands of people for each cancer found— and it is possible that the people most at risk for lung cancer would be as resistant to getting a chest X ray as they are to giving up smoking.

If you don't have lung cancer but smoke, *quitting now* is the most important cancer preventive measure you can take. It is never too late to stop smoking. The lungs have a remarkable ability to heal themselves, and damaged tissues often return to normal within two to four years after smoking cessation (the tissues of heavy smokers may require longer). Neither diet nor exercise nor anything else will counteract the damage if you continue to smoke.

Even if you have already been diagnosed with lung cancer, there are benefits in quitting, though doing so will not reverse the cancer. Continuing to smoke can lessen the benefits of therapies, as well as increase the risk of other conditions such as stroke or coronary heart disease. Also, continuing to smoke will mean continuing to expose others in your household to risk of lung cancer and other respiratory ailments.

Treatment of lung cancer requires the strongest means available to the medical profession. Surgery to remove part or all of an affected lung is often followed by prolonged radiation and multidrug chemotherapy. The side effects of these treatments can be significant, including postoperative pain, nausea, loss of appetite, bone marrow suppression, and many other effects.

In one type of lung cancer, "small cell" cancer, surgery is usually not performed, except for a biopsy. The reason that this type of cancer is called "small cell" is that the cells are indeed smaller than other lung cancer types. For reasons unknown, these cells are very quick to spread beyond the reach of surgery. For small cell lung cancer, chemotherapy and radiation therapy are given in hopes of stopping the disease, both in the lung and elsewhere in the body.

Several nutritionally based studies are in progress around the world to try to prevent lung cancer. These are actually *chemoprevention* rather than dietary trials, in which specific nutrients are used as drugs to try to interrupt the process of cancer formation. Most of these trials are using antioxidants, including vitamins A and E and synthetic derivatives of vitamin A.

The National Cancer Institute of the United States, in cooperation with investigators in Finland, has initiated one of the largest human clinical trials ever attempted. Heavy smokers are participating in this study, which is examining vitamin A and vitamin E separately and together as preventives for lung cancer. Results should be available by 1994. Other lung cancer studies include the CARET trial, conducted in the United States. This trial seeks to enroll by 1996 more than 15,000 heavy smokers and persons exposed to asbestos. These persons will participate in tests of beta carotene and retinol (two vitamin A substances) to prevent lung cancer. In China, preliminary work has been done to set up a lung cancer chemoprevention trial in tin miners, who are at risk for this cancer. This trial will use vitamin A, beta carotene, vitamin E, and selenium. In another study, high-dose vitamin A has been given safely to a group of people who have already undergone treatment for lung cancer. Early results of this study are promising, because vitamin A appears to prolong the period between conclusion of cancer therapy and recurrence of disease.

None of these trials is expected to show maximum effect of vitamins as chemopreventives as long as the participants continue to smoke. To benefit fully from the vitamins, it will be necessary for the smokers to quit smoking. This is because, as mentioned earlier, the carcinogenic effects of smoking overwhelm any good and healthy things that smokers do for themselves.

Nevertheless, I mention these important trials because they illustrate why squamous cell cancers should be categorized as cancers of *undernutrition*. As you probably noticed, the trials described above all involve *adding* something, usually a vitamin, to the diet. The same principle applies to the diseases discussed below (i.e., head and neck cancer, cervical cancer, and bladder cancer).

With regard to lung cancer, a working hypothesis that appeals to me is this: Tobacco smoke affects lining cells of the body to produce a relative deficiency of agents, such as vitamin A, that control differentiation of cells. These cells do not differentiate properly; they grow, perhaps under the influence of other tobacco-related growth factors, into a cancer. Still other factors may then come into play to cause metastases. In this scenario, tobacco is an instigator of the process, but it is possible that severe undernutrition (i.e., lack of vitamin A and other compounds) could occur without tobacco use, with the same results. This would account for the observation in epidemiological studies that low vitamin A intake correlates with lung cancer.

Vitamin E deficiency also causes disruption of squamous cells. Pellagra, a disease caused by multiple dietary deficiencies, is characterized by a number of changes, some of which occur in lining cells, including both atrophy (shrinkage) and hypertrophy (growth) of the cells lining the gut as well as the skin. This is why vitamins A and E are being used in lung cancer chemoprevention trials to combat possible precancerous changes.

Most lung cancers are the squamous variety; some are adenocarcinomas. Adenocarcinomas of the lung may also be caused by smoking, but not much is known about the relationship between nutrition and this cancer type.

HEAD AND NECK AND ESOPHAGUS CANCER

Head and neck cancer arises in the lining cells of the throat and mouth, including the lips, tongue, upper part of the esophagus, and the upper airway structures. They are predominantly squamous cell cancers and account for about 40,000 cases and 11,000 deaths in the United States yearly. If you have been diagnosed with head and neck cancer, you are undoubtedly aware of the seriousness of this type of disease. The site of the cancer can make an enormous difference in the chances of survival. Ninety-two percent of persons who are treated for lip cancer survive five years or longer, but only 10 percent of persons treated for esophageal cancer survive five years. Other sites fall between these extremes.

Apart from the fact that cure is often elusive in these diseases, the location of tumors can interfere significantly with your ability to eat by simple obstruction. Treatment may remove the source of obstruction but may, at the same time, present new challenges to nutrition. The necessary surgical procedures may require removal of segments of the digestive apparatus permanently, or these segments may be disabled by the side effects of chemotherapy or radiation for prolonged periods. Some of the side effects are loss of salivary gland function and resulting dry mouth, mucositis, nausea, and tooth loss.

As I mentioned earlier, head and neck cancers are associated, like lung cancer, with tobacco use, including chewing tobacco or snuff, as well as smoking. Unlike lung cancer, however, head and neck cancers are also strongly associated with alcohol consumption. Smoking without alcohol consumption can cause head and neck cancer, as can the use of alcohol without smoking, but the risk is increased even more by this combination. Some researchers have also found a link between head and neck cancer and marijuana smoking, with or without the use of alcohol, mostly in people under the age of thirty.

Early head and neck lesions are *highly curable* when surgery, radiation therapy, and/or chemotherapy are used. More advanced head and neck cancers are treated with the same types of regimens, but results are not as good. Researchers have noted that chemotherapy can have dramatic short-term results, so there are trials of what is called "neo-adjuvant" chemotherapy in progress. This method involves giving powerful doses of chemotherapy *before* surgery, to shrink the lesions and allow the surgeon to perform less extensive surgery. Thus far, the findings are encouraging. Neo-adjuvant chemotherapy offers the advantage of less disfigurement, and survival rates in persons who get neo-adjuvant chemotherapy are about equivalent to the rates obtained by other methods. This approach may, in some cases, make it possible to spare the larynx and other structures, but assessment of the long-term outcome of these methods requires several more years of study.

There are certain warning signs that make impending head and neck cancer evident to an examining physician. Leukoplakia is a white "plaque" that appears on the mucous membranes of the mouth. Erythroplakia is a red, velvety lesion that also appears on mouth tissues. Neither of these is itself cancerous, but *either* signals the need for a biopsy and careful follow-up inspections by a physician (they are premalignant lesions).

People with leukoplakia or erythroplakia are good subjects for chemopreventive trials. About three decades ago, researchers learned that topical applications of vitamin A could reverse oral leukoplakia.

Since then, oral vitamin A (i.e., taken as a tablet instead of applied directly) also has been found to be effective. Currently, clinical trials are in progress to evaluate vitamin A derivatives in this regard. It appears that synthetic derivatives of vitamin A are more effective than the natural vitamin A precursor, beta carotene. Unfortunately, the synthetic derivatives are more toxic, causing skin and eye irritation as well as increased blood lipid levels.

As with many cancers, second primary tumors can occur in persons who have had head and neck cancer. According to a widely accepted theory, squamous cells exposed to carcinogens (such as tobacco smoke) for long periods of time undergo what is called field cancerization. This means that surrounding cells over a wide area (for example, the entire mouth and throat) become premalignant. Over time, some cells in this field progress to malignancy, and treatment becomes necessary. If the treatment is successful, that cancer is gone, but others can develop in other parts of the field. Persons who refuse to stop smoking or drinking, even after diagnosis of a head and neck cancer, are especially susceptible to further cancers of the head and neck, lung, or esophagus. Beta carotene, synthetic vitamin A derivatives, and other chemopreventive drugs are being tested in both the United States and Europe for their ability to prevent second primary tumors of the head and neck, and early results are encouraging. An exciting study was published late in 1993 from China (a joint NCI/Chinese project) that documented a decreased rate of esophageal and stomach cancer in subjects at high risk who took vitamins A and E along with selenium.

CANCER OF THE CERVIX

Cancer of the cervix is grouped with other tumors of undernutrition for several reasons: The disease is more common among women of low socioeconomic status (in whom dietary patterns are likely to be poor); risk of the disease has been linked with certain nutritional deficits; and decreased risk has been associated with high intake of particular foods. Specifically, a diet low in beta carotene and vitamin C increases risk, and consumption of large amounts of fruits and vegetables decreases risk. For these reasons, cervical cancer is the target of a number of nutrition-based prevention clinical trials. There are, however, other important risk factors for cancer of the cervix, including early age at first intercourse, having multiple sex partners, and exposure to certain sexually transmitted viruses (e.g., the human papillomaviruses).

Over the past several decades, the number of women diagnosed with invasive cervical cancer has decreased. In 1992, there were about 13,500 new cases of invasive cervical cancer and about 4,000 women died from this disease. In contrast, in 1958, 8,500 women died from cancer of the cervix. This decline in deaths is due in part to the widespread use of the Pap smear, a procedure in which a small sample of cells is taken from the cervix and preserved on a slide for examination under a microscope by specially trained technicians. The procedure takes only a few minutes and is usually performed along with a pelvic examination. Done by a skilled professional, the Pap smear normally causes very little discomfort, if any. The presence of malignant cells on the slide sample indicates cervical cancer.

Just as a developing head and neck cancer may have warning signals such as leukoplakia or erythroplakia, developing cervical cancer also presents certain warning signs, but in very early stages, these signs can only be seen on a Pap smear. This is one of several reasons for doing Pap smears so often. If your Pap smear indicates certain changes in the cells of your cervix, such as dysplasia or inflammation, your physician should monitor your progress very carefully, with repeated Pap smears or with further studies and treatment.

Even when the diagnosis is definitively cervical cancer, in most women the disease can be cured. The cure rate is almost 100 percent if the disease is found while it is still in situ (i.e., it has not yet invaded surrounding cells). Every year, about 50,000 women in the United States are diagnosed with in situ cervical cancer. When all stages of diagnosis are taken into account, the five-year survival rate for cervical cancer is 66 percent.

Though 66 percent is a good survival rate, 100 percent is obviously far more desirable. This is why the Pap smear is one of the most important tests a woman can get to maintain her health. The American Cancer Society recommends an annual Pap smear and pelvic exam for women who are or have been sexually active or have reached age eighteen. After three or more consecutive satisfactory normal annual exams, the Pap test may be performed less frequently, at the physician's discretion.

The type of treatment necessary for cervical cancer depends on the stage of disease at diagnosis. Early (in situ) disease can be treated by local removal of the disease by surgery, cryotherapy (freezing), or electrocoagulation (heating by an electric current). More advanced disease requires more extensive surgery and/or radiation therapy.

Several centers are now testing beta carotene, vitamin A derivatives, vitamin C, and folic acid to see if these compounds can reverse premalignant changes in the cervix, in much the same way that vitamin A reverses premalignant oral lesions. Some of these trials are using direct application of preventive compounds to the cervix. Others are evaluating agents that can be taken orally. Early evidence is that cervical dysplasia (which can progress to cervical cancer) can be reversed.

BLADDER CANCER

Cancer of the urinary bladder is relatively common, found more often in men than in women. In 1992, more than 51,000 people were diagnosed with the disease, and about 9,500 died from it.

As in other squamous cell cancers, smoking is a significant risk factor. Carcinogens in smoke pass through the lungs and into the blood. As the kidneys cleanse these carcinogens from the blood, they are deposited in the urine. Thus stored in the bladder, the carcinogens act on the lining cells of the bladder to stimulate cancer. Persons who are employed in certain industries (dye making, rubber manufacturing, or leather processing) are also at increased risk for this cancer.

Bloody urine is a common warning signal of bladder cancer. Diagnosis is accomplished by cystoscopy, a procedure in which an instrument is inserted into the bladder so that the physician can directly visualize the condition of the bladder and take samples of suspicious areas for biopsy.

When bladder cancer is found early, the five-year survival rate is 90 percent, but this falls to just 9 percent once the disease has metastasized. The type of treatment that is appropriate depends on the stage at diagnosis. Surgery, radiation therapy, chemotherapy, or a combination of these may be needed. Trials of neo-adjuvant chemotherapy (drugs given before surgery to shrink the tumor) are underway. There is very little data on chemoprevention of bladder cancer. Avoidance of tobacco remains the most effective preventive measure.

Skin Cancer

Skin cancer is by far the most common cancer of all. More than 700,000 cases occur each year in the United States, but only about 32,000 of these are of the life-threatening type, malignant melanoma. The rest are highly curable basal cell or squamous cell cancers. Overall, 8,800 deaths occur yearly from skin cancer, and the majority of these—6,700 cases—are from melanoma.

The most important risk factor for skin cancer is excess sun exposure. People with fair skin are at the highest risk, and the disease is uncommon (but not unheard of) in black persons. Other risk factors include exposure to arsenic, radium, or coal tar.

Skin cancer has increased at an alarming rate in the past decade. There are several reasons for this. One of the most important may be that air pollution is slowly destroying the protective layer of ozone that envelops our planet. The larger the "holes" in the ozone grow, the greater the level of damaging sun rays that can reach the earth and the people who inhabit it. Another important factor is lifestyle. At the very same time that the ozone layer is shrinking we have become sun worshippers, casting off more and more of our clothing. A shirt, a hat, a pair of slacks can mean the difference between a safe experience in the sun and one that lays the groundwork for future cancer.

Sun protection, including an adequate sunblocking agent (look for an SPF rating of 15 or greater), is important at every age. Infants and children have very tender skin and should be protected by adequate clothing and shading, as well as by sunscreen. Sun exposure (and especially sunburn) in the teenage years is very dangerous. That mark of perverse, youthful pride after mowing the lawn or a day at the beach—a peeling burn—is evidence that the skin has been seriously damaged. Elders also should be very careful about sun exposure, because as we age, our skin becomes more sensitive. So everyone—from infants to great-great-grandparents—should avoid excess sun exposure, including reflected light from pools or water. The hours from 10:00 A.M. to 2:00 P.M. are the worst.

I wish that tanning booths could be a thing of the past. At their very best, they are a serious hazard to healthy skin, and in many states, they are entirely unregulated, with neither equipment inspections nor training for the operating personnel.

Everyone should be alert for skin cancer. The warning signals include any change in pigmentation of a mole or other pigmented spot, or the new appearance of any such spot. Other signs are scaling, bleeding, oozing, itching, and pain. Any unexplained skin change should prompt a visit to the doctor. This includes a sudden change in color or size of a mole, but *any* change is important. It's important to note that skin cancer, including melanoma, can arise on any part of the skin, and its location will not necessarily correlate with sun-damaged areas. For example, a person who has experienced years of "red neck" sunburns while gardening or fishing may develop a melanoma in a remote location that was usually protected, such as the thigh (in fact, the thigh is one of the more common sites for melanoma). Skin cancers can be hidden in the scalp as well, so your health-care provider should check everywhere—even the soles of your feet—at least annually, and you should be performing monthly skin examinations at home.

How can benign changes in the skin be discerned from suspicious or malignant changes? Only a biopsy can tell for certain, but there is an "ABCD" rule that physicians use when considering whether a lesion is melanoma, the deadliest type of cancer:

A = Asymmetry. One half of the lesion is not like the other half.
B = Border irregularity. The lesion's edges are notched, ragged, or blurred.
C = Color is not uniform.
D = Diameter is greater than 6 millimeters.

Treatment for skin cancer depends upon the type of cancer—squamous cell, basal cell, or melanoma—which must be determined by biopsy. If found early, squamous cell and basal cell tumors can be removed by freezing, electrodesiccation, or surgery. More extensive surgery and possibly radiation therapy are used in more advanced cases.

Melanoma is especially dangerous because it can spread very quickly to distant sites. This type of cancer requires complete surgical removal of all of the primary tumor. Over time, physicians have refined their concepts of how much surrounding skin (surgical margin) must be removed to be sure that all of the tumor has been eradicated; consequently, there is a trend toward less extensive initial surgery. Lymph node dissections used to be routine, but are becoming less common. Systemic chemotherapy has not been very effective in advanced melanoma, but recent preliminary experience with cisplatin and alpha interferon has been somewhat encouraging.

If treated early, basal cell cancers and squamous cell cancers can usually be cured. Five-year survival of melanoma is about 90 percent of persons with early lesions, but this falls dramatically to 14 percent if the disease has metastasized.

Consistent with the "field cancerization theory" (see the section on head and neck cancers, above), a major risk factor for basal cell or squamous cell skin cancers is having had a previous skin cancer of these types.

Interestingly, squamous cell skin cancer is now linked, along with other squamous cell cancers discussed in this chapter, with smoking. Since radiation from the sun damages the DNA in cells, it's possible that the combination of sun damage and cigarette smoking may be as lethal as the combination of smoking and alcohol consumption.

Skin cancer has been the target of several chemoprevention clinical trials. Studies of people with xeroderma pigmentosum, an inherited defect in the mechanisms that normally repair sun damage to the skin, are providing some interesting leads. Skin cancer is very common in persons with xeroderma pigmentosum. A vitamin A type of compound has been tested and proven effective in preventing new nonmelanoma skin cancers in persons with this defect; however, the same compound did not prevent basal cell cancer in individuals who do not have xeroderma pigmentosum. Beta carotene was also ineffective in preventing new basal cell cancers in persons who did not have xeroderma pigmentosum. Until more is known through such studies, the best preventive measure is protection from sun exposure.

AN EATING PLAN FOR PEOPLE WITH SQUAMOUS CELL CANCERS

As with other diseases we have discussed, nutritional changes have the best chance of helping in early stages of disease and in premalignant lesions. Metastatic cancers have a poor chance of responding to dietary changes. Chapter 8, "Solving Nutrition Problems and Improving Well-being During Treatment," gives useful advice on eating during treatment. Consult with your doctor before making any dietary changes.

EAT MORE FRUIT AND VEGETABLES

Several investigators have linked consumption of fruit and vegetables to a decreased risk of both squamous cell and adenocarcinomas of the lung and other squamous cancers. Vitamin C, beta carotene, or some other factor may account for this. No particular kind of fruit or vegetable has been singled out as more important than others. Fresh, raw fruits and vegetables may have more of an effect than cooked ones. This is because the vitamins in many fruits and vegetables may deteriorate quickly after being exposed to air or heat.

Studies have shown that risk of adenocarcinoma of the lung is decreased when the diet includes vegetables, fruits, and soy products. Fruit consumption has also frequently been seen as protective for many other cancers, including cancer of the esophagus, mouth, larynx, pancreas, stomach, bladder, colorectum, cervix, ovary, endometrium, and breast. Vegetables have a somewhat less powerful effect.

As discussed, a number of vitamins and other compounds are being tested as chemopreventives, both in those who are at risk of cancer and in those who have been treated for cancer, to prevent recurrences. Perhaps when these trials are complete, it will be possible to be precise in recommending the amounts of particular vitamins, minerals, or trace elements that are needed to provide maximum protective effect. If fruits and vegetables protect against squamous cancer, it is reasonable that they support recovery as well. There is not much solid data on this, however, although studies are in progress.

In the meantime, I think the evidence for a diet rich in fruits and vegetables is strong enough to support increasing these substantially in your diet (see chapter 9, "Three Months to a New Eating Plan," for how to do it). Since such a diet is almost always high in fiber and low in fat, you should also enjoy other anticancer and anticardiovascular disease benefits. Eat a considerable amount of fruits and vegetables and make sure you choose from a wide variety.

If you are at risk for squamous cancers or in recovery, I recommend that you increase your consumption of fruits and vegetables to eleven or more servings a day. Be sure to vary the fruits and vegetables, both so you don't get tired of any one type and so you gain the widest range of healthful elements. Think of these as changes for a lifetime, not just while you're fighting cancer. The recipes at the back of this book provide a good sampling of tasty and attractive ways to prepare fruits and vegetables.

REDUCE DIETARY FAT

Although the squamous cell cancers are cancers of undernutrition, a high-fat diet can still pose a problem. For example, investigators have found a positive relationship between consumption of high-fat foods and the risk of lung cancer in both men and women. Smoking, as would be expected, increased the risk in persons who ate the greatest amounts of fat. Processed meats, dairy products, eggs, and certain desserts (fruit pies, custard, cream pies) were the foods most strongly associated with increased risk. In addition to being high in calories, the fat can be converted to cholesterol, a process that may activate certain oncogene products (as discussed in chapter 2, "The Connection Between Cancer and Diet"). Cholesterol and some fatty acids may also change immune function and cell membrane composition.

Vegetables and fruits will provide high levels of vitamin C and A, but a low-fat diet may be relatively low in the antioxidant vitamin E. Consider asking your doctor for a vitamin E supplement.

LIMIT CONSUMPTION OF FOODS CONTAINING NITRATES AND NITRITES

Nitrites and nitrates in processed meat may be involved in cancer. For this reason, one dietary guideline is to limit consumption of foods that contain these substances.

MAINTAIN A HEALTHY WEIGHT

If you are getting chemotherapy or radiation for squamous cell cancer, it is quite likely that the doses and duration will be high and prolonged. You may face anorexia, nausea, mucositis, diarrhea, and other nutritional challenges. Chapter 8 gives tips on how to overcome these problems. Remember, an increased intake of food, compared to what is normal for you, is *not* the goal. Changing the types of food you eat, away from fats and toward fruits and vegetables, is important, as is maintaining adequate nourishment during treatment.

If you are overweight, do not worry if a small weight loss occurs. This is to be expected on a low-fat diet based on fruits and vegetables. If you are like most heavy Americans, a little weight loss can be healthy.

Do not become so anxious that you "force-feed" yourself to try to gain weight. As we discussed in chapter 2, such overfeeding may be associated with net harm, not benefit. Strive for a diet low in fat, high in fiber, fruits, and vegetables.

AVOID *ALL* TOBACCO EXPOSURE

Most important of all, do not smoke any tobacco products, and avoid exposure to *all* tobacco, including passive or secondhand smoke (smoke inhaled because someone else is smoking).

Recommendations for Squamous Cancers

BASIC PLAN:

1. Increase fruits and vegetables to eleven or more servings per day.

2. Lower fat intake to 25 percent of daily calories or less. (See chart page 112 and add 5 percent.)

RATIONALE:

Fruits and vegetables contain antioxidant vitamins and many other chemopreventives. A low-fat diet may deprive squamous cells of needed energy.

Specific Foods and Nutrients You Should Stress in Your Diet:

Fruits and vegetables, as recommended above. Be sure to choose from a wide variety.

Allium vegetables (garlic, onions, leeks) contain compounds with anticancer activity (see chapter 5, "For People with Colorectal Cancer"). Some data exists to support the broad spectrum effects of garlic against squamous cancers.

Consider asking your doctor for a vitamin E and a multivitamin supplement. This may boost immunity in older patients, as might an increased intake of foods containing beta carotene (see page 38).

PART 3

HOW TO MAKE OUR NUTRITION PLAN WORK FOR YOU

8

SOLVING NUTRITION PROBLEMS AND IMPROVING WELL-BEING DURING TREATMENT

&

W hen you are in treatment for cancer, you may find that it is more difficult to get the nutrition you need. Some therapies, although not all, can have side effects, including nausea, sore mouth, constipation, and fatigue, that pose their own nutritional challenges. Nutritionists and people with cancer have discovered many simple solutions to these problems. This chapter shares dozens of these approaches so that you can experiment and find the ones that work for you. Ann Foltz, R.N., Ph.D., contributed most of these ideas.

Good nutrition is especially important during therapy to help maintain your strength, prevent body tissues from breaking down, and help rebuild the normal tissues that have been affected by the treatments.

At fifty-six, Erma Smith had spent most of her life caring for her husband and their home. These tasks brought her great satisfaction and joy, but they took on even greater importance when her husband, Leon, was diagnosed with Alzheimer's disease. As you know, cancer never occurs in a vacuum. Whatever troubles are going on in your life will continue to challenge you, even as you battle with cancer. So it was with Erma, whose diagnosis was colon cancer. Friends took over Leon's care while Erma underwent surgery, but everyone—and most of all, Erma—knew that no one could care for him as well as she could.

To attempt to eradicate any cancer cells that remained after the surgery, it was necessary for Erma to have a series of chemotherapy treatments. The powerful drugs that were used for her cancer—5-FU and levamisole—caused some loss of appetite, abdominal pains, and mouth soreness. Though Erma had done well with the trauma of surgery, these relatively moderate side effects of chemotherapy made it nearly impossible for her to eat solid foods. Without quick intervention, she faced weight loss and weakness.

The solution to the mouth soreness was amazingly simple: buttermilk used as a mouthwash, which helped heal the tender tissues. Once her mouth had begun to heal, she went on a liquid diet and ate pureed foods. With just these changes, Erma maintained her strength and weight so well that she was able to continue the chemotherapy and continue to care for her husband.

A simple solution, a big difference.

FINDING THE RIGHT SOLUTION

Under the microscope, cancer is an impersonal collection of cells, but when cancer is active in a human body—your body—it is a highly personal experience. Every person has a different set of biological, emotional, and spiritual strengths and weaknesses. Cancer and its treatment will pose very different problems from one individual to another, and even from day to day for any one person.

Depending on the way you are feeling, the stresses you are juggling, and the availability of your support system, a problem-solving method may work one day and fail the next. This is why looking for solutions to the challenges of cancer is more like random dialing than looking up a telephone number in a directory. But by experimenting, you will arrive at solutions that work for you.

Most of the suggestions in this section are for people who want to maintain, not lose, weight, and who are not on special diets for other illnesses.

In applying any of these or other methods for dealing with nutritional problems during your recovery, there are three things to keep in mind. First, don't wait until the problem is out of hand. Begin to manage the problem as soon as it arises. Second, be flexible about your choices, even from day to day. You may find that pot roast—your all-time favorite—is suddenly unappealing. Use food alternatives and choices that appeal to you *at this time.* And third, include your health-care providers in what you are doing. It's important to keep them informed of your nutritional problems and how you are coping with them. If you are unable to apply the measures described in this section, or despite these measures you are eating less, talk with your doctor or nurse. There may be medications to help you get through the rough times and back on the path to recovery.

And always remember that, given enough time, treatment side effects will get better. Don't lose your hope or fighting spirit.

FATIGUE

Many things can cause fatigue in persons with cancer, including cancer treatments (surgery, radiation, chemotherapy, biologic response modifiers, or immunotherapy), fevers or infections, anxiety or depression, loss of sleep, and personal worries.

In some ways, fatigue can be more difficult to deal with than pain. When you are in pain, there is no question that the problem *is* pain. You know exactly where it hurts, you know which part of your body must be protected or rested until the pain stops, and you know or can ask for specific measures to deal with the pain, such as relaxation techniques, heat or cold applications, and pain medications. Fatigue, however, is more insidious.

You may begin your day feeling sprightly, ready to take on the world (well, all right, ready to do a load of laundry), but before breakfast is finished, you've suddenly lost interest in the plans to go to the grocery store, fixing lunch looms like a mountain-climbing expedition, and your favorite TV talk show is more than you can cope with. The sound of a loved one's voice may inexplicably make you angry, and in the middle of pulling on your shoes, you just want to roll back into bed—not to sleep, but just to lie there.

This kind of misery can work havoc with your diet. It can interfere with your ability to plan, shop for, and prepare nutritious meals. It can render you uncharacteristically finicky, craving scrambled eggs or pudding or tea and toast at every meal because these are effortless to prepare and digest.

Fatigue can also isolate you. It's very difficult to explain to others how exhausted you feel, especially when you're too tired to think straight and you're tangled up in being angry at your body for betraying you like this.

The first step to dealing with fatigue is to recognize that the name of the problem is fatigue, not laziness or a sudden, unexplained case of slovenliness. You are the same organized, competent person you were before your cancer; however, fatigue is standing between you and all you would normally accomplish.

Next, act to prevent fatigue, beginning with simplifying the work you would normally do. As you well know, simplifying may be not so simple to do. One of the special tortures of being sick is that you will be spending a lot of time at home, surrounded by endless reminders of work to be done. How long has that window been cracked? It would take only ten minutes to fix it, if you could just get the energy to go to the hardware store. . . . Look at the dust on those rugs. If only you could get the vacuum cleaner out of the closet!

Prioritize. The window has probably been cracked for months. It will be there next month and the month after, and you will tend to it when you can. The rugs might be a more pressing concern, especially if dust makes you itch and sneeze—what a perfect task for one of your grandchildren, or a neighborhood teen who's eager to earn a little cash. If such tasks seem to be mounting up, a good way to hold them at bay is to lie down on the sofa with a pencil and paper and make a list of all the things you're going to tend to when you feel better. Then put them out of your mind for now. Focus on the task you can do best, which is tending to your health and your nutritional needs.

Strategies for Meal Planning and Preparation

- Instead of shopping, use your time and energy to plan meals and write out a grocery list. Enlist someone to do the shopping for you. In some parts of the country, grocers are reviving the idea of home delivery, which would relieve you of the physical exertion in this task.
- If you do food shop for yourself, consider shopping in smaller stores (this is true for hardware, clothing, and other types of purchases, too); you'll be able to park closer, shop faster, and eliminate the temptation to shop until you drop.
- When you cook, plan ahead. If possible, have someone get everything you'll need (the big bowl, the electric mixer, the ingredients) out and on the counter for you. An indispensable tool in the kitchen is a high stool, or a chair at a comfortable level for your work surface. A barstool with a back is very nice for this purpose.
- Take advantage of morning, when you are most likely to feel alert. You may want to make breakfast your main meal of the day. Your appetite may also be better in the morning.
- If possible, divide tasks into parts that can be done between rest periods. For example, run vegetables in the food processor right after breakfast—and store them, covered, in the refrigerator until ready to use. A slow-cooking Crockpot is an excellent tool, especially if your fatigue typically worsens in the afternoon. (Another advantage of Crockpots is that the cooking odors stay inside

the pot, which will be a relief if odors have become a problem for you.)

- If you are working outside the home during your recuperation, take advantage of weekends for cooking. Would you normally go to a cafeteria at lunchtime? If the food selections are healthful (i.e., not laden with fat), consider bringing a sandwich for lunch (which is very easy to fix) and buying a carry-home supper from the cafeteria.

- When cooking, choose the part of the meal preparation that's interesting to you, and do that part. Leave the rest to another family member or use a commercial product. Spaghetti sauce from a bottle is a perfectly acceptable alternative to made-from-scratch, as are canned stews, soups, and frozen dinners and pizzas—as long as the fat content is low. Keep in mind that many of these products are high in sodium, so if you are on a low-sodium diet, these may not be appropriate for you. Combine canned, low-fat, low-salt soup with 3 ounces of chicken or fish and ladle over toast for a quick and easy dinner. Accompany these quick dinners with skim milk and fresh fruit.

- Steer clear of complicated menus. Meat loaf is much easier to prepare than porcupine meatballs; a roasted whole chicken is much simpler than a fricassee and will yield leftovers for additional meals. There's no need to fix mashed potatoes *and* stuffing *and* fresh rolls; make a large portion of one of these items.

- If you feel you can handle it, make a large batch of a single item (for example, a triple portion of meatless lasagna) and freeze the extras. Instead of cooking just a portion of rice, spaghetti, macaroni, or noodles, it takes just a tiny bit more energy to cook a lot, and these batches freeze exceptionally well in sealable plastic bags. It's amazing how simple it is to prepare a macaroni-and-cheese dish if the macaroni is already cooked.

- Check into the availability of Meals-on-Wheels services in your area.

- Eat small, nutritious snacks all day. Eating six small meals may not require either the larger effort to prepare or the energy and time to eat.

PLAN REST PERIODS

- You may need only one, or you may need four or five a day. Try to rest *before* you become really tired; this will enable you to do more over the course of the day. A rest period should be at least twenty to thirty minutes long. Be wary of sleeping during the day, though, as it may interfere with your ability to sleep at night.
- Sitting down to write out the bills is not resting. Stretch out and use the time to meditate, listen to music, give some attention to a pet, watch television, do some light reading, or to do nothing at all.
- You might also experiment with variations of your normal sleep schedule, such as going to bed earlier or sleeping later. Be sure to guard against mixing up your days and nights; sleeping late can mean staying up later and pretty soon you may find yourself sleeping all day and staying up all night.

MORE STRATEGIES FOR FIGHTING FATIGUE

- Some persons with cancer swear that vitamins give them more pep. While this is not a proven method, you might discuss this option with your health-care provider. Some patients think that B_{12} gives them energy; others have found that some of the commercial tonics with vitamins, minerals, and iron help give them energy and appetite. Note, however, that the alcohol content of some of these is significant. In any case, avoid *megadoses* of vitamins, which in some cases can be toxic.
- When you are struggling with fatigue, the last thing you'll feel like doing is exercising, but mild exercise can be very helpful, especially if your fatigue is the result of periods of enforced inactivity (such as hospitalization) or depression. Walking and swimming are excellent. Before beginning any exercise program, however, check with your doctor.
- Let others help. Many people volunteer who are genuinely inter-

ested in helping you. If you do not take them up on their offer, it may not come again!

- Finally, keep busy, if only in little ways. This period of relative confinement might be a genuine opportunity to get those boxes of family photos organized into albums or to take up a new handicraft. Such activities will help you to pass the time and keep your spirits up, and could tempt you into new interests that will help you overcome fatigue.

NAUSEA AND VOMITING

While nausea and vomiting are the bane of many cancer patients' existence, it is important to note that many cancer drugs do *not* cause vomiting, and that there are a number of other drugs to treat nausea and vomiting. One of them, made available in the early 1990s, is ondansetron, which provides complete or near-complete relief of nausea for many people.

Ondansetron or other antinausea medications may be administered before or with your chemotherapy treatment, thus blocking nausea and vomiting before they start. So you may never experience nausea or vomiting, despite high doses of chemotherapy. Or you may experience a little nausea, which can be relieved with other antinausea drugs. Or you may have nausea or vomiting until you are well into your course of treatment.

Your health-care provider will probably order some antinausea medicine for you; if not, ask for some. If you find it is helpful, and your physician agrees, consider taking it the night before a treatment, taking it again right before treatment, and continuing to take it as ordered around the clock on the day following treatment. Check with your doctor before setting this or any schedule for taking medication. Remember that most antinausea medications have side effects, including light-headedness, dry mouth, sleepiness, and muscular twitching, depending on the drug and the dose.

For those who cannot obtain relief with ondansetron or other antinausea drugs, nausea can be a major obstacle to good nutrition, especially if vomiting occurs. Fortunately, vomiting usually ceases after the day of treatment, though in some cases, the effects are longer lasting.

Chemotherapy is not the only cause of nausea or vomiting. Radiation of the head, gastrointestinal tract (stomach, small bowel, or large bowel), or pelvis can cause nausea, especially in the later stages of treatment. Emotional aspects of illness and treatment can make nausea or vomiting worse; for example, some people undergoing treatment become nauseated or begin vomiting when they see the building where they receive treatment. This is called "anticipatory nausea." Food or other odors, especially odors associated with the clinic (alcohol, for example), can set off waves of nausea. Anxiety can cause reduced appetite or nausea, as can fatigue (see the previous section on fatigue). Also, drugs other than anticancer drugs, such as pain medications and antibiotics, can contribute to nausea.

Try the strategies below. As with most other aspects of cancer and its therapy, your needs are unique, so you should experiment to see what works best for you.

DIET STRATEGIES FOR FIGHTING NAUSEA AND VOMITING

- First, try eating at different times in relation to treatment. Some people feel better eating before their treatment is given; others do better by not eating or by eating several small meals during the day. ("Eating" may mean just a few crackers, not a full meal.)
- Another tactic is to eat "consolation" foods—foods that have, in the past, helped you overcome an upset stomach. For some people, soups will do it. Others like carbonated beverages or tea.
- Avoid sugar-free drinks. Sugar does have some good uses! In this case, it helps to slow down the activity of your gastrointestinal tract.
- Whatever you try, begin with fluids. Clear, cool, caffeine-free

beverages are usually well tolerated (ginger ale, flavored gelatin, clear broth, etc.). Sip liquids slowly.

- Avoid liquids at mealtimes. Take them thirty to sixty minutes before eating.
- After the fluids seem to be settling your stomach, eat *small amounts* of food every thirty minutes or so until you are sure that things will stay down. *Eat slowly.* Try plain, high-carbohydrate foods, such as toast and crackers. Avoid high-fat items (butter, peanut butter, cheese).
- Smaller portions of low-fat food seem to be easier to digest and get through the stomach faster. With this kind of fare, however, be sure to eat more often in order not to compromise your calorie intake.
- If you feel nauseated, eat salty foods rather than sweet ones, especially if you have been vomiting.
- Eat dry foods such as toast and crackers, especially soon after getting up in the morning. (Every woman who has used this for morning sickness can tell you it usually works!)
- If you can track a time during the day when nausea is more likely to occur, try not to have your favorite food around then because the two may become associated, and after the therapy is over, you will be turned off by the sight and smell of the food. (One group of researchers turned this phenomenon to some patients' advantage by focusing unpleasant associations on an unfamiliar food. Before chemotherapy, a number of patients were given some halvah, a Middle Eastern sweet that is unfamiliar to most Americans. The persons who experienced nausea or vomiting associated this unpleasantness with halvah. Before long, most were able to return to their normal diet without experiencing nausea or vomiting—but they couldn't stand the sight of halvah!)
- If the smell of food makes you feel nauseated, planning ahead may help you to cope. Cold foods are likely to be easier to tolerate than hot ones, because these will have less odor. Having cold plates (such as gelatin salads or sandwiches) prepared in advance will spare you the queasiness of having to handle food.
- Sit up or lie propped up in bed for twenty or thirty minutes after eating. Do not lie down flat for at least two hours after eating.

More Strategies for Fighting Nausea and Vomiting

- Sucking on a lemon drop or peppermint candy or chewing gum can reduce nausea during chemotherapy administration.
- Clean your mouth and teeth more often.
- You may find that a cold towel applied to the back of the neck helps reduce nausea.
- Dress in loose clothing and open the windows if the smell outside is wonderful and it is not cold.
- Again, distraction can be helpful. Play some favorite tapes, or do some chores. Taking a walk, especially in fresh air, may help.

Appetite Loss (Anorexia)

The medical term for appetite loss is *anorexia.* It can result from the cancer itself, or from cancer treatment. If the source of the problem is the cancer itself, you may find that treatment of the cancer alleviates the anorexia.

Appetite loss associated with treatment comes in many varieties. Some people note a little queasiness on the day of chemotherapy or during the radiation therapy schedule, while others experience almost total loss of appetite from the first day of therapy. You may do well for several weeks or months, then suddenly have symptoms.

It is important to try to sort out whether you are less willing to eat because you don't feel hungry, or are too tired or nauseated to eat. If the problem is one of the latter, see the section above. Just "not feeling hungry," though, requires different management methods.

Ways to Cope with Loss of Appetite

- Persons with anorexia sometimes find that the problem is least troublesome at breakfast. If this is true of you, you should make the most of this meal. Try a breakfast of your favorite cereal and sliced fresh fruit, skim milk with ⅓ cup nonfat powdered milk added to it, egg substitute scrambled with favorite vegetables, decaf coffee or tea, and dry toast with apple butter.

- In general, many persons with cancer find that keeping a little bit of food in the stomach is helpful, so you may want to eat more than three meals a day, or have snacks, spacing them by about three hours.
- Keep a variety of choices in small portions on hand. This will be more economical in the long run, because you won't be throwing out food. Use easily prepared foods to make your mini-meals, especially if you must do the food preparation yourself: nonfat frozen yogurt, graham crackers, low-fat frozen dinners, soups, cereal, nonfat "ice cream," and nonfat pastries.
- A simple fool-the-eye trick is to serve meals on smaller plates or in small bowls. Using a smaller fork may feel silly at first, but it really can help you to slow down, relax, and savor each bite.
- Have a snack before bedtime. Milk and milk products can help maintain your weight and also help you get to sleep (your mother was right about the warm milk!). Of course, if you are one the many people who cannot digest milk, you should find a substitute (see section on lactose intolerance, pages 165–66).
- Cooking is hard work and can tire you so much that you will lose interest in eating. The odors of cooking may cause nausea or reduce your appetite. If you are able to handle the cooking, follow the suggestions for planning and preparation in the section on fatigue. Planning and preparing meals in advance, at the times when you are feeling up to it, will be especially helpful, and freezing miniature portions will provide a break for you on days when you're feeling swamped.
- If you are not up to cooking, this is the time to call on family and friends. Be sure to explain that small portions—a cup of baked macaroni, a cup of homemade soup—is more enticing to you than a full-sized casserole. Friends and neighbors will be delighted that something as simple as putting aside small portions of a meal prepared for their own family can be a big help to you.
- If you need additional help, an excellent resource is Meals-on-

Wheels, which provides carry-in service of prepared foods in some areas. Some church groups also offer such support. A social worker (usually available through your health provider, clinic, or cancer center) should be able to help you locate and arrange for such services. Check with your local hospital, too; meals prepared there will probably be lower in fat and salt. The advantage of these types of services is that you won't have to think about food, handle food, or deal with the odors until the meal arrives. Another alternative that may be available are meals in a community setting, where you can visit with other people while you eat.

• Drink lots of liquids. If you do not, you may become dehydrated, which in itself can cause nausea or loss of appetite. If you have anorexia but do not have a dry mouth (see page 172), concentrate on drinking *between* meals. Fluids at mealtimes, especially cold ones, may make you feel full and cause you to eat less of your meal.

ADDING NUTRIENTS

If you are eating poorly during treatment, the following can help increase calories and sometimes fiber, vitamins, and minerals, too.

• Add a tablespoon of sugar to recipes when you bake or cook.
• If you can tolerate milk, substitute skim milk for water whenever possible.
• Thicken a glass of milk with a generous scoop of powdered milk or nonfat "ice cream."
• If you are preparing your milk for regular use from powdered milk, use extra powder, and let the mixture sit in the refrigerator (at least several hours) so that the powder will completely dissolve and flavor will develop fully. Use evaporated skim milk to decrease fat intake.
• Try blending nonfat frozen dessert with ginger ale for a shake. Or blend nonfat powdered milk with nonfat yogurt and fresh fruit, such as strawberries or bananas.

- Add dried fruits to snacks or baked goods. Some nice combinations are prunes with peanut butter, and raisins or apricots in muffins or on cereal.
- Add high-protein foods to your favorite comfort foods. For instance, if spaghetti and meatballs is a comfort food, add nonfat dry milk powder to the meatball mixture along with the oatmeal. This will increase calories and protein without compromising flavor.
- Commercially prepared concentrated food supplements are available in liquids, powders, and puddings, and these can be used in many ways. Ask your doctor or nurse about these.

TIPS FOR INCREASING PROTEIN AND CALORIES

To Add Protein:

- Add skim milk powder to the regular amount of milk in all recipes.
- Use fortified milk (blend together 1 cup of nonfat milk powder and 1 quart of skim milk) for cooking and drinking.
- Add milk powder to hot cereal, cold cereal, egg substitute for scrambled eggs, meatballs and meat loaf, and casserole dishes.
- Make a milk shake with fortified milk, fresh fruit, and frozen nonfat yogurt.

To Add Calories:

- Add oatmeal and wheat bran to casseroles, meatballs, and meat loaf.
- Add powdered coffee creams (made without coconut or palm oil) to soup, milk shakes, and hot cereals.
- Bread meat, chicken, and fish with nonfat coatings such as matzo meal, cornflake crumbs, plain homemade French bread crumbs, or cornmeal.
- Add raisins, figs, dates, dried apples, and dried pears to cereals.

OTHER STRATEGIES

- Some people find that exercise makes them ravenous; others find that exercise shuts their appetite down. If you are exercising regularly, pay attention to how it affects your appetite. If exercise stimulates your appetite, exercise before eating. If exercise decreases your appetite, wait an hour or so after eating to work out.
- If you are taking oral pain medicine, schedule your meal or snack about thirty minutes after you take the medicine, since both pain and pain medicine can interfere with appetite.
- Brushing your teeth or freshening your mouth before meals can help clear the "fuzzies" from your taste.
- Get comfortable! If you have been spending a lot of time in bed, try to get up for meals, even if you must take them on the sofa. Sit with pillows as needed. The change of environment will make things seem brighter and will turn mealtimes into a positive experience.
- Make the meal look inviting with garnishes and lots of color. A meal of fish, mashed potatoes, and cauliflower looks very bland. Change it to fish with red-and-green-pepper sauce, baked potato with chives and nonfat yogurt dressing, and zucchini and yellow squash, steamed in julienne strips. For dessert, have low-fat custard topped with fresh strawberries. Beautiful!
- The companionship of friends, family, or coworkers will not only help you feed your body, but will also feed your soul as well. If you must dine alone, turn on some music or keep company with a favorite show on television.

CHANGES IN TASTE

Both chemotherapy and radiation treatments can cause changes in taste. You may find that your sense of taste is decreased or missing altogether, or that foods taste odd. If you are experiencing alterations in or loss of taste, talk with your doctor or nurse. Sometimes a zinc deficiency, which can accompany some cancers and treatment, is the basic problem, and this can be remedied with a supplement.

Strategies for Overcoming Changes in Taste

- Tart candies may reduce the sensations of bitter or sour taste during chemotherapy administration. Peppermint or lemon drops may be especially helpful. If these seem to work for you, get the low-sugar type to reduce the chance of tooth decay (as explained later, tooth decay can be a special problem during certain types of treatment).
- Extra sugar, spices, or seasonings or a commercial salt substitute may perk up your taste buds. A rule of thumb is to increase seasonings by a quarter at first, and continue with increments if you notice an improvement in your ability to taste.
- A common complaint is that red meat tastes "metallic" to persons undergoing chemotherapy. Marinating meats in low-salt soy sauce or Italian salad dressing may help; however, if it still tastes unpleasant, switch to chicken, fish, or beans for protein.
- The taste of cool or cold foods (frozen nonfat yogurt, nonfat puddings, gelatin salads) may seem to change less. Stay with familiar foods and beverages; it's better to experiment later, when your taste is back to normal.
- Frequent mouth care will help with taste changes, but avoid commercial mouthwashes, because they are likely to contain alcohol, which can dry out the mouth.
- A common fungus (Candida or thrush) can grow in the mouth during treatment and interfere with taste. If you have a white coating on your tongue, ask your doctor for some medicine for this. It can be treated easily.

CHANGES IN SMELL

Chemotherapy and radiation treatments can change the way foods smell to you, which in turn affects their taste. The first sign of this may be a general decrease in appetite because foods don't have the odor or taste you expect. To deal with this problem, see the sections above on loss of appetite and taste changes. In general, however, avoid foods that smell different or unpleasant to you. Later in your recovery, your sense of smell should return to normal, and you will be able to resume your normal diet and favorite foods.

WEIGHT GAIN

Weight gain can occur during cancer treatment, but why this is so is not well understood. It may be related to the effects of chemotherapy on the body's hormones, or to the direct effect of hormone medication, such as the therapies given for some cases of breast cancer, prostate cancer, or lymphoma.

Some people gain weight during chemotherapy because their bodies are retaining water, while others gain because their appetites increase or they crave certain foods. Some who have struggled for years to lose or maintain weight must put dieting aside to deal with cancer, and this change can result in weight gain. Some gain because they snack constantly to settle their stomachs.

Often weight gain is due to fluid retention. Cut down your sodium intake, since too much sodium can cause you to retain fluids. No more than 3 grams of sodium a day—1 teaspoon is optimal. The average American consumes 6 to 10 grams, because salt is added to many foods, and because so many of us add salt at the table before tasting the food. Make it a habit to check food labels for sodium, and cut down on your sodium. Note that prepared foods are often high in sodium, as are many over-the-counter medicines, such as some antacids.

If you find that you are gaining weight, you should discuss this with your health-care provider. Together, you can decide whether the weight gain is a problem and what the causes and best treatments are for you. For some people, mild diuretics or limiting salt intake may be suggested if water retention is the problem. Others may need dietary counseling.

WEIGHT LOSS

Weight loss is not uncommon in cancer. Many factors, such as anxiety, fatigue, changes in taste or smell, and depression, can contribute. Cancer itself can also cause weight loss. As explained in chapter 2, "The Connection Between Cancer and Diet," cancer alters the way your body processes food.

Special supplements may help you maintain your weight. Some supplements are designed to be eaten; others are given intravenously. In considering the use of these products, it's important to note that increased calorie consumption is not always helpful or desirable. Research with people who have more advanced disease has shown that increasing weight by eating or using nasogastric tube feedings or intravenous fluids may not be helpful (see chapter 2). Be sure your doctor is aware of any plans you have to markedly increase calorie intake.

With all the stresses that cancer causes, it sometimes happens that a family or individual will "tune out" by focusing on one aspect of the illness, and weight is a very handy one. "Encouragement" can become a crusade, as family members try to get the person with cancer to eat more to offset the weight loss. While everyone's intentions are the best, the results can be unfortunate, because not only is the patient not helped, but communication becomes difficult. If necessary, enlist your health-care provider's assistance in explaining your needs to family members.

MILK (LACTOSE) INTOLERANCE

Many adult African Americans, Asians, Native Americans, and some whites have difficulty digesting cow's milk. It is not uncommon for people to lose the ability to digest milk sugar (lactose) as they get older. When people with "lactose intolerance" drink milk or eat milk products, they may experience gas, abdominal pain and cramps, bloating, diarrhea, or nausea. The distress may occur within minutes, and sometimes lasts for hours. If this has happened to you, you probably have decreased your intake of milk products already. In that case, you can skip this section, unless you would like to try milk again.

If you were able tolerate milk and milk products well before treatment, but you feel bloated or have diarrhea after eating milk products now, then the treatment is probably responsible for the change. Cancer treatment—especially radiation therapy to the abdomen and some chemotherapy agents—can interfere with the production of enzymes that help in lactose digestion. For most people, the condition reverses itself over time; meanwhile, you may find some of the following measures helpful.

- Avoid milk and cheese products, except processed (acidophilus) milk and most cheddar cheeses.
- Many people can tolerate nonfat yogurt and buttermilk because the lactose is changed in them. Try eating small amounts of these products.
- Remember that milk is a common ingredient in other foods, even bread. French or Vienna-style breads do not contain milk.
- There are products that you can take to facilitate lactose digestion. Some are available over the counter; others must be obtained by prescription. Discuss these alternatives with your physician.
- Try milk substitutes, such as soy milk. These are especially useful as milk substitutes in cooking. Plain soy milk may taste too chalky for use as a beverage, but there are excellent flavored varieties, including chocolate and vanilla, and these are available in low-fat varieties.

• There are also a number of lactose-free food supplements that you can use to make puddings or milk shakes.

TOOTH DECAY

Radiation therapy to the mouth or throat can directly damage teeth. Tooth decay can also result indirectly when chemotherapy or radiation treatment produces a sore mouth or tongue, leading people to interrupt normal toothbrushing and flossing. A third source of tooth decay is dry mouth.

It is a good idea to see your dentist *before* beginning cancer therapy, so that any existing cavities or other problems can be taken care of in advance. If you need dental care after you have started treatment, *be sure to tell your dentist that you are undergoing cancer therapy,* because it may be important for your dentist and physician to communicate about your special needs, or you may need antibiotics before dental care, as a preventive measure against infection.

In any case, keep your routine mouth care going during therapy. If mouth soreness does develop, there are helpful suggestions on pages 175–76 of this chapter. Your health-care provider may suggest special toothbrushes, toothpastes, mouthwashes, or other measures, especially if your blood work shows a low platelet count.

STOMACH IRRITATION OR HEARTBURN

Stomach irritation can be caused by radiation to the area of the esophagus or the stomach. Some chemotherapy drugs, notably steroids, can chemically irritate the stomach as well. Of course, unrelated conditions may also cause you to have a burning sensation in the stomach, so your health-care provider should be notified if you are having this problem. Before calling, however, try to determine whether the discomfort is better, the same, or worse after eating. This information will help with diagnosis. Here are some ways to keep stomach irritation to a minimum.

- Food can act as a buffer for many drugs that can cause some irritation, so take medication with food, unless specifically instructed not to. It doesn't have to be a large amount of food. A few crackers, a small glass of skim milk, or a slice of toast will be sufficient.
- Sit up for twenty minutes after eating. This reduces the chance that stomach acid will wash up from the stomach to the esophagus, causing heartburn.
- There are many over-the-counter medications that reduce heartburn (Maalox, Riopan, Gelusil, etc.). Again, this is a choice to be discussed with your health-care provider, because there are differences among these medications.

CONSTIPATION

Constipation can be a problem during your recovery from cancer. Sometimes constipation results from anticancer drugs (especially vincristine [Oncovin]) or from pain-relieving drugs. Changes in your activity level or eating patterns can also cause constipation. If you increase the amount of fiber in your diet, for example, but not fluids, you will become constipated. More fiber means more stool, which requires more fluids to stay soft.

It is important to discuss any bowel changes with your doctor or nurse. Call for advice if your bowel pattern becomes very different from what is usual for you (for example, if you normally have one bowel movement each day, but instead have bowel movements only every two or three days). You should also notify your health-care provider if you have alternating constipation and diarrhea or if you have loose stools for more than two or three days. Otherwise, the following self-care should relieve the problem.

- Include food high in fiber in your diet. Eat more fruit, especially raisins, prunes, peaches, and apples. Some people find a glass of warm prune juice, taken at night, to be very effective.
- Eat more vegetables, raw or cooked: squash, broccoli, carrots, and celery. Cooking does not alter fiber content significantly, but leave the skin on when possible, since that is the major source of fiber in many vegetables.
- Eat whole-grain cereals and breads. Oat bran is effective against constipation and is delicious in muffins and rolls. Uncooked rolled oats can be sprinkled over other cereals to increase fiber. Another way to use whole oats is to grind them in a food processor or blender and substitute the resulting oat flour for a portion of wheat flour in waffles or pancakes.
- Bran, such as wheat bran, has many uses. It can be added to baked goods, casseroles, or cooked or cold cereals. High-fiber wafers (FiberMed, FiberAll) and high-fiber powders (Citri-Cel, Metamucil, and others) may be especially helpful if you are unable to eat an adequate amount of vegetables, fruits, and cereals.
- Drink lots of fluids. First, check with your doctor to be sure that you can drink without restrictions, then drink eight to twelve glasses of liquids a day. Try to think of drinking this over your sixteen-hour day—that's about a half glass every hour! If you are having trouble with your appetite and weight loss, choose fruit nectars or punches, drink between meals, and freeze juices or nectars to eat as a quick sherbet or "slush." Some people find that hot beverages (warm prune juice, hot coffee or tea, or even plain water) stimulate the bowel.
- Exercise. It's true that exercise is difficult if you are feeling tired. On the other hand, constipation can be caused by lack of exercise and can in turn cause you to feel more tired. So exercise is both a preventive measure and a solution. Walking is excellent exercise, especially since you can pace yourself to whatever level of exertion you feel you can handle. If you are confined to bed, ask your doctor or nurse for some bed exercises.

- Establish a pattern. We are creatures of habit in many ways, even to the time of a bowel movement. Choose a time when you can be undisturbed. Be sure that you have adequate support while you are sitting; if necessary, use pillows or rolled towels to brace yourself or to get comfortable. Take your time. Focusing too much on your purpose can cause tension, so use distraction (the bathroom is a great place to store catalogs for browsing!). Take care not to strain; if you're not having a good result, continue with the other measures and try again later in the day.

- Laxatives should be used as a last resort, sparingly, and with the approval of your physician. Ask your health-care provider about using bulk-forming laxatives or stool softeners, or choosing the least harsh product. If you do use medication, try to take it at about the same time during the day; that will help you establish a pattern.

DIARRHEA

Diarrhea (frequent, loose stools) can result from surgery of the small or large bowel (when large sections of the bowel are removed), radiation therapy to the stomach or pelvis, and some chemotherapy medications. It can also be caused by some antinausea medicines, especially metoclopramide (Reglan).

Antibiotics, which kill off some of the "good" bacteria in your body as well as the "bad" bacteria, may also cause diarrhea. If this is the source of your problem, and you are not intolerant of milk products, try eating a little active-culture yogurt several times a day, which will restore the "good" bacteria. At the same time, follow the measures described below for maintaining fluids.

When the cause of diarrhea is surgery, the problem corrects itself to some degree, but you may also have to accommodate to the situation by drinking more fluids.

Diarrhea may be associated with radiotherapy. In some persons, it continues to be a problem during recovery; in others, it stops when treatment is concluded. Diarrhea associated with chemotherapy or antinausea medication can last one or two days after administration of your treatment.

In any case, if diarrhea lasts more than three days, contact your health-care provider.

Diarrhea causes loss of body fluid. At its extreme, it can cause dehydration, so it is important to increase intake of water and appropriate beverages. By appropriate, I mean beverages that are free of caffeine, which can stimulate bowel activity and further dehydrate you.

REPLENISHING LOST FLUIDS

• Avoid caffeinated coffee and tea; flavored teas are good substitutes, especially if you add a little sugar. The sugar may help quiet the bowel activity and can be a quick source of energy at a time when you are probably not able to eat normally. For the same reason, if you choose carbonated beverages—which some people find restorative, when used in moderation—use sugar-sweetened, not diet, kinds. A recently introduced alternative to carbonated sodas is mineral water with fruit juices, which is both bubbly and tasty. Small amounts of fruit juices are good for variety, but avoid prune juice, which can worsen diarrhea.

• A number of commercial beverages are available to replenish fluids during exercise or physical labor, and these can be useful in dealing with diarrhea. If you have not used these before, buy a small trial amount first, to see if the taste appeals to you.

• Whichever beverages you choose, start slowly, increasing the amounts gradually. Too much liquid, too soon, can add to the problem! Begin with "clear" liquids—that is, anything you can see through. This includes many of the fluids noted above. Since both cold beverages and hot beverages tend to increase bowel activity, keep your drinks close to room temperature. Open carbonated beverages and let them go "flat" before drinking if you have a lot of gas.

- For many years, hospitals have been successfully using the "BRAT" diet for patients with diarrhea. It is often used for pediatric patients but I'm sure the name is just from the first letter of each food! **B**anana, **R**ice (plain white, no fat or salt added), **A**pplesauce (unsweetened), and **T**oast (dry).
- When your bowel movements reduce in frequency, try fluids and foods that have more substance (soup and nectars, for example). Use foods that you have found easy to digest in the past. Eat small meals, and add to the food choices slowly.
- Be careful about milk when you have diarrhea. It is not uncommon to become intolerant of milk products when you are on chemotherapy or taking antibiotics. If you want to try milk, consider the acidophilus type. Soy milk, which comes in many flavors as well as plain, is another good alternative.
- Some people find that crackers, with peanut butter or cheese, are helpful. Other "light" foods, like nonfat scrambled egg substitutes, mashed potatoes, nonfat cottage cheese, bananas, nonfat yogurt, and toast, may settle well. Sometimes cereals will do, but avoid high-fiber types. Cooked cereals, such as cream of rice or cream of wheat, are especially gentle to the stomach. Avoid greasy or highly spiced foods and foods that are high in fiber. Chapter 9, "Three Months to a New Eating Plan," has a list of high-fiber foods.

OTHER STEPS TO MANAGING DIARRHEA

- A number of medications can alleviate diarrhea. Kaopectate, Imodium, and Donagel are available over the counter. Each of these contains different ingredients, so ask your doctor which to take.
- Reduce your activity level and rest often.
- If your diarrhea continues despite these measures, or if there is blood in the stool, contact your physician or nurse promptly.

RECTAL SORENESS

Both constipation and diarrhea can cause rectal soreness. There are several measures that you can take at home to relieve this problem.

- For simple first aid, soak in a tub of very warm water or in a "sitz" bath (a basin that attaches to the toilet seat). Follow this with an application of Nupercainal, Preparation H, Anusol, or other similar over-the-counter preparations.
- Because toilet tissue can be irritating, use Tucks moisturized towelettes or similar products for personal hygiene. A very inexpensive alternative is to wet a swatch of cotton or quilted cotton square (available in cosmetics departments) with witch hazel. This also makes a good poultice; applied for two or three minutes, it can be very soothing.
- If you are experiencing rectal dryness, which is common in constipation, apply a dab of Diaperene, A and D ointment, or K-Y jelly *before and after* each bowel movement.
- If you are having a great deal of trouble with this problem, talk with your doctor or nurse. There are some specialty creams (Sween products, for example) that may offer additional protection. Occasionally, severe rectal soreness can mean an abscess—this requires medical attention so call your doctor promptly if this develops.

DRY MOUTH (XEROSTOMIA)

Radiation treatments may reduce saliva production, resulting in dry mouth. This condition goes away with time in some cases; in others, unfortunately, it does not. Members of the radiation therapy team (the doctor, nurse, or registered technologist) can tell you about the duration of dry mouth in your case.

In persons receiving chemotherapy, dry mouth can be caused by antinausea drugs, but this effect is usually limited to the time during which the medication is used.

DRINKING AND EATING

* Whatever the source of the problem, the obvious first step in alleviating it is to increase liquids: eight or more glasses a day. Carry a large cup or bottle wherever you go (the type used by athletes—with a cap and a straw—is great). You may find that nectars work particularly well since they are thicker than other juices. Be cautious, however, with acidic juices such as tomato juice or orange juice; these cause a burning sensation for some people. Also, beware of spices; these may irritate your mouth.
* Dry mouth can certainly make it more difficult to meet your nutritional needs. You may find a soft diet easier to swallow. Try cream soups, mashed potatoes, nonfat yogurt, noodles, macaroni and cheese, nonfat scrambled egg substitutes, nonfat puddings, gelatins, cereals, and milk shakes (made with evaporated skim milk, soy milk, or regular milk plus nonfat "ice cream"). Casserole dishes, especially when they contain gravy or sauce, may be easier to eat: lasagna, chicken à la king, corned beef hash, quiche.
* Make all of your food moist. Let dry cereal soak in milk. Soak breads in milk or other beverages or sauces. Add gravies to meat, chicken, and fish, and add sauces to vegetables. Eat canned fruit with the juice.
* You may want to try blenderized food, but this method is not without its problems. Preparation can be time-consuming, and the resulting mixture may have an unfamiliar or "off" color or odor.
* There are several food supplements or replacements that you might want to try. Your doctor or nurse can usually supply samples. If these are to your liking, they can be ordered with a prescription and often are covered by insurance.
* The temperature of foods and drinks may affect the amount of

dryness you feel. Most people feel that cool or lukewarm foods are easier to swallow than hot foods. Still others find that very cold food is better.

DENTAL CARE

Dry mouth can lead to dental caries (cavities), so it is very important to keep your mouth as moist as possible and maintain good oral hygiene. The healthier and more comfortable your mouth, teeth, and gums are, the more likely it is that you will be able to maintain good nutrition.

- If you are having radiation therapy to the neck or mouth, discuss with your doctor whether you need to see a dentist. In addition to your normal mouth care regimen, your dentist may suggest daily use of a fluoride mouth wash.
- Clean your mouth often and carefully. Rinse your mouth before and after meals, using plain water or a glass of water with ½ teaspoon salt and ½ teaspoon of baking soda. This will alleviate some of the cottony feeling of mouth dryness, as well as decrease the risk of caries.
- Avoid commercial mouthwashes, because most of these contain alcohol, which dries the mouth even more. Lemon and glycerine swabs can be irritating and drying, so avoid these as well.
- If you notice any sores or "patches" in your mouth, notify your doctor or nurse promptly—early intervention can prevent worse problems from developing.

OTHER MEASURES FOR DRY MOUTH

- In addition to increasing fluids, try chewing sugar-free gum or sucking sugar-free candies, to stimulate your salivary glands. Lemon drops are acidic, but many people find them helpful.

- Try ice chips, but don't chew on the ice (chewing ice can cause tooth problems). Similarly, Popsicles or frozen juices (such as cherry or grape, not orange) may provide some relief.
- There are products that are similar to saliva, called artificial saliva. Again, your doctor or nurse may have a sample or can order a small amount for you to try.
- Don't overlook your environment, which is an important source of moisture. Adding moisture to the air is especially important at night, when you won't be drinking fluids. This does not have to be an expensive proposition. If you have vents on the floor or low on the walls, or if you have old-fashioned radiators, a pan of water near the vent or beneath the radiator will do the trick (just remember to refill it each day!). A humidifier (available at the drugstore) is a good solution for your bedroom; make sure to keep it clean to avoid spreading harmful mold or bacteria into the air.

SORE MOUTH (STOMATITIS, MUCOSITIS)

Some day—hopefully soon—scientists will be able to target cancer therapies directly to cancer cells, completely bypassing the body's healthy cells. Until that time, one of the great nuisances of chemotherapy or radiotherapy is stomatitis, an irritation of the tender tissues of the mouth. Soreness may be general, with some redness throughout the mouth. You may also see a few or many small ulcers. In some cases, the ulcerated area may actually extend throughout the gastrointestinal tract. Unlike mouth dryness—which is sometimes permanent—this condition will eventually go away.

Whether slight or extensive, you should report this problem to your physician or nurse, who may decide to put you on medication. You should also adapt your diet as follows.

A Nonirritating Diet

- Cold foods may be easier to tolerate and swallow, so use gelatins, nonfat frozen yogurt, fat-free "ice cream," Popsicles, nonfat puddings, cold soups, and slushes liberally.
- Liquids and soft foods may also be less irritating. Avoid "rough" and scratchy foods; for example, substitute soft bread for toast and crackers. Scrambled egg substitutes and nectars should go down easily.
- Avoid spicy foods.

Other Measures

- Tobacco and alcohol can increase mouth pain. Avoid them.
- Remember that most commercial mouthwashes contain alcohol and should be avoided.
- Dentures can also irritate your mouth. Leave them out if you can, except when eating.
- Clean your mouth frequently, using a soft toothbrush or, if this is too abrasive, a cotton swab.
- Rinse several times a day. A saltwater gargle (1 teaspoon salt in 6 to 8 ounces warm water) can provide short-term relief.
- Over-the-counter liquid antacids, swished and swallowed before eating, can reduce burning pain. There are also some mouthwash products available by prescription only—ask your doctor or nurse about these, or about pain medication, if this is needed. When using pain medication, take it about thirty minutes before meals so it will have time to begin working before you start to eat.
- Plain buttermilk used as a mouthwash (swish and swallow) will frequently soothe irritated mouth tissue.

RECIPES FOR SPECIAL NEEDS

Dorothy Slater and Mary Hitchings, registered dietitians, have developed these recipes to help you fulfill your nutritional needs and to make you more comfortable during treatment. Each has been enjoyed by others in treatment.

Potato-Carrot Soup
YIELD: 4 SERVINGS

1²/₃ cups diced onion
1½ cups peeled, diced potato
1 cup diced celery
²/₃ cup diced parsnip
⅓ cup diced carrot

1 clove garlic, minced
2¼ cups chicken broth, fat-free, no added salt
¼ teaspoon salt
⅛ teaspoon black pepper

1. Place vegetables and ½ cup of the chicken broth in a 3-quart microwave-safe container. Cover with plastic wrap and microwave on high for 15 to 20 minutes or until vegetables are tender, stirring every 5 minutes. Or place in a 3-quart saucepan over high heat and bring to a boil. Reduce heat and simmer, covered, for 45 to 60 minutes or until vegetables are tender.

2. Stir in remaining 1¾ cups chicken broth. In batches, puree in food processor or blender until smooth.

3. Return to microwave container or saucepan. Add salt and pepper. Cover and reheat in microwave or on stove.

Per serving (1 cup):
fat grams 6
fiber grams 5
calories 183
protein grams 4
carbohydrate grams 40
sodium milligrams 227

rich in vitamin A
good source of fiber
good for sore or dry mouth
lactose-free

Tomato-Yogurt Soup

YIELD: 5 SERVINGS

4 cups plain nonfat yogurt
1/4 cup salsa
2 medium ripe tomatoes, peeled,
    seeded, and diced

3 whole scallions, chopped
1/8 teaspoon garlic powder
Fresh cilantro to taste

1. Combine all ingredients and process in a blender or food processor until smooth. Serve at room temperature or chilled.

Per serving:
fat grams trace
fiber grams 1
calories 111
protein grams 11
carbohydrate grams 16
sodium milligrams 182

good for sore or dry mouth
tart
spicy
cool

Curried Squash Soup

YIELD: 3 SERVINGS

2 pounds winter squash (Hubbard
    or butternut)
2 teaspoons unsalted butter
1 1/2 cups chopped onion
1/2 cup chopped celery
1 large apple, preferably McIntosh,
    peeled, cored, and chopped
Salt substitute to taste

Black pepper to taste
Curry powder to taste
1 tablespoon chicken broth, fat-free,
    no added salt or water
1 bay leaf
1 cup nonfat buttermilk
2 teaspoons lemon juice

1. Preheat oven to 375 degrees.
2. Pierce squash with a sharp knife in several places and bake for 30 minutes or until tender.
3. Melt butter in a medium saucepan. Add onion, celery, apple,

salt, and pepper. Cover and cook over low heat for 5 minutes, stirring occasionally. Add curry powder, broth or water, and bay leaf, increase heat to high, and bring to a boil. Reduce heat, cover, and simmer for 30 minutes. Discard bay leaf.

4. When squash is cool, peel, discard seeds, and cut into chunks.

5. In batches, puree broth and squash in a food processor or blender until smooth.

6. Return to saucepan. Add buttermilk and lemon juice. Adjust seasonings and heat, but do not allow to boil.

Per serving (1 cup):	*rich in vitamin A*
fat grams 5	*good for dry mouth*
fiber grams 5	*tart*
calories 236	*spicy*
protein grams 7	
carbohydrate grams 46	
sodium milligrams 109	

Zucchini and Potato Soup
YIELD: 4 SERVINGS

2 teaspoons unsalted butter
2 cups chopped onion
1 large clove garlic, minced
2 pounds zucchini, unpeeled, thinly sliced
2 medium potatoes (about ¾ pound), peeled and sliced
2 cups chicken broth, fat-free and no added salt
1½ tablespoons white wine vinegar
4 teaspoons tarragon
Salt substitute to taste
Black pepper to taste
1 cup plain nonfat yogurt

1. Melt butter in large Dutch oven over high heat and add the onion and garlic. Sauté until onions become translucent, about 3 minutes. Add zucchini, potatoes, chicken broth, vinegar, 1 teaspoon each of the tarragon, salt, and pepper. Bring mixture to a boil, then reduce heat, cover, and simmer for 30 minutes. Set aside to cool.

2. In batches, puree warm soup in food processor or blender until

smooth. Transfer puree to serving bowl, cover, and chill for at least 1 hour.

3. In a small bowl, mix together the yogurt and the remaining 1 tablespoon tarragon. Ladle soup into bowls and top each serving with a heaping spoon of seasoned yogurt.

Per serving (1 cup):   *good for dry mouth*
fat grams 4   *tart*
fiber grams 5   *cool*
calories 181
protein grams 8
carbohydrate grams 33
sodium milligrams 50

High-Fiber, Low-Fat Milk Shake

YIELD: 4 SERVINGS

3 cups skim milk   *1 medium apple, unpeeled, sectioned*
¼ cup 100 percent bran cereal   *or 1 cup fresh strawberries or*
¼ teaspoon cinnamon   *1 banana or 1 medium pear or*
½ teaspoon vanilla extract   *peach*

1. Freeze 2½ cups of milk in an ice-cube tray overnight.
2. Put cubes into blender and add ½ cup milk, bran, cinnamon, vanilla, and fruit. Whirl until blended.

Per serving (1 cup):   *good for sore or dry mouth*
fat grams 1   *tart*
fiber grams 3   *cold*
calories 93
protein grams 8
carbohydrate grams 17
sodium milligrams 178

Orange Strawberry Shake

YIELD: 4 SERVINGS

2 cups orange juice
1½ cups apricot nectar

1 cup frozen strawberries

1. Combine all ingredients and process in blender until smooth.

Per serving (1 cup):
fat grams trace
fiber grams 3
calories 169
protein grams 2
carbohydrate grams 44
sodium milligrams 6

rich in vitamin C
good for dry mouth
lactose-free
tart
cold

Orange Banana Shake

YIELD: 1 SERVING

1 cup orange juice
1 small ripe banana
¼ cup instant nonfat milk powder

½ cup ice cubes
¼ cup club soda

1. Combine orange juice, banana, milk powder, and ice cubes. Process in blender until mixture is thick and ice cubes are crushed.
2. Add club soda and serve at once.

Per serving (all):
fat grams 1
fiber grams 0
calories 276
protein grams 9
carbohydrate grams 63
sodium milligrams 109

rich in vitamin C
good for sore or dry mouth
tart
cold

Mango Treat

YIELD: 2 SERVINGS

1 ripe mango, peeled and sliced
1 banana, peeled and sliced
1 cup skim milk

1 cup nonfat plain yogurt
2 ice cubes (plus additional if
    desired)

1. Combine all ingredients and process in blender until consistency of a thick milk shake.
2. Divide into 2 glasses. Add more ice if desired and serve.

Per serving (1 cup):
fat grams 3
fiber grams 7
calories 228
protein grams 12
carbohydrate grams 46
sodium milligrams 155

rich in vitamin C
rich in vitamin A
good source of fiber
good for sore or dry mouth
cold

Buttermilk Punch

YIELD: 3 SERVINGS

This cool, thick, nutritious punch is great as a snack, for breakfast, or at bedtime. It is easy to make and can be varied with fruits, juices, and nectars. If buttermilk is not one of your favorites, you will be pleased to discover that its flavor cannot be distinguished from the fruit flavors.

For a variation, add ½ cup of your favorite fruit to the mixture in the blender: watermelon, cantaloupe, papaya, kiwi, chopped apples, apricots, cranberries, blackberries, raspberries, strawberries, or one very ripe banana.

3 ounces (6 tablespoons) frozen,
    unsweetened pineapple juice (or
    orange juice)

2 cups nonfat buttermilk
Fresh mint sprigs (optional)

1. Combine ingredients in blender and process until thick and creamy.

2. Serve over ice, garnished with fresh mint if desired.

Per serving (1 cup):   *good for sore or dry mouth*
fat grams .6   *tart*
fiber grams .5   *cold*
calories 131
protein grams 6.6
carbohydrate grams 23
sodium milligrams 173

Frozen Yogurt Fruit Snack
YIELD: 5 SERVINGS

2 cups nonfat vanilla yogurt   *¼ cup lemon or lime juice*
6 ounces frozen apple juice concen-   *2 cups any other unsweetened juice*
   trate

1. Combine yogurt, apple juice concentrate, and lemon or lime juice in a blender and whirl. Add the unsweetened fruit juice and mix well.

2. Pour into molds and freeze.

Per serving (1 cup):   *rich in vitamin C (when made with*
fat grams trace   *orange juice as the other unsweetened*
fiber grams trace   *juice)*
calories 167   *good for dry mouth*
protein grams 6   *tart*
carbohydrate grams 36   *cold*
sodium milligrams 74

Apple Yogurt Snack

YIELD: 2 SERVINGS

1 cup plain nonfat yogurt
1 cup unsweetened applesauce
½ teaspoon cinnamon

1 teaspoon sugar (optional)
2 teaspoons unprocessed bran

1. Combine the yogurt, applesauce, cinnamon, and sugar if desired. Refrigerate at least 2 hours.

Add the bran just before serving, stirring well.

Per serving (1 cup):
fat grams .5
fiber grams 3
calories 141
protein grams 7
carbohydrate grams 30
sodium milligrams 170

good for sore or dry mouth
cool

9

THREE MONTHS TO A
NEW EATING PLAN

ટે.

I n previous chapters, we discussed *why* changing your eating
habits can help your remission if you have cancer or reduce your
risk of getting cancer. The two chapters that follow will tell
you *how* to do it.

There is lots of good news in this chapter—particularly the re-
assurance that you will not feel "food deprived." You will learn that
"healthy" can also be "tasty."

This chapter will tell you how to make sustained, long-term
changes in your eating patterns. Dietary change, to be maintained,
must be gradual, not abrupt. You can't go from a high-fat diet to a
low-fat, high-fiber pattern overnight. If you go too fast, you will feel
deprived and will not continue; furthermore, if you are cooking for
a spouse or family, you may have a rebellion on your hands. If you
increase fiber too quickly, you may have gas and other discomforts,
too. The plan here will help you gradually and comfortably make the
long-term changes that will make all the difference for you.

First, we will talk about the overall eating plan and then we'll lay
out a three-month plan for gradual change. You'll also learn how to
eat appropriately in restaurants. After your first three months are
over, you'll learn how to tally up your progress by counting fat and
fiber grams.

After you have your basic three-month plan down, you can learn much more in the following chapter about how to make healthy changes in your diet. In that chapter, you will learn techniques and tips for choosing the right foods in the grocery store, and for cooking them so that you will enjoy great taste as well as the best nutrition.

THE BASIC CANCER RECOVERY EATING PLAN

As we've seen, reducing your risk for a cancer recurrence and preventing it in the first place involve a similar nutritional plan. Whether you are dealing with colon cancer, breast cancer, prostate cancer, or a squamous cell cancer of the lung or other site, the basic eating recommendations are the same:

- Less fat
- More fiber
- More vegetables
- More fruits
- More whole grains

Fortunately, these nutritional goals help each other out. When you reduce fat, you'll find you automatically increase grains, vegetables, and fruits, gaining fiber and valuable vitamins. In fact, it is very difficult to sustain a diet that is both high-fiber and high-fat.

If you have breast cancer and your goal is to adopt a very low-fat diet, your food choices will almost automatically include more fiber, thus resulting in a double benefit because, according to recent research, increased dietary fiber may also inhibit breast cancer.

If you have had colon cancer and want to increase your fiber to 30 to 35 grams per day, you will learn to choose more cereals, fruits, vegetables, and water, and quite naturally, your fat consumption will fall. Again, you will gain a double benefit, because decreased fat consumption also seems to inhibit new colon cancer.

Although clinical data are scarce on prostate cancer, it has been shown in epidemiologic studies that prostate cancer, like breast cancer, is associated with a high-fat diet. Theoretically, lowering fat intake should favorably affect hormone levels in men and delay recurrence. For these reasons, a low-fat diet is reasonable and prudent for men with early prostate cancer.

If you are recovering from a squamous cell cancer and decide to choose more vegetables and fruits for their chemopreventive components, a decrease in fat and an increase in fiber is almost automatic. This is good for several reasons. Low-fat and high-fiber intake have been associated with decreased primary squamous cell cancer risk, *and* the low-fat, high-fiber eating pattern should reduce the risk of second primary (separate) cancers that can occur in persons who have had a first cancer.

A low-fat, high-fiber diet is also good for preventing other diseases, especially heart disease, high blood pressure, stroke, and diabetes; therefore, for an adult, low-fat and high-fiber choices are a win-win approach.

PICTURING THE OVERALL DIET

Now you are ready to put techniques of proper eating into practice.

There's a new nutrition tool that can help you visualize how your diet will fit together. In 1992, the United States Department of Agriculture replaced the Four Basic Food Groups concept that we all grew up with with a new concept called the Food Guide Pyramid. The Food Guide Pyramid is a useful reference when balancing quantities of different types of foods.

One of the goals of the Food Guide Pyramid is to help everyone reduce their risk of cancer and other major diseases, so it's no surprise that the recommendations can help you with your particular goal of cancer recovery and prevention. The pyramid emphasizes lowering fat and increasing fiber, fruits, and vegetables.

Food Guide Pyramid

A Guide to Daily Food Choices

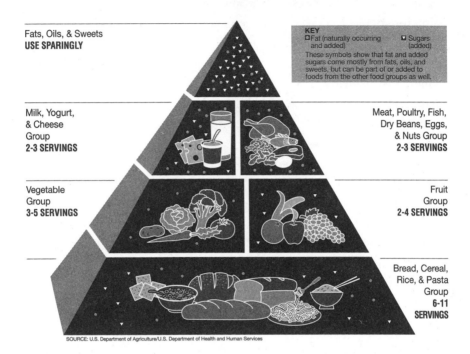

Fats, Oils, & Sweets
USE SPARINGLY

KEY
□ Fat (naturally occurring   ▨ Sugars
   and added)   (added)
These symbols show that fat and added
sugars come mostly from fats, oils, and
sweets, but can be part of or added to
foods from the other food groups as well.

Milk, Yogurt,
& Cheese
Group
2-3 SERVINGS

Meat, Poultry, Fish,
Dry Beans, Eggs,
& Nuts Group
2-3 SERVINGS

Vegetable
Group
3-5 SERVINGS

Fruit
Group
2-4 SERVINGS

Bread, Cereal,
Rice, & Pasta
Group
**6-11
SERVINGS**

SOURCE: U.S. Department of Agriculture/U.S. Department of Health and Human Services

Use the Food Guide Pyramid to help you eat better every day. . .the Dietary Guidelines way. Start with plenty of Breads, Cereals, Rice, and Pasta; Vegetables; and Fruits. Add two to three servings from the Milk group and two to three servings from the Meat group.

Each of these food groups provides some, but not all, of the nutrients you need. No one food group is more important than another — for good health you need them all. Go easy on fats, oils, and sweets, the foods in the small tip of the Pyramid.

To order a copy of "The Food Guide Pyramid" booklet, send a $1.00 check or money order made out to the Superintendent of Documents to: Consumer Information Center, Department 159-Y, Pueblo, Colorado 81009.

U.S. Department of Agriculture, Human Nutrition Information Service, August 1992, Leaflet No. 572

The two lower tiers of the pyramid indicate those foods we should choose most often; bread, cereal, rice, pasta, vegetables, and fruits should be the dominant part of our diet. Meat, poultry, and fish are less important in this scheme. Fats and oils are to be eaten only sparingly, as they appear naturally in fruits, vegetables, grains, and lean cuts of meat. As does our eating plan, the pyramid leaves you room to indulge from time to time. The important thing is to remember which foods form the broad base, which the middle, and which the narrow peak. Use the pyramid as a reminder of general principles, refining the plan to suit the particular needs of someone with your form of cancer (see disease-specific chapters).

Over the three meals and however many snacks of each day, you *must* include no *fewer* than:

- Six to eleven servings of complex carbohydrates, such as bread, pasta, and rice. (These are low-fat or nonfat foods—as long as you don't add margarine, butter, or other high-fat dairy substances to them.)
- Six to eleven servings of vegetables and fruits (at least six for people with most cancers, eleven for people with squamous cancer).
- Three servings of nonfat dairy products, which may include nonfat milk, nonfat yogurt, nonfat "sour cream," nonfat cream cheese, and nonfat cottage cheese.

You *may* include:

- Never more than 6 ounces of lean meat daily.
- Nonfat desserts and snack substitutes to prevent feelings of deprivation—anything from fat-free potato chips to fat-free brownies (see "Recommended Snack Foods" chart, page 205).

Do six to eleven servings of complex carbohydrates sound like a lot of food? Or six to eleven servings of vegetables and fruits? As you can see in the chart called "How Much Is a Serving?" page 191, many serving sizes are probably smaller than you think.

Also, these goals are not really at all hard to achieve in a diet that is not based on meat. Two pieces of bread with each meal (toast, rolls, etc.), a bowl of cereal at breakfast or other time of the day, a couple of servings of pasta at lunch or dinner, and a serving of rice or a bread snack will quickly add up to your minimum daily grain total. Two fruit snacks and fruit on cereal, plus two vegetables with lunch and dinner, take care of the fruit and vegetable requirement with no trouble. When you review this day's meals in terms of serving amounts, you can see that there is plenty of volume here. If you eat *at least* the prescribed amounts, you will not be hungry and usually just won't have room for fatty foods. Also, you will be surprised how quickly you lose the desire for fat. Please remember that you can eat as much fruit and vegetables and grains as you wish.

To reduce total fat, it is necessary to reduce meat portion sizes, but not to eliminate meat entirely. If you are used to 10-ounce servings of meat, a 3-ounce serving will seem small at first, but soon will be enough as you increase vegetables, fruits, and grains. Three ounces of meat is about the size of a deck of cards or your palm.

LABEL READING

If you want to change what's in your diet, you have to know what's inside the foods you buy. For all canned, frozen, or otherwise processed foods, label reading is essential to your eating plan.

Whenever I approach this topic, I think of the story of a young woman who had a known, lifelong, and serious allergy to a particular food. Her allergy was recognized in early childhood, so she was taught by her parents and physician to always refuse this food. She did well until she went away to college, and with her friends frequented a local eatery that was famous for its chili. The restaurant boasted that the chili was successful because of its "secret ingredient." Who would ever have imagined that the secret

HOW MUCH IS A SERVING?

Food	One Serving
Bread	
Regular (90 calories per slice)	1 slice
Diet (45 calories per slice)	2 slices
Pasta	½ cup (cooked)
Rice	⅓ cup (cooked)
Vegetables	
Raw, leafy	1 cup (about the size of a fist)
Chopped, cooked	½ cup
Fruits	
Apple or Orange	1 (size of tennis ball)
Banana	1 small
Canned, unsweetened	½ cup
Dairy	
Nonfat milk	1 cup
Nonfat yogurt	1 cup
Nonfat cheese	1 ounce (a piece of cheese about the size of the last joint of your thumb)

ingredient was peanut butter, the very substance that she was allergic to? The tragic ending for the story is that after one spoonful of the chili, the young woman went into anaphylactic shock and nearly died.

The moral of this story is that you would be amazed at what's in some of the prepackaged, commercially prepared, and restaurant foods that we eat. Some type of sugar (sucrose, corn sweeteners, etc.) is added to just about everything. Another omnipresent ingredient is fat. Many food manufacturers have become more sensitive about what *type* of fat they use, and have stopped using lard and other saturated fats, but other fats are still there. Monosodium glutamate is often added to processed foods as a "flavor enhancer." Many

Nutrition Facts

Serving Size ½ cup (114g)
Servings Per Container 4

Amount Per Serving

Calories 90   Calories from Fat 30

	% Daily Value*
Total Fat 3g	5%
Saturated Fat 0g	0%
Cholesterol 0mg	0%
Sodium 300mg	13%
Total Carbohydrate 13g	4%
Dietary Fiber 3g	12%
Sugars 3g	
Protein 3g	

Vitamin A	80%	•	Vitamin C	60%
Calcium	4%	•	Iron	4%

* Percent Daily Values are based on a 2,000
  calorie diet. Your daily values may be higher or
  lower depending on your calorie needs:

	Calories	2,000	2,500
Total Fat	Less than	65g	80g
Sat Fat	Less than	20g	25g
Cholesterol	Less than	300mg	300mg
Sodium	Less than	2,400mg	2,400mg
Total Carbohydrate		300g	375g
Fiber		25g	30g

Calories per gram:
Fat 9   •   Carbohydrate 4   •   Protein 4

people, myself included, react to MSG with nausea, itching, diarrhea, and other symptoms. You will not know you are eating MSG unless you read food labels.

Clearly, to know what is in your food, you have to read the labels. Reading and understanding the labels of every product is absolutely essential to making proper purchases. This is time-consuming and sometimes frustrating when you first start doing it, but as you develop your own list of what's acceptable and what's not good for you, it will get easier.

The most important parts of the label for our purposes are the fat and fiber contents and certain vitamins and minerals (in particular, beta carotene and calcium). So, pay special attention to these parts of the label as we go along.

The task of being an informed food shopper has been greatly eased by new government regulations on food labeling. Until recently, each food manufacturer decided what constituted a serving size, and descriptive terms—lite, light, lo-fat, fat-free, etc.—were confusing and, in some cases, deceptive. The United States Food and Drug Administration set out to solve these problems. As the FDA explained in its publication, *Backgrounder,* of January 11, 1993: "The purpose of food label reform is simple: to clear up confusion that has prevailed on supermarket shelves for years, to help consumers choose more healthful diets, and to offer an incentive to food companies to improve the nutritional qualities of their products." Early in 1993, the Food and Drug Administration published the final regulations for the 1990 Nutrition Labeling and Education Act (NLEA). These regulations have dramatically changed food labels, so that nutritional content will be clear, serving sizes uniform, and health claims scientifically based. As the FDA says, "Grocery store aisles are on their way to becoming avenues to greater nutritional knowledge."

Let's look at the new label format. (See opposite.)

With the old label, the percentage of U.S. Recommended Daily Allowance for protein, certain vitamins, and minerals *may* be given. Fiber can appear separately, for example: "Each ½ cup serving contains 13 grams of dietary fiber."

The new label *must* show the percentage provided of U.S. Recommended Daily Values, based on a 2,000-calorie diet, for certain vitamins and minerals, and for fat, cholesterol, sodium, total carbohydrates, and fiber. It will also show maximum recommendations for fat, cholesterol, sodium, and carbohydrates, based on a 2,500-calorie intake.

Both the old and the new labels give information to help you alter your diet to fight cancer, but the new label has some distinct advantages:

- Because the portions are standard now, the new label makes it possible for you to pick up different brands and compare their nutritional contents.

- The new label emphasizes nutrients that we consume too much of (fat, for example), rather than those nutrients we used to tend to get too little of (vitamins and minerals).
- The new label helps you understand how a particular food fits into your total daily diet.
- Both the old and new labels state fat-gram and fiber-gram content, but the new label also includes fat *calories,* making it easier to calculate the percentage of calories in a food that is derived from fat.

Let's explore that last point further. The key number you need for reducing fats is the daily *fat-gram content* I recommend for your diet. The percentage of total calories coming from fats will help you decide whether to buy the product.

As the new label will remind you (at the bottom), each gram of fat contains 9 calories. Here's how to calculate the percentage of calories from fat in one serving of a product.

- If the product has an old label, start by multiplying the number of fat grams by 9.
- If the product has a new label, the calculation will be done for you, on the line "calories from fat."
- With both labels, you still must calculate what percentage of the total calories is fat calories. Using the new label above, each serving has 260 calories, 120 calories from fat. Dividing 120 by 260, you learn that 46 percent of the calories come from fat!

When reading labels, especially for fat, you have to look beyond the words in large print—*Light! Less fat!*—to the fine print. For example, bologna or turkey marked "92% fat-free" can still get most of its calories from fat. Instead of reading the front of the label, look for the fine print that tells *number of grams of fat per serving.*

Label reading does take time, but it is necessary, including some spot-checking after you've developed some experience with what's acceptable and what's not. A patient once pointed out to me how important it is to keep reading the labels. She bought a certain brand of popcorn, and the label said it had 18 percent fat. A few months later, she bought the same brand, and the label said it had 45 percent fat. The lesson is clear: Read the label, not just the brand name.

THE FIRST THREE MONTHS

You have now learned the basic principles of the eating plan, something about serving sizes, and how to read food labels. Now we will go into the specifics of the eating plan.

It is important to move gradually so the changes in your diet will be permanent. A reasonable goal is to change your eating patterns over a period of about three months. Here is the basic plan:

Month 1: *Get the fat out of breakfast* (as much as possible). Learn label reading and substitutions.

Month 2: *Eliminate fat snacking.*

Month 3: *Reduce fat to a minimum at lunch and dinner,* whether prepared at home or eaten out, by learning low-fat meal planning, selection, and preparation.

Let's get an overview of how you'll do it, then look in depth at each month.

THE FIRST CHALLENGE IS BREAKFAST

Have you ever thought about how television commercials portray breakfast? The Great American Breakfast is so cherished in our nation's folklore that advertisers sometimes invoke either the Farm Breakfast—the whole family is seated around a groaning board of eggs, bacon, and waffles—or the Why You Should Feel Guilty about Not Having the Farm Breakfast. The latter is especially popular right now, because advertisers know that our mornings are more dash-out-the-door than second-cup. We've already relinquished many of our families' lunches and dinners to the school cafeteria, the corporate diner, or the nearest restaurant. Now even breakfast is eaten on the run, via a toaster pastry, a quick stop at a drive-in window, a roll from the office automat, or worse yet, nothing at all.

While we would all benefit from better breakfast habits, during recovery from cancer it is imperative to take charge of breakfast. For one thing, your appetite may be best in the morning, and it's important to take advantage of that timing. If this is true for you, breakfast will be your biggest meal, and you need to make it right. This can be done.

THE SECOND TASK IS TO SWITCH TO NONFAT SNACKS

For some of us, between-meal snacks account for as much as *one fourth of our calorie intake.* If you are not careful, this can amount to a huge load of fat. Fortunately, there are now many nonfat snack foods you can buy, as well as fresh oranges, apples, carrots, and other fruits and vegetables. One of your eventual goals will be to include six to eleven servings of fruits and vegetables each day, and between-meal snacking is an excellent way to work these into your diet.

THE THIRD MONTH'S CHALLENGE IS LUNCH AND DINNER

The recipes in the back of this book will be particularly helpful in this regard. In addition to these, I'll be sharing tips on reducing fat in your favorite recipes and describing how to choose low-fat frozen dinners for those times when you're too tired to cook from scratch.

TAKE IT SLOW

Even if you're feeling feisty and ready to make drastic changes, I recommend sticking to this three-month plan. A gradual change can be carried out more thoughtfully and can be better sustained. If you tackle this as a crash course, you may soon miss your high-fat meals and lapse into old habits. Remember that you are dealing with a lot right now. If you are on a treatment, taking chemotherapy or radiation therapy, or recovering from surgery, you will need extra time to adjust. Taking one step at a time in changing your diet can make the difference between feeling beautiful or feeling burdened.

After the third month, it will be time to proceed to counting grams of fat and fiber. This will make it possible, if you wish, to keep tabs on your intake of fiber and fat as precisely as possible. Counting grams may not be really necessary, however. If you master the basics of low-fat meals and snacks, you may find that it's sufficient to count fat grams for a week or less, until you acquire experience with how much to eat. Once you've accomplished that, you may only need to spot-check occasionally to be sure you haven't done any backsliding. Our goal is to show how you can adopt the low-fat, high-fiber habit for a lifetime of healthy eating without having to constantly worry about grams.

MONTH 1—GETTING THE FAT OUT OF BREAKFAST

Breakfast will be changed in weekly changes over a month. That Great American Breakfast of bacon, eggs, buttered toast, whole milk, and maybe a Danish is absolutely *loaded* with fat. *Almost all of this fat can be removed and you can still have a very satisfying meal.* Since cereals, skim milk, and "fat-free" products still contain a small amount of fat, it is impossible to get 100 percent of the fat out of breakfast—but it is possible to dramatically reduce the fat in this important meal. In doing so, you will remove a significant portion of the daily fat burden. We will proceed over four weeks, showing you how and what to substitute to get the fat out of breakfast. You will learn how simple substituting will be, as long as you can substitute fat-free foods.

WEEK 1: SUBSTITUTIONS

INSTEAD OF: Scrambled eggs (1 egg = 5 grams fat, and who eats just one?)

CHOOSE: Your favorite cereal at least four days of the week (2–3 grams of fat) OR nonfat egg substitute no more than 3 days (¼ cup = 0 gram fat) OR 2 egg whites to equal 1 egg (0 gram fat) in any recipe. (Note, however, that some cereals are high in fat, particularly granola and cereals with nuts.)

INSTEAD OF: Bacon (1 strip = 3.5 grams fat)

CHOOSE: Low-fat processed meat, such as lean Canadian bacon (1 ounce = 0.9 gram fat) OR baked (cooked) ham (1 slice = 0.5 gram fat), no more than three days, and remember that this will count toward your 6 ounces per day of allowed meat, and that sodium content may be high.

INSTEAD OF: Buttered white toast (1 slice with 1 teaspoon butter = 5 grams fat) or a commercial biscuit, some of which have 7 grams fat each

CHOOSE: Whole wheat toast with jelly or jam (1 slice = 0.9 gram fat) OR fat-free cream cheese product or fat-free margarine (1 ounce = 0 gram fat) OR fat-free and cholesterol-free Danish (0 gram fat)

INSTEAD OF: Whole milk on cereal (1 cup = 8.9 grams fat)
CHOOSE: 2% milk on cereal (1 cup = 4.7 grams fat)

INSTEAD OF: 1 ounce whole milk in coffee (2.4 grams fat)
CHOOSE: 1 ounce 2% or skim milk in coffee (0.6 gram fat)

Note: Include at least one fruit high in vitamin C, such as strawberries, oranges, or grapefruit. You may use juices freely, but remember that fruit juice generally lacks fiber, so *also eat a fruit.*

Also note: Week 1 is still low in fiber, but fiber content will increase in Week 2.

When you choose to have an egg, bacon, buttered toast, and

coffee with whole milk, the total is *15.9 grams fat.* If you eat two eggs and have a cup of whole milk, the fat content climbs to *29.8 grams fat.* By using the substitution list, the total is 7 *grams fat.*

WEEK 2

Maintain the substitutions of Week 1 except *substitute 1% for 2% milk,* thus saving 2 grams fat or more (1 cup of 1% milk = 2.4 grams fat; 1 ounce in coffee = 0.3 gram fat).

To *increase fiber, try a fortified cereal* with a moderate fiber content (approximately *4 grams fiber* content will do). To each serving of cereal, *add 2 tablespoons of a high-fiber cereal that contains 10 grams fiber* or more per serving (see "Fat and Fiber in Cereals," page 202). An alternative is to add the same amount of high-fiber cereal to a serving of nonfat yogurt.

With these additions or substitutions, if you continue with the plan for Week 1 plus the changes for Week 2, your breakfast now has about *5.5 grams fat,* and the fiber content of your diet has been increased considerably.

WEEK 3

Maintain the same substitutions but use *skim milk* (1 cup = 0.4 gram fat; negligible fat in 1 ounce) and add a *serving of high-fiber cereal (fiber content 10 grams* or more), perhaps with a small amount of your favorite cereal that contains 2 grams fat or less. Add sugar and cinnamon if you wish, and don't forget the fruit! An alternative is 1½ Apple and Raisin Bran Muffins (see recipe section, pages 340–41) for 10 grams fiber; if eaten instead of cereal, drink a glass of skim milk or eat a cup of nonfat yogurt to replace the milk in the cereal. How about a round of applause? This week's breakfast has about *3 grams fat* and over *10 grams fiber!*

Note that the amount of fiber in breakfast can be adjusted to keep your fiber intake in your range. For example, if you have six servings of fruits and vegetables in a day (12 grams fiber) and six servings of grains (12 grams fiber), then a 10-gram fiber cereal will bring your total to 34 grams. A note of caution: If you attempt to follow the recommendations to the maximum—i.e., eleven servings of grains, eleven servings of fruits and vegetables, a serving of high-fiber cereal—you will be getting about 50 grams of fiber daily. This may cause gas and theoretically some loss of minerals, so shoot for 25 to 35 grams daily.

WEEK 4

In general, this is a good *week for reinforcement* of what you've learned, so continue the pattern for Week 3; however, if your concern is colon cancer, you may want to have a high-fiber cereal daily, along with six fruits and vegetables and six grains, to increase the fiber amount to achieve a daily total fiber content of 30 to 35 grams. Of course, you can have a low-fiber cereal (for example, 4 grams), but then to reach the daily total you need more fruits, vegetables, and grains (average 2 grams per serving)—a total of thirteen to fifteen servings of fruits, vegetables, and grains. (Note: Your fiber goal may be less than 30 to 35 grams, depending on your physician's advice and your tolerance for the fiber.) *Do not exceed 35 grams fiber unless instructed to do so by your doctor.*

At this point, you have reduced the grams of fat from almost 16 (the typical American breakfast) to *about 3 grams.* You have increased the fiber from essentially 0 grams to *more than 10 grams.* This is a major accomplishment. Congratulations!

Eating high-fiber cereal at breakfast is a key way to get the fiber you need each day. It is hard to go from bacon and eggs straight to a high-fiber selection, so this is why I recommend going from low-, to moderate-, to high-fiber cereal over three weeks.

To know what kinds of cereals are low, moderate, or high in fiber, you must read the labels. Some of the choices are listed in the chart

"Fat and Fiber in Cereals" (see page 202), but there are many more cereals in the grocery store.

The average American diet contains 10 to 14 grams of fiber daily, so you need about 20 more grams to reach 30 to 35 grams daily. Over the three months of this plan, you will be moving toward one serving of high-fiber cereal (8 to 11 grams) plus six fruits and vegetables (about 12 grams fiber), which equals about 20 grams a day minimum. Then, six servings of carbohydrates (about 12 grams fiber) will get you up to 32 grams fiber. With a lower-fiber cereal (2 to 4 grams), you still have over 25 grams of fiber for that day.

The gradual fiber increase may cause uncomfortable amounts of gas; however, your intestines will usually adapt in a few weeks. Though increased fiber prevents constipation, it can also be a cause of constipation, because fiber absorbs water in the gut. For this reason, *it's important to increase your intake of water* to keep things moving and to decrease cramps. If you find that you just can't adjust to certain foods, then eat smaller servings of them, or try other foods.

Check the label for the size of a cereal serving. As you can see on the table, serving sizes vary. Most are about ⅓ cup. A whole cup of a high-fiber cereal at one time—which would contain a whopping 25 to 33 grams fiber—might cause abdominal distress if you are not used to it.

If you do not enjoy cereal for breakfast, it is fine to eat the ⅓ to ½ cup of high-fiber cereal during the day, when you get home from work, before you cook supper, for lunch or at bedtime, on nonfat yogurt or a potato or mixed in nonfat "ice cream." Again, Apple and Raisin Bran Muffins are delicious and high in fiber. However you choose to consume your higher-fiber cereal, do it as prescribed over three weeks.

It is *not* healthy to skip breakfast entirely. You need the nourishment and the fiber. Again, don't forget the importance of fruit for breakfast.

A final word: The idea is to reduce total fat, not to feel deprived and punished. Some of my patients with cancer have absolutely refused to give up their morning bacon and eggs. If this is your case, make another meal—lunch or dinner—the fat-free meal. But give the suggestions a good try—you may well find that you enjoy them.

FAT AND FIBER IN CEREALS

	FAT GRAMS	FIBER GRAMS
HIGH-FIBER EXAMPLES		
Kellogg's Bran Buds (⅓ cup)	0–1	11
Kellogg's All-Bran (⅓ cup)	0.5	8.5
General Mills Fiber One (½ cup)	1.0	13
MEDIUM-FIBER EXAMPLES		
Kellogg's Bran Flakes (¾ cup)	0.5	4
Kellogg's Raisin Bran (¾ cup)	0.7	4
LOWER-FIBER EXAMPLES		
General Mills Cheerios (1¼ cups)	1.8	2
Post Grape-Nuts Flakes (⅞ cup)	0.8	1.9
Post Grape-Nuts	0.1	1.8
Kellogg's Corn Flakes (1¼ cups)	0.1	0.3
Kellogg's Special K (1⅓ cups)	0.1	0.2
Post Hearty Granola (¼ cup)	4.1*	0.1
FORTIFIED CEREAL EXAMPLES		
Just Right		
Crunchy nugget (1 cup)	1.5	3
Fruit and nut (¾ cup)	1.0	2
Total		
Raisin bran (1 cup)	1.5	5
Whole grain (¾ cup)	1	2.5
Corn flakes (1⅓ cups)	0.5	1
Product 19 (1 cup)	0	1

* Some cereals do have a considerable amount of fat. Cereals that exceed 2 grams fat per serving are not acceptable for this plan.

MONTH 2: GETTING THE FAT OUT OF SNACKS

Now it's time to concentrate on another heavy source of fat: snack foods. America has become a nation of browsers and grazers. We extend the usual three meals a day with our snacks. As I mentioned earlier, for some of us, snacks account for as much as one fourth of our total calorie intake, so making these snacks relatively fat-free can have a substantial impact on the day's fat intake.

Snacking throughout the day is not really a new practice. Our ancestors did not sit down to three square meals a day; they grazed or snacked, eating small amounts when they could. So

---

FRUITS FOR SNACKS OR ANYTIME

Fruit is virtually fat-free. Think of fruit as no-fat and mostly high in fiber (average about 2 grams fiber per serving).

FRUIT*	FAT GRAMS	FIBER GRAMS
Apple (1 medium)	0.5	2.8
Applesauce (½ cup)	0.2	1.4
Apricots (3 medium)	0.4	1.4
Banana (1)	0.6	1.6
Blackberries (½ cup)	0.3	3.3
Blueberries (1 cup)	0.6	4.4
Cantaloupe (1 cup)	0.4	0.5**
Cherries, raw (½ cup)	0.7	1.1
Dates (10)	0.4	4.2
Grapes (½ cup)	0.3	0
Oranges (1)	0	1.9
Pear (1)	0.7	4
Pineapple (1 cup)	0.7	2.4
Prunes (10)	0.4	4
Strawberries (1 cup)	0.6	2.8

Note: To simplify your calculations, from now on you can use for all fruits and vegetables 0 grams fat and 2 grams fiber.

**Cantaloupe is full of vitamins, though low in fiber.

snacking is not a bad new habit, just an old necessity revived, largely in response to the hectic pace at which we live. There are some nutritional theories that it is actually healthier to eat more, smaller meals, and you may find that smaller meals cause less nausea during treatment. This is all the more reason to make snacks healthy.

In general, a fat-free snack is one that has no added oil or fat; however, some fruits and vegetables naturally contain a lot of fat. Avocados, for example, are very high in natural fat (27 grams apiece).

If you choose the right kinds of snacks, they will help you achieve your nutritional goals for fiber (fruit, vegetables, and grains). Choose snack foods with your total daily diet in mind.

It helps that there are abundant raw fruits and vegetables available in our markets almost year-round. Selections such as oranges, carrots, and apples are just about perfect. They contain important vitamins and fiber and almost no fat. A carrot, for example, is loaded with beta carotene, has 1 gram fiber, and contains only 0.1 gram fat. Fruits and vegetables are also full of flavor and interesting textures, so they are satisfying in every way.

Snack foods other than fruits and vegetables are not "bad" *if they are fat-free* (*fat-free* means that the food contains less than 0.5 gram fat per serving, and no added fat or oil). For example, pure chocolate contains no cholesterol and no sugar. The problem is that we add sugar and fat to chocolate. So, if you like chocolate, enjoy it. Moderation is the key, but always read the label. As with any snack food, don't eat so much that it kills your appetite for more nutritious snacks and the necessary fruits and vegetables.

Thanks in part to the pressure that informed and health-conscious consumers have put on food manufacturers, there is now an amazing array of no-fat snack products, including fat-free potato chips, fat-free "cream cheese" products, almost fat-free nachos and tortilla chips and fat-free "ice cream" products and yogurt. So it's unlikely you'll feel deprived. Again, reading the label is very important, especially if you have other health problems and special diet needs. Be aware that some of these lack fiber (and in some cases, nutritional value) as well as fat. Some of these

RECOMMENDED SNACK FOODS

Note: Consult the package for serving sizes if not given.

FOOD	FAT GRAMS	FIBER GRAMS
Pretzels (1 ounce)	0.7	1
Popcorn (1 cup), fat-free microwave or air-popped—Don't add butter!	0.2	1
Fat-free saltines (½ ounce)	0	0.5
Fat-free baked tortilla chips	0.7	1
Fat-free black bean and pinto bean dips (2 tablespoons) and salsa	0	1
Nonfat soft frozen yogurt	0	0
Nonfat "ice cream" (may be labeled as "frozen dairy dessert" or "dairy product")	0	0
Fat-free potato chips	0	1
Angel food cake	0	0.5
Instant pudding made with skim milk	0.2	0

snacks contain a lot of salt. Fortunately, manufacturers are catching on to the whole picture of good nutrition, so many offer several versions of their products. Fat-free potato chips and tortilla chips, for example, can be purchased in several flavors (with various amounts of salt, depending on the recipe) or entirely salt-free. It seems that each grocer takes a different approach to where these items will be stocked, so if you can't find them in the "diet foods" section, check the aisle where the fat-laden snack foods are, or ask at the information desk.

What about cookies and other goodies? *If they are nonfat* (for example, selections from the many types of fat-free cookies that are now available, or pretzels) *count them as a bread serving toward your daily total of six to eleven servings.*

As with the other changes you are making, switching to no-fat snacks will take some time and thought. It's more difficult to set a specific schedule for snacks, because snacking is by nature more spontaneous and the choices are too numerous to list.

Remember, we are talking about *snacks.* Our goal is fat-free *snacking.* To give you a little more freedom at lunch and dinner, you can have an occasional *dessert,* and some of the things that will not qualify as a snack could qualify as a dessert. Also, if you choose a fatty snack, you can compensate by having a fat-free dessert. Always watch portion sizes of fat-containing snacks.

Snack Substitutions

INSTEAD OF:	HAVE ONE SERVING:
½ cup chocolate pudding 4.5 grams fat/0 gram fiber	Fat-free chocolate pudding 0.2 gram fat/0 gram fiber
½ cup ice cream 16 grams fat/0 gram fiber	Fat-free "ice cream" or yogurt 0.2 gram fat/0 gram fiber
½-inch slice pound cake 6 grams fat/1 gram fiber*	Angel food cake 0 gram fat/0.5 gram fiber
1 oatmeal raisin cookie 8 grams fat/1 gram fiber	Fat-free cookie 0 gram fat/1 gram fiber*
1 cream puff custard 9 grams fat/0 gram fiber	Fat-free pastry 0 gram fat/0.5 gram fiber*
1 Danish pastry 8–20 grams fat/0.5 gram fiber*	Fat-free pastry 0 gram fat/0.5 gram fiber*
1 ounce potato chips 12–14 grams fat/0.5 gram fiber*	Fat-free potato chips 0 gram fat/0.5 gram fiber*
1 ounce tortilla chips 8 grams fat/1 gram fiber	Fat-free tortilla chips 0.5 gram fat/1 gram fiber*
Commercial icings 15 grams fat/0 gram fiber	No-fat frostings 0 gram fat/0 gram fiber*

*Estimated; brands vary—read the labels.

MONTH 3: LUNCH AND DINNER

By the end of Month 2, you will have achieved control of breakfast and snack foods. Since about 30 percent of calories come from breakfast and 20 percent or more from snacks, half or more of your calorie intake is now fat-free or nearly so. You are consistently substituting nonfat dairy products for high-fat ones, cereal or nonfat egg substitutes for eggs, and nonfat snacks and fruit for fat-laden junk food. You are well on your way to a low-fat, high-fiber eating pattern, and you haven't suffered from food deprivation at all, because you have learned to substitute wisely.

You are also now *reading labels automatically* on every food item you buy (review the earlier section in this chapter if necessary) and may even have had the pleasant experience of friends' asking you for advice and suggestions about healthy eating.

Lunch and dinner remain. The basics of eating right at lunch and dinner are the same as for breakfast and snacks—low fat, high fiber. Wise shopping and ingredient substitutions are the same for all meals and snacks. Lunch and dinner do pose certain new challenges, however. They are: putting meat in its place, eating more fruits and vegetables, exploring new recipes, and adapting your favorite recipes.

PUTTING MEAT IN ITS PLACE

The first step is to start thinking of meat in a new way. Instead of thinking, "What side dishes can I put around my main meat course?" think, "What meat will I like with my pasta, rice, or vegetables?" It's important to think of meat as a condiment, not the main focus of the meal. And remember: Meat is optional; it doesn't have to be part of your diet every day.

> Over the course of the day, you should not exceed 6 ounces of lean meat. The proper portion size for one serving of meat is 3 ounces, about the size of a deck of playing cards. *Note:* You don't have to eat as much as 6 ounces, or any meat at all.

The way you cook meats makes a difference, too. Trim away all visible fat. Remove the skin from poultry before cooking. Try broiling and microwaving instead of frying.

Experiment with stir-fries and casseroles, which tend to use meat as a condiment, yet are very satisfying. Beware of casserole recipes

---

LEANER MEATS

Beef Choose bottom round, eye of round (about 8.5 grams fat per 3-ounce serving), top round (5.5 grams fat/3 ounces), sirloin (7.5 grams fat/3 ounces), or tenderloin (8 grams fat/3 ounces).

Pork Lean tenderloin is a good choice (4 grams fat/3 ounces).

Veal All veal, except breast. Veal cutlet (4 grams fat/3 ounces), rib chops (4 grams fat/3 ounces), or loin chops (7.5 grams fat/3 ounces).

Chicken White meat without skin (4 grams fat/3 ounces; by comparison, white meat with skin has 9 grams fat/3 ounces, dark meat without skin has 8.5 grams fat, and dark meat with skin has 13.5 grams fat).

Turkey White meat without skin (2.5 grams fat/3 ounces; by comparison, white meat with skin has 7 grams fat, dark meat without skin has 6 grams fat, and dark meat with skin has 10 grams fat).

Duck Without skin (9.5 grams fat/3-ounce serving; with skin this meat has a whopping 24 grams fat/3 ounces).

Seafood *Low-fat* choices (1 gram fat/3 ounces) include bass, bream, cod, crappie, flounder, grouper, haddock, halibut, mahimahi, perch, pike, red snapper, rockfish, scrod, speckled trout, sunfish, sole, and fresh tuna. *Shellfish* (clams, crayfish, lobsters, scallops, and shrimp) have less than 2 grams fat/3 ounces. Oysters have 4 grams fat/3 ounces. *Medium-fat* choices (5 grams fat/3 ounces) are angelfish, bluefish, catfish, croaker, fresh sardines, kingfish, mackerel, orange roughy, shark, swordfish, trout, whitefish, and yellowtail. *High-fat* (8 to 10 grams fat/3 ounces) are pompano, salmon, and wahoo.

This information on leaner meats is from *Eat for Health Meat Guide,* USDA Agriculture Handbook 8-13, and unpublished USDA veal and lamb data.

that rely on butter and rich sauces, though. Many good low-fat casseroles are high in vegetables and grains. Stir-frying lots of vegetables with a little meat (about three parts vegetables to every one part meat) can be accomplished nicely with nonstick vegetable spray or with chicken broth, wine, fruit juice, or water rather than oils. It's also a good idea to plan at least two meat-free meals a week.

If you and your family are accustomed to eating lots of meat, putting meat in its proper place will be a drastic change, but it won't be as difficult as you might anticipate. If you are following the rest of the plan, you will all feel full and satisfied.

EAT MORE FRUITS AND VEGETABLES

Lunch and dinner are the meals when we typically eat most of our fruits and vegetables, so when the time comes to focus on these meals in Month 3, you also need to focus on ways to work more of these valuable foods into your diet.

In general, fresh fruits and vegetables are probably best, not only because they offer the fullest nutritional value, but also because they simply taste better, raw or prepared. However, there is nothing wrong with using canned or frozen vegetables and fruits, especially if the convenience makes it possible to eat properly at a time when food preparation is more than you can handle. But watch out for added sodium in canned vegetables.

I recommend you increase your consumption of all fruits and vegetables to a total of at least six servings a day, and preferably more, and eleven servings if you have squamous cancer. The purpose of this increase is to take advantage of their chemopreventive content (which is explained in chapter 2, "The Connection Between Cancer and Diet"), as well as their fiber. One of the most desirable chemopreventives is beta carotene but there are dozens of others. Some fruits and vegetables have more fiber than others; to simplify your calculations, assume each fruit or vegetable serving contains 2 grams fiber and 0 gram fat.

EXPLORING NEW RECIPES

Located at the end of this book are over a hundred absolutely delicious recipes for breakfast, lunch, dinner, desserts, and snacks. Created by Chef Mark Erickson, each of these recipes combines low-fat and high-fiber eating principles with exceptional taste and ease of preparation. Chef Erickson's recipes are deceptively elegant; having tried these in my own home, I found that most take only about twenty minutes to put together.

Each recipe has been analyzed for major nutrient content. The recipes are grouped for convenience as follows.

- Soups and Chowders
- Pastas, Pasta Salads, and Pizzas
- Grains and Beans
- Poultry, Seafood, and Meat
- Vegetables and Vegetable Salads
- Desserts
- Breads
- Breakfasts and Brunches
- and a collection of versatile sauces, accompaniments, and other base recipes

Oh, go ahead and peek at the dessert section now. See? You are not going to be taste-deprived.

Although many of the recipes will seem familiar—from New England Clam Chowder to Corn Pudding to Warm Brownie Cake— many others will be new types of dishes that you should explore and work into your repertoire. For example, there are marvelously satisfying bean dishes, lots of grain recipes, fruit-based desserts, and meatless main dishes in the collection.

FROZEN DINNERS

There are many low-fat frozen dinners and entrees, though I don't encourage habitual use of these. For one thing, they can be expensive. They are handy when you don't feel like cooking and can be quite acceptable if you add a raw or cooked vegetable, a fruit, bread, and skim milk or nonfat yogurt. Look for products with 5 or less grams of fat. Watch the sodium content if you need to decrease sodium. Fiber content is becoming uniformly more available on the labels, since this is part of the new food labeling act.

LEARN NEW COOKING TECHNIQUES

In the next chapter, you will learn many new lower-fat ways to cook, including ways to modify your favorite recipes. This month is a good time to start adapting the way you cook.

EATING OUT

Now you've passed through the first three months of making real changes in your eating habits. You've tackled breakfasts, snacks, lunches, and dinners. But there's something out there that can be a real threat to your eating prescription—restaurants. Considering that some people eat out three to five times a week or more, the high-fat, low-fiber choices that predominate can be a real challenge. However, many restaurants (40 percent in a recent poll) now offer low-fat choices, and even if the menu doesn't point out low-fat items, it is still possible to make acceptable choices and to control portion sizes.

Here are some tips for eating out.

ASK WHAT DISHES CONTAIN

Since you can't read any labels on restaurant food, what do you do? You ask. Ask the waiter what an item contains. If it has cheese, sour cream, or butter in it, for example, request that this be left out or that the dish be prepared with no more than 1 tablespoon of the ingredient per serving. If the sauce is the problem, ask for the sauce "on the side" or deleted altogether. Tell the server you are looking for low-fat items and ask for suggestions. Be assertive enough that he or she understands. Restaurants do want satisfied customers and usually will try to accommodate you. If not, go elsewhere next time.

DON'T GO IN STARVING

Eat some fruit or cereal before leaving home. This is equivalent to the adage about never going to the grocery store hungry, because you will overspend. If you can't avoid going in hungry, ask for some bread (preferably whole-grain and without butter, of course!) before ordering.

EMPHASIZE VEGETABLES, FRUITS, AND COMPLEX CARBOHYDRATES

Remember to minimize meat and to maximize vegetables, fruits, and complex carbohydrates. Use the salad bar—even some fast-food places offer these now. Get lots of the fresh vegetables and fruits, but avoid the dressed salads (coleslaw, potato salad, etc.) and the dressings. Most places that provide a salad bar have low-fat or nonfat salad dressings, so if you don't see these, ask. You can make a delicious meal of vegetables, side dishes, and a salad.

WATCH OUT FOR LARGE MEAT PORTIONS

Almost all restaurants serve meat portions larger than 3 ounces. If your plate arrives with a huge piece of meat on it, ask for a doggie bag *before* you eat and place the excess in the bag for use later. This removes temptation. You also could offer some to your companions, or leave some uneaten on your plate. If you feel you can't resist it, pour salt and pepper on it to ensure it remains uneaten as the meal progresses. It is not necessary to trade your health for a politely cleaned plate. The cook is not going to be unhappy if you eat only a little, or even if you don't eat at all.

EAT WHAT'S RIGHT FOR YOU

It is a treat to eat out, especially if you have been ill. Try to enjoy the ambiance and the companionship as well as the food. Remember, you don't have to wash the dishes! Don't make yourself feel guilty later by ordering without thinking. If your companions are having gobs of fatty foods, enjoy their company while you stick to what is healthful for you. And if there is a particularly desirable item on the menu, such as a dessert, the "rule of 10" is a good one to follow. If dessert looks like a 10 on a scale of 1 to 10, order it. If the first bite is a 10, take another. If this one is a 10, take another. If still 10, go ahead and eat it. If, however, the rating falls to 8 or less after a few bites, stop.

Ethnic can be excellent. The increasingly popular Chinese and Mexican restaurants offer both challenges and opportunities. In a Chinese restaurant most dishes are made to order, so special requests can usually be granted, such as asking for very lean meat and extra vegetables. Avoid breaded sweet-and-sour dishes, fried egg rolls, and fried wontons. They are usually deep-fried. Also avoid dishes with nuts, duck, fried rice, and pan-fried noodles. Choose instead steamed dishes such as pork or teriyaki beef or chicken and rice. White rice—one of the complex carbohydrates that you need—is always served.

Mexican restaurants will often immediately bring you fried chips with salsa. This can be a problem, because you can eat all the salsa you want, but the chips are laden with fat. Try to eat only ten or so, then move them away. Good choices here are chicken or beef enchiladas, burritos, Mexican salad, and black bean soup. You can always ask that sour cream and cheese be left out of dishes, as well.

WHAT TO DO ABOUT FAST FOOD

Many fast-food chains now offer more healthful choices, so select from these. Always avoid fried items. Even fish is fatty when fried, especially when sauces—which are usually mayonnaise-based—are added. A small hamburger with mustard and ketchup and a tomato is not a bad choice. Some chains have low-fat shakes that are okay, but if in doubt, ask to see the label of the container (unlike larger restaurants, the fast-food chains can often do this; some even have nutrition information about their products available).

Fast-food chains now have breakfast items. Without a doubt, their biscuits taste wonderful, but they are not only loaded with fat, they beg for butter. So it's best to avoid the biscuits. Pancakes with syrup are okay. Fat-free muffins or bagels are fine, and cereal with skim milk is great.

Delis can be hazardous, but if you are very choosy, you can safely navigate their menus. Avoid vegetarian sandwiches with cheese and ask that the cheese be left out of other types of sandwiches. Ask for a takeout box when you place your order, because it's almost certain that the portion on your sandwich will exceed 3 ounces. Request "no mayonnaise or dressing." Mustard and ketchup are fine. When choosing a sandwich, remember that corned beef is high in fat (16 grams per 3 ounces). A Reuben sandwich is also high in fat (30 grams). A roast beef sandwich has 17 grams of fat. White-meat turkey breast on whole-grain bread is a better choice (5 grams of fat). At 10 grams of fat, one slice of cheese-only pizza looks deceptively innocent next to these high-fat meat sandwiches. Avoid ice cream; instead, choose nonfat yogurt or nonfat "ice cream" products.

TRAVEL

Most airlines will prepare a low-fat meal for you if you request it when making your reservation or twenty-four hours in advance of your flight. Margarine or mayonnaise may still appear on the tray, however. Don't eat it, and refuse the free nuts. If you forget to place your special request, or the airline doesn't have your order, you can eat your salad plain, take the skin off chicken or remove visible fat from the meat, and skip the dessert.

What to Do If You Get Off Track

Changing any habit is difficult, and you will probably experience a day when the whole plan goes out the window or, over a week or two, you find yourself backsliding to your old food choices. One of the best ways to deal with this is to plan for it now, while you are making up your mind to choose this healthy nutritional method. *If you lapse into old patterns, forgive yourself for it, then pick up where you left off.* Keep trying. Before you know it, you will find that the program has become part of your routine. Over time, foods that are high in fat will eventually taste too greasy or too rich for your educated palate, and it will seem very natural and pleasant to reach for something low in fat.

If the backslide becomes a plunge that lasts for more than two weeks, start over at the beginning, reintroducing the fiber and reducing the fat over three to four weeks. Not only will this give your body a chance to readjust, it will give you a chance to refresh your memory on the details of the program.

Checking Your Progress with Fat- and Fiber-Gram Counting

I believe you can learn to reduce fat and increase fiber in your diet without keeping a log of anything for very long, but to get started correctly, you may find it helpful to count fat and fiber grams. Once you learn what and how much to eat, you can continue to count if you wish, or can just spot-check occasionally.

Thanks to the new food labeling regulations described earlier in the section "Label Reading," it's possible to achieve reasonably precise fat- and fiber-gram counting. In case you're feeling a bit like a pioneer, this trail has already been blazed: Hundreds of women participating in breast cancer prevention trials have used the fat-gram counting technique for five years to hold the fat-calorie component of their diet to 20 percent.

First, let's review why fat and fiber grams are important. Fat is "dense" in calories compared to other major nutrients (1 gram fat = 9 calories; 1 gram carbohydrate or protein = 4 calories). So, if you eat less fat, you eat fewer calories, even if you replace each gram of fat deleted with a gram of carbohydrate. It is more complicated to replace fat with meat protein, because all meat contains some fat, even if all visible fat is removed. As discussed in chapter 2, "The Connection Between Cancer and Diet," both fat and calories may stimulate tumor growth, and some research indicates that protein may do so, too.

It is impossible to give you here a simple, accurate, universally applicable prescription for a fat-gram total and fiber-gram total, because each person's size, health status, and current eating habits are different, and because this science is in some ways still rudimentary. Nevertheless, it is possible to work with what is generally known to be true. The process is rather involved, however, and it is best to get help from your physician or nutritionist in developing an individualized eating plan. The section "For the Doctor" at the end of this book includes guidelines.

Several national organizations recommend you eat no more than 30 percent of your daily total calories as fat to reduce your risk of cancer. My prescription to combat disease recurrence is that you consume 20 percent or less of your total calories from fat if you have breast cancer, colon cancer, and prostate cancer, and 25 percent or less for other cancers.

Let's say you're aiming for 20 percent or less of calories from fat and your fat-gram goal works out to be 34 grams per day or less. Under my plan, you will achieve this level *after* the three-month period described above, not immediately. After three months, when you have taken the fat out of breakfast and snacks and are eating low-fat lunches and dinners, reaching your fat-gram goals is almost automatic, especially if you are using Chef Erickson's recipes.

If you are not there after three months (perhaps because you are eating out a lot), the Fat and Fiber Gram Calculator on page 218 will be helpful. Another chart shows the fat and fiber in commonly eaten snack foods and appropriate substitutes for those that have too much fat (page 206). Remember to read labels.

QUICK READINGS ON ADDED FATS

- 1 teaspoon of butter adds **4 grams of fat** to a slice of bread.
- 2 teaspoons of butter to grill a sandwich adds **8 grams of fat.**
- 1 tablespoon of salad dressing adds 7 **grams of fat** to 1 cup of salad.
- 1 tablespoon of mayonnaise adds 11 **grams of fat** to a sandwich.
- Pan-frying adds **6 grams of fat** to a 3-ounce serving of meat, poultry, or fish.
- Deep-frying adds 15 **grams of fat** to a 3-ounce serving of breaded meat, poultry, or fish.
- 3 tablespoons of gravy adds **2 grams of fat** to a 3-ounce serving of meat, poultry, or fish.
- 2 tablespoons of cheese of cream sauce adds 10 **grams of fat** to ½ cup of vegetables or potatoes.
- Marinating or stir-frying adds 4 **grams of fat** to ½ cup of vegetables.
- Deep-frying adds **8 grams of fat** to ½ cup of vegetables or potatoes.

A fiber-gram goal is easier to calculate than a fat-gram goal. Fiber amounts vary somewhat with height, weight, and calorie intake— less if you are shorter and more if you are taller. For fiber, I suggest 30 to 35 grams per day for colon cancer, and *at least* 25 to 30 grams

FAT AND FIBER GRAM CALCULATOR

Note: These are averages to help you easily estimate fat and fiber intake. For processed foods, read labels.

	FAT GRAMS	FIBER GRAMS
Food		
Fruit (small)	0	2
Vegetables (1 cup raw, ½ cup cooked	0	2
with light sauce or butter	2	2
with heavy sauce	10	2
stir-fried/marinated	4	2
Legumes (½ cup)	1	5
(beans, peas, lentils) with light sauce or butter	3	5
with heavy sauce or cheese	10	5
Grains (½ cup or 1 slice bread)	2	2
lightly buttered	4	2
heavily buttered	10	2
Nuts (1 ounce or 10–20 nuts)	15	2
Nonfat dairy products (1 cup)	0	0
Meat, fish, poultry* (3 ounces)	8	0
breaded and fried	23	0

*See chart on page 208 for meats, fish, and chicken.

for breast and other cancers. I do not recommend exceeding 35 grams of fiber per day.

Label reading will help you attain this goal as will the use of Chef Erickson's recipes. If your fiber goal is 30 to 35 grams, I strongly recommend you get this from fruits, vegetables, and whole grains, *not from food supplements* such as pills or powders. If you eat five complex carbohydrate servings and five fruit and vegetable servings a day, for example, this equals about 20 grams of fiber. Adding a high-fiber cereal at 12 grams equals 32 grams, and you've reached your daily total.

A Summary of the Eating Plan for the First Three Months

Month 1

Days 1 and 2

- Read chapter 9.
- Reread this chapter and the chapter pertinent to the disease you have or are interested in.

Day 3 or As Soon as Possible

- Discuss what you have learned and the proposed dietary changes with your physician, to be sure he or she approves—and understands that you want to make these changes to *add* to your treatment, not to replace standard treatment.

Day 4

- Begin the process of getting fat out of breakfast by preparing a grocery list and shopping. Include the following:

  —High-fiber cereal (see list, page 202, for examples; you may find another brand you like better, but be sure it is low-fat [2 grams of fat or less per serving] or nonfat. *Read the label.*)

—Favorite fortified cereal (2 grams of fat or less per serving)
—2% milk
—Egg substitutes—if you don't want cereal every day
—Jam, jelly, fat-free margarine, fat-free cream cheese—for toast
—Whole wheat bread
—Vitamin C fruit—oranges, grapefruits, strawberries, mangoes, etc.
—Fruit juice—if you like, but a glass does not count as a fruit because it has no or low fiber

Days 5 to 7

- Prepare first breakfast: One serving of your favorite fortified cereal with 2% milk; add 1 tablespoon of high-fiber cereal. Use sugar if you wish, or cinnamon and brown sugar. If you are diabetic, use proper sugar substitutes. Make wheat toast (as much as you want) and add jelly, jam, or fat-free cream cheese or fat-free margarine. Have at least one of the fruits you bought, and have your usual coffee with 2% milk (or half the amount of whole milk or cream you usually use). Fruit juice is fine. Have egg substitutes if desired (aim for three days or less per week of these substitutes).
- Start your walking program. If recovering from surgery or if you are taking radiation or chemotherapy, start gradually—to the corner and back, for example—with your doctor's okay. If you are able, walk five minutes daily or ten minutes three times a week.

Week 2

- Make another grocery list:

  - High-fiber cereal—vary brands if you wish, but your choice must have 2 grams or less fat per serving
  - Favorite fiber cereal (2 boxes)
  - 1% milk

    — Ingredients for Apple and Raisin Bran Muffins: (see pages 340–41 for recipe)

    — More nonfat condiments for toast (jam, jelly, fat-free cream cheese, fat-free margarine)

    — More whole wheat bread

    — More fruit

    — Fruit juice, if you like

- This week, add 2 tablespoons of high-fiber cereal to your favorite cereal. Fat-free egg substitutes can be eaten three days maximum per week, if desired, but don't let them substitute for servings of high-fiber cereals or fat-free, high-fiber muffins. Drink coffee and juice as desired. Use 1% milk in your coffee if desired. If the increased amount of fiber in your diet causes gas and cramps, increase your water and juice consumption to six to eight glasses a day.
- Continue to have one or more fruits at breakfast.
- Increase walking *as tolerated* to ten minutes, four to five times a week, or fifteen minutes three times a week.

Week 3

- Make another shopping list:

    — High-fiber cereal

    — Favorite fortified cereal

    — Fat-free muffins or ingredients

    — Skim milk

    — More whole wheat bread, condiments, fruit

    — High-fiber nonfat muffins

- This week, eat one serving of high-fiber cereal at least four of the days but preferably five or six. Continue fruit, coffee, juice. Use egg substitute on days when you're not eating high-fiber cereal, or your favorite cereal with 2 tablespoons of high-fiber cereal added, or 1½ Apple and Raisin Bran Muffins (10 grams fiber).

You may have these muffins on any or all days to substitute for the high-fiber cereal.

- Increase walking to twenty minutes daily or forty-five minutes three times a week. If it rains, walk in a mall as much as you're able.

Week 4

- Continue as in Week 3 to consolidate your almost fat-free breakfast pattern and your walking routine. Vary the cereal types to avoid boredom.

MONTH 2

You now have the fat out of breakfast. This month you will get the fat out of snacks (don't worry about lunch and dinner yet—they come in Month 3).

Week 1

- Prepare another grocery list:

  - Restock breakfast items as needed and continue fat-free breakfasts.
  - Buy carrots, and fruits in season.
  - See snack substitutions list (page 206) for no-fat snacks, and purchase those you like.

- At snack time, eat fruits and raw vegetables—at least one carrot and one fruit. Including your breakfast fruit, this is three fruits and vegetables a day. Have other snack foods in moderation. Your ultimate goal is at least six to eleven fruits and vegetables a day.

- Continue walking from now on—twenty minutes daily or forty-five minutes three times a week.

Week 2

- Continue your one carrot snack, but add to it two fruit snacks. This brings your total to four fruits and one vegetable a day. Have other no-fat snacks as desired, in moderation. Note: Large fruits count as two servings; a one-serving apple or orange is about the size of a tennis ball.

Week 3

- Continue with at least one carrot snack and increase to three fruit snacks and other no-fat snacks as desired. This equals six fruits and vegetables per day, counting the one at breakfast. You may use fat-free dips, such as salsa, fat-free cream cheese, or fat-free sour cream, for your veggies.

Week 4

- Continue with at least one carrot snack and increase to four fruit/vegetable snacks. You may not want other no-fat snacks at this point. With the breakfast fruit, you are up to six fruits and vegetables a day. With vegetables at lunch and dinner, you have reached the goal of six to eleven servings a day, easily.

MONTH 3

Now you're ready to tackle lunch and dinner.

- Make a new shopping list:

  - Fat-free breakfast items, as before
  - Fruits in season
  - Fresh, frozen, or canned vegetables
  - Pasta, rice, and other favorite complex carbohydrates
  - Nonfat dairy products (yogurt, skim milk nonfat "ice cream,"
etc.)
  - Lean meats
  - Also, items needed to make Chef Erickson's recipes for the
    week

- Your goal at the end of this month is six to eleven complex carbohydrates (remember that any of the fat-free snack pastries in the chart on page 206 are carbohydrates [grains], as are the breakfast cereals); six to eleven fruits and vegetables; three nonfat dairy products; and no more than 6 ounces of lean meat daily. (If you do exceed 6 ounces per day, you should make it up the next day with a vegetarian lunch and/or dinner.)
- Remember: Practice substitution and moderation, wherever and whenever possible.
- At the end of Month 3, you will be eating six to eleven fruits and vegetables (about 10 to 20 fiber grams), six to eleven servings of complex carbohydrates per day (12 to 22 fiber grams), and one serving of high-fiber cereal or 1½ Apple and Raisin Bran Muffins four or more days per week (10 to 13 grams of fiber). If you eat the maximum servings of all these, you could be eating too much fiber (50-plus grams). You should vary the amount of fiber-containing foods *to match your fiber-gram goal.* For example, if your goal is 30 to 35 grams daily, then five fruits and vegetables and six complex carbohydrates (total of 22 fiber grams) plus the high-fiber cereal equal 32 to 35 grams of fiber. If you have an egg substitute at breakfast, then eleven fruits and vegetables (22 fiber grams) and six complex carbohydrates (12 grams) is enough—or vice versa—eleven complex carbohydrates and five fruits and vegetables.
- If your goal is 25 grams or more, vary fiber intake accordingly,

but don't exceed 35 grams a day. You can reach 25 grams by eating six fruits and vegetables (12 grams) and seven carbohydrates (14 grams), or by one bowl of high-fiber cereal (10 grams), four fruits and vegetables (8 grams), and four carbohydrates (8 grams), for example.

• Congratulations—you're there!

10

CHOOSING AND
COOKING HEALTHY
FOODS

?&

TECHNIQUES FOR BEGINNING
THE RIGHT EATING PLAN

1. If you're trying to cut out fats, the place to start is by identifying the existing sources of fat in your diet.

- Check what you normally eat against the fat-gram counter (see page 404) to identify the fats you normally consume. Two good places to start are your pantry and refrigerator.

- Make a realistic determination of how much fat you are actually consuming. Make a list of all the fat sources you've stocked (½ pound cheese, ½ pound butter, etc.)—then one month later, list the quantities that still remain (accounting for restocking, of course) to give yourself an idea of how much of these fat sources you eat in a day, a week, a month.

- Come to an understanding of yourself and your needs. Make a list of the foods you feel you simply couldn't give up, and another list of the foods you really enjoy but wouldn't mind limiting or changing to fit the plan. Then review the lists of suggested substitutions, with the goal of getting the fat out of your *personal fat weaknesses,* such as cheeses, salad dressing, or ice cream.

- If you eat more than 1 ounce of cheese per day, begin to gradually decrease the amount (and fat grams)—not by eliminating cheese, but by substituting *nonfat* cheese.

2. Focus on healthy new choices.
- Fruits
- Vegetables
- Legumes and beans
- Grains
- Nonfat substitutions
- Nonfat snacks (see tables on pages 203 and 206)

3. Sharpen your shopping techniques.
- Read labels.
- Eat before you shop to prevent binge buying.
- Buy the lowest-fat brand available of any food.
- Buy nonfat substitutes when these are available, such as nonfat cheese, cake, "ice cream" products, candy (divinity, sugar candy, orange slices, for example), milk, yogurt, "cream cheese," "sour cream," mayonnaise, crackers, salad dressings, potato chips, and tortilla chips. As with any foods, there are differences among brands, so experiment until you find the brands you like. For many of these products, the price is approximately the same as products with fat, so it will be educational and healthful to use these for your entire family, not just for yourself.
- Stock up! This will help you on days when you are not feeling well, or when you are feeling tempted to backslide on your eating plan. Good items to keep on hand are nonfat or very low-fat pasta sauces, beans, tuna (packed in water), low-salt and low-fat chicken broth, nonfat cheese, frozen vegetables, and pastas. When you cook, double or triple portions and freeze the excess.
- There are many other hints for good grocery shopping in the next section.

4. Plan ahead.
- Shop wisely. A basic shopping list is provided in the next section. Over time, you may adapt it to fit your preferences and needs—

but always work from a list. This assures that you will make the proper purchases, and as consumer tests have shown, it will save money.

- Keep a list or notebook of foods that need to be replaced. Enlist your family's aid, asking them to note anything that they use up.
- If going out with friends to eat and shop, offset the inevitable extra fat grams by eating salads, veggies, fruit, and nonfat yogurt. If possible, have some cereal before you leave—this will take the edge off your appetite and help you resist temptation. The section entitled "Eating Out" in the previous chapter has some tips for restaurant dining.

5. Organize your refrigerator, pantry, menu plans, and approach to cooking, and take advantage of timesaving methods and equipment, such as your microwave.

- Think *simple*—for example, if you have the items from the basic shopping list on hand, you can create an almost instant meal by combining frozen veggies (spinach would be excellent!), cooked pasta, and nonfat cottage cheese. Chef Erickson's recipes are both delicious and simple to prepare.
- Assemble ingredients and equipment before you begin the task of cooking—this will save you many steps.
- Use the microwave to decrease the cooking time of vegetables and meats. A good rule of thumb is that microwave cooking requires one fourth the time that conventional cooking takes. So, if you would normally bake a dish for thirty minutes, the appropriate microwaving time would be seven to nine minutes. This rule does not apply to rice and some packaged goods; follow the instructions on the box. You may need to do some experimenting to get cooking times just right for your tastes.

6. Review your progress from time to time. For example, take stock of your eating goals at the end of Month 2 on the eating plan described in chapter 9.

- Review the new, nonfat substitutions in your refrigerator and pantry.
- If there are high-fat items still hiding in the corners, discard

them. Another tactic is to freeze such foods in individual servings in bags; for example, freeze butter in teaspoon-sized slices so you are not tempted to spread too much on bread. Bacon is used in some of Chef Erickson's recipes; freeze slices individually.

- List all of the fruits and vegetables that have replaced products with hidden fats.
- Take a moment to congratulate yourself for every first step of success, and for all the fat grams you've saved. The impact you are having on your health may be far greater than these simple changes suggest. For example, research has shown that for each 1,000 grams of increased fat intake per month, a person with breast cancer increases the risk of death from that illness 1.4 times.

7. Be firm in your resolve, but gentle with how you carry out that resolve. If you really want a particular food, remember that you are not cornered by your eating plan—in fact, your plan sets you free to exercise several options:
- Use the "rule of 10" (see page 213 in chapter 9).
- Consume the food in moderation.
- Make up for the extra fat grams by planning an extra nonfat meal for the following day—then stick to that plan.

Smart Shopping Tips

Many of the techniques for starting your new eating plan concern grocery shopping, so let's start there, too. Smart grocery shopping is crucial—because what you bring home is what you are going to eat.

- Buy whole-grain breads with 2 grams fat or less per serving. A whole bagel or English muffin, for example, has 2 grams fat.
- Buy only nonfat crackers (soda crackers, saltines).

- Choose cereals with 2 grams fat or less, preferably fortified, but remember to check the fiber content as well. Stock up on cereals with 8 grams or more fiber per serving.
- Make meat a secondary, not primary, shopping focus. Meat is now a condiment, not the most important meal element.
- Buy ground turkey, beef, or veal only if ground by the butcher for you, after taking off all fat. (To save money, buy quantities when on sale, then freeze 3-ounce portions to use later as needed.)
- Select tuna, sardines, and salmon packed in water rather than in oil.
- Frozen fish (plain, not battered or breaded) is also acceptable.
- If you buy low-fat luncheon meats, buy only those that have 2 grams of fat or less per serving. *Avoid luncheon meats with nitrates.*
- Beans are an excellent, inexpensive food. They are available in a rainbow of varieties, are simple to cook, and can be prepared entirely fat-free. They are wonderful in soups, stews, pasta, salads, rice salads, and succotash, or made into spreads. For a comparison of available protein in beans, meats, and fish, see the table below. Canned beans are good to have on hand when you are too tired to cook, but they are often prepared with fat, especially saturated fat. If you use canned beans, pork and beans, Senate bean soup, or vegetarian refried beans, skim the fat off (the yellow-white substance on top) after the can has been in the refrigerator for an hour or two, or in the freezer for fifteen minutes. The taste is the same and you eliminate a few fat grams. Also, rinsing canned beans reduces salt and "gas."

COMPARING BEANS, MEATS, AND FISH—YOU DECIDE

AMOUNT	FOOD	PROTEIN GRAMS	FAT GRAMS	FIBER GRAMS
1 cup	Lentils	17.9	0.7	6
1 cup	Kidney beans	15.4	0.3	6
3 ounces	Chicken	25	5	0
3 ounces	Beef round	22	6	0
3 ounces	Bass	16	3	0

- There are several brands of low-fat soups. Broth-based soups are usually lowest in fat. Store them in the refrigerator, unopened, and skim the fat off the top before heating.
- Buy nonfat milk and milk products: nonfat sour cream and yogurt, nonfat cheese, nonfat "ice cream," nonfat cottage cheese, nonfat cream cheese.
- Use nonfat margarine—it is available and tastes fine.
- Buy lots of pastas, but avoid cheese-filled types.

THE PRODUCE SECTION

When shopping, spend lots of time in the produce section. Consider experimenting with one or two fruits or vegetables that you don't usually have.

One of the secrets to success with your eating plan will be to base your menus on fruits and vegetables in season. They are always best just after they are harvested. The longer it takes them to get to market, the more they lose color, flavor, texture, and nutrients. Local farmers' markets tend to carry produce that has been grown nearby, which will be much fresher than that which has been trucked across the country. If you do not have access to such a market, try to shop where you know the produce has been properly cared for. The way to tell this is to take an overall look at the vegetable and fruit displays—what's your impression? Are the squash mottled, the fruits shriveled, and the green beans and carrots flabby? Are the apples routinely bruised and the bananas overripe? What about the lettuce—has it seen better days? You'll be able to tell if this is the best place to shop.

If there is a farmers' market in your local area, you will probably find a wider and fresher variety at better prices there. This can be especially helpful if you are one of the many cooks who have learned that it is very efficient to cook in large quantities once a week or once a month, then freeze portions for meals over the coming weeks. Inviting friends or family to share in the cooking will help you avoid fatigue.

A BASIC SHOPPING LIST

PRODUCE

Carrots—for the whole family, chopped and whole
Italian or cherry tomatoes (the latter require no slicing)
Sweet and Idaho potatoes
Lettuce, cabbage, onions (prechopped, if available)
Garlic (whole)
Other salad-bar produce, with no fat added
Green, red, yellow peppers
Fresh beans, broccoli, cauliflower, squash, corn

FRUITS (FRESH OR FROZEN)

Mangoes
Strawberries
Grapefruit
Oranges
Apples
Grapes
Kiwi
Raspberries
Other fruits in season
Unsweetened applesauce (substitute for fat in cooking)

BEANS
(DRIED AND CANNED; LITTLE OR NO SALT, IF POSSIBLE)

Black beans
Garbanzos
Kidney beans
Pinto beans
Lentils

BREADS, GRAINS, SNACK ITEMS
(WHOLE-GRAIN WHENEVER POSSIBLE)

Pita bread

Tortillas (lowest fat possible)

Bagels

English muffins

Nonfat, high-fiber muffins (5 grams fiber)

Rice, brown or white

Pastas

Cereals—a favorite fortified cereal and a cereal with 8 grams fiber
  or more per serving

Nonfat pastries

Nonfat cookies, nonfat cakes, nonfat crackers

Pretzels

Nonfat tortilla chips

Nonfat potato chips

Nonfat popcorn

DAIRY

Skim milk

Nonfat cottage cheese

Nonfat ricotta cheese

Nonfat cream cheese

Nonfat sour cream

Nonfat cheese (grated and ready to use)

Nonfat Parmesan

Nonfat yogurt

Egg substitute (read the label—avoid the ones with fat added)

Canned soups—reduced fat and sodium

Nonfat margarine

Meats (Fresh or Frozen)

For cuts, see chart "Leaner Meats" in chapter 9 (page 208)
Low-fat fish
Boneless, skinless chicken
Turkey breast—sliced
Low-fat beef
Lower-fat pork
Ground turkey, beef or veal (from lean cuts, with fat cut off)

Saving Time and Energy in the Grocery Store

Take advantage of the many new services that grocery stores now offer. In the produce section, you will find precleaned and chopped vegetables, shredded and prewashed cabbage for coleslaw, and ready-to-serve fruits. Many stores now maintain a completely stocked salad bar, including fat-free dressing. In some stores, the seafood department will steam your purchases, free of charge, and others will work from your list to gather and deliver your order.

You may be interested to know that the recently enacted Americans with Disabilities Act (ADA) entitles you to special assistance with your shopping if you feel you need it. The ADA has heightened the awareness of retailers to the needs of persons who are disabled, and in fact, mandates that establishments that serve the public make their services accessible to the disabled. You are, of course, a person on the road to recovery, and you may not be thinking of yourself as "disabled." But cancer and its treatment can be temporarily disabling. So if you are not feeling able to shop, you can ask at the service desk for assistance. "Assistance" can include giving your list to a clerk, who will collect your items for you while you wait (of course, as a courtesy to the store, it helps to make such requests at times when it isn't usually crowded). Many stores now offer wheelchairs or battery-powered vehicles for their customers' convenience; don't be shy about using these.

On days when you have obligations that will tire you or take you out of your home, such as a visit to the doctor, have some low-fat, lower-sodium frozen dinners on hand, or stop by the grocery store to pick up steamed seafood and a salad. A little planning can keep you away from the fast-food establishments, at a net savings of *many* fat grams.

STOCKING YOUR KITCHEN

Chef Erickson has provided this basic list for a well-stocked kitchen. All of Chef Erickson's recipes can be prepared with the items from this list.

HAND TOOLS

Vegetable peeler
Paring knife
Chef's knife
Bread knife
Rubber spatula
Measuring cups and spoons
Nylon pancake turner
Wire whisk
Pastry brush
Rolling pin
Potato masher
Vegetable grater
Fat-separating measuring cup (two spouts)

POTS AND PANS

Nonstick sauté pans, 6-inch and 10-inch
Saucepans: 1-quart, 2-quart, 3-quart, 4-quart
Coarse sieve

Fine sieve
Colander
Roasting pan
Stockpot, 3-gallon
Sheet trays
Cake rack
Nonstick muffin tin
Pancake griddle
Pan grill (ribbed cast-iron skillet)
Pie pan, 9-inch
Baking pan, 9-by-12-inch
Assorted mixing bowls
1-quart loaf pan
9-inch, 7-inch, 8-inch square cake pans
4-quart stewing pan or casserole
Individual soufflé molds
1½-quart soufflé dish
9-inch cheesecake pan

MISCELLANEOUS

Paper coffee filters
Portion scale
Pizza stone (or unglazed, untreated quarry tiles from your tile
   store)
Metal or bamboo skewers
Butcher's twine or cotton string
Cotton dishcloths

APPLIANCES

Blender
Meat thermometer
Immersion blender (optional)

Food processor (optional)
Pasta machine (optional)
Ice cream freezer
Microwave oven (optional)

STORING FOODS SAFELY

The shelf life of foods is an important factor at any time, but when you are dealing with cancer and cancer therapy, it becomes even more important. Since you may already be feeling finicky about foods, anything that has been on the shelf long enough to lose its color, texture, or flavor—or to develop off flavors—will not only spoil your appetite for the moment, but could leave you queasy for the rest of the day. Also, this is no time for a bout with food poisoning.

The way to prevent food spoilage or waste is to cook in small quantities, *or* cook in greater quantities, then immediately package the excess in freezer-proof containers, label and date, and put in the freezer promptly. Leftovers that have been in the refrigerator for a week are not good candidates for freezing and reheating.

To prevent waste and spoilage, maintain the appropriate temperatures (40 degrees F in the refrigerator, 0 degrees F in the freezer), and stock items in sections: (1) labeled and dated leftovers, in clear containers, which should be nearest the door so they won't get buried; (2) produce; (3) nonfat dairy products; (4) meats; (5) beverages; (6) sauces and condiments. Foods and liquids will expand when frozen, so allow room for this in the container. Make containers as airtight as possible.

Refer to the chart "How Long Does It Keep?"

HOW LONG DOES IT KEEP?

FOOD	APPROXIMATE REFRIGERATOR LIFE	APPROXIMATE FREEZER LIFE
Beef, mutton, veal, venison		
Cooked	3 days	2 months
Ground (cooked)	2 days	2 months
Ground (raw)	2 days	3 months
Steaks/roasts	3 days	9 months
Breads		
Quick baked	1 week	2 months
Yeast baked	1 week	4–8 months
Yeast unbaked	1–2 days	2 weeks
Cheese		
Cottage	Expiration date	1 month
Hard, semihard	Varies	6–12 months
Fish/Shellfish		
Crab/oysters	1–2 days	3–4 months
Fish (cooked)	1–2 days	2–3 months
Fish (raw)	1–2 days	3–4 months
Shrimp (cooked)	1–2 days	2–3 months
Shrimp (raw)	1–2 days	6 months
Fruits (PPFF)		
Citrus	1 week	3–4 months
Noncitrus (cooked)	1 week	12 months
Noncitrus (uncooked)	1 week	12 months
"Ice cream" product		1 month
Lamb		
Chops/roasts (cooked)	3–4 days	3 months
Chops/roasts (raw)	3–4 days	3 months
Ground (cooked)	1–2 days	2 months
Ground (raw)	3–5 days	3 months
Milk	Expiration date	1 month
Onions (raw, chopped)	2 days	3–6 months
Pizza	2–3 days	1 month

HOW LONG DOES IT KEEP? (cont.)

FOOD	APPROXIMATE REFRIGERATOR LIFE	APPROXIMATE FREEZER LIFE
Pork		
Ground (cooked)	1–2 days	2 months
Ground (raw)	3–5 days	3 months
Chops/roasts (cooked)	3–4 days	2 months
Chops/roasts (raw)	3–4 days	6 months
Poultry		
Pieces	1–2 days	8 months
Whole (raw)	1–2 days	12 months
Sandwiches (no mayonnaise)	3 days	1 month
Sherbet		1–3 months
Soups/stews	1 week	6 months
Vegetables		
Fresh	1 week	
Cooked	1 week	1 month
PPFF		12 months

Note: PPFF means "properly prepared for freezing," which varies widely for different fruits and vegetables. An excellent, inexpensive annual guide for freezing of all types of foods (as well as for home canning) can be obtained by writing for the *Ball Blue Book: The Guide to Home Canning and Freezing,* which is published by Ball Corporation, Consumer Products Division, Consumer Affairs, 345 South High Street, Muncie, Indiana 47305-2326.

Also note: Garlic, potatoes, and onions should not be refrigerated.

The following items do not freeze well: egg whites, fruit jelly in sandwiches, mayonnaise, meringue, prepared dishes containing bell peppers, onions, cloves, or synthetic vanilla, potatoes cooked in stews or soups, and raw vegetables.

SUBSTITUTING INGREDIENTS TO CUT FAT

By substituting ingredients, there's a lot you can do to adapt your favorite recipes for lunch and dinner to your new eating plan.

For example, a wonderful trick is to substitute applesauce for fat in baking. This works in pancakes, most muffin and nut bread recipes, and in brownies and cakes. The rule is to substitute in equal amounts—if your recipe calls for ½ cup fat, substitute ½ cup applesauce. The resulting reduction in fat can be dramatic. For example, the low-cholesterol directions for a popular pancake mix, including 1 tablespoon oil, yield pancakes with 5 grams of fat per serving. If you substitute 1 tablespoon of applesauce, the pancakes will have only 1 gram of fat per serving. And they're just as delicious. Serve these with fruit and syrup, and they are fat-free!

Here are some other examples of recipe adaptation.

GRANDMA'S DELICIOUS BUT FAT-LADEN LASAGNA
(10 SERVINGS)

INGREDIENTS	FAT GRAMS	FIBER GRAMS
½ pound lean ground beef	11	0
½ pound Italian sausage	56	0
½ cup chopped onion	0	0.6
1 clove garlic	0	0
32 ounces spaghetti sauce (canned)	44	0
8 ounces lasagna noodles	4.2	1.7
2 cups part-skim ricotta cheese	40	0
½ cup grated Parmesan cheese	12	0
3 cups part skim mozzarella cheese	108	0
Total per serving	28	0.2

This is how we grew up—28 grams of fat in a serving of lasagna! And that's with lean ground beef and part-skim cheeses, so you can imagine how high the count could go. What follows is the revised list of ingredients. The results are still delicious, but look at the difference in the fat and fiber contents.

ENLIGHTENED LASAGNA (10 SERVINGS)

INGREDIENTS	FAT GRAMS	FIBER GRAMS
½ cup chopped onion	0	0.6
2 10-ounce packages frozen spinach	0	6
2 cups nonfat cottage cheese	0	0
1 tablespoon grated Parmesan cheese	3	0
3 cups nonfat mozzarella cheese	0	0
8 ounces lasagna noodles	4.2	1.7
3 cups tomato sauce	0	2.0
2 cloves garlic, chopped	0	0
Total per serving	0.7	1

The enlightened method eliminated 27.3 grams of fat—and no one misses them! (Note also that Grandma's recipe involved meat that she had to brown in a pan before adding it to the sauce. This method of cooking retains the fat.)

Here's one way to adapt a packaged meal to reduce the fat content to about one fifth of the original recipe. As you can see, the product lacks fiber, so it would be important to round out this meal with high-fiber selections—for example, apple slices, a slice of high-fiber bread, and carrot sticks.

INGREDIENT SUBSTITUTIONS THAT CUT FAT

- Replace each whole egg in baking with two egg whites.
- Use nonfat yogurt instead of sour cream, heavy cream, oil, or mayonnaise to give velvety smoothness to dressings, sauces, and drinks. For cooked dishes that require sour cream, substitute the same amount of nonfat yogurt *plus* 1½ teaspoons of flour.

- Make nonfat Yogurt Cheese (see recipe, pages 386–87) and use in place of cream cheese to top bagels or to make cheesecake, or use nonfat cream cheese.
- Use evaporated skim milk in coffee or hot tea, cream-based soups, stews, and salad dressings.
- In baking recipes, replace whole milk with skim milk or no-fat buttermilk.
- Substitute an equivalent portion of applesauce for oil in muffins, sweet breads, cakes, and brownies. (Another way to do this is to

SMARTER SKILLET CHICKEN (4 SERVINGS)

INGREDIENTS	FAT GRAMS	FIBER GRAMS
¾ pound boneless, skinless chicken breast	12	0
Nonstick vegetable spray (for chicken)	1	0
Seasoning and rice packet	1	1
Nonstick vegetable spray (for rice— according to package directions)	1	0
2 egg whites OR egg substitute equivalent to 2 eggs	0	0
Total per serving	3.8	0.3

SKILLET CHICKEN HELPER (4 SERVINGS)

INGREDIENTS	FAT GRAMS	FIBER GRAMS
¾ pound boneless, skinless chicken breast	12	0
1 tablespoon margarine (for chicken)	12	0
Seasoning and rice packet (included in the package)	1	1
2 tablespoons margarine (for rice)	24	0
2 eggs	10	0
Total per serving	14.8	0.3

substitute an equivalent portion of nonfat yogurt; however, applesauce seems to give more satisfactory results.)
- Substitute unsweetened cocoa for baker's chocolate.
- Reduce ½ cup nuts in recipes to 1 tablespoon nuts.
- Replace ground beef with ground turkey and chicken (made to order by your butcher, without skin) in recipes. Reduce the meat to 3 ounces per person.

HEALTHY COOKING TECHNIQUES

It doesn't do you any good to select lean chicken breast if you then deep-fry it! Once you've selected healthy ingredients, you have to cook them in a way that keeps their fat content low. From an anticancer standpoint, cooking techniques are healthy if they add as few fats as possible.

Also, when cooking meat, avoid high-temperature methods such as frying, broiling, and grilling. Choose instead lower-heat (under 300 degrees), high-moisture methods such as stewing or braising—or use the microwave. The reason is the recent findings that high heat gives rise in meat to a variety of substances that have been shown to cause cancer in experimental animals. This subject is now under intensive investigation. Be sure, however, to cook all meats thoroughly to kill bacteria.

Here are some healthy, low-fat cooking techniques:

COATING THE PAN

- Use nonstick vegetable spray instead of butter, oil, or margarine to coat pots and pans. Better yet, use nonstick pans.
- Use a pastry brush if you must apply fats; use a cooking spray instead, whenever possible.

OVEN FRYING

Marinate or dip vegetables (for example, eggplant, tomatoes, or squash), meat, fish, poultry, or potatoes in a blend of nonfat yogurt, egg whites, and nonfat mayonnaise. Shake in a bag with nonfat bread crumbs, cornflake crumbs, or crumbs from crisp rice cereal, adding appropriate herbs as desired. Spray the baking pan and/or food with cooking spray, or brush with butter or margarine (no more than ¼ teaspoon per serving). Bake in oven at 300 degrees until done.

An alternative to this oven frying is to heat a nonstick coated frying pan until hot. Spray it with cooking spray. Add coated meat or vegetables and cook over medium heat until done, turning once.

When using the oven-frying or stovetop frying methods, serve the meat or vegetables on top of sauce, so that the outside of the food stays crisp.

BAKING

Baking in parchment paper makes it possible to prepare meat, fish, fruits, and vegetables with no additional fat. Place marinated fish or meat on a parchment square (about 8 inches square). For each part fish or meat, place two parts veggies on top. Fold up the packet and place it on a cookie sheet sprayed with cooking spray. Bake at 300 degrees until steam puffs up the paper square (about fifteen minutes). A sample recipe is chicken covered with thin slices of carrots, onions, and basil with Creamy Herb Salad Dressing (see page 374). Aluminum foil can be substituted for parchment.

STIR-FRYING

Stir-frying is an excellent, low-fat way to prepare vegetables, fish, meat, or poultry. In this method, the foods are cooked by the heat of the pan, not the heat of oil. The foods are stirred in the pan to promote cooking, preserving the color, texture, and nutrition. This method lends itself well to creativity.

A good basic rule is to use 3 cups vegetables to every 1 cup meat, fish, or poultry. The meat should be cooked first, in the pan or wok in ideally no more than 1 teaspoon of oil. Ginger or scallions stirred into the oil adds a nice flavor. Remove the meat from the pan when done, then add vegetables, and stir-fry briefly (cooking too long will make them soggy). Return meat to complete the stir-frying. For a tasty thickener, add spices to cornstarch and a small amount of wine, water, or stock.

To save clean-up effort, after cooking rinse the pan or wok immediately with very hot water and return it to the heat to dry.

POACHING

This is an excellent, gentle way to prepare fish (including shellfish), meat, or poultry without fat. The liquid, which should be gently simmering (not boiling), gains flavor from the food and gives flavor and moisture to the food. Fish or shellfish should be started in cold liquid, which makes it possible to cook the fish evenly. For poaching, fish can be wrapped in cheesecloth, which will hold the fish together and prevent the skin from bursting. Meat poaches beautifully if not left in too long; overpoaching makes the meat tough and the broth unclear. Poached poultry is very delicate.

STEWING

Whenever possible, cook soups and stews several hours or a day ahead, refrigerate until the fat solidifies on top, then skim it off. If you're in a hurry, you can add ice cubes to the stock or meat drippings and pour it all into a fat-separating measuring cup.

MICROWAVING

One of the handiest tools for quick fixes is the microwave. Don't overlook its value in defrosting foods, as well as reheating and cooking. To reheat frozen leftovers, begin on high to soften, then reduce the power to 50 percent. When reheating the rice, noodles, casseroles, and vegetables, you should add 1 tablespoon water per serving. Fish that is steamed in the microwave tastes poached. Microwave-poached chicken in stock is good in soups or salads (not as an entree). If your microwave is sufficiently large, you can cook a turkey breast down in it until it's half-done, and then cook it breast up in a conventional oven until done; the results are brown, crisp, and juicy. (A turkey larger than 12 pounds may be too large for most microwaves.) If you have questions about turkey preparation, the packaging often lists a toll-free number to call.

MAKING SAUCES

- Add nonfat dry milk to soups and sauces for richness without the fat or cream.
- To make a delicious very-low-fat meat sauce, set the cooked meat aside where it will stay warm. Pour the drippings into a fat-separating measuring cup and let set until the fat floats to the top; pour off the defatted liquid and save. Pour the defatted drippings back into the pan. Cook to reduce by half. Dissolve a small amount of cornstarch in a little water or wine and pour into barely simmering juices. Cook briefly; extending boiling will thin the sauce.
- Thicken soups and sauces or defatted pan drippings with vegetable purees instead of a butter-flour "roux." To make a puree, whirl carrots, sweet potato, potato, tomato, or leek in the food processor or blender, then simmer until the volume decreases, to concentrate the taste.

Cooking Beans

Beans can be prepared entirely fat-free. They should be washed carefully, removing any stones, grit, and debris, then soaked overnight in cold water or for one hour in water that has been brought to a boil. (Lentils and split peas do not require presoaking.) Soaking and discarding the water the beans soaked in before cooking has been suggested as a way to reduce the gas that beans cause in some people.

Cooking times for beans vary, but most are cooked within one hour. If you are adding seasoning vegetables (onions, garlic, green pepper), these can be sautéed in a nonstick pan with a spritz of nonstick spray, or cooked in the bean liquid along with the beans. One pound of large, dry beans (for example, kidney beans) is equivalent to 5½ cups cooked. One pound of small, dry beans equals 2 to 3 cups cooked. One cup of uncooked lentils equals about 2½ cups cooked. One cup of uncooked split peas equals 2½ to 3 cups cooked.

Refried beans are a wonderful, very quick south-of-the-border treat with fat-free tortilla chips and salsa. To refry without fat, use a nonstick pan coated with cooking spray. If you add cheese in your refried beans, choose nonfat cheese and sprinkle a thin layer on top, instead of blending it in—you'll use less cheese this way.

Steaming Vegetables

Steaming vegetables is the best way—short of serving them raw—to retain nutrients and avoid fat. The liquid should boil, but never touch the food. Steaming is a wonderful way to produce flavorful vegetables, but if you want to boil them instead, save the stock for cooking pasta or rice afterwards.

Microwaving is another way to steam foods (see the table on pp. 249–50). Vegetables lose less water-soluble nutrients when microwaved than when steamed. Cut vegetables into equal-sized pieces. When cooking vegetables or fruits whole, be sure to pierce them with a knife to allow steam to escape (if you forget this step, you

STEAMING VEGETABLES

VEGETABLE	STEAMING TIME (MINUTES)
Artichokes	30–60
Asparagus	3
Beets	30
Broccoli	3–5
Brussels sprouts	15
Cabbage	7
Carrots	3–5
Cauliflower	3–5
Corn, on cob	3
Corn, kernel	3
Greens, leafy	20
Green beans	3
Parsnips	5–15
Peas	2
Peppers	3
Summer squash	3
Winter squash	45

risk an explosion of the food in the microwave, which is both messy and potentially injurious). Most vegetables should be microwaved in a baking dish with 2 tablespoons of water added, covered, then cooked on high. Seasonings or sauces should be added after cooking.

ENHANCING FLAVORS

Until your palate becomes accustomed to the leaner, healthier foods you are now emphasizing in your diet, less fat may seem the same as less flavor. Be creative, using wines, fruit juices, herbs, spices, balsamic and other vinegars, and low-fat sauces (see Chef Erickson's recipes) to enhance flavors. Some tips appear on pp. 250–51.

MICROWAVING FRESH VEGETABLES

Note: For frozen vegetables, follow directions on the package.

Cooking Time (minutes)	Standing Time (minutes)	Fat Grams	Fiber Grams
Artichoke—2; cook in parchment paper			
8–10	5	0.2	2
Asparagus—1 pound (5 servings); add 2 tablespoons water			
4–7	1	0.3	1.6
Green beans—1 pound; add 2 tablespoons water			
5–7	2	0.2	2.1
Broccoli—1 pound; slit stalks; add 2 tablespoons water			
6–8	2	0.2	0.6
Brussels sprouts—10 ounces (tub); add 2 tablespoons water			
5–7	2	0.2	4.1
Carrots—1 pound; sliced; add 2 tablespoons water			
6–8	1	0.1	2.5
Cauliflower, cut—1 pound; add 2 tablespoons water			
6–8	2	0.1	2.3
Cauliflower, whole—1½ pounds; add 2 tablespoons water			
11–13	3	0.5	2
Corn on the cob—2 ears; remove husk, sprinkle with water			
3–4	3	4	2
Eggplant, cubed—1 pound; add 2 tablespoons water			
6–8	1	0	2
Eggplant, whole—1¼ pounds; pierce with fork			
4–7	3	0.5	2

MICROWAVING FRESH VEGETABLES (cont.)

Note: For frozen vegetables, follow directions on the package.

COOKING TIME (MINUTES)	STANDING TIME (MINUTES)	FAT GRAMS	FIBER GRAMS
Onions—1 pound; add 2 tablespoons water			
4–8	2	0.2	2.2
Parsnips—1 pound; sliced; add 2 tablespoons water			
6–8	2	0.2	2.1
Peas—1½ pounds; add 3 tablespoons water			
5–7	1	0.2	2
Potatoes, new—2 servings, each 6–8 ounces; pierce with fork			
6–8	5	0.2	2
Potatoes, sweet or Idaho—2; pierce with fork			
4–6	5	0	4
Snow peas—1 pound; add 2 tablespoons water			
4–6	1	0.2	2
Squash, summer; 1 pound; add 2 tablespoons water; pierce with fork			
4–6	1	0.2	2
Squash, winter; 1 pound; pierce with fork			
6–8	5	0.2	2

- Instead of butter and sour cream, flavor food with herbs, spices, vinegar, or fresh lemon juice. If you do use dairy products, use ½ teaspoon butter, nonfat margarine, or nonfat sour cream.
- Enhance the flavor of plain vegetables with balsamic vinegar, tomato sauce, lemon juice, nonfat margarine, or Creamy Herb Salad Dressing (see page 374) instead of butter.
- Some butter-in-a-shaker products might contain some fat, but several of these are nonfat and are a good way to season vegeta-

bles, popcorn, and other foods that customarily would be buttered. Read the label carefully.

- Nonfat salad dressings make wonderful marinades, promoting both flavor and tenderness.
- Chef Erickson's sauces also make wonderful marinades. Use them as glazes during cooking.

USING HERBS AND SPICES

Herbs are especially useful for kitchen magic. For meals that are cooked ahead, save all or part of the herb additions until warming the food for serving. To get the maximum flavor from herbs, chop just before using.

You can build a collection of herbs from the grocery store, but growing your own is an immensely satisfying, low-key activity that you might consider, especially if you're not up to bigger gardening tasks.

Some herbs will grow in pots on a sunny windowsill, and most will thrive in a postage-stamp garden. Some herbs, like thyme and oregano, are perennials and will come up year after year. Fresh-picked basil will transform a ho-hum spaghetti sauce into a culinary event—and this sturdy plant quickly produces more than one family can use at a time. Mint—an old Southern favorite—is also vigorous and hardy; the weedings make great "new neighbor" or "thanks for being patient while I grumbled about my miseries" gifts (by the way, the proper way to make mint iced tea is to steep fresh, washed leaves in the boiling water with tea—that sprig on the side of the glass is just for show). There are many other herbs available in seed packets or sprouted for you at your local nursery.

The chart has a summary of the standard uses for herbs, but don't let these limit you; experimenting is what it's all about. All the recipes in this book use fresh herbs unless otherwise specified. Just remember that fresh herbs tend to be milder in flavor than dried herbs. A good basic rule is to double the amount of fresh herbs; if

SUGGESTED USES FOR HERBS AND SPICES

To flavor:	Use:
Fruits and vegetables	Basil, caraway, chives, cinnamon, cloves, dill, ginger, marjoram, mint, nutmeg, oregano, paprika, rosemary, savory, tarragon, thyme
Meats	
Beef	Chives, garlic, oregano
Lamb	Basil, garlic, mint, oregano, rosemary
Pork	Coriander, ginger, sage, thyme
Poultry	Garlic, oregano, rosemary, sage
Seafood	Dill, fennel, tarragon, thyme
Pasta	Basil, chives, garlic, parsley, thyme
Potatoes	Chives, garlic, paprika, pepper, rosemary
Salads	Basil, chervil, chives, dill, marjoram, mint, parsley

the recipe calls for 1 teaspoon dried marjoram, you should use 2 teaspoons fresh marjoram.

COOKING IN A HURRY

Every cook has shortcuts for those days when there just isn't time, energy, or interest in serious cooking. This is fine—as long as the shortcut doesn't take you to the fast-food place for a cheeseburger, fries, and milk shake. As mentioned earlier, most of Chef Erickson's recipes take only twenty minutes to put together.

One of the quickest ways to puncture your resolve to cook and eat properly is to go to the kitchen and find that you have everything on hand—*except* the pasta, or the cottage cheese, or another basic ingredient. That's why the basic shopping list and careful record keeping are so important. Even so, you can often start with the basic idea, substitute items, and create something entirely new. Here is an example of a low-fat fix.

MAÑANA-IS-HERE-AND-I'M-STILL-NOT-READY SUPPER

1 or 2 cans vegetarian chili
1 can stewed tomatoes (Mexican-style is even better)
Tortillas

If the chili contains fat, put the can(s) in the freezer for 5 minutes, then open and skim off the fat. Mix the chili and tomatoes in a sprayed, nonstick pan; simmer until the tomato liquid is reduced by half. Toast tortillas 5 to 7 minutes. Great accompaniments: salad and a dollop of nonfat "sour cream." Supper's ready!

11

SUPPORTING CANCER RECOVERY WITH EXERCISE AND SEXUALITY

ᐧᐧ

S
ince your health-care team is focusing on other aspects of your care, exercise may never come up in your visits to the clinic or physician's office. Chances are that this will be just fine with you at first, because it is not likely to be high on your list of priorities then. As your treatment proceeds, though, you may well have questions both about exercise itself and how it can complement your nutritional plan.

The Federal Centers for Disease Control and Prevention have estimated that almost 60 percent of Americans over age eighteen are physically inactive, increasing their risk of severe diseases. So if you have not been very physically active you are not alone.

A NEW DEFINITION OF EXERCISE

What does the word *exercise* suggest to you? Do you see young, muscular people flying down a snowy slope? Or a middle-aged person huffing and puffing on a treadmill? Do you hear the phrase, "No pain, no gain"?

Let's toss those notions out of the window and start with a sensible new definition: Exercise is moving your body or parts of your body through space, at any pace that suits you, and it can be done in a bed, on a floor, in a wheelchair, or anywhere else you happen to be. Exercise has different meanings at different ages and at different phases of your life (or, as the beautiful words of the *Desiderata* suggest, "Surrender gracefully the things of youth"). And if it hurts, you're overdoing it.

Think of stretching your arms, bending your knees, flexing your ankles gently in bed, perhaps to a slow and lovely piece of music.

Think of walking a tiny distance today, perhaps from your bed to the bathroom. Imagine walking from your bed, to the bathroom, to the living room tomorrow. Fantasize walking all the way to the front porch on the next day, and into the garden on the fourth.

Moving your body through space is important for many reasons. It stimulates your circulation and respiration, and the resulting increase in oxygen throughout the body gives you a mental, emotional, and physical lift. Exercise helps maintain a healthy blood pressure. It is absolutely essential to muscle tone, including the most important muscle, your heart. Exercise improves joint mobility and strengthens bone. The risk of developing osteoporosis is increased by inactivity, especially bed rest for prolonged periods. This can be countered by properly performed exercise.

Exercise is also a marvelous way to purge yourself of the invisible poisons that build up through stress: anxiety, fear, sadness, anger. Exercise can stimulate a picky appetite, eliminate fatigue, and assist your body in achieving sound and restorative sleep.

Walking, for most people, is an excellent exercise. It involves the large muscles of the arms and legs, which increases circulation and strengthens the heart. It also promotes an increase in lean body mass and makes bones stronger. As your strength and endurance increase, so will your self-esteem and confidence. You may find that a walk makes you hungry and relaxes you so you enjoy your mealtime. Other benefits of exercise in combatting cancer are given later in the chapter.

When you are dealing with cancer, moving your body through space will get you out of the bed or off the sofa, especially if you have a partner to encourage you. It will take you to other parts of your home or neighborhood and give you a whole new perspective on your situation. It will alleviate *boredom,* which is not so much a state of mind as it is a painful emotion that we feel when our routine is scaled back by hours and hours of cancer treatments.

Finally, exercise burns up fat stored in the body, and for that reason, it has a very important place in any well-rounded program of nutrition. This is especially true if there is excess weight to be dealt with. People are often surprised to hear that many individuals with cancer *gain* weight. For example, as discussed fully later, hormonal therapy and chemotherapy for breast cancer can cause weight gain. The weight gain can be discouraging for the person who experiences it, and can cause additional stumbling blocks to recovery. Exercise can help overcome these problems.

SPECIAL ROLES OF EXERCISE IN CANCER

Aside from the general benefits of exercise, there are benefits that are particular to cancer.

First, as pointed out in chapter 2, "The Connection Between Cancer and Diet," excess calories themselves may be detrimental. If so, burning off calories by exercise would be a preventive measure. Studies suggest that it may be very important for women with breast cancer to decrease overall body fat. Exercise is one way to achieve this.

Several studies have looked at exercise as a way of overcoming cancer cachexia, the condition in some cases of advanced cancer when a person suffers debilitating loss of weight and strength, even when eating an adequate amount of food. Exercise may help in two ways. One, exercise can improve the body's conversion of glucose to useful energy. And two, exercise may make the body more sensitive to insulin. This is an important feature when insulin resistance develops in association with cancer cachexia, causing the body not to use sugar well. (See chapter 2.)

Some fascinating findings are coming out of studies of the Zuni Indians in New Mexico, who have a phenomenally high rate of diabetes. The Zunis are the oldest Americans. They have lived in this country for longer than any other tribe, and throughout their history, they were runners. Relay races and other forms of running were integral to their culture for over a thousand years. Some time in this century, the tradition was dropped. Soon after, the incidence of diabetes in these people rose sharply, and in fact, it has nearly decimated the tribe.

Studies of genetic patterns among the Zunis have uncovered the culprit in their diabetes: a gene that made it possible for the Zunis to extract a great deal of energy from the body's nutritional stores; thus, they were able to run long distances, very thriftily using up the available energy. *Once they ceased running, the healthy purpose of the gene was thwarted, and diabetes developed.* Though many of the elderly cannot benefit from these findings, the tribe is making great strides in reviving running, especially among schoolchildren, in hopes of forestalling or avoiding the disease.

These findings certainly provide sobering food for thought about the relationship between health and exercise. As the Zunis have learned to control diabetes with proper diet, weight control, and especially exercise, so are persons with cancer learning to use these measures to help prevent cancer or its recurrence.

When scientists attempt to study the relationship between exercise and cancer cachexia, their work is complicated by the fact that the study participants have far-advanced disease. Nevertheless, I think that over time we will find the two to be related, and it's safe to say that, when done in moderation and with your physician's permission, exercise is not likely to cause harm.

It is reasonable that exercise, by decreasing body fat and increasing lean body mass, will help create a more favorable hormonal balance in early breast cancer and perhaps other hormonally sensitive cancers. Of course, strengthening the lungs, heart muscles, and bones should help with any chronic disease.

Several studies have shown that physical activity may indeed protect against certain types of cancer in animals. Experiments have shown that *moderately* exercised animals have fewer chemically induced breast cancers than did either sedentary or highly exercised animals. Exercise has also been shown to reduce carcinogen-induced colon tumors in physically active rats, compared to sedentary animals.

One study in humans looked at more than 17,000 college graduates over more than three decades. In this group, physical activity (measured by walking, stair climbing, and sports participation) was associated with a decreased risk of developing colon cancer, if the activity level was high (more than 2,500 calories expended per week).

Exercise may help prevent colon cancer because it helps prevent chronic constipation. Exercise helps things keep moving along in several ways.

- Laboratory studies have shown that walking increases the speed at which waste matter moves through the colon. As explained earlier, this decreases the time that potentially carcinogenic materials are in contact with the cells of the colon. (In fact, excessive exercise may speed things up too much, because in long-distance runners, diarrhea is sometimes a problem.)
- The vagus nerve, which controls waves of contraction and release in the intestines, is stimulated by aerobic exercise.
- Exercise has been found to raise blood levels of prostaglandins, which among other things increase movement of food through the colon.
- Exercise increases levels of gastroenteropancreatic hormones, which also are associated with movement of wastes through the colon.

Besides speeding food through the gastrointestinal tract, exercise may also help prevent colon cancer in other ways.

- Exercise may increase levels of interleukins (substances involved in immunity). Decreased levels of interleukins in animals have been associated with tumor growth and spread.
- Exercised animals also have increased levels of several antioxidant compounds, which may have a protective effect in colon cancer.
- Exercise can reduce cholesterol levels, which may decrease bile acid formation and help prevent colon cancer.

That's quite a list of rather complicated ways that exercise may help prevent colon cancer. Clearly, the relationship between exercise and cancer is complex, and learning more about it is important. Available data do not allow a precise judgment about whether exercise can prevent the recurrence of disease after treatment. In a breast cancer recurrence prevention project, we are looking at the effects of walking as an adjunct to diet, but it will be a while before we have the results of this study.

Though all of these findings are fragments, rather than fully formed pieces of the cancer puzzle, I think that it is very prudent to adopt a regular program of exercise as a way of helping to prevent recurrence if you have had cancer treated for cure. Even if the program does nothing to actually prevent recurrence, exercise clearly makes the body stronger, including the heart, lungs, muscles, and bones.

YOUR EXERCISE PROGRAM

It's important to discuss any plans for exercise with your health-care provider. But even if your physical capacity is very limited, you can improve your quality of life by exercising.

As soon as you are up to it, walking is an excellent way to exercise. Walking requires little in the way of gear (a pair of sneakers or walking shoes will do), has a fully adjustable speed range (go as fast or as slow as you feel is right for you), can be done anywhere (do it in your front yard or on a mountaintop), and can be done in total solitude or by the thousands.

I think your chances of long-term success are much better if you have an exercise partner. In your neighborhood or park, a walking buddy provides good company, an added margin of safety, and assistance for you in the event you become tired. Many places now have walking groups that get together at local malls, rain or shine, and often these excursions conclude with coffee or tea and good conversation. (In my community there is a group that calls itself the Walkie-Talkies, which is an excellent description of how they divide their time.)

If you live near an ocean or lake or have access to a pool, a wonderful way to get a double return is to walk in water, which provides buoyancy and support for your body and uses more energy without putting more stress on the body.

You should be cautious about walking if you have a problem with weight-bearing bones, especially metastatic disease in these bones. In this case, your physician's input will be vital to your decisions about exercise, and it may be helpful to include a physical therapist in the planning and developing of a program that is safe and beneficial for you.

In the chart below are some of the common activities you can do and a rough estimate of calories expended in each (the exact amount of calories used depends on your body size, your metabolic rate, and the intensity of the activity).

As you can see, the number of calories expended in an hour of walking is substantial and not much different from biking or tennis. Not everyone can play tennis, but almost everyone can walk, even when undergoing chemotherapy or radiotherapy. This is why I recommend walking as the best exercise.

If you decide that walking is appealing and appropriate for you, and your physician agrees, start out slowly. *Your physician's approval is always important, but is especially needed if you have any cardiac or skeletal problems.* Always begin with a warm-up, walking slowly for about five minutes, and then stretch your leg muscles lightly. Walk twenty minutes three times a week to start. Increase this to forty-

ACTIVITY	ESTIMATED CALORIES USED PER 30 MINUTES
Walking	150
Golf	150
Biking	150
Singles tennis	175
Table tennis	100

five minutes three times a week or an equivalent amount daily (i.e., five to ten minutes every day). At the end of your walk, cool down by walking slowly for another five minutes. Walk with a partner if you can.

Swimming is also an excellent exercise. So is dancing, and it can provide time to be close to your spouse or partner.

INTIMACY AND SEX

There's another side of "getting physical" that will be affected by your cancer. And like walking and other forms of exercise, it too can help your recovery—in psychological ways.

In facing cancer you also will be facing one of the greatest challenges to your relationships with others, especially to your spouse or significant other. There will be many issues to deal with, from the shock of hearing the diagnosis and fear about one's mortality, to the reality of losing time from work or home endeavors in order to take treatments, to the unwelcome task of getting everyone else—like the insurance company—to do their part so you can keep your household afloat.

Even if your cancer is localized and you are assured of a cure, both you and your partner will find yourself grappling with sobering questions about life and death—your own and each other's. As we've discussed in other chapters, treatment for cancer with surgery, radiation, and chemotherapy can cause many side effects, including fatigue and physical discomforts. If you are undergoing treatment for prostate cancer or have lost a breast, if you have lost your hair to chemotherapy, you must deal with the deepest questions of self-image, masculinity/femininity, and what roles these play in your most intimate relationship.

If this were a script for a TV movie about the problems cancer causes, instead of a book for people with the real thing, we'd probably cast everyone as good-looking, supportive, understanding, patient, resourceful, and loving. Depending on how long we have between commercials, we'd present little vignettes of angry words, anxious moments, and struggle, then neatly resolve them in time for the late news.

I'm sure you know that's totally unrealistic. The truth is that cancer and its treatment will have an impact on your daily life, including sexual patterns and intimate relationships with your spouse. In fact, sexual activity may cease for a while. For one thing, your spouse may fear causing you more pain and discomfort. For another, your own anger at being sick and guilt feelings about how cancer is affecting your family may make you want to curl up in a closet.

There is some very good news for you. Though your relationship will go through some stormy moments (or scarier still, some long, thunderous silences), *chances are that you will get through this together.* Studies have shown that couples who have a basically sound relationship before one of the partners is diagnosed with cancer will emerge from the cancer experience at least as close as before, and possibly much closer and stronger. And in some struggling relationships, the reality of cancer puts everything else in perspective. People can learn to appreciate one another better as they deal with the challenges of this disease, especially if they strive for open communication, patience, and empathy.

After treatment, as you develop your eating and exercise plans, you will find that it is very helpful to make changes together. We've talked about how much having an exercise partner increases the chances you'll stick with it. Dietary changes, too, are better adopted when the whole household makes them, especially if cutting down on fats and increasing fiber are the cornerstones of your plan. If your diet is to address some special need not shared by your partner, it can be adapted. But all in all, a healthy exercise and nutrition plan will help reduce your partner's risk of developing cancer, while helping to support your recovery.

By rebuilding your dietary patterns, exercising together, and working through a mountain of problems together, you have already begun the work of forging a stronger partnership, in all aspects of life. Eventually you will be ready to rekindle your intimate relationship as well—not only to overcome whatever problems the cancer caused, but also to renovate dull patterns that may have crept into your relationship over the years.

Interestingly, many cancer survivors describe cancer as an opportunity, as well as an ordeal. In support of that, I propose to you that during your illness, you and your spouse or partner have probably been collecting good memories as well as bad, and you have developed new relationships—perhaps even friendships—with members of your health-care team and other families dealing with cancer. Together, you and these new people in your life have appreciated, as no one else can, what's really important in life.

In my work in oncology, I have seen many couples go through this, and I am especially impressed at how the spouse of the person with cancer must—and usually does—work through the same challenges and feelings that the patient does. It can bring people much closer together and result in a better sex life.

Since so much of your time in treatment has been spent dealing with "heavy" issues, the period after treatment is just right for reflecting on your early courtship and the laughter and excitement of that time. What made your spouse happy then may still work now—and no one knows better than you what the intimate and emotional needs of your spouse are. Don't feel you have to focus right away on a deep discussion of troubling issues. There will be times when this comes up naturally.

During therapy, you and your spouse spent a lot of time chair-bound, bed-bound, or house-bound. This can become a frame of mind if you let it. Get out of the house together. Go to a movie. Pack up your breakfast and picnic in the park. Take a weekend drive to the mountains or the shore, and stay in a motel. If at first you don't feel ready for sex, you can still share feelings and emotions with your spouse, reconnect emotionally, and hold each other.

If either of you feels fear or concern about the possibility of feeling or causing pain or injury to areas that were treated surgically, consult with your health-care provider.

Both your needs and your spouse's needs may change as healing occurs. Build from one love-sharing session to the next and be alert to these changing needs. Touch and compassion may be sufficient at first. You may find that taking turns giving and receiving pleasure is less threatening until you are reacquainted and more sure of yourselves. As the relationship renews, be honest with each other. Again, you have an opportunity to discard some "old stuff" that somehow worked its way into your relationship and became routine. Don't assume that what you have always done is the best way for the present.

Tell each other what you like and don't like. If you are uncomfortable with being touched (for example, in scarred areas), gently lead your partner to what you need. Music and wine and candlelight can be especially helpful to alleviate lingering tensions. Foreplay will reconnect you emotionally and allow you to express your caring for each other. Take all the time you need and savor these moments together. You've earned it.

PART 4

RECIPES AND MENUS

RECIPES

≷❧

T oo many times, when people think of eating healthfully, they think about what they'll have to give up. I want you to be able to think instead about the marvelous culinary adventures that lie ahead. With that goal, I went to one of our country's most talented young chefs, Mark Erickson, and asked him to create a collection of imaginative recipes that would suggest wonderful new ways to eat healthfully.

These recipes will help you reduce dietary fats, increase fiber, and eat a wide variety of fruits and vegetables with their various benefits. (Low fat has been defined as approximately 20 percent of calories as fat.) Some of the recipes can also help with special needs (see chapter 8, "Solving Nutrition Problems and Improving Well-being During Treatment").

At the end of the collection are some sauces, condiments, and other versatile base recipes. These are components of some of the other dishes in the book, but they can also be used in many other ways. Think of them as basic building blocks in your low-fat kitchen.

Some of the recipes are quite elegant, but you'll find that they are less difficult and take much less time than they look. There are a few recipes in the collection that take a bit more time—for holidays and celebrations and for times when you want to make yourself something extra special, or someone who loves you wants to make something special for you.

There is an aspect of nutrition that cannot be accounted for in a recipe, and that is the magic that occurs in each cook's hands. Maybe it has to do with the ghosts of conversations hanging in the air or the angle at which sunlight comes through the kitchen windows. We hope that you will enjoy making these recipes. And we know that if you don't feel up to doing your own cooking, any friend or family member you ask for help will be greatly reassured by having a meaningful role in your care and recovery. Please remember that if you are on a sodium restricted diet, some of the recipes in this book should be modified to reduce their salt content.

Soups and Chowders

Chicken Paprikash Soup

YIELD: 10 SERVINGS

This hearty broth is garnished with a zip of yogurt.

1 teaspoon oil

1 cup minced onions

2 cloves garlic, minced

1 pound skinless, boneless chicken
   breast, in ½-inch dice

4 tablespoons Hungarian paprika

2 tablespoons grated lemon zest

1½ teaspoons caraway seeds,
   crushed

8 cups chicken broth

1 cup all-purpose flour

1 teaspoon baking powder

1 egg

½ cup skim milk

½ teaspoon salt

⅛ teaspoon white pepper

¼ cup chopped parsley

5 ounces nonfat yogurt

1. Heat oil in a large saucepan over high heat and add the onions and garlic. Sauté until onions become translucent, about 2 minutes. Add the chicken and continue to cook for 5 minutes, or until the chicken meat begins to brown slightly. Add the paprika, lemon zest, and caraway and continue to cook until an aroma of the seasonings rises from the pan. Add the chicken broth and bring to a simmer.

2. In a small bowl, combine the flour, baking powder, egg, skim milk, salt, and pepper. Work with a spoon until a stiff paste develops. Using two small spoons scoop dumplings the size of lima beans into the simmering soup. When all the batter is used, allow soup to simmer for 15 minutes. Remove from heat.

3. Add the parsley. Adjust the seasoning.

4. Serve, topping each bowl with a tablespoon of yogurt. Or refrigerate and reheat as needed.

Per serving (1 cup):

fat grams 3

fiber grams 1

calories 157

protein grams 18

carbohydrate grams 14

sodium milligrams 336

Old-fashioned Chicken Vegetable Soup with Rice

YIELD: 10 SERVINGS

For many, chicken soup is the quintessential comfort food. This will keep for up to a week in the refrigerator, so it can be prepared well in advance and reserved for a day when you don't feel like cooking. It can also be frozen.

1 whole chicken	*1 teaspoon salt*
3 quarts cold water	*1 carrot, peeled and diced*
2 bay leaves	*2 ribs celery, diced*
10 peppercorns	*1 leek, diced*
Pinch of thyme leaves	*1 cup brown rice*
2 tablespoons parsley stems	*1/4 cup chopped parsley*

1. Remove the skin and cavity fat from the chicken. Place in a 6-quart soup pot and add the cold water. Place over medium heat and bring to a boil. Immediately reduce to a very light simmer. Use a spoon or ladle to skim off the fat and impurities that float to the surface.

2. Place the bay leaves, peppercorns, thyme leaves, and parsley stems in a small square of cheesecloth or clean cloth toweling. Use a small piece of string to tie the cloth in a loose bundle to enclose the herbs. Add the herb bundle and the salt to the simmering liquid. Partially cover the pot.

3. After about 1½ hours of simmering, carefully remove the chicken from the broth. This may be best accomplished by pouring it through a colander, as the chicken will be very tender at this point. Place the chicken in a large pan and allow to cool. Discard herb bundle.

4. Return the broth to the heat. Add the vegetables and rice and simmer for 20 minutes.

5. When the chicken is cool enough to handle, carefully pull the meat from the bones in large pieces, being careful to remove any cartilage. Cut the meat in bite-sized pieces, and add to the broth.

6. Chill the soup overnight, then skim off any fat that collects on the surface. To serve, heat, then sprinkle each bowl with chopped parsley.

Per serving (1 cup):

fat grams 3

fiber grams 0.6

calories 149

protein grams 14

carbohydrate grams 15

sodium milligrams 622

Summer Gazpacho
YIELD: 6 SERVINGS

Gazpacho is so refreshing on a hot summer day or evening. Although the recipe below is specific, feel free to add, subtract, or substitute some of the vegetables. Just make sure that the tomatoes are really ripe or you will be better off using canned tomatoes instead.

If you wish, you can add cooked shrimp, crabmeat, or crayfish.

1½ pounds very ripe tomatoes, peeled and seeded (or 3 cups drained diced canned tomatoes)

3 scallions, chopped

½ green bell pepper, seeded and chopped

1 Italian long hot pepper

½ cucumber, peeled, seeded, and chopped

¼ red onion, chopped

4 cloves garlic, peeled

¼ cup chopped parsley

¼ cup chopped basil

1½ teaspoons olive oil

2 tablespoons red wine vinegar

1 cup tomato juice

1 teaspoon salt

¼ teaspoon black pepper

2 slices Italian bread, cubed and baked in the oven until brown and crisp

1. Place the tomatoes, scallions, peppers, cucumber, onion, garlic, parsley, and basil in a food processor and chop until quite smooth but still retaining some texture.

2. Pour the vegetables in a bowl and add the remaining ingredients except the croutons. Mix well and refrigerate for several hours. Garnish with the bread croutons when serving.

Per serving (1 cup):

fat grams 2

protein grams 3

fiber grams 3

carbohydrate grams 17

calories 87

sodium milligrams 221

Hearty Lentil Soup

YIELD: 10 SERVINGS

Lentil soup is a meal in itself. Store it in small freezer containers for quick lunches. If you have a microwave at work, pack it in little microwave-proof containers to take along with you.

1 teaspoon oil

2 tablespoons cider vinegar

1/2 cup diced lean ham

1 cup uncooked lentils

1/2 cup diced onion

6 cups chicken broth

1/2 cup diced carrots

1 bay leaf

1/2 cup diced celery

Pinch of thyme

1 clove garlic, minced

1/4 teaspoon black pepper

1 tablespoon tomato paste

1 teaspoon dry mustard

1. Heat oil in a medium saucepan over low heat and add the ham and vegetables. Sauté until onions become translucent, about 2 minutes.

2. Add the tomato paste and vinegar and continue to cook for 3 minutes.

3. Add the lentils, broth, bay leaf, and thyme. Raise heat and bring to a boil. Reduce heat and simmer for 20 minutes.

4. Remove from heat, discard bay leaf, and season with pepper and mustard.

Per serving (3/4 cup):

fat grams 2

protein grams 11

fiber grams 3

carbohydrate grams 14

calories 111

sodium milligrams 299

Pinto Bean Soup

YIELD: *10 SERVINGS*

This soup with the taste of the American Southwest cries out for a wedge of warm corn bread.

1 pound dry pinto beans	*2 cups chicken broth*
2 strips bacon, chopped	*1 bay leaf*
2 onions, chopped	*¼ teaspoon thyme*
1 red bell pepper, seeded and chopped	*2 teaspoons chili powder*
	1 teaspoon cumin
1 green bell pepper, seeded and chopped	*¼ teaspoon black pepper*
	1 teaspoon salt
4 cloves garlic, minced	*2 tablespoons cider vinegar*
8 cups water	*¼ cup chopped cilantro or parsley*

1. Rinse the beans. Cover with cold water and allow to soak overnight. Drain.

2. Heat a heavy-bottomed 1-gallon soup pot over high heat. Add bacon and cook until it has released its fat but has not yet browned. Add the onions, peppers, and garlic and continue to cook for a few minutes until the onions become translucent.

3. Add the remaining ingredients except the vinegar and cilantro or parsley. Bring to a boil and reduce to a simmer. Simmer slowly for 1½ hours.

4. Discard the bay leaf and puree about half of the soup in a blender or food processor. Mix the puree back into the soup and stir in the vinegar and cilantro. Serve.

Per serving (1 cup):

fat grams 4	protein grams 10
fiber grams 11	carbohydrate grams 29
calories 183	sodium milligrams 325

Sweet Potato Soup

YIELD: *10 SERVINGS*

Sweet potatoes make this soup wonderfully rich. Garnish with croutons or some chopped raisins and a few slivers of toasted almonds.

You can substitute butternut squash or pumpkin for the sweet potatoes.

3 pounds sweet potatoes	*1½ quarts chicken broth*
1 cup diced pumpernickel or rye bread (about 2 slices)	*1 bay leaf*
	Pinch of thyme
1 teaspoon safflower oil	*1 tablespoon fresh gingerroot, peeled and chopped*
2 cloves garlic, minced	
1 cup coarsely chopped onion	*1 cup evaporated skim milk*
½ cup coarsely chopped celery	*½ teaspoon salt*

1. Preheat oven to 350 degrees. Bake the whole sweet potatoes until tender. When cool enough to handle, peel and mash the potatoes. Reserve.

2. While the potatoes are baking, on a cookie sheet alongside toast the bread cubes until crisp; set aside.

3. Heat oil in a large saucepan over low heat and add the garlic, onions, and celery. Cook slowly until the vegetables are tender, about 10 minutes.

4. Add the broth, bay leaf, thyme, and sweet potato pulp, and bring to a simmer. Simmer for 20 minutes.

5. Add ginger, evaporated skim milk, and salt and return to a simmer. Remove from heat, discard bay leaf, and puree in a blender or food processor. Strain.

6. Serve topped with the pumpernickel or rye bread croutons.

Per serving (¾ cup):

fat grams 2	protein grams 7
fiber grams 2	carbohydrate grams 23
calories 134	sodium milligrams 333

Corn and Crab Chowder

YIELD: 10 SERVINGS

This is a lower-fat version of a soup popular all along the Atlantic coastal states where corn and blue crabs are plentiful in the summer.

1 tablespoon unsalted butter

1 onion, coarsely chopped

2 ribs celery, coarsely chopped

6 cups chicken broth

1/4 teaspoon thyme

1 bay leaf

8 ears fresh corn on the cob

2 cups potatoes, peeled and diced

1 cup evaporated skim milk

1/2 teaspoon salt

1/4 teaspoon white pepper

1/4 pound fresh crabmeat

1/4 cup minced chives or scallion
tops

1. Heat butter in a large saucepan over high heat. Add the onions and celery and sauté a few minutes until the onions become translucent.

2. Add the chicken broth, thyme, and bay leaf. Bring to a boil and reduce to a simmer.

3. Cut the kernels from the corn. Place half of the cut corn in the simmering soup and simmer for 20 minutes. Discard bay leaf. Puree the soup in a blender or food processor and strain through a coarse sieve. Return the soup to the pan and bring back to a simmer. Add the remaining corn and the diced potatoes. Allow to simmer for 15 minutes.

4. Add the evaporated skim milk, salt, and pepper and return to a simmer. Remove from the heat and add the crabmeat.

5. Top with minced chives or scallion tops and serve.

Per serving (3/4 cup):

fat grams 3

fiber grams 5

calories 176

protein grams 11

carbohydrate grams 30

sodium milligrams 319

New England Clam Chowder

YIELD: 10 SERVINGS

If you ever want to stir up trouble in New England, just ask a group of people how thick chowder should be—then run. Feel free to add or subtract flour (the thickener) to cast your personal vote.

This chowder gets its richness from the evaporated skim milk, which replaces cream in the original.

This soup doesn't freeze well, but you can refrigerate several days' worth.

3 5-ounce cans chopped clams,
   including juice
Clam juice or chicken broth as
   needed
1 strip bacon, chopped
1 onion, chopped
¼ teaspoon thyme

1 bay leaf
¼ cup flour
1 cup evaporated skim milk
1 large potato, peeled and diced
¼ teaspoon black pepper
Salt to taste

1. Drain clams, reserving juice. Set aside. Add enough chicken broth to reserved clam juice to bring measure of liquid to 4 cups. Set aside.

2. Heat a heavy-bottomed 1-gallon soup pot over high heat. Add bacon and cook until it has released its fat but not yet browned. Add the onion and sauté a few minutes until translucent. Add the thyme, bay leaf, and clam juice. Bring to a boil and reduce to a simmer.

3. Carefully whisk together the flour and evaporated skim milk preventing any lumps. Pour the mixture into the simmering clam juice and whisk until smooth. Return to a simmer. Add the diced potatoes and simmer for 20 minutes.

4. Discard bay leaf and add the reserved drained clams. Adjust seasoning before serving with pepper and salt if needed.

Per serving (¾ cup):

fat grams 3
fiber grams 1
calories 139

protein grams 13
carbohydrate grams 15
sodium milligrams 263

Swiss Chard and White Bean Chowder
YIELD: 10 SERVINGS

For the Swiss chard, you may substitute kale or beet greens. To have small amounts of bacon on hand for occasional use in recipes like this one, freeze strips individually in separate bags for future use.

1 cup dry white beans
1 strip bacon, diced
1 cup diced red onion
4 cloves garlic, minced
2 teaspoons minced fresh rosemary
   or ½ teaspoon dried
2 quarts chicken broth

1 bunch Swiss chard (about 1
   pound), stems diced, leaves
   shredded
1 pound red-skinned potatoes,
   scrubbed and diced
¼ cup chopped parsley
½ teaspoon salt
½ teaspoon white pepper

1. Rinse the beans. Cover with cold water and allow to soak overnight. Drain.

2. Heat a heavy-bottomed 1-gallon soup pot over high heat. Add bacon and cook until it begins to brown. Add the onions and garlic and continue to cook for a few minutes until the onions become translucent. Add the rosemary and chicken broth and bring to a boil. Simmer for approximately 45 minutes. Add the Swiss chard and potatoes and continue to simmer for an additional 30 minutes. Remove from heat.

3. Add the parsley and adjust the seasoning with salt and pepper.

Per serving (1¼ cups):

fat grams 3
fiber grams 3
calories 176

protein grams 11
carbohydrate grams 28
sodium milligrams 408

Pastas, Pasta Salads, and Pizzas

Pasta Dough

YIELD: 6 SERVINGS (3/4 POUND)

Although it is possible to buy excellent premade and dried pastas, there are times when one prefers to do it from ground zero. Be sure you have a pasta machine to roll out this dough as rolling pasta by hand is more of a workout than you may want.

You may produce variations of this basic pasta dough by replacing half of the egg whites with ¼ cup of either tomato paste, cooked and pureed spinach, water with a pinch of saffron, or even Red Pepper Sauce (see pages 376–77). Or you can flavor the dough with grated lemon zest or fresh herbs.

4 egg whites
⅔ cup semolina flour

1 cup bread flour

1. Combine all ingredients in a food processor fitted with a steel blade. Process until mixture has the consistency of cornmeal. Remove from the processor and press into a ball. Cover and allow to rest for ½ hour.

2. Divide dough into 3 equal pieces. Roll through the pasta machine at its thickest setting. Fold in half and reroll through the thickest setting again. Repeat with other two pieces.

3. Reduce setting and roll as before. Continue to reduce setting and repeat rolling process until desired thickness is achieved.

4. Cut or shape pasta as desired and divide into 6 servings (2 ounces each).

Per serving (2 ounces):

fat grams .362

fiber grams 1

calories 148

protein grams 7

carbohydrate grams 28

sodium milligrams 37

Whole Wheat Drop Noodles

YIELD: 10 SERVINGS (2 POUNDS)

These are what Europeans call "spatzle." Although there are dozens of ways to form the little dumplings, the method below is one of the easiest.

These noodles are especially good with stews. You can reheat them in the microwave, covered with plastic wrap.

3 egg whites

1½ cups all-purpose flour

1 cup whole wheat flour

¼ teaspoon nutmeg

½ teaspoon salt

¼ teaspoon white pepper

1½ cups skim milk

1. Bring a large pot of water to a boil.
2. Combine egg whites, flours, nutmeg, salt, pepper, and 1 cup of the skim milk in a bowl. Mix until the mixture forms a smooth, heavy paste. Add the remaining skim milk and mix well. Beat the mixture until it begins to show signs of elasticity.
3. Pour the batter into a colander. Using a rubber spatula, work the mixture through so that it drops into the boiling water in long strands.
4. When the water returns to a boil, remove from heat and drain the contents by pouring it through the empty colander.
5. Either serve hot or spread the noodles out onto a baking tray and allow to cool before refrigerating or freezing for later use. Divide into ⅔ cup servings.

Per serving (⅔ cup):

fat grams 0.5

fiber grams 2

calories 122

protein grams 6

carbohydrate grams 24

sodium milligrams 143

Macaroni and Cheese
YIELD: 4 SERVINGS

A lighter version of the all-American favorite.

1 cup dry macaroni
1 cup skim milk
4 ounces nonfat cheddar cheese,
   grated

2 tablespoons cornstarch
¼ teaspoon salt
Pinch of cayenne pepper

1. Cook the macaroni in 1 quart of boiling water in a 2-quart saucepan until tender. Drain but do not rinse.

2. Return the macaroni to the pan and add the milk. Place over moderate heat and bring to a simmer.

3. In a small bowl toss the grated cheese and cornstarch together. Slowly stir the cheese mixture into the simmering milk. When the milk returns to a simmer and the cheese has melted, remove from the heat and add salt and cayenne.

4. Serve as is, or pour into a 1-quart casserole and allow to cool. Bake uncovered at 350 degrees until top is browned, about ½ hour. Cut into 4 servings.

Per serving:
fat grams 0.5
fiber grams 1
calories 149

protein grams 9
carbohydrate grams 26
sodium milligrams 444

Pasta with Broccoli Pesto
YIELD: 2 SERVINGS

Typical pesto sauces are loaded with oil. This lighter version keeps that wonderful taste of summer, and provides a vegetable serving, too.

1 tablespoon olive oil

8 cloves garlic, thinly sliced

2 cups chopped fresh broccoli

¼ cup chicken broth

½ teaspoon salt

⅛ teaspoon black pepper

¼ cup packed fresh basil leaves

2 cups pasta (fusilli, penne,
   linguine, etc.)

¼ cup grated Parmesan cheese

1. Heat olive oil in a medium sauté pan over high heat and add the sliced garlic. Cook until the garlic becomes light tan—only a few seconds. Add the broccoli and chicken broth immediately and cook over high heat until broccoli is tender, about 3 minutes.

2. Pour contents of pan into a blender, add the salt, pepper, and basil, and blend at high speed until smooth.

3. Cook the pasta in a large quantity of boiling water until tender. Drain, but do not rinse, and place in a bowl.

4. Pour broccoli sauce over pasta, sprinkle with half of the Parmesan, and toss. Top with remaining Parmesan and serve. Divide into 2 servings.

Per serving:

fat grams 12

fiber grams 8

calories 544

protein grams 22

carbohydrate grams 88

sodium milligrams 322

Fettuccine Primavera

YIELD: 4 MAIN-DISH SERVINGS

Even though *primavera* means "springtime," this popular pasta dish is appealing any time of the year. Feel free to vary the vegetables to include your favorites.

Normally primavera is prepared from a reduction of heavy cream, which makes it rich but puts it out of the realm of low-fat cooking. This version uses Enlightened White Sauce and Neufchâtel cheese to provide a rich texture without the fat.

½ tablespoon unsalted butter

¼ cup diced onions

2 cloves garlic, minced

½ cup thinly sliced carrots

¼ cup diced peppers

1 cup sliced mushrooms

½ cup fresh or frozen peas or snow
   peas

1 cup asparagus, cut into ½-inch
   pieces

½ cup Enlightened White Sauce
   (see page 375)

¼ cup Neufchâtel cheese (or low-
   fat cream cheese)

1 tablespoon chopped fresh tarragon
   or parsley

¼ teaspoon white pepper

8 ounces dried fettuccine

4 tablespoons grated Parmesan
   cheese

1. Heat butter in a large sauté pan over medium heat and add the onions and garlic. Cook a few minutes until the onions become translucent. Add the carrots and sauté lightly. Add the peppers and mushrooms and continue to sauté. Add the peas or snow peas, asparagus, and Enlightened White Sauce, and bring to a simmer. Remove from heat and add the Neufchâtel cheese, tarragon or parsley, and pepper.

2. Cook the fettuccine in a large quantity of boiling water until tender. Drain but do not rinse and place the pasta in a bowl.

3. Pour the vegetable sauce over the pasta and toss well. Divide into 4 portions and serve topped with Parmesan cheese.

Per serving:

fat grams 8

fiber grams 5

calories 383

protein grams 17

carbohydrate grams 61

sodium milligrams 695

Country-style Pasta
YIELD: 2 SERVINGS

This quick pasta is a great way to produce a hearty meal when your time is limited.

1 cup dry pasta (bowtie, fusilli, penne, rigatoni)

2 teaspoons olive oil

1/4 cup diced prosciutto ham

1/2 cup chopped onion

2 cloves garlic, chopped

2 cups packed coarsely shredded escarole

1 cup drained, cooked white beans (canned)

1 tomato, seeded and chopped

1 cup chicken broth

1/4 teaspoon black pepper

2 tablespoons chopped fresh basil

1/4 cup grated Parmesan cheese

1. Cook the pasta in a large quantity of boiling water until tender. Drain, rinse, and reserve.

2. Heat the olive oil in a 2-quart saucepan over moderate heat. Add the prosciutto and fry for 1 minute. Add the onions and garlic and allow to cook until the onions become translucent, about 4 minutes. Add the escarole and cook until it wilts, about 2 minutes.

3. Add the beans, tomato, cooked pasta, and chicken broth and bring to a simmer. Cook for about 5 minutes until the flavors are well incorporated.

4. Remove from the heat and add the pepper and basil.

5. Divide into 2 servings and top each with the Parmesan cheese.

Per serving:

fat grams 11

fiber grams 12

calories 504

protein grams 29

carbohydrate grams 73

sodium milligrams 714

Fusilli Pasta with Pan-grilled Chicken and Red Pepper Sauce

YIELD: 4 SERVINGS

Since there is evidence that foods grilled directly over burning fuels such as charcoal and wood produce carcinogens, I recommend you avoid traditionally grilled foods. Unfortunately, by avoiding grilled foods we eliminate a very good low-fat cooking technique.

I've found that we can produce some of the same appeal of grilled foods by the use of a "pan grill." A pan grill is a cast-iron skillet that has a ribbed cooking surface. As the meat is cooked, excess fat drains away from the food while the ribs give the surface of the meat a nice scored appearance.

To keep the food from sticking, lightly coat the pan grill with nonstick vegetable spray and never scrub it with anything more abrasive than a soapy washcloth. Store it with a light film of vegetable oil rubbed on its surface to prevent rusting.

½ teaspoon salt
⅛ teaspoon white pepper
1 tablespoon lemon juice
2 cloves garlic, minced
12 ounces chicken breasts, boneless and skinless
3 cups fusilli pasta
1 cup Red Pepper Sauce (see pages 376–77)

2 tablespoons chopped fresh basil
3 tablespoons ripe olives (preferably Kalamata), pitted and coarsely chopped
¼ cup grated Parmesan cheese (or crumbled mild chèvre goat cheese)

1. Place salt, pepper, lemon juice, and garlic in a shallow bowl. Add the chicken breasts and coat with the marinade. Allow to marinate for at least 1 hour. Preheat broiler or grill.

2. Cook the pasta in a large quantity of boiling water until tender. Drain but do not rinse, and keep hot.

3. Heat Red Pepper Sauce in a large saucepan. Add the basil and olives. Combine sauce and cooked pasta and toss until well coated.

4. Remove chicken breasts from marinade and pat dry. Pan-broil for 4 to 5 minutes on each side or until the outside is golden brown and the pink color is almost gone in the center.

5. Divide the pasta between 4 serving plates and sprinkle with cheese. Slice cooked chicken breasts into finger-sized pieces, arrange over pasta, and serve.

Per serving:

fat grams 6
fiber grams 3
calories 392

protein grams 35
carbohydrate grams 47
sodium milligrams 426

Penne à la Vodka

YIELD: 4 SERVINGS

Here's a hearty but simple warm pasta dish. Even though the recipe calls for heavy cream it still gets only 19 percent of its calories from fat. If you desire less fat you can replace the heavy cream with evaporated skim milk.

1 teaspoon olive oil	1/2 teaspoon salt
4 cloves garlic, minced	1/8 teaspoon white pepper
1 cup minced onions	1/4 cup heavy cream
2 cups canned diced tomatoes (no-salt-added variety)	6 cups penne pasta (or macaroni, fusilli, radiatore, etc.)
2 tablespoons chopped fresh basil	1 ounce vodka, peppered if
1 teaspoon red chili flakes	available (optional)

1. Heat olive oil in a medium saucepan over medium heat and add the garlic and onions. Sauté a few minutes until onions become translucent. Open the tomatoes and drain the juice from the can into the onions. Adjust heat to high and allow to simmer and evaporate until the liquid is reduced to about 1/2 cup (one quarter of its original volume). When reduced add the diced tomatoes, basil, chili flakes, salt, pepper, and heavy cream. Return to a simmer.

2. Cook the pasta in a large quantity of boiling water until tender. Drain but do not rinse.

3. Add the cooked pasta and heat through. Adjust the seasoning, add the vodka, and divide into 4 servings.

Per serving:

fat grams 8	protein grams 12
fiber grams 5	carbohydrate grams 68
calories 410	sodium milligrams 292

Stewed Orzo

YIELD: 8 SERVINGS (3 CUPS)

Orzo is a Greek pasta that looks like rice.

To the finished dish, you can add some diced cooked shrimp or scallops. Another variation is to add some sautéed mushrooms.

2 teaspoons olive oil

½ cup minced onions

1 clove garlic, minced

1 cup orzo or riso pasta

½ cup white wine

1½ cups chicken broth

¼ cup evaporated skim milk

½ teaspoon salt

¼ cup grated Parmesan cheese

1. Heat olive oil in small saucepan over high heat. Add the onions and garlic and sauté a few minutes until onions become translucent.

2. Add orzo or riso pasta and stir with a spoon to evenly coat grains with the vegetables and oil. Add the white wine and ½ cup of the chicken broth. Bring to a simmer and stir. When liquid has been absorbed add another ½ cup of the broth, return to a simmer, and continue to stir. Repeat with the remaining broth.

3. When the last addition of stock has been absorbed so that the contents of the pan have the consistency of stew, add the evaporated skim milk and salt. Return to simmer and remove from heat.

4. Stir in the Parmesan cheese and serve.

Per serving (3/8 cup):

fat grams 2

fiber grams 1

calories 122

protein grams 5

carbohydrate grams 17

sodium milligrams 229

Marinated Mushrooms and Orzo à la Grecque
YIELD: 10 SERVINGS

This is a simple salad that can be a side dish or light meal.

2 quarts water	10 coriander seeds, crushed
8 ounces orzo or riso pasta	1/4 cup chopped parsley
1 pound mushrooms, sliced	1/4 cup chicken broth
1 red onion, sliced	1 tablespoon olive oil
1/4 cup lemon juice	1 tablespoon red wine vinegar
1/2 cup Greek olives, pitted and	1/2 teaspoon salt
chopped	1/4 teaspoon black pepper
4 cloves garlic, minced	

1. Bring 2 quarts water to a boil in a large saucepan. Add the orzo or riso pasta and cook for 10 minutes. Drain and rinse under cold water.

2. Place in a mixing bowl and add the remaining ingredients. Mix until well incorporated and allow to marinate for at least 1/2 hour before serving.

Per serving (1/2 cup):

fat grams 3	protein grams 4
fiber grams 2	carbohydrate grams 22
calories 129	sodium milligrams 190

Oriental Noodle and Vegetable Salad
YIELD: 12 SERVINGS

Ramen or soba noodles can be found in most supermarkets in the oriental food section. Here they are combined with oriental vegetables and flavorings for a very fresh taste. This salad tastes best for the first twenty-four hours.

8 ounces ramen or soba noodles
2 cups fresh bean sprouts
2 cups snow peas
2 cups fresh shiitake mushrooms, sliced
1 red bell pepper, sliced
1 cup celery, thinly sliced at an angle
1 cup thinly sliced scallions

1/4 cup light soy sauce
2 tablespoons fresh gingerroot, peeled and chopped
4 cloves garlic, chopped
1 tablespoon sesame seeds
1/2 cup chicken broth
1 tablespoon sesame oil
2 tablespoons vinegar (preferably rice wine vinegar)

1. Cook the noodles in boiling water according to the instructions (do not use the flavoring packet if one was provided in the package).

2. Drain the noodles but do not rinse and place in a large mixing bowl. Add the remaining ingredients and toss well.

Per serving (1/2 cup):

fat grams 3
fiber grams 3
calories 117

protein grams 5
carbohydrate grams 19
sodium milligrams 368

Pasta and Shrimp Salad

YIELD: 8 SERVINGS

Summer meals of chilled pasta salads are not only healthy but easy as well. Serve on a bed of lettuce.

2 cups snow peas
4 cups penne or shell pasta, cooked
1 cup small cooked shrimp (if desired, purchase already cooked)
1 red bell pepper, sliced

1/2 cup Creamy Herb Salad Dressing (see page 374)
1/4 cup chopped fresh parsley
1 teaspoon salt
1/4 teaspoon white pepper

1. Place snow peas in a microwavable container and sprinkle with 1 teaspoon water. Cover and cook at high heat for 1 minute. Drain and cool. Or place in a steamer on the stove over boiling water for 1 minute.

2. Combine all ingredients in a mixing bowl and toss carefully.

3. Chill before serving.

Per serving (1 cup):

fat grams 1   protein grams 11

fiber grams 2   carbohydrate grams 25

calories 158   sodium milligrams 340

Pizza Dough

YIELD: ONE 12-INCH OR FOUR 7-INCH PIZZAS

Pizza is one of the most misunderstood foods. Although it can be high in fat, if you choose your toppings carefully, it can be a low-fat culinary masterpiece. Create your own favorite version with a thick vegetable- or tomato-based pureed sauce, lean meats (precooked), vegetables (raw, cut in small pieces), and nonfat cheese (used sparingly).

Pizzas baked on preheated clay tiles or a pizza stone develop a crispier crust. Since the tile or stone is porous, the steam produced by the dough as it cooks escapes and is absorbed into the stone. Sprinkling the pizza tile or stone with a little cornmeal just before setting the pizza on it helps as well. If you don't have or can't find a pizza stone, simply line a baking tray with clean unglazed quarry tile from your local flooring store.

You can also buy frozen pizza dough at your market, but check the label because some brands contain fat.

½ teaspoon honey   *¼ teaspoon salt*

1 cup lukewarm water (not hot)   *2 cups bread flour*

1 package active dry yeast

1. Combine honey, water, and yeast in a mixing bowl. When a foam appears on the surface, add the salt and approximately ¾ of the flour. Stir until a smooth, heavy dough is formed. Knead in the remaining flour and form into a ball.

2. Place dough in a bowl, cover with a towel, and let rise in a

warm place until doubled. Reknead the dough until smooth again.

3. Divide the dough and carefully stretch into four 7-inch disks or one 12-inch disk.

4. Top and bake according to recipe instructions.

Per serving (one 7-inch pizza):

fat grams 0.6	protein grams 7
fiber grams 2	carbohydrate grams 49
calories 235	sodium milligrams 137

Tomato, Mozzarella, and Basil Pizza

YIELD: 4 SERVINGS

You can also make this as one big pizza.

4 uncooked 7-inch pizza shells
  (see pages 289–90)
¼ cup Tomato Sauce (see pages
  378–79)
2 cups Oven-dried Tomatoes (see
  pages 380–81) or 4 fresh ripe
  tomatoes

¼ cup chopped fresh basil
4 ounces grated low-moisture skim
  mozzarella cheese
¼ cup grated Parmesan cheese

1. Place a pizza stone in the oven and preheat to 450 degrees.

2. Set each pizza shell onto a dinner plate lightly dusted with cornmeal. Spread Tomato Sauce onto the top of each shell. Arrange Oven-Dried Tomatoes on sauce. Scatter basil, mozzarella, and Parmesan cheese over all.

3. Carefully slide the pizzas onto the hot stone and bake for 12 to 15 minutes or until the cheese is browned and the dough is crisp. Lift off stone with a metal spatula and place on a cutting surface. Cut into wedges and serve.

Per serving (1 pizza):

fat grams 8	protein grams 21
fiber grams 9	carbohydrate grams 70
calories 431	sodium milligrams 756*

* Higher in sodium than ideal. DO NOT EAT if fluid retention or hypertension is a problem.

White Clam Pizza

YIELD: 4 SERVINGS

Pizza need not be topped with red sauce and cheese. As long as you use low-fat toppings, you can let your imagination and palate run wild.

You can make one big pizza instead of four little ones.

4 uncooked 7-inch pizza shells (see pages 289–90)	2 tablespoons chopped fresh basil
1 tablespoon olive oil	¼ teaspoon black pepper
4 cloves garlic, minced	¾ cup drained minced clams
	¼ cup grated Parmesan cheese

1. Place a pizza stone in the oven and preheat to 450 degrees.

2. Set each pizza shell onto a dinner plate lightly dusted with cornmeal.

3. In a small bowl, mix together olive oil, garlic, basil, and pepper and spread onto the top of the pizza shells. Sprinkle the shells with chopped clams and Parmesan cheese.

4. Carefully slide each pizza onto the hot stone and bake for 12 to 15 minutes or until the cheese is browned and the dough is crisp. Lift from stone with a metal spatula and place on a cutting surface. Cut into wedges before serving.

Per serving (1 pizza):

fat grams 6	protein grams 17
fiber grams 2	carbohydrate grams 52
calories 338	sodium milligrams 266

Grains and Beans

Barley Risotto

YIELD: 6 SERVINGS

True risotto is an Italian rice stew prepared by cooking a special high-starch rice called "arborio" with rich broth, butter, and Parmesan cheese. After some experimentation I've found several other grains that produce similar results, one of the best being barley.

This is a satisfying stand-alone meal. It also goes with nearly any meat dish, or can be served as the base to a baked or broiled fish as well. It reheats well, but may need additional water or broth.

1 teaspoon olive oil	1/4 cup evaporated skim milk
1/4 cup diced onion	1/2 teaspoon salt
1/4 cup diced carrots	Pinch of white pepper
1/4 cup diced celery	1 teaspoon chopped fresh rosemary
1/2 cup pearled barley	or parsley
2 cups chicken broth	2 tablespoons grated Parmesan
1 bay leaf	cheese

1. Heat oil in a small saucepan and add onion, carrots, and celery over moderate heat. Sauté a few minutes until onion becomes translucent.

2. Add barley and stir well.

3. Add 1/4 of the broth and the bay leaf, and bring to a simmer. Stir thoroughly to keep the barley from sticking together. When all the liquid is absorbed, add another 1/4 of the broth and continue to stir over the heat. Repeat until all of the liquid is added and continue to cook until the barley is tender (approximately 15 minutes total).

4. Add the evaporated skim milk, salt, and pepper. When the

contents of the pan take on the consistency of porridge, remove from the heat. Remove bay leaf and add the rosemary or parsley and Parmesan cheese. Serve hot.

Per serving (¹/₂ cup):

fat grams 2

protein grams 5

fiber grams 3

carbohydrate grams 16

calories 96

sodium milligrams 295

Barley and Mushroom Salad
YIELD: 12 SERVINGS

Discover barley, which in this recipe becomes light, fluffy, and delicious.

This salad will keep for several days in the refrigerator.

1 teaspoon safflower oil

¹/₂ cup minced onion

2 cloves garlic, minced

1 cup pearled barley

3³/₄ cups chicken broth

12 ounces fresh mushrooms, sliced

1 medium leek, split in half, washed, and sliced into ¹/₂-inch ribbons

1 cup grated carrots

¹/₄ cup chopped parsley

1 teaspoon salt

¹/₂ teaspoon white pepper

2 teaspoons olive oil

2 teaspoons red wine vinegar

1. Preheat oven to 325 degrees.

2. Heat the safflower oil in an oven-proof medium saucepan and add the onion and garlic. Sauté a few minutes, until the onion becomes translucent. Add the barley and 3 cups of the chicken broth and bring to a simmer.

3. Cover tightly and bake for 1 hour. Fluff the barley with a fork.

4. Pour the hot barley into a bowl and add the mushrooms, leeks, and carrots. Toss lightly and allow to cool.

5. Add the remaining ³/₄ cup chicken broth and the rest of the ingredients. Mix well and serve at room temperature or chilled.

Per serving (¹/₂ cup):

fat grams 3   protein grams 4

fiber grams 4   carbohydrate grams 21

calories 119   sodium milligrams 248

Grain Burgers

YIELD: 5 SERVINGS

Hamburgers get their flavor from the fat that is ground into them. When the fat is reduced to acceptable quantity, some people find the meat unpleasantly dry. Instead, try a moist and flavorful alternative to the hamburger with this recipe. You can freeze the burgers; thaw before cooking.

¹/₂ cup boiling water

¹/₂ cup dry bulgur wheat

1 tablespoon natural peanut butter (ground peanuts)

3 ounces tofu, mashed

1 tablespoon light soy sauce

¹/₄ teaspoon garlic powder

¹/₄ teaspoon onion powder

2 tablespoons all-purpose flour

¹/₄ cup bread crumbs

5 hamburger buns

1 tomato, sliced

5 leaves lettuce

5 tablespoons Kraft Free imitation mayonnaise (see note on page 305)

1. Pour boiling water over bulgur wheat and allow to sit until cool.

2. Add peanut butter, tofu, soy sauce, garlic powder, onion powder, flour, and bread crumbs. Mix well until the mixture reaches a consistency that will form into patties.

3. Heat a skillet over high heat and coat lightly with nonstick vegetable spray. Press mixture into 5 patties and sauté on both sides until browned and crisp, about 5 minutes. (The burgers do not have to cook through—just brown.)

4. Place each patty on a toasted hamburger bun and garnish with tomato, lettuce, and imitation mayonnaise.

Per serving (1 burger):

fat grams 5	protein grams 10
fiber grams 6	carbohydrate grams 46
calories 261	sodium milligrams 662*

* Watch sodium for the rest of the day or do not eat if edema is a problem.

Brown Rice Pilaf

YIELD: 4 SERVINGS

Brown rice has more fiber than white, but you can use plain white converted rice if desired with the same ratio of rice to liquid.

Make extra to heat in the microwave for a convenient meal accompaniment later in the week.

1 teaspoon unsalted butter	*2 cups chicken broth*
½ cup diced onion	*1 bay leaf*
1 cup brown rice	*½ teaspoon salt*

1. Preheat oven to 350 degrees.
2. Heat butter in a small oven-proof saucepan over high heat. Add the onions and sauté a few minutes until they become translucent. Add the rice and continue to sauté until the rice begins to brown slightly, about 5 minutes.
3. Add the broth, bay leaf, and salt. Bring to a boil. Cover tightly and bake in oven for 20 minutes.
4. Remove the pan from the oven and uncover. Discard the bay leaf and fluff the rice with a fork. Divide into 4 portions and serve hot.

Per serving:

fat grams 3	protein grams 6
fiber grams 2	carbohydrate grams 38
calories 202	sodium milligrams 378

Brown Rice with Braised Chickpeas

YIELD: 4 SERVINGS

1 cup dried chickpeas or pinto
 beans
1½ teaspoons olive oil
4 cloves garlic, minced
½ cup chopped scallions
½ cup diced red bell pepper
1 cup cubed eggplant
1 cup canned diced tomato,
 drained

1 teaspoon red chili flakes
1 cup water
½ teaspoon salt
2 tablespoons chopped fresh basil or
 parsley
3 cups Brown Rice Pilaf (see
 above) prepared with water or
 vegetable stock instead of chicken
 broth if nonmeat dish is desired

1. Soak chickpeas or pinto beans in cold water overnight. Drain.
2. Preheat oven to 300 degrees.
3. Heat olive oil in an oven-proof, 1-quart saucepan or Dutch oven with a tight-fitting lid over high heat. Add the garlic, scallions, and peppers and cook for 3 minutes. Add the eggplant, tomato, red chili flakes, chickpeas or pinto beans, and water and bring to a simmer. Cover tightly and place in the oven.
4. Braise for 2 hours or until peas are very tender. Remove from oven and add the salt and basil or parsley.
5. Divide into 4 portions and serve over Brown Rice Pilaf.

Per serving:

fat grams 8	protein grams 18
fiber grams 14	carbohydrate grams 75
calories 431	sodium milligrams 965*

* Do not eat if fluid retention, hypertension, or problems with elimininating salt are present.

Bulgur Wheat Salad

YIELD: 12 SERVINGS

This is a tasty variation on the Middle Eastern dish tabbouleh. Bulgur, which is simply cracked wheat, has a pleasant nutty flavor when prepared this way.

2 cups bulgur wheat
3 cups boiling water
4 tomatoes, coarsely chopped
1/4 cup lemon juice
2 tablespoons olive oil
1/4 cup chopped fresh mint
1 teaspoon salt

1/2 teaspoon black pepper
4 cups drained chickpeas (canned)
1 cucumber, peeled and sliced
2 green bell peppers, seeded and
   sliced
1 cup sliced scallions

1. Place bulgur in a large bowl. Add boiling water and stir. Allow to rest until cooled.

2. Add remaining ingredients and toss.

3. Chill and serve.

Per serving (1 cup):

fat grams 4
fiber grams 10
calories 211

protein grams 9
carbohydrate grams 38
sodium milligrams 193

Baked Polenta

YIELD: *10 SERVINGS*

Polenta is a type of Italian porridge made from cornmeal. In this recipe, it is cooled then baked until crispy brown.

Polenta is a wonderful food to discover, since its creamy texture defies its low calorie content and high fiber. It takes on other flavors well—try it with salsa and/or black beans.

1 1/2 cups chicken broth
1 1/2 cups skim milk
1 cup cornmeal
1 teaspoon salt

1/2 teaspoon white pepper
1/4 cup grated part-skim
   mozzarella cheese

1. Place chicken broth and skim milk in a small saucepan over low heat and bring to a simmer.

2. Slowly add the cornmeal, stirring constantly to avoid lumps. Bring back to a simmer and add the salt and pepper. Simmer at a low temperature for 20 minutes, stirring constantly.

3. Remove from heat and pour mixture into a pie pan lined with plastic wrap. Chill uncovered until firm, about 1 hour.

4. Preheat oven to 375 degrees.

5. Cut into 10 wedges like a pie, place on a nonstick surface such as a cookie sheet or pie plate, and top with mozzarella. Bake until browned, approximately 15 minutes.

6. Serve immediately while still hot.

Per serving (1 wedge):

fat grams 2	protein grams 5
fiber grams 1	carbohydrate grams 12
calories 78	sodium milligrams 296

Hoppin' John Salad
YIELD: 12 SERVINGS

Traditionally, Hoppin' John is a Southern dish of black-eyed peas and rice often served at New Year's for good luck. The same combination makes a great salad.

1 cup brown rice	*1 cup chopped scallions*
2 cups water	*½ cup chicken broth*
1 teaspoon salt	*1 tablespoon olive oil*
1½ cups black-eyed peas, drained	*1 tablespoon cider vinegar*
(canned)	*1 teaspoon black pepper*
4 ounces diced lean ham	

1. Preheat oven to 350 degrees.

2. In an oven-proof saucepan over high heat, combine brown rice, water, and salt and bring to a simmer. Cover tightly and bake in oven for 20 minutes. Remove from oven and scoop rice into a large mixing bowl. Allow to cool to room temperature.

3. Add remaining ingredients and mix thoroughly. Allow to marinate at least ½ hour before serving.

Per serving (¹/₂ cup):

fat grams 2	protein grams 5
fiber grams 3	carbohydrate grams 17
calories 108	sodium milligrams 245

Black Bean Salad

YIELD: 9 SERVINGS

This salad is great with Corn Pudding and Barbecued Shrimp.

3 cups canned black beans, drained	*¹/₂ cup chopped green pepper*
2 cups cooked white rice	*¹/₂ cup chopped red onion*
1¹/₂ tablespoons olive oil	*1 teaspoon chopped garlic*
1 ounce vinegar	*¹/₄ cup chopped cilantro*
2 ounces chicken stock	*1 teaspoon salt*
¹/₂ cup chopped scallions	*¹/₄ teaspoon white pepper*
¹/₂ cup chopped red pepper	

1. Combine all ingredients.
2. Allow to marinate for one hour before serving.

Per serving (¹/₂ cup):

fat grams 2	protein grams 5
fiber grams 4	carbohydrate grams 24
calories 140	sodium milligrams 279

Black Bean and Cornmeal Loaf

YIELD: 6 MAIN-DISH SERVINGS OR
12 APPETIZER SERVINGS

This loaf makes a great appetizer or vegetarian main dish. It makes an excellent meat-free entree (if you use water rather than chicken broth) for once a week or after a high-fat day.

2 cups water or chicken broth
1/2 teaspoon salt
3/4 cup cornmeal
1 cup boiling water
1/4 cup sun-dried tomatoes
1 teaspoon olive oil
1/2 cup diced red bell pepper
1/2 cup diced green bell pepper
1/2 cup diced red onion

3 cloves garlic, minced
2 tablespoons chopped cilantro
1 cup cooked or canned black
  beans, drained
Cornmeal as needed
6 tablespoons Yogurt Cheese
  (see pages 386–87)
6 ounces Fresh Salsa (see pages
  381–82)

1. Over high heat, bring water or chicken broth and salt to a boil in a medium saucepan. Reduce heat to low. Whisk in cornmeal in a slow steady stream. Simmer for 10 minutes. Remove from heat and reserve.

2. Place the sun-dried tomatoes in a small bowl and cover with 1 cup boiling water. Allow to steep until cool. Drain and discard the water; dice the tomatoes.

3. Heat olive oil in a sauté pan over high heat. Add the red peppers, green peppers, red onion, and garlic, and sauté a few minutes, until onion becomes translucent. Add the sun-dried tomatoes, cilantro, and black beans and heat through. Remove from heat. Add cooked vegetables to cooked cornmeal and mix well.

4. Line a 2-quart loaf pan with plastic wrap. Pour the mixture into the loaf pan and tap the pan against a flat surface to eliminate any air pockets. Refrigerate overnight to allow to cool and set.

5. With a sharp knife, slice the loaf into 12 slices, allowing 2 slices per main-dish serving. Lightly dust the surfaces of the slices with cornmeal.

6. Heat a nonstick skillet over high heat and coat lightly with nonstick vegetable spray. Sauté the slices on both sides until lightly browned.

7. Serve hot, topping each portion with Yogurt Cheese and Fresh Salsa.

Per serving (2 slices):
fat gram 1
fiber grams 5
calories 161

protein grams 8
carbohydrate grams 30
sodium milligrams 328

Lentil Ragout
YIELD: 5 SERVINGS

Lentils are a win-win food—not only do they taste great, but they are good for you as well. Protein-rich, low-cholesterol lentils are high in fiber, too. Unlike most beans and legumes, lentils don't have to be presoaked, so they're also convenient. Try this savory stew as a main course or along with pan-broiled salmon or lamb.

You can use any type of lentils for this recipe, but if you can find the French Green Lentils (Lentilles du Puy), grab them for this recipe. They are a bit more expensive, but they are smaller and firmer so that even after cooking, they pop when bitten into rather than just fall apart—imparting a much richer flavor!

1 strip bacon, finely chopped	*½ teaspoon salt*
¼ cup minced onions	*⅛ teaspoon white pepper*
¼ cup minced carrots	*1 bay leaf*
¼ cup minced leeks	*½ teaspoon thyme*
¼ cup minced celery	*½ teaspoon caraway*
2 cloves garlic, minced	*½ teaspoon grated lemon peel*
1 tablespoon tomato paste	*¼ cup Brown Stock (see pages*
1 tablespoon vinegar	*385–86)*
½ cup lentils	*1½ teaspoons cornstarch*
1½ cups chicken broth	*2 tablespoons water*

1. Heat a small saucepan over high heat. Cook bacon until crisp. Add the onions, carrots, leeks, celery, and garlic and sauté lightly approximately 2 minutes. Add the tomato paste and cook 3 minutes, or until the vegetables begin to turn light brown.

2. Add the vinegar, lentils, broth, and seasonings, reduce heat to low, and cook at a light simmer until lentils are tender, approximately 25 minutes.

3. Discard the bay leaf and add the Brown Stock. Return to a simmer.

4. In a small bowl, mix together the cornstarch and the water.

Add to the saucepan. When the contents return to a simmer, remove the pan from the heat.

   5. Serve warm.

Per serving (½ cup):

fat grams 2   protein grams 8

fiber grams 3   carbohydrate grams 17

calories 112   sodium milligrams 354

Poultry, Seafood, and Meat

Chicken Breast in Tortilla Sauce

YIELD: 4 SERVINGS

In many parts of the United States, Mexican restaurants are now even more popular than Italian ones. This Mexican-influenced dish can be prepared in advance and reheated.

1 pound boneless, skinless chicken breasts
4 teaspoons chili powder
1/2 teaspoon salt
2 cloves garlic, minced
1/4 cup chopped onion
1 tomato, chopped
1 6-inch corn tortilla, torn into small pieces

1 tablespoon tomato paste
1/8 teaspoon ground cumin
1 cup chicken broth
1 tablespoon chopped fresh cilantro
1/4 avocado, diced
4 tablespoons Yogurt Cheese (see pages 386–87)
2 tablespoons diced tomato
2 cups cooked white rice

1. Season chicken breasts with 2 teaspoons of the chili powder and 1/2 teaspoon of the salt. Heat a nonstick skillet over medium heat and add the chicken breasts. Sauté on both sides until they are a rich brown color, about 10 minutes. Remove the chicken from the pan and reserve.

2. Return the skillet to the heat and add the garlic, onion, and tomato. Sauté lightly about 4 minutes. Add the tortilla pieces, tomato paste, ground cumin, and the remaining 2 teaspoons chili powder.

3. Add the chicken broth and bring to a simmer. Allow to

simmer slowly for 15 minutes. Remove from the heat and pour the contents of the pan in a blender. Add the cilantro and salt and blend until very smooth.

4. Place the chicken breasts in the skillet and pour the sauce over the breasts. Place over a moderate heat and bring the sauce to a boil. Reduce to a simmer and allow to cook for 4 minutes or until the chicken breasts are cooked through.

5. Divide the breasts evenly onto 4 serving plates and garnish with the avocado, Yogurt Cheese, and tomato. Serve over warm rice.

Per serving:

fat grams 7	protein grams 33
fiber grams 4	carbohydrate grams 40
calories 357	sodium milligrams 686

Mexican Tortilla Pie

YIELD: 8 SERVINGS

This dish is a distant relative of lasagna, with the noodles replaced by tortillas and the tomato sauce by salsa.

Layer it up in a cake pan without baking if you want to keep it in the freezer until needed.

1 pound boneless, skinless chicken breasts, cut into 1-inch cubes	2 cups pinto beans, drained (canned)
2 cups sliced mushrooms	3 10-inch flour tortillas
1 onion, chopped	1½ ounces Monterey Jack cheese, grated
2 green bell peppers, seeded and chopped	1 cup salsa
2 tablespoons jalapeño peppers, seeds removed, minced	

1. Heat a 10-inch oven-proof skillet over high heat and coat lightly with nonstick vegetable spray. Add the chicken meat and sauté until browned on all sides. Remove from the pan and reserve.

2. Add the mushrooms, onions, peppers, and jalapeño to the pan

and sauté a few minutes, until the onions become translucent. Remove from pan and reserve.

3. Add the pinto beans to the pan and heat thoroughly. Using a spatula or a fork, crush the beans while heating them until the beans begin to "cake" in the pan. Add half of the cooked vegetables to the beans and mix. Remove and reserve.

4. Preheat oven to 350 degrees. Rinse the skillet and coat lightly with nonstick vegetable spray. Line the bottom of the pan with one of the flour tortillas. Add the bean and vegetable mixture and spread in an even layer. Cover with approximately half of the grated cheese.

5. Place another flour tortilla in the pan over the bean mixture and add the chicken meat and the remaining vegetables. Drizzle the meat with approximately half of the salsa.

6. Cover the chicken and vegetable mixture with the last flour tortilla. Coat the top with an even layer of the remaining salsa and top with the remaining cheese.

7. Place the skillet in oven and bake for approximately 35 minutes. Remove from the oven, slice into 8 wedges, and serve hot.

Per serving (1 wedge):

fat grams 5	protein grams 21
fiber grams 7	carbohydrate grams 28
calories 236	sodium milligrams 223

Curried Chicken Salad Pita Sandwich

YIELD: 4 SERVINGS

For a long time, I've tried to find a substitute for 98-percent-fat mayonnaise, and have not been satisfied by my attempts to make one from scratch, or by the products on the market. Finally, there's one I can recommend—Kraft Free. You can make many of your old favorite recipes simply by replacing the traditional mayonnaise with this new product.

2 tablespoons mango chutney or
    other bottled chutney
1 tablespoon curry powder
1/3 cup Kraft Free imitation
    mayonnaise
2 tablespoons plain nonfat yogurt

1/2 pound diced cooked chicken meat
1/4 cup diced celery
1/4 cup chopped scallions
4 pita bread rounds, sliced in half
    and opened to form "pockets"

1. Place chutney, curry powder, imitation mayonnaise, and yogurt in a food processor or blender and process until smooth. Transfer to a mixing bowl.

2. Fold chicken meat, celery, and scallions into dressing until well incorporated.

3. Spoon salad into 8 pita halves. Serve.

Per serving (2 pita halves):

fat grams 5	protein grams 23
fiber grams 2	carbohydrate grams 42
calories 229	sodium milligrams 568

Tandoori-style Cornish Hen

YIELD: 4 SERVINGS

In the Indian cooking technique called tandoori, foods are marinated with spices, skewered, and roasted in an extremely hot clay oven until they're crisp outside and juicy inside. Tender but crispy chicken without frying! Although you don't have a tandoori oven at home, you can get similar results with this recipe. Serve with mango chutney and brown rice.

1/2 cup nonfat yogurt
1/4 cup lemon juice
1 tablespoon grated fresh gingerroot
2 garlic cloves, minced
1 1/2 teaspoons cayenne pepper
1 teaspoon ground cumin

1/4 cup chopped fresh cilantro
1 teaspoon salt
2 1 1/2-pound Cornish hens
2 cups cooked brown rice
1/4 cup Mango Relish

1. In a bowl, combine yogurt, lemon juice, ginger, garlic, cayenne, cumin, cilantro, and salt.

2. Remove wing tips from Cornish hens and carefully pull the skin from the entire bird. Trim any visible fat. With a sharp knife make about eight 1-inch slashes into the meat of each bird. Split the Cornish hens in half and place in a small pan.

3. Pour the yogurt-based marinade over the chicken halves. Refrigerate overnight.

4. Preheat oven to 300 degrees.

5. Remove Cornish hens from marinade, allow to drain slightly, and place on broiler rack. Bake for 45 minutes or until the hens are done (pierce with a fork to make sure the juices run clear and free of any pink). The surface will be a reddish brown.

6. Remove from oven and serve over brown rice and garnish with Mango Relish.

Per serving (½ Cornish hen):

fat grams 8	protein grams 26
fiber grams 4	carbohydrate grams 47
calories 362	sodium milligrams 637

Broiled Swordfish with Black Bean Sauce and Mango Relish

YIELD: 4 SERVINGS

This slightly spicy dish has an island flavor. Serve with Brown Rice Pilaf (see page 295). You can also make this dish with other meaty fish steaks such as tuna or marlin.

4 4-ounce swordfish steaks	*¼ cup chopped scallions*
1 tablespoon lime juice	*2 cups Black Bean Sauce (see page*
½ teaspoon salt	*371)*
1 tablespoon chopped cilantro	*1 cup Mango Relish (see page*
	379)

1. Place swordfish steaks in a shallow pan. Combine the lime juice, salt, cilantro, and scallions and pour over fish. Turn fish

several times to coat with marinade and refrigerate for at least 1 hour.

2. Meanwhile, prepare the Black Bean Sauce and Mango Relish.

3. Preheat a broiler to high and coat the grate lightly with nonstick vegetable spray. Place fish under broiler and cook 4 to 5 minutes on each side or until the fish is browned and flaky but not dry.

4. Pool the Black Bean Sauce in the center of a platter or 4 plates, place the fish over the sauce, and top with Mango Relish.

Per serving:

fat grams 7	protein grams 29
fiber grams 6	carbohydrate grams 22
calories 259	sodium milligrams 818

Citrus Baked Snapper

YIELD: 4 SERVINGS

This is a quick and simple way to bake a fillet. For the snapper, you can substitute halibut, grouper, bass, or other lean, white-fleshed fish.

4 4-ounce skinless snapper fillets	*2 tablespoons chopped fresh basil or*
1 orange	*parsley*
1 grapefruit	*1/2 teaspoon salt*
1/4 cup dry bread crumbs	*1/4 cup white wine*
1 1/2 teaspoons olive oil	*1/4 cup canned evaporated skim*
1 teaspoon lemon juice	*milk*

1. Preheat oven to 300 degrees.

2. Place the fish fillets in one layer in a baking dish. Peel the orange and grapefruit, cut into sections, and arrange alternating wedges over the fish.

3. Combine the bread crumbs, olive oil, lemon juice, basil or parsley, and salt and scatter the mixture evenly over the fish fillets and citrus sections.

4. Pour the white wine into the bottom of the baking dish.

5. Bake for approximately 15 minutes or until the fish is done at the center and slightly browned on top.

6. Transfer fish and fruit from baking dish to plates. Pour liquid from baking dish into a small saucepan and bring to a simmer. Simmer until it coats the back of a spoon, about 3 to 5 minutes. Remove from heat and add the evaporated skim milk. Pour around fish and serve.

Per serving:

fat grams 4	protein grams 26
fiber grams 2	carbohydrate grams 13
calories 193	sodium milligrams 405

Barbecued Shrimp on Marinated Cucumbers
Y I E L D : 4 S E R V I N G S

This is a great summer dish that goes together easily. Serve with Black Bean Salad and Corn Pudding.

1 large cucumber, peeled and sliced
  thinly
½ teaspoon salt
½ tablespoon white wine vinegar
2 teaspoons sugar
1 tablespoon chopped dill
1 pound large shrimp, peeled and
  deveined

2 ounces Cowboy-style Barbecue
  Sauce (see pages 373–74)
4 ⅔-cup servings Black Bean
  Salad (see page 299)
4½-cup portions Corn Pudding
  (see pages 326–27)

1. Combine cucumber and salt. Cover and refrigerate for at least 1 hour. Drain cucumbers and add the white wine vinegar, sugar, and dill.

2. Preheat broiler. Thread shrimp onto four bamboo skewers. Brush with a small amount of the Cowboy-style Barbecue Sauce and broil for 2 minutes or until the sauce begins to caramelize. Turn the skewers and repeat for 2 minutes on second side. Brush with more

sauce and repeat browning until the shrimp are done (about 6 minutes total).

3. Place a bed of the cucumbers onto 4 plates and set the skewers over the top. Serve with Black Bean Salad and Corn Pudding.

Per serving:

fat grams 7	protein grams 35
fiber grams 8	carbohydrate grams 50
calories 398	sodium milligrams 1,093

Cioppino

YIELD: 4 SERVINGS

Cioppino, a fish stew, is inherently low in fat but packed with flavor. It makes a great do-ahead party dish since you can proceed through step 2 and hold or refrigerate it until a few minutes before serving. When the guests are about to sit down bring it back to a light simmer then add the seafoods and finish.

Serve this dish with a mixed salad and Red Pepper Bread Croustades (see pages 339–40).

1½ teaspoons olive oil
1 clove garlic, minced
1 leek (white and medium-green parts only), split, rinsed, and thinly sliced
½ red bell pepper, seeded and chopped
½ green bell pepper, seeded and chopped
1 bulb fennel, diced (reserve top)
1 tablespoon tomato paste
½ cup white wine
1 teaspoon saffron
3 cups clam juice or fish stock
1½ teaspoons grated orange peel

8 small red-skinned potatoes, scrubbed and quartered
1 tomato, peeled, deseeded, and chopped
1 teaspoon salt
¼ teaspoon white pepper
¼ cup chopped fresh tarragon
1 tablespoon chopped fennel top
2 tablespoons chopped fresh basil
12 clams, washed
12 mussels, washed and debearded
12 large shrimp, peeled and deveined
½ pound fresh tuna, monkfish fillet, or sea bass, cut into 1-inch cubes

1. Heat olive oil over medium heat in a medium saucepan and add garlic and leeks. Sauté until the leeks become tender, about 4 minutes. Add the peppers, fennel, and tomato paste and continue to sauté for 3 minutes.

2. Add the wine, saffron, clam juice or fish stock, orange peel, and potatoes and simmer until the potatoes are tender, about 20 minutes.

3. Add the tomato, the seasonings and herbs, clams, mussels, and shrimp and continue to simmer until the mussels and clams have opened (about 1 minute). Add the cubed fish. Divide into 4 portions and serve immediately.

Per serving:

fat grams 6	protein grams 26
fiber grams 4	carbohydrate grams 32
calories 281	sodium milligrams 1,032

Beef and Ale Stew with Sourdough Dumplings
YIELD: 6 SERVINGS

This hearty but low-fat stew is sure to please a meat eater. Since this dish reheats well, you can make a large batch and put some aside in the freezer (make sure the dumplings are immersed in the sauce).

¼ cup whole wheat flour

1 teaspoon salt

½ teaspoon black pepper

1½ pounds very lean beef such as bottom round, cut into 1½-inch cubes

1 teaspoon safflower oil

3 onions, sliced

4 cloves garlic, minced

2 bottles dark ale or beer

1 bay leaf

½ teaspoon fresh thyme or ¼ teaspoon dried

1 teaspoon fresh rosemary or ½ teaspoon dried

1 tablespoon brown sugar

DUMPLINGS:

8 slices sourdough bread, cut or
    torn into ½-inch pieces
½ cup all-purpose flour
1 teaspoon baking powder
½ cup skim milk

3 egg whites
½ teaspoon salt
½ cup chopped scallions
2 tablespoons chopped parsley

1. Preheat oven to 325 degrees.

2. Combine flour, salt, and pepper in a plastic bag and add the cubes of beef. Shake the bag to coat the meat with the mixture.

3. Heat oil in a nonstick skillet over high heat. Add a few pieces of beef at a time and brown the meat on all sides. When the meat is browned, remove it from the pan and reserve while the next batch is browning.

4. When the last of the meat has been browned and removed from the pan, add the onions and garlic. Reduce heat to low. Sauté slowly until the onions take on a rich caramelized color and are very tender, about 10 minutes.

5. Return the beef to the pan and add the ale, bay leaf, thyme, rosemary, and brown sugar. Cover tightly and place in the oven for 1 to 1½ hours or until the meat is fork tender but not falling apart. Remove from the oven and discard the bay leaf. Adjust seasoning with salt and pepper if needed.

6. To make the dumplings, place bread in a bowl and toss with flour and baking powder. Add milk, egg whites, salt, scallions, and parsley. Mix all ingredients together, let stand for 5 minutes, then mix again. Scoop the mixture into balls the size of a walnut onto a tray.

7. Add dumplings to the stew and allow to simmer until they have firmed up and absorbed some of the liquid from the stew, approximately 10 minutes. Serve hot.

Per serving:
fat grams 11
fiber grams 3
calories 490

protein grams 41
carbohydrate grams 48
sodium milligrams 944

Venison Sauerbraten with Gingersnap Gravy

YIELD: 8 SERVINGS

Venison is delicious and is being heralded as a healthy meat because it is very low in fat. Farm-raised venison has become widely available and is extremely good.

This dish is a good way to introduce venison to the uninitiated since the wine and vinegar marinade help tame the wild flavor. Serve with 24 ounces of cooked egg noodles (8 ounces raw) or Whole Wheat Drop Noodles (see page 279), and Braised Red Cabbage (see page 324).

2 pounds venison bottom round or leg roast
1 onion, chopped
1 carrot, chopped
1 rib celery, chopped
5 cloves garlic, peeled
2 cups red wine
2 tablespoons red wine vinegar
1 teaspoon salt
1 teaspoon black peppercorns

2 bay leaves
1/4 teaspoon thyme
1 tablespoon minced or chopped parsley stems
1 tablespoon safflower oil
2 tablespoons tomato paste
1 cup chicken or beef broth
1/2 cup gingersnap cookies, finely chopped in a blender or food processor

1. Trim the venison of all visible fat and sinews and place in a nonreactive 3-quart stewing pan with a tightly fitting oven-proof lid. Add the onion, carrot, celery, garlic, wine, vinegar, salt, peppercorns, bay leaves, thyme, and parsley stems. Cover, place in the refrigerator, and allow to marinate for at least 48 hours, turning the venison twice daily.

2. Preheat oven to 300 degrees.

3. Remove the venison and strain the solids from the marinade. Reserve all.

4. Using a large skillet, heat the oil over high heat and sear the venison on all sides. Remove the meat and set aside. Add the drained solids from the marinade and sauté until the vegetables brown slightly. Add the tomato paste, reduce the heat to medium, and continue to sauté until the tomato paste begins to brown and

adhere to the vegetables. Add the marinade to the pan and remove from the heat.

5. Place the meat in the stewing pan and pour the contents of the skillet over the top. Add the broth, place the pot over a high heat, and bring to a boil. Reduce the heat to a simmer and cover with the lid.

6. Place the pot in the oven and braise for 1 to 1½ hours or until the venison is fork tender.

7. Remove the meat from the pan and strain the liquid. Discard the solids.

8. Bring the liquid to a simmer and whisk in the gingersnap crumbs. Allow to simmer for 10 minutes and adjust the seasoning.

9. Slice the venison across the grain of the meat in ¼-inch slices and arrange on a serving platter. Ladle the gravy over the meat and serve.

Per serving:

fat grams 8

protein grams 41

fiber grams 2

carbohydrate grams 27

calories 351

sodium milligrams 387

Braised Stuffed Flank Steak Roll
YIELD: 6 SERVINGS

Although this recipe looks like a lot of work it is really quite simple. A thorough reading of the method before preparation lessens the fright factor.

This seems to taste even better if cooked one day and reheated the next. It also freezes quite well as long as it is not presliced.

1½ pounds beef flank steak,
   trimmed of all visible fat and
   sinews
1 onion, minced
1 rib celery, minced
2 cloves garlic, minced
1 bay leaf
½ teaspoon chopped fresh thyme
½ teaspoon chopped fresh rosemary
10 slices Italian bread
2 egg whites

1 teaspoon salt
¼ teaspoon white pepper
¼ cup chopped parsley
1 tablespoon tomato paste
½ cup red wine
2 cups beef broth
2 tablespoons cornstarch, diluted in
   a small quantity of water
¼ cup chopped fresh herbs (parsley, tarragon, chives, chervil)

1. Trim flank steak into a rectangle approximately 7 inches by 10 inches. Save all beef trimmings and set aside. Using a long and very sharp knife, slit the flank steak open along one of its long edges. Continue slitting and rolling the top layer of meat back until the flank is nearly cut into two layers and is held together by a ½-inch seam along the other long edge (do not cut all the way through creating two pieces). Pound the meat lightly into an even layer.

2. Coat a skillet with nonstick vegetable spray and heat over a high heat. Add the onions, celery, and garlic, and sauté a few minutes, until the onions become translucent. Add the bay leaf, thyme, and rosemary, and remove from the heat. Pour vegetables onto a plate and allow to cool. Discard bay leaf.

3. Preheat oven to 350 degrees. Dice the bread into ⅜-inch cubes and lay out onto a cookie tray. Bake until evenly toasted to a golden brown. Remove and set aside.

4. Place the reserved beef trimmings in a blender or food processor and chop to a coarse texture.

5. In a large bowl combine the cooked vegetables, toasted bread, chopped beef, egg whites, salt, pepper, and parsley. Work the mixture with your hand until it is well incorporated and sticks together, but the cubes of bread are still noticeable.

6. Place the stuffing on the pounded flank and spread it out so that it forms an even layer covering the entire surface. Tightly roll the flank steak jelly-roll fashion so that the grain of the meat runs

the length of the roll. Use thick cotton string or butcher's twine to tie the roll tightly in about 5 or 6 evenly spaced places.

7. Preheat oven to 300 degrees.

8. Heat an oven-proof skillet over high heat. Lightly coat with nonstick vegetable spray. Brown the roll on all sides. Reduce the heat and add the tomato paste to the pan. Use the meat to spread the tomato paste around in the pan and cook slowly until the tomato paste is browned and smells sweet. Add the wine and beef broth and bring to a simmer. Cover the pan tightly and place in oven for 1 hour, turning the roll occasionally. When the meat is cooked through and fork tender, remove from oven and allow to rest in its braising juices for 15 minutes. Carefully lift the flank roll to a cutting board. Place the braising juices over a high heat and bring to a boil. While whisking the pan, add the cornstarch and bring back to a simmer. Remove from the heat and add the herbs. Adjust the seasoning with salt and pepper.

9. Slice the flank steak into 12 slices, 2 per portion, and place on a platter or plates. Pour a small amount of sauce over the slices and serve any remaining sauce in a gravy boat.

Per serving (2 slices):

fat grams 7	protein grams 32
fiber grams 2	carbohydrate grams 34
calories 338	sodium milligrams 610

Baked Stuffed Summer Squash
YIELD: 4 SERVINGS

This dish has a Middle Eastern flare. Serve it with a simple green salad or with Corn Pudding and vegetables. If you prefer, you can substitute lean beef, pork, or veal for the lamb.

4 *medium yellow squash or*
   zucchini

¼ *cup diced onions*

2 *cloves garlic, minced*

½ *cup chopped raisins*

2 *cups cooked brown rice*

1 *tablespoon pine nuts, toasted and*
   chopped

½ *pound lean ground lamb (ask*
   the butcher to give you ground
   leg muscle)

2 *tablespoons chopped cilantro or*
   parsley

1 *teaspoon curry powder*

1 *teaspoon salt*

¼ *teaspoon black pepper*

2 *tablespoons grated Parmesan*
   cheese

1. Split squash in half lengthwise and carefully scoop out seeds with a teaspoon to give the squash halves a boat shape. Reserve pulp and seeds. Trim bottoms of the halves so that they will sit flat and place them on a baking tray.

2. Coarsely chop reserved pulp and seeds from squash by hand or briefly pulse in a food processor. Heat a medium sauté pan over low heat and add the onions, garlic, and chopped squash and cook until tender, about 10 minutes. Place on a plate and chill in the refrigerator about 30 minutes.

3. Preheat oven to 350 degrees.

4. In a bowl, combine the raisins, rice, pine nuts, lamb, cilantro or parsley, curry powder, salt, pepper, and cooked and chilled vegetables. Mix until well incorporated and mixture sticks together.

5. Divide the mixture between the hollows of the eight squash halves. Dust the tops of the squash with the Parmesan cheese and bake for approximately 25 minutes or until the mixture is cooked through.

Per serving (2 squash halves):

fat grams 8

fiber grams 6

calories 338

protein grams 22

carbohydrate grams 48

sodium milligrams 631

Blackberry-glazed Pork Tenderloin
Y I E L D : 4 S E R V I N G S

The tart blackberry sauce complements the rich flavor of the pork. Good accompaniments are Mashed Sweet Potatoes with Ginger and Asparagus Glazed with Orange.

In the summer, you can serve slices of the glazed tenderloin cold.

This recipe uses the pan grill described in the recipe for Fusilli Pasta with Pan-grilled Chicken and Red Pepper Sauce (see pages 283–84).

1 pound pork tenderloin, trimmed of all visible fat and sinews
¼ teaspoon salt
Pinch of black pepper
½ cup Blackberry Ketchup (see page 372)

3 cups Mashed Sweet Potatoes with Ginger (see page 330)
24 pieces (4 portions) Asparagus Glazed with Orange (see page 323)

1. Preheat oven to 300 degrees.
2. Season the pork tenderloin with salt and pepper. Heat a pan grill over high heat and coat lightly with nonstick vegetable spray. Place pork in pan and allow to cook until brown, about 4 minutes. Roll 90 degrees and cook again. Repeat until the outside is browned on all sides.
3. Remove the pork to a broiler pan with a pan below to catch juices as it roasts. Liberally brush the outside of the pork loin with Blackberry Ketchup, reserving what's left, and roast for 20 minutes, occasionally brushing with more ketchup, until the pork feels quite firm when squeezed, or its internal temperature reaches 160 degrees.
4. Remove the pork from the oven and allow to cool slightly. Meanwhile, heat the remaining ketchup.
5. Slice the pork and fan onto 4 warm dinner plates. Scrape all the juices and drippings from the pork into the Blackberry Ketchup sauce and stir. Ladle the warm sauce over the pork loin and serve with the sweet potatoes and asparagus.

Per serving:

fat grams 11   protein grams 32

fiber grams 6   carbohydrate grams 59

calories 447   sodium milligrams 724

Veal and Sun-dried Tomato Meat Loaf with Basil Sauce

YIELD: 6 SERVINGS

The old American favorite meat loaf becomes leaner and more special here by using ground veal and flavorful sun-dried tomatoes.

½ cup sun-dried tomatoes

1 cup boiling water

½ cup skim milk

½ cup diced onions

2 cloves garlic, minced

2 cups whole wheat bread crumbs (4 slices bread)

1 pound lean ground veal (look for 95 percent lean, or buy veal and have the butcher cut off all visible fat before grinding)

½ teaspoon salt

¼ teaspoon black pepper

2 egg whites

½ cup chopped fresh basil

1 tablespoon cornstarch, diluted in a small amount of chicken broth or water

3 cups Brown Rice Pilaf (see page 295)

1. Place the sun-dried tomatoes in a small bowl and cover with boiling water. Allow to steep until cool. Drain and discard the water; finely chop the tomatoes.

2. Preheat oven to 350 degrees.

3. In a small saucepan over medium heat, place 1 tablespoon of the skim milk, and the onions and garlic. Cook a few minutes until the onions become translucent. Add the remaining milk and heat until warm. Add the bread crumbs and remove from the heat. Stir until it becomes a thick paste. Transfer to a dinner plate and chill.

4. In a large bowl, combine the chopped tomatoes, bread paste, veal, salt, pepper, egg whites, and half of the basil. Mix until it sticks together.

5. Place the mixture into a 9-by-12-inch pan and shape into a rectangular loaf approximately 10 inches long.

6. Bake 30 to 35 minutes or until the internal temperature reaches 160 degrees.

7. Remove the meat loaf from the pan.

8. Place the drippings from the pan into a small saucepan and bring to a boil. While whisking, add just enough of the cornstarch-and-water mixture to thicken the juices to a sauce consistency. Remove from the heat and add the remaining basil. Adjust the seasoning if necessary.

9. Slice the meat loaf into 6 slices and serve with the sauce and Brown Rice Pilaf.

Per serving (1 slice):

fat grams 7	protein grams 23
fiber grams 4	carbohydrate grams 40
calories 309	sodium milligrams 710

Veal and Eggplant Casserole

YIELD: 6 SERVINGS

This dish is inspired by a traditional Greek dish called moussaka. By broiling the eggplant rather than frying it in oil and being careful with the contents of the custard-style topping, it meets our low-fat goals.

I like this dish even better if it is cooked a day in advance. It's also a lot easier to cut when chilled. Simply reheat in the microwave. It's a good idea to recrisp the topping under the broiler for a moment before serving.

1 large eggplant, about 2 pounds
1 pound lean ground veal
1 onion, diced
4 cloves garlic, minced
1 red bell pepper, diced
1 green bell pepper, diced
1 cup Tomato Sauce (see pages 378–79) or canned tomato sauce
1/4 teaspoon cinnamon
1/8 teaspoon allspice
1 bay leaf
1 teaspoon dried oregano
1/4 teaspoon salt
1/4 teaspoon black pepper
1/4 cup all-purpose flour
1 1/2 cups skim milk
1/2 cup grated Parmesan cheese
1/2 cup chopped basil
3 egg whites

1. Preheat broiler to high. Slice eggplant lengthwise into 3/8-inch-thick slices. Place eggplant slices on broiler rack and brown on both sides. Remove from heat and reserve.

2. Lightly coat a skillet with nonstick vegetable spray and add veal. When the meat is first added it will give off a great deal of moisture. As it cooks the moisture will evaporate and the meat will begin to brown. Chop the meat as it browns, to break clumps. When the veal is lightly browned, add the onions, garlic, and peppers. Sauté until the onions are translucent. Add the Tomato Sauce, cinnamon, allspice, bay leaf, oregano, salt, and pepper. Bring to a simmer and cook for 15 minutes, stirring often to prevent scorching. Remove from heat, discard bay leaf, and reserve.

3. Combine the flour and skim milk in a small saucepan and place over medium heat. Stir constantly until contents thicken and come to a boil. Simmer lightly for 10 minutes and remove from heat. Add the Parmesan cheese and basil and mix well. Place the egg whites in a small bowl and beat lightly. Pour the hot liquid over the eggs while whisking. Reserve.

4. Preheat oven to 350 degrees.

5. Lightly coat a 9-by-9-inch pan with nonstick vegetable spray. Line the bottom of the pan with 1/3 of the browned eggplant as you would pasta for lasagne. Run the slices up the sides so they hang slightly over the edge of the pan. Place 1/2 of the meat sauce in the pan and spread evenly. Layer another 1/3 of the eggplant so that it just covers the meat sauce. Add the remaining meat sauce and repeat with the eggplant. Flap over any eggplant that hangs over the edge

of the pan so that it completely seals the layers. Pour the cheese sauce over the top.

6. Bake for 1 hour or until the cheese sauce is well browned. Remove from the oven and allow to cool slightly before cutting into 6 servings.

Per serving:

fat grams 6

fiber grams 8

calories 249

protein grams 25

carbohydrate grams 27

sodium milligrams 618

Vegetables and Vegetable Salads

Asparagus Glazed with Orange

YIELD: 4 SERVINGS

Instead of butter, add a flavorful and beautiful citrus glaze to vegetables. Try this method with broccoli and snow peas, too.

24 medium asparagus, peeled
1 tablespoon water
¼ cup chicken broth
2 tablespoons orange juice

1 tablespoon grated orange peel
1 teaspoon cornstarch
¼ teaspoon salt
Pinch of white pepper

1. Place asparagus in a microwave-proof dish and drizzle with 1 tablespoon water. Seal the dish tightly with plastic wrap and set aside.

2. Combine the chicken broth, orange juice, orange zest, cornstarch, salt, and pepper in a small saucepan and place over medium heat. Bring to a boil, then remove from the heat.

3. Microwave the asparagus on high power for 2 minutes or until the asparagus is tender but not limp. (Or place asparagus in a steamer basket over briskly boiling water and steam for about 2 minutes.) Open the plastic seal and drain off any excess liquid.

4. Pour the orange sauce over the asparagus and serve.

Per serving (6 asparagus spears):
fat grams 0
fiber grams 1
calories 28

protein grams 3
carbohydrate grams 5
sodium milligrams 183

Braised Red Cabbage

YIELD: 8 SERVINGS

This is a hearty vegetable that hits the spot on a cold fall or winter day.

Since the cabbage is cooked until tender this is one vegetable dish that can be frozen successfully.

½ strip bacon, chopped

½ onion, diced

1 clove garlic, minced

2 pounds red cabbage, thinly shredded

1 apple, peeled, cored, and chopped

½ cup red wine

1 tablespoon red wine vinegar

3 tablespoons brown sugar

3 whole cloves

¼ baking potato, peeled then pureed in a food processor or grated on a hand grater

1 teaspoon salt

¼ teaspoon white pepper

1. Place bacon in a nonreactive large saucepan and set over high heat. Allow the bacon to fry until the pieces start to become crisp. Add the onions and garlic and sauté a few minutes until the onions become translucent. Add the cabbage, apple, wine, vinegar, sugar, and cloves. Stir over high heat until the cabbage wilts and the liquids come to a boil. Cover and allow to simmer over low heat for 20 to 25 minutes, stirring frequently.

2. Uncover the pan and while stirring add the raw potato puree. Allow the cabbage to return to a simmer and thicken. Cook for 5 minutes. Season with salt and pepper, remove the cloves, and serve.

Per serving (½ cup):

fat grams 2

fiber grams 3

calories 89

protein grams 2

carbohydrate grams 18

sodium milligrams 175

Carrot Custard

YIELD: 10 SERVINGS

Every time I've served these carrot custards I've had the same surprised response: "That was too good to be carrots."

If you want to get fancy, you can bake the custards in little
individual cups and turn them out onto the plates just before serving. (Bake 45 minutes at 275 degrees.)

1½ pounds carrots, peeled and   *1 tablespoon sugar*
   coarsely chopped   *½ teaspoon salt*
4 egg whites   *⅛ teaspoon white pepper*
4 ounces evaporated skim milk

   1. Boil carrots in lightly salted water until very tender, about 15
minutes. Allow to cool slightly.

   2. Preheat oven to 325 degrees.

   3. Transfer carrots to a blender or food processor and add remaining ingredients. Puree to a very smooth consistency.

   4. Pour into a lightly oiled 2-quart baking dish.

   5. Place the baking dish in a larger pan and add boiling water to
larger pan to a depth of 1 inch. Place the pans in oven and bake for
30 minutes or until a knife inserted in the custard comes out clean.

   6. Spoon onto plates.

Per serving (3 ounces, or 6 tablespoons):

fat grams 0   protein grams 3
fiber grams 2   carbohydrate grams 10
calories 50   sodium milligrams 112

Middle Eastern Carrot, Orange, and Raisin Salad

YIELD: 10 SERVINGS

Carrot and raisin salad is nothing new, but too often it is weighed
down with heavy mayonnaise dressing. This Middle Eastern–
inspired recipe is much lighter and more refreshing, and it is loaded

with vitamin C. Our testers loved this one! The salad will keep for several days in the refrigerator.

2 navel oranges	1 tablespoon chopped fresh mint
1 teaspoon grated orange peel	1/2 cup raisins
1 pound carrots, peeled and very finely shredded	1 tablespoon olive oil
	1/4 cup nonfat yogurt
1 garlic clove, minced	1/2 teaspoon salt
1/2 teaspoon ground cumin	1/4 teaspoon cayenne

1. Peel and section the oranges.

2. Combine the orange peel, orange segments, and remaining ingredients, and allow to marinate for at least 1 hour before serving.

Per serving (1/2 cup):

fat grams 2	protein grams 1
fiber grams 2	carbohydrate grams 14
calories 70	sodium milligrams 128

Corn Pudding
YIELD: 8 SERVINGS

This is a wonderfully comforting dish. It heats very well in the microwave. Serve it with almost any main dish. It is at its best at the peak of corn season.

3 cups fresh corn (cut from the cob) or frozen	1/4 cup cornmeal
	2 eggs
1 teaspoon olive oil	2 tablespoons fresh basil, chopped
1/2 cup chopped scallions	1/2 teaspoon salt
2 cloves garlic, minced	1/4 teaspoon black pepper
1 cup evaporated skim milk	1/4 cup bread crumbs

1. Place corn in a blender or food processor and chop until partially pureed. Reserve.

2. Heat oil in a small saucepan over low heat and add the scallions

and garlic. Cook for 2 minutes. Add the corn puree and evaporated skim milk. Bring to a simmer. Whisk the contents of the pan and add the cornmeal in a slow steady steam. Return to a light simmer and cook for 10 minutes. Remove from heat and allow to cool to room temperature.

3. Preheat oven to 350 degrees.

4. To the corn mixture, add the eggs, basil, salt, and pepper.

5. Lightly coat a small casserole with nonstick vegetable spray and add the corn pudding mixture. Top with the bread crumbs.

6. Place the casserole in a slightly larger pan and add boiling water to the outer pan to a depth of 1 inch. Place the pans in the oven and bake for 35 minutes or until a knife inserted into the pudding comes out clean. Serve hot.

Per serving (½ cup):

fat grams 3	protein grams 7
fiber grams 3	carbohydrate grams 20
calories 124	sodium milligrams 207

Jicama Slaw
YIELD: 4 SERVINGS

Jicama is often referred to as Mexican potato. It is brown on the outside and white on the inside with a flesh that has the texture and some of the starchiness of potato, but a pleasingly sweet flavor.

Feel free to throw in some strips of sweet red and green bell peppers if you like.

The slaw will keep for several days in the refrigerator.

2 cups peeled and grated jicama
(1 medium)
½ cup grated carrot
2 tablespoons fresh lime juice
1 tablespoon sugar

2 tablespoons chopped cilantro
½ cup Yogurt Cheese (see pages
386–87)
¼ teaspoon salt

1. Mix together all ingredients. Allow to marinate for ½ hour before serving.

Per serving (½ cup):

fat grams 0

fiber grams 1

calories 70

protein grams 4

carbohydrate grams 14

sodium milligrams 184

Barbecue Oven Fries

YIELD: 4 SERVINGS

This is a great way to produce low-fat french fries.

You can eliminate the barbecue spices if you want a more traditional flavor.

2 large baking potatoes

1 teaspoon chili powder

Pinch of dried oregano

¼ teaspoon garlic powder

¼ teaspoon onion powder

2 teaspoons safflower oil

½ teaspoon lemon juice

¼ teaspoon salt

1. Preheat oven to 475 degrees.

2. Scrub potatoes thoroughly and wipe dry. Slice lengthwise, ½ inch thick. Lay the potato slices down and cut into ½-inch-wide sticks.

2. In a medium bowl, combine the chili powder, oregano, garlic powder, and onion powder. Add the potato sticks and toss until evenly coated. Add the safflower oil and lemon juice and toss again until well coated.

3. Lay the potato sticks on a rack on a baking tray. Bake for about 35 to 40 minutes, turning occasionally. When the potatoes are evenly browned, remove from oven and season with salt before dividing into 4 servings.

Per serving:

fat grams 3

fiber grams 4

calories 185

protein grams 4

carbohydrate grams 38

sodium milligrams 152

Fresh Potato Salad
YIELD: 6 SERVINGS

No, this is not the typical "grandmother's style" potato salad. But it's fresh and delicious, and will let you enjoy one of life's little pleasures without the guilt.

2 pounds red-skinned potatoes, scrubbed

¼ cup shallots, peeled and halved

2 cloves garlic, minced

2 tablespoons minced fresh chives

2 tablespoons chopped fresh parsley

1 tablespoon chopped fresh tarragon or parsley (if fresh tarragon not available omit from recipe rather than using dried terragon)

1 tablespoon Dijon mustard

1 tablespoon olive oil

1 tablespoon red wine vinegar

½ cup chicken broth

½ teaspoon salt

¼ teaspoon white pepper

1. In medium saucepan, cover potatoes with cold water. Bring to a boil and cook 15 to 20 minutes or until tender. Remove from heat and drain. Set aside.

2. Meanwhile, combine remaining ingredients in a bowl and mix.

3. When potatoes are just cool enough to handle, slice them into ¼-inch slices and add them to bowl. Toss carefully to prevent breaking the potato slices excessively.

4. Serve the salad while still slightly warm. Or refrigerate it until used.

Per serving (¾ cup):

fat grams 2

fiber grams 2

calories 162

protein grams 4

carbohydrate grams 32

sodium milligrams 203

Mashed Sweet Potatoes with Ginger

YIELD: 6 SERVINGS

Anyone who claims not to like sweet potatoes needs to try these. The ginger lends a nice accent without being too obvious, but feel free to add more if you like.

Serve these with the Blackberry-glazed Pork Tenderloin (see pages 318–19) or with any slightly sweet/sour dish.

2 medium sweet potatoes
1 medium white potato
¹/₂ cup canned evaporated skim milk

1 tablespoon chopped fresh gingerroot
¹/₄ teaspoon salt
¹/₄ teaspoon white pepper

1. Wash the potatoes and place in a medium saucepan with enough cold water to cover by at least 1 inch. Bring to a boil and reduce to a simmer. Cook until potatoes are fork tender, about 20 minutes. Drain.

2. In a small saucepan over low heat, combine the evaporated skim milk with the ginger. Allow to steep together for approximately 10 minutes. Strain out and discard ginger.

3. Peel the potatoes while still quite hot and mash with a sturdy whisk or a potato masher. Once the potatoes are free of lumps, add the strained evaporated skim milk and the remaining ingredients and whip until smooth.

Per serving (¹/₂ cup):

fat grams 0
fiber grams 2
calories 95

protein grams 3
carbohydrate grams 21
sodium milligrams 120

Mashed Potatoes with Caramelized Onions

YIELD: 8 SERVINGS

Mashed potatoes are a great American comfort food. If you're used to preparing mashed potatoes with cream and butter, try this new version, with the sweet flavor of slowly browned onions.

1 tablespoon olive oil
1 cup minced onions
1½ pounds potatoes, low-starch or boiling variety

½ cup evaporated skim milk
½ teaspoon salt
¼ teaspoon white pepper

1. Preheat oven to 300 degrees.

2. Heat olive oil in an oven-proof sauté pan over high heat and add the onions. Reduce the heat to medium and cook the onions, stirring frequently, until they begin to brown. Place the pan in the oven and bake until the onions become a dark golden brown, stirring frequently. Remove from oven and reserve.

3. Meanwhile, place unpeeled potatoes in a saucepan and cover with cold water. Place on high heat and bring to a simmer. Simmer 20 to 25 minutes or until the potatoes are very tender. Drain and allow to cool just enough so that they may be handled. Peel the potatoes and return to the pan. Mash the potatoes with a masher or with a stiff whisk.

4. Heat the evaporated skim milk and add to the potatoes. Whip the potatoes until smooth. Add the caramelized onions, salt, and pepper. Mix well and serve.

Per serving (½ cup):

fat grams 2
fiber grams 1
calories 85

protein grams 3
carbohydrate grams 15
sodium milligrams 155

Potatoes au Gratin
YIELD: 8 SERVINGS

No culinary repertoire is complete without a version of potatoes au gratin, not even one that follows strict fat guidelines.

1 cup skim milk

1 cup evaporated skim milk

1 pound potatoes, peeled, sliced
  1/8 inch thick

1 garlic clove, minced

1/2 teaspoon salt

1 tablespoon cornstarch, diluted with
  a small amount of water

1/3 cup grated Swiss cheese

1/4 cup bread crumbs

1/4 cup grated Parmesan cheese

1. Combine skim milk, evaporated skim milk, potatoes, garlic, and salt in a medium saucepan and bring to a boil. Allow to simmer lightly until potatoes are tender, about 15 minutes (be careful to not allow milk to scorch in bottom of pan).

2. Preheat oven to 350 degrees.

3. When potatoes are tender, add the cornstarch and stir until thickened. Remove from heat and stir in the Swiss cheese.

4. Pour potatoes into an 8-by-8-inch baking dish. Combine bread crumbs and Parmesan cheese and scatter over surface top.

5. Bake for 25 minutes or until the potatoes are lightly browned. Serve immediately or refrigerate and reheat portions in microwave as needed.

Per serving (2-by-4-inch square):

fat grams 3	protein grams 7
fiber grams 1	carbohydrate grams 20
calories 134	sodium milligrams 273

Butternut Squash with Ginger and Garlic
YIELD: 4 SERVINGS

The name butternut squash is no mistake. It is a vegetable with a rich flavor yet very little fat.

Try this recipe with a broiled or roasted chicken.

1 teaspoon olive oil
½ tablespoon garlic, minced
1 tablespoon minced fresh
   gingerroot
3 cups butternut squash, peeled,
   seeded, and cut into ½-inch
   cubes

¼ teaspoon salt
Pinch of white pepper
2 tablespoons grated Parmesan
   cheese
1 tablespoon chopped fresh parsley

1. Combine olive oil, garlic, and ginger in a large sauté pan with a tight-fitting lid and place over medium heat uncovered. When a strong aroma of garlic rises from pan, in about 30 seconds, add the butternut squash, salt, and pepper. Stir well and cover tightly to steam the squash. Reduce heat to low and cook for 5 minutes until the squash is tender (be careful to not allow squash to brown).

2. Turn the squash out into a serving dish and top with the Parmesan and parsley before serving.

Per serving:

fat grams 2	protein grams 3
fiber grams 4	carbohydrate grams 17
calories 88	sodium milligrams 186

Vegetable Stew with Couscous and Harissa

YIELD: 4 SERVINGS

This is a Moroccan-influenced dish that can be served either as a main dish or an accompaniment to Tandoori-style Cornish Hen (see pages 306–307) or grilled chicken. The "harissa" is the sauce made from the last three ingredients.

1 cup dry couscous

1½ cups boiling water

½ teaspoon salt

1 teaspoon olive oil

½ onion, diced

4 cloves garlic, minced

½ red bell pepper, cut into matchsticks

½ carrot, cut into matchsticks

½ zucchini, cut into matchsticks

½ yellow squash, cut into matchsticks

10 ripe olives (Kalamata if available), pitted

6 artichoke hearts, cut into small wedges (canned are acceptable if rinsed of oil and drained)

½ cup drained chickpeas (canned)

1 tablespoon pine nuts, toasted

2 tablespoons raisins

1 tomato, chopped

⅛ teaspoon cumin

½ teaspoon curry powder

½ cup chicken broth (or water for vegetarian style)

2 teaspoons cornstarch

1 teaspoon lemon juice

3 tablespoons chopped cilantro

¼ cup Red Pepper Sauce (see pages 376–77)

2 teaspoons Tabasco sauce

1. In a small bowl, combine couscous, boiling water, and salt. Cover tightly with plastic wrap and set aside.

2. Heat the olive oil in a large sauté pan over high heat. Add the onion and garlic and sauté a few minutes until the onion becomes translucent.

3. Add the red pepper, carrot, zucchini, and yellow squash and sauté for 3 to 4 minutes. Add the olives, artichoke hearts, chickpeas, pine nuts, raisins, tomato, cumin, and curry powder and sauté for 2 more minutes.

4. In a small bowl, combine the chicken broth, cornstarch, lemon juice, and 2 tablespoons of the cilantro. Add to the vegetables. Stir with a spoon until the contents of the pan come to a simmer. Remove the pan from the heat.

5. In a small bowl, combine the Red Pepper Sauce, Tabasco sauce, and remaining 1 tablespoon cilantro.

6. Divide the couscous into 4 mounds on serving plates or pasta bowls. Drizzle the sauce over the couscous. Ladle the vegetable stew over the couscous and serve.

Per serving:

fat grams 5 protein grams 9
fiber grams 7 carbohydrate grams 43
calories 244 sodium milligrams 513

Breads

Bran Bread

YIELD: 2 LOAVES (40 SLICES)

Good bread is good for the body. You'll find that when you eat good bread, you won't need to slather it in butter to make it taste like something. Many people have found that kneading yeast breads is good for the soul, too.

This bread is a flavorful way to introduce more bran into your diet.

1 package active dry yeast
1/3 cup warm water
2 2/3 cups water, room
   temperature
2 tablespoons olive oil

5 1/2 cups unbleached all-purpose
   flour
2 cups bran
2 1/4 teaspoons salt

1. Stir the yeast into the warm water in a large bowl. When a foam becomes visible on the surface, add the room-temperature water and the olive oil.

2. In a separate bowl, combine the flour, bran, and salt. Stir 2 cups at a time into the liquid until a smooth, heavy dough is formed. Knead in the remaining flour by hand and work for 8 to 10 minutes until a smooth, elastic dough is formed. Form the dough into a ball and place in a clean dry bowl. Cover with a towel and let rise in a warm place until doubled, about 1 hour.

3. Reknead the dough until smooth again and divide into 2 pieces. Shape the dough into rounds or oblong loaves and place on a floured surface. Allow to rise for 45 minutes until the loaves are light and spongy.

4. Preheat oven to 425 degrees. Bake the loaves for 20 minutes,

then reduce the heat to 375 degrees and bake for another 20 minutes. Cool the loaves on a rack.

Per serving (¹/₂-inch slice):

fat grams 1   protein grams 2
fiber grams 1   carbohydrate grams 15
calories 76   sodium milligrams 121

Honey Whole Wheat Bread

YIELD: 2 LOAVES (40 SLICES)

This loaf makes great sandwich bread. Try it toasted, too.

The dough will develop a better crust if brushed or sprayed with water just before, and several times during, the baking. A clean plant sprayer makes this extra step a snap.

1¹/₂ packages active dry yeast   *7 cups whole wheat flour*
4 tablespoons honey   *3 teaspoons salt*
3 cups warm water

1. Stir the yeast and honey into ¹/₄ cup of the warm water in a large bowl. When a foam becomes visible on the surface add the remaining water.

2. In a separate bowl, combine the flour and salt. Stir 2 cups at a time into the liquid until a smooth, heavy dough is formed. Knead in the remaining flour by hand and work for 8 to 10 minutes until a smooth, elastic dough is formed. Form the dough into a ball and place in a clean dry bowl. Cover with a towel and let rise in a warm place until doubled, about 2 hours.

3. Divide into 2 pieces and carefully shape the dough into rounds without overhandling. Allow to rise for 45 minutes until the loaves are light and spongy.

4. Preheat oven to 450 degrees. Bake the loaves for 10 minutes, then reduce the heat to 400 degrees and bake for another 25 minutes. Cool the loaves on a rack.

Per serving (1/2-inch slice):

fat grams 0   protein grams 3

fiber grams 3   carbohydrate grams 17

calories 78   sodium milligrams 162

Baked Cheddar and Scallion Spoonbread

YIELD: 4 SERVINGS

A spicy version of the old Southern grits soufflé.

2 cups skim milk   *1/2 cup chopped scallions*
1/4 cup cornmeal   *2 egg whites*
1/4 teaspoon salt   *Pinch of cream of tartar*
Pinch of white pepper   *1/4 cup grated cheddar cheese*

1. Preheat oven to 350 degrees.

2. Place skim milk in a small saucepan over high heat and bring to a simmer. While whisking, add the cornmeal in a slow steady stream. Bring back to a boil and reduce the heat to low. Simmer lightly for 15 minutes. Remove from heat and add the salt, pepper, and scallions.

3. Place the egg whites and cream of tartar in a clean dry mixing bowl and beat until it forms soft peaks.

4. Fold egg whites into the cornmeal base just until incorporated.

5. Lightly coat a 7-by-7-inch baking dish with nonstick vegetable spray. Add the spoonbread batter and scatter the cheese evenly over the top.

6. Bake for 20 minutes or until the batter is risen and firm. Slice into quarters.

Per serving:

fat grams 3   protein grams 9

fiber grams 1   carbohydrate grams 15

calories 121   sodium milligrams 269

Skillet Corn Bread

YIELD: *12* SLICES

A lot of the soups and salads can be made into complete meals with a good piece of corn bread.

Keep this bread covered and in the refrigerator since it contains very little fat and will dry out quickly.

2 cups cornmeal	*2 tablespoons sugar*
2 cups all-purpose flour	*1 teaspoon salt*
2½ tablespoons baking powder	*2 cups buttermilk*
2 teaspoons baking soda	*5 eggs*

1. Preheat oven to 400 degrees. Place a cast-iron or heavy metal 10-inch skillet in the oven.

2. Combine dry ingredients in a bowl. In a separate bowl combine the buttermilk and eggs.

3. Make a well in the dry ingredients and add the buttermilk and egg mixture. Gently stir the wet ingredients into the dry ingredients until a smooth batter is formed (do not overmix).

4. Lightly coat the hot skillet with nonstick vegetable spray. Add the corn bread batter. Bake for 20 minutes or until a toothpick inserted in the center comes out clean. Turn the bread out from the skillet and cool on a rack. Slice into 12 wedges.

Per serving (1 wedge):

fat grams 3	protein grams 8
fiber grams 2	carbohydrate grams 39
calories 219	sodium milligrams 590

Red Pepper Bread Croustades

YIELD: *4* SERVINGS

These bread crisps make good accompaniments for soups and pastas. Make up a basket, set them out on the table, and watch them disappear.

8 slices Italian bread
½ cup Red Pepper Sauce (see pages 376–77)
2 tablespoons grated Parmesan cheese

1. Preheat oven to 400 degrees.
2. Spread one side of each slice of bread with the Red Pepper Sauce and place sauce side up on a baking tray. Sprinkle with the grated Parmesan cheese.
3. Bake until the bread is crisp and the cheese and sauce have slightly browned.

Per serving (2 slices):

fat grams 1	protein grams 7
fiber grams 1	carbohydrate grams 36
calories 188	sodium milligrams 582

Apple and Raisin Bran Muffins

YIELD: 12 SERVINGS

This is a great way to take your bran cereal "on the road" for a busy morning.

Make them up and freeze them, then zap them in the microwave before hitting the door.

3 cups bran cereal (such as All-Bran)
⅓ cup flour
¼ cup brown sugar
2 tablespoons baking powder
1 teaspoon cinnamon
2 teaspoons grated lemon peel
1 apple, peeled, cored, and chopped
½ cup raisins
¾ cup skim milk
3 egg whites
2 tablespoons applesauce

1. Preheat oven to 400 degrees.
2. Place the bran cereal, flour, brown sugar, baking powder, cinnamon, and lemon peel in a blender or food processor and chop until the mixture has the texture of cornmeal. Transfer to a large mixing bowl.

3. Place apple and raisins in the blender or food processor and chop to a fine dice. Add to the dry ingredients and mix to combine.

4. Make a well in the bowl of dry ingredients and add the skim milk, egg whites, and applesauce. Mix until well incorporated but do not overmix.

5. Drop batter into 12 muffin tins that have been coated lightly with nonstick vegetable spray.

6. Bake until risen and browned, about 25 minutes.

Per serving (1 muffin):

fat grams 0.5	protein grams 5
fiber grams 7	carbohydrate grams 32
calories 121	sodium milligrams 222

Orange Muffins
YIELD: 12 MUFFINS

Too often, breakfast muffins are loaded with shortening or vegetable oil to make them moist and tender. This recipe makes a nice tender muffin with a refreshing flavor while keeping the fat in check. Try other citruses, too, such as lime or grapefruit.

2 cups all-purpose flour	*1/3 cup orange juice*
1/4 cup sugar	*4 tablespoons grated orange peel*
2 teaspoons baking powder	*1/2 teaspoon vanilla extract*
1/4 teaspoon salt	*3 tablespoons unsalted butter,*
1/2 cup skim milk	*melted*
1/3 cup buttermilk	*1 cup powdered sugar*
1 egg	*1 tablespoon nonfat yogurt*

1. Preheat oven to 400 degrees.

2. In a large mixing bowl, combine the flour, sugar, baking powder, and salt. Mix well.

3. In a separate bowl combine the skim milk, buttermilk, egg, orange juice, 3 tablespoons of the orange peel, vanilla extract, and melted butter.

4. Make a well in the center of the dry ingredients and pour in

the wet ingredients. Mix gently, being careful not to overmix, until just combined.

5. Divide the mixture into 12 muffin cups or liners that have been coated lightly with nonstick vegetable spray. Bake for approximately 25 minutes or until muffins are browned and a knife inserted into the middle comes out clean. Remove the muffins from the pan.

6. In a small bowl, combine the powdered sugar, yogurt, and remaining 1 tablespoon orange peel. Beat until smooth. Spread mixture over warm muffins and allow to cool before serving.

Per serving (1 muffin):

fat grams 4   protein grams 3
fiber grams 1   carbohydrate grams 31
calories 169   sodium milligrams 119

Breakfasts and Brunches

Swiss Muesli

YIELD: 4 SERVINGS

This combination of cereal and fruit is packed with fiber and taste. Make it the evening before, and wake up to a great start for your day.

1½ cups old-fashioned oatmeal
1 cup skim milk
½ cup nonfat yogurt
¼ cup raisins
1 ripe banana, mashed with a
   fork

2 tablespoons brown sugar
½ teaspoon cinnamon
1 tablespoon chopped walnuts
1 cup fresh berries (strawberries,
   raspberries, blueberries)

1. Combine the oatmeal, skim milk, yogurt, raisins, banana, brown sugar, cinnamon, and walnuts in a bowl. Refrigerate overnight.

2. Spoon into 4 dishes and top with fresh berries before serving.

Per serving: 1 cup
fat grams 2.5
fiber 3.78
calories 196

protein grams 7
carbohydrate grams 39
sodium milligrams 201

Breakfast Shake
YIELD: 2 SERVINGS

This "power" drink is like a breakfast in a glass. Try combining other fruits such as papaya and orange, or apple and raspberry.

1 cup nonfat yogurt
1/2 banana, peeled and sliced
1/2 cup strawberries

1 tablespoon honey
1/4 cup bran cereal

1. Place all of the ingredients into a blender and blend on high speed for 20 seconds.
2. Divide between 2 tall glasses and serve.

Per serving:
fat grams 2
fiber grams 5
calories 168

protein grams 8
carbohydrate grams 34
sodium milligrams 179

Savory Egg Cups
YIELD: 4 SERVINGS

An elegant dish for serving guests at a brunch, or for a holiday meal.
There are a number of no-cholesterol, nonfat egg substitutes on the market.

2 pieces phyllo dough
1/4 cup tomatoes
1 1/2 cups nonfat egg substitute
1/4 cup Mushroom "Bacon"
  (see pages 379–80)

2 tablespoons minced chives
1/4 teaspoon salt
Pinch of black pepper
4 teaspoons Yogurt Cheese
  (see pages 386–87)

1. Preheat the oven to 350 degrees. Place a single sheet of phyllo dough on a dry cutting surface. Working very quickly so that the dough does not dry out and become brittle, cut the sheet into a 6 equal-sized squares. Stack the squares 3 layers deep with a slight twist between each so that the stacks resemble sunbursts. Press the

stacks into 4 cups of a dry muffin tin or in individual oven-proof dishes and mold the dough into the corners to create dough cups. (Each sheet will produce 2 cups.) Repeat the process until all the dough is used. Bake the cups until they are golden brown, about 12 minutes. Remove the phyllo cups from the molds and place one on each plate.

2. Lightly coat a skillet with nonstick vegetable spray and place it over moderate heat. Add the tomatoes and egg substitute and cook slowly, stirring constantly, as for scrambled eggs. When cooked to the desired doneness, remove the pan from the heat and add the Mushroom "Bacon" and chives, and adjust the seasoning with salt and pepper.

3. Spoon the mixture into the phyllo cups and top with the Yogurt Cheese. Serve immediately.

Per serving:

fat grams 1	protein grams 9
fiber grams 1	carbohydrate grams 6
calories 71	sodium milligrams 206

Vegetable Quiche
YIELD: 8 SERVINGS

Quiche is not trendy the way it once was, but it's still a great dish for brunch or for a family who doesn't all eat at the same time. Feel free to vary the vegetables as long as you keep the ratio of eggs to milk intact.

8 ounces (*½ recipe*) *Ricotta Pastry* (*see pages 387–88*), *no sugar or vanilla*
1 cup mushrooms, sliced
½ red bell pepper, seeded and diced
½ green bell pepper, seeded and diced

½ cup chopped tomato
½ cup diced lean ham
1 cup skim milk
½ cup nonfat egg substitute
½ teaspoon salt
⅛ teaspoon white pepper
¼ cup grated nonfat cheddar cheese

1. Preheat oven to 350 degrees.

2. Roll pastry and line a 9-inch pie pan with the dough. Crimp edges and prick dough with tines of a fork. Place an empty pie tin inside the dough-lined tin, and bake for 15 minutes. Remove extra tin and allow to cool.

3. Toss mushrooms, red and green peppers, tomato, and ham together and place in bottom of pie shell.

4. Combine skim milk, egg substitute, salt, and pepper and pour over the vegetables. Scatter top with cheddar cheese.

5. Bake 35 minutes or until the tip of a knife inserted into custard draws out clean.

6. Allow to cool for about 5 minutes before cutting into 8 wedges and serving.

Per serving:

fat grams 2	protein grams 9
fiber grams 1	carbohydrate grams 15
calories 120	sodium milligrams 535

Apple, Raisin, and Cheese Breakfast Blintzes

YIELD: 4 SERVINGS

A healthy and delicious alternative to eggs and pancakes for brunch. Try other fruits and spices, too—for example, dried sour cherries or blueberries in place of the raisins.

These can be made in advance and frozen if desired.

2 *Granny Smith apples, peeled and diced*	¼ *cup low-fat cream cheese (Neufchâtel)*
1 *tablespoon brown sugar*	¼ *cup part-skim ricotta cheese*
½ *cup raisins*	8 *Whole Wheat Crêpes (see pages*
¼ *teaspoon cinnamon*	*388–89)*

1. Place apples, brown sugar, and raisins in a small sauté pan and cook over a low heat until apples are soft. Remove the pan from the heat, add the cinnamon, and allow to cool.

2. Soften the cream cheese for 1 minute in a microwave set at low power (defrost). Fold the ricotta cheese and the cooked apples and raisins into the cream cheese.

3. Preheat oven to 325 degrees.

4. Place the crêpes on a flat surface and divide the mixture down the center of each crêpe. With each crêpe, fold the bottom flap up, then fold in the two sides, and finally fold down the top flap, like an envelope. Place the blintzes seam side down in a baking dish. Heat in oven for 15 minutes and serve. Or refrigerate overnight and heat the next day.

Per serving (2 blintzes):

fat grams 5	protein grams 7
fiber grams 4	carbohydrate grams 44
calories 240	sodium milligrams 146

Crêpes with Apricot and Cheese Filling
YIELD: 4 SERVINGS

These crêpes make a great breakfast sweet, replacing fat-laden Danish pastries and sweet rolls.

Since they freeze well, make up a batch and wrap them in small packages for easy thawing in the microwave.

¼ cup dried apricots	4 tablespoons honey, divided
1 cup water	2 tablespoons chopped walnuts
1 teaspoon grated lemon peel	8 Whole Wheat Crêpes (see pages
¼ cup low-fat cream cheese	388–89)
(Neufchâtel)	

1. Place apricots and water in a small saucepan and bring to a boil. Remove from heat, cover tightly, and allow to steep until water has cooled.

2. Preheat oven to 350 degrees.

3. Drain apricots and place in a food processor or blender with the lemon peel, cheese, and 2 tablespoons of the honey. Process until

very smooth, stopping occasionally to scrape down sides of bowl with a rubber spatula.

4. Lay crêpes out on a flat surface and divide apricot mixture on them. Spread mixture in an even layer on each. Roll crêpes into tight cigarette rolls and line up in a small cake pan. Drizzle the crêpes with remaining 2 tablespoons honey and sprinkle chopped walnuts over the surface.

5. Bake until rolls are heated through and walnuts are slightly glazed, about 15 minutes. Serve warm.

Per serving (2 crêpes):

fat grams 3	protein grams 5
fiber grams 2	carbohydrate grams 37
calories 186	sodium milligrams 79

Cornmeal Pancakes with Yogurt and Berries
YIELD: 6 SERVINGS

You'll be surprised by how moist and smooth cornmeal pancakes are. Cornmeal is a good source of fiber and complex carbohydrates.

1 cup flour
1 cup cornmeal
2 teaspoons baking powder
1 teaspoon baking soda
4 tablespoons sugar, divided
Pinch of salt
1 cup skim milk

½ cup buttermilk
1 egg
1 cup Yogurt Cheese (see pages 386–87)
1 pint fresh berries (strawberries, blueberries, raspberries)

1. In a large mixing bowl, combine the flour, cornmeal, baking powder, baking soda, 2 tablespoons of the sugar, and salt.

2. In a separate bowl combine the skim milk, buttermilk, and egg.

3. Make a well in the bowl of dry ingredients and add the wet ingredients. Carefully stir the wet ingredients into the dry ingredients, being careful not to overmix.

4. Combine the Yogurt Cheese and the remaining 2 tablespoons sugar.

5. Heat a griddle or sauté pan over medium heat. Coat lightly with nonstick vegetable spray. Ladle about ¼ cup batter per cake onto the griddle. Turn when bubbles form on the raw surface of the cakes. Cook second side until lightly browned.

6. Arrange the cakes on plates and top with the berries and the sweetened yogurt.

Per serving (3 pancakes):

fat grams 2	protein grams 10
fiber grams 5	carbohydrate grams 53
calories 273	sodium milligrams 371

Peach and Ricotta Pancakes
YIELD: 6 SERVINGS

This brunch recipe produces a wonderful twist on the old hotcake. Try other fruits, too, such as plums, nectarines, or even berries.

Since the egg whites will go flat if stored, make only one day's worth of mix at a time.

1 cup flour
1 teaspoon baking powder
½ teaspoon baking soda
¼ teaspoon salt
2 tablespoons sugar
½ cup part-skim ricotta cheese
¼ cup skim milk
1 tablespoon unsalted butter,
  melted

1 teaspoon grated lemon peel
2 fresh peaches, peeled, pitted, and
  chopped
1 egg white
1 cup Berry and Amaretto Break-
  fast Syrup (see page 370) or
  maple syrup

1. In a medium mixing bowl, sift together the flour, baking powder, baking soda, salt, and sugar.

2. In a separate bowl, combine the ricotta, skim milk, butter, and lemon peel.

3. Fold the peaches into the wet mixture.

4. Place the egg white in a clean, dry bowl and beat until soft peaks form. Carefully fold the egg white into the batter.

5. Heat a griddle or sauté pan over medium heat. Lightly coat with nonstick vegetable spray. Ladle about ¼ cup batter per cake onto the griddle. Turn when bubbles form on the raw surface of the cakes. Cook second side until lightly browned.

6. Arrange the cakes on plates and top with Berry and Amaretto Breakfast Syrup or your favorite breakfast syrup.

Per serving (3 pancakes):

fat grams 4	protein grams 6
fiber grams 2	carbohydrate grams 44
calories 234	sodium milligrams 257

Pumpkin and Bran Pancakes with Apple Butter and Maple Syrup

YIELD: 6 SERVINGS

Pumpkin makes a great flavoring for pancakes. These fiber-packed pancakes are great for brunch on a chilly day.

You can make up a bunch and freeze them.

1 cup oat bran	*1 teaspoon vanilla extract*
1 cup flour	*1 cup nonfat yogurt*
1 teaspoon baking soda	*2 tablespoons safflower oil*
1 teaspoon baking powder	*4 egg whites*
2 tablespoons brown sugar	*½ cup apple butter*
2 tablespoons pumpkin puree	*½ cup maple syrup*

1. In a large mixing bowl, combine the oat bran, flour, baking soda, baking powder, and brown sugar. Mix thoroughly.

2. Combine the pumpkin puree, vanilla, yogurt, and oil. Add to the dry ingredients and mix until just combined, being careful not to overmix.

3. Place the egg whites in a clean, dry bowl and beat until medium peaks are formed. Carefully fold the egg whites into the batter.

4. Heat a griddle or sauté pan over medium heat. Coat lightly

with nonstick vegetable spray. Ladle about ¼ cup batter per cake onto the griddle. Turn when bubbles form on the raw surface of the cakes. Cook second side until lightly browned.

5. Top each pancake with a scoop of apple butter and a drizzle of maple syrup, and serve.

Per serving (2 pancakes):

fat grams 6

protein grams 6

fiber grams 4

carbohydrate grams 61

calories 295

sodium milligrams 217

French Toast
YIELD: 4 SERVINGS

Baking French toast makes it light like a soufflé, but if you'd rather not fire up the oven, you can cook it all the way on top of the stove.

Make sure you soak the bread long enough—nothing is worse than French toast that's dry at the core.

True French bread contains only flour, water, yeast, and salt; check the label and avoid brands made with shortening.

1 cup skim milk
½ cup nonfat egg substitute
¼ cup sugar
½ teaspoon cinnamon
½ teaspoon vanilla extract
16 slices French bread, 1 inch thick

1½ teaspoons unsalted butter
4 tablespoons Yogurt Cheese (see pages 386–87)
½ cup Berry and Amaretto Breakfast Syrup (see page 370), Cider Sauce (see pages 372–73), or maple syrup

1. Preheat oven to 350 degrees.

2. In a medium bowl, combine milk, egg substitute, sugar, cinnamon, and vanilla and beat until well combined.

3. Place bread slices in a 9-by-12-inch pan and pour custard mixture over them. Allow to soak for approximately 5 minutes, then carefully turn over and allow to soak for an additional 5 minutes.

4. Melt butter in a large skillet over moderate heat. Add the soaked bread slices and cook until golden brown on the first side. Turn the slices and place the pan in the oven. Bake for 12 minutes or until the slices are puffed and resilient to the touch.

5. Top each slice with a dollop of Yogurt Cheese and a drizzle of syrup.

Per serving (4 slices):

fat grams 3	protein grams 9
fiber grams 1	carbohydrate grams 46
calories 245	sodium milligrams 271

Desserts

Glacé

YIELD: 6 SERVINGS

If ice cream is your weakness, this simple dessert base will be the single most effective item in the battle to keep desserts low in fat yet still appealing. Keep the insert of a Donvier-style freezer in your freezer, and a container of this base in your refrigerator, and you can make fresh glacé in minutes.

You can add all sorts of flavorings to the basic recipe before freezing. Try 2 tablespoons freeze-dried coffee, 1 cup Raspberry Sauce (see page 376), 1 tablespoon cinnamon, 1½ cups chunky applesauce with cinnamon and raisins, or even 1½ cups canned pumpkin puree with a little pumpkin-pie spice for a holiday twist.

2 cups part-skim ricotta cheese　　*1½ cups maple syrup or sugar*
3 cups nonfat yogurt　　*1 tablespoon vanilla extract*

1. Puree the ricotta cheese in a blender or food processor until silky smooth. Stop the machine several times and scrape the sides of the bowl to ensure that all of the cheese is processed.

2. Add the remaining ingredients and process until incorporated.

3. Refrigerate until needed or freeze in an ice cream freezer according to the manufacturer's specifications.

Per serving (3 ounces, or 6 tablespoons):
fat grams 3　　protein grams 6
fiber grams 0　　carbohydrate grams 24
calories 144　　sodium milligrams 71

Warm Brownie Cake

YIELD: 6 SERVINGS

Nobody will believe you when you tell them that the richness of this dessert comes from prunes!

1 ounce unsweetened chocolate
1/4 cup canned prune puree
2 tablespoons skim milk
2 egg whites
1 teaspoon vanilla extract
1/2 cup sugar
1/4 teaspoon salt

1/4 cup all-purpose flour
2 tablespoons unsweetened cocoa
  powder
1 tablespoon chopped walnuts
2 cups fresh berries
12 ounces frozen nonfat yogurt,
  vanilla or other

1. Preheat oven to 350 degrees.
2. Melt chocolate in a microwave at low power setting for 2 to 3 minutes, or in a double boiler on top of the stove over low heat.
3. Combine prune puree, skim milk, egg whites, vanilla, sugar, and salt. Mix thoroughly. Add the chocolate and mix.
4. In a separate bowl, mix together flour, cocoa, and walnuts. Carefully fold into prune and chocolate mixture, being careful not to overmix.
5. Lightly coat 6 small soufflé cups or oven-proof coffee cups with nonstick vegetable spray. Divide mixture into cups.
6. Bake for 25 minutes or until firm to the touch. Allow to cool slightly before serving with the berries and frozen yogurt.

Per serving:
fat grams 5
fiber grams 4
calories 229

protein grams 6
carbohydrate grams 41
sodium milligrams 140

Burgundy Poached Peach with Its Sherbet

YIELD: 8 SERVINGS

In this elegant dessert, the liquid used to poach the fruit is then made into a sherbet to serve alongside. Cherries or pears can be used instead of peaches.

4 large fresh freestone peaches

2 cups red burgundy wine

½ cup plus 2 tablespoons sugar

1 cinnamon stick

4 cloves

15 black peppercorns

1 cup Yogurt Cheese (see pages 386–87)

8 sprigs fresh mint

1. Bring a large pot of water to a boil. Set up a bowl of ice water. Plunge the peaches into the boiling water for 20 seconds and quickly remove and drop in the ice water. Use a paring knife to pull the peel away from the flesh of the peach. Split the peaches in half and remove the pit.

2. Combine the wine, ½ cup of the sugar, cinnamon stick, cloves, and peppercorns in a medium saucepan. Add the peach halves, place over medium heat, and bring to a very slight simmer. Poach for 8 to 10 minutes. Remove from heat and allow to cool to room temperature in the liquid. Remove peaches from poaching liquid and refrigerate.

3. Strain the poaching liquid and place in a shallow baking dish. Place the baking dish in the freezer. Stir the poaching liquid every 15 minutes as it begins to freeze. When the mixture becomes firm enough, scrape it with the edge of a spoon to create a smooth but slushy texture.

4. Combine Yogurt Cheese with the remaining 2 tablespoons sugar.

5. Place a scoop of the frozen wine sherbet in the bowls of 8 champagne glasses or goblets. Place a peach half over the top of each and garnish with a tablespoon of sweetened yogurt and a sprig of fresh mint. Serve.

Per serving:

fat grams 0.5

fiber grams 1

calories 139

protein grams 2

carbohydrate grams 23

sodium milligrams 23

Peach Crisp

YIELD: 9 SERVINGS

Fruit crisps can be very low in fat if one is careful with the amount of fat incorporated into the topping. Serve plain or with raspberry Glacé (see page 353).

This recipe works well with a variety of different fruit other than peaches; for example, plums, nectarines, apples, or pears.

½ cup plus ⅓ cup brown sugar   *⅓ cup rolled oats*
1 tablespoon all-purpose flour   *1 tablespoon whole wheat flour*
½ teaspoon grated lemon peel   *½ teaspoon cinnamon*
2 pounds peaches, pitted and sliced   *1 tablespoon unsalted butter*

1. Preheat oven to 375 degrees.
2. Combine ½ cup of the sugar, flour, lemon peel, and fruit in a bowl and mix thoroughly. Place mixture into an 8-by-8-inch baking dish.
3. Combine the remaining ⅓ cup sugar, rolled oats, whole wheat flour, and cinnamon in a mixing bowl. Melt butter and mix thoroughly with the dry ingredients.
4. Sprinkle the topping over the fruit in the baking dish.
5. Bake for 45 minutes or until the topping is golden brown.
6. Allow to cool slightly before dividing into 9 servings.

Per serving:

fat grams 2   protein grams 1
fiber grams 2   carbohydrate grams 34
calories 148   sodium milligrams 9

Warm Berry Stew

YIELD: 4 SERVINGS

In the spring when berries are top quality, plan a meal around this dessert. If you like, you can serve this with a garnish of fresh mint.

2 cups fresh raspberries, strawberries, and blueberries
1 cup Raspberry Sauce (see page
376)
1 teaspoon vanilla extract

1½ teaspoons unsalted butter
1 tablespoon toasted almonds
12 ounces frozen vanilla yogurt or
lemon sherbet

1. Clean, hull, and wash all berries. Quarter the strawberries.
2. Place the Raspberry Sauce in a small saucepan and heat to a simmer. Add the vanilla extract and the berries. Bring the pan back to a simmer. Remove from the heat and add the butter, swirling until the butter is melted into the berries.
3. Divide the stew into 4 soup plates. Scatter the toasted almonds over the surface.
4. Place a scoop of frozen yogurt or sherbet in center. Serve immediately.

Per serving:

fat grams 5	protein grams 2
fiber grams 5	carbohydrate grams 46
calories 229	sodium milligrams 42

Apple Strudel

YIELD: 5 SERVINGS

Phyllo dough makes an easy flaky wrapper for apples or other fruits such as plums, pears, and peaches. It's hard to believe the dough is so lean.

This is one recipe that does not refrigerate well once it is baked, but you don't have to bake the whole thing at one time either.

You can serve this with a nonfat frozen yogurt and some Raspberry Sauce (see page 376).

1 pound Granny Smith apples, peeled, cored, and sliced

1/4 cup golden raisins

1/4 teaspoon cinnamon

1/8 teaspoon nutmeg

1/8 teaspoon ground cloves

2 tablespoons brown sugar

2 sheets frozen phyllo dough, thawed in the refrigerator overnight

1 tablespoon unsalted butter, melted

2 tablespoons cake crumbs or bread crumbs

1. Combine apples, raisins, cinnamon, nutmeg, cloves, and sugar in a large saucepan and cook until apples are tender and excess liquid is evaporated, about 12 minutes (do not overcook). Spread the apples out onto a sheet tray and chill in the refrigerator.

2. Preheat oven to 400 degrees.

3. Lay a clean dish towel onto a flat surface and unfold one of the phyllo sheets onto it. Carefully brush the surface with 1 teaspoon of the butter. Dust it evenly with the crumbs and place the second sheet over the first. Butter the second sheet with 1 teaspoon of the butter.

4. Place the apples running along one of the long edges of the dough in a mound 3 inches wide. Using the towel to pick up the dough, roll the dough around the apples into a tight cigar shape. Stop rolling when the roll is just about to roll over the far edge. Cradle the strudel in the cloth and transfer to a baking sheet, placing it so that it lays on its seam.

5. Brush the outside with the remaining butter.

6. Slash the top of the strudel with a sharp knife, marking 5 equal servings.

7. Bake for 20 to 25 minutes or until the dough is nicely browned.

8. Slice into the premarked servings and serve.

Per serving:

fat grams 3

fiber grams 3

calories 138

protein grams 1

carbohydrate grams 29

sodium milligrams 34

Banana and Caramel Custard Pie
YIELD: 8 SERVINGS

Although this dessert is for a pie, you can take the same pudding and serve it simply in a bowl or use it as filling for an angel food cake.

1½ cups graham cracker crumbs	3 egg yolks
¾ cup sugar	1 teaspoon vanilla or banana
1 egg white	extract
1½ cups skim milk	1 pound bananas
3 tablespoons cornstarch	

1. Preheat oven to 350 degrees.

2. Combine graham cracker crumbs, ¼ cup of the sugar, and egg white and mix well. Press into a 9-inch pie pan and bake for 10 minutes. Cool and set aside.

3. Place the remaining ½ cup sugar in a small saucepan and place over high heat. Allow to cook until the sugar melts and a rich brown caramel color develops. Remove from the heat and *very carefully* add 1 cup of the skim milk. Allow the pan to set for a few minutes until the crisp sugar loosens from the bottom of the pan. Return to heat and bring to a light simmer. Simmer until the caramel is dissolved into the milk.

4. Combine the 3 tablespoons cornstarch with the remaining ½ cup milk and the egg yolks in a bowl and mix well. Slowly pour the hot caramel milk over the egg yolk mixture while stirring with a whisk. Return the mixture to the saucepan and place back over a low heat. Stir constantly until the mixture reaches a simmer and becomes thick. Remove from heat and add the extract. Set aside.

5. Peel and quarter the bananas. Arrange the banana pieces in the bottom of the pie shell. Pour the caramel custard over the bananas and put in refrigerator to cool and set at least 3 hours.

6. Cut into 8 pieces and serve.

Per serving:

fat grams 5	protein grams 3
fiber grams 2	carbohydrate grams 54
calories 270	sodium milligrams 172

Upside Down Pear Pie

YIELD: 10 SERVINGS

This is an easy dessert especially if you have the dough made up in advance.

A close relative of the famous French pastry called "tarte Tatin," this recipe uses pears instead of apples and a lighter dough to keep the fat content down.

This is very good with 2 ounces of cinnamon Glacé (see page 353) on the side of each portion.

½ cup sugar
1 tablespoon unsalted butter
6 Bartlett pears, peeled, cored, and
    sliced

10 ounces Ricotta Pastry (see pages
    387–88)

1. Preheat oven to 350 degrees.
2. Heat a large, nonstick oven-proof skillet over high heat. Scatter sugar over surface of pan and allow to cook to a light caramel color. Add butter and sliced pears and cook lightly until pears are well coated with caramel and softened (there should be no excess moisture in the pan at this point). Remove pan from heat. Arrange pears in pan to form a flat, evenly distributed layer.
3. Roll Ricotta Pastry out into a 12-inch disk. Lay dough over pears and lightly press to inside edge of pan. Lightly score surface of dough to allow steam to escape.
4. Place skillet over a high flame and cook until a light caramel aroma escapes from the pan, about 5 minutes.
5. Bake about 20 minutes or until dough is rich brown. Remove from oven and loosen dough from edges of pan. Place a cake platter over pan and invert pan and platter together so that pie falls pear side up onto platter.
6. Cut into 10 wedges and serve.

Per serving:
fat grams 5
fiber grams 3
calories 249

protein grams 5
carbohydrate grams 48
sodium milligrams 169

Cherry Rice Pudding Brûlée

YIELD: 6 SERVINGS

This is a cross between rice pudding and crème brûlée.

Instead of kiln-dried cherries, you can use other dried fruits available such as blueberries, cranberries, apricots, and good old raisins.

¼ cup nonconverted rice	½ cup kiln-dried cherries
1 quart skim milk	1 tablespoon grated orange peel
¾ cup sugar	1 teaspoon vanilla extract
⅛ teaspoon nutmeg	¼ cup brown sugar

1. Preheat oven to 300 degrees.

2. Combine rice, milk, ½ cup of the sugar, and nutmeg in a 1½-quart casserole. Place over high heat and bring to a boil. Bake, uncovered, for 2 hours, stirring every 15 minutes.

3. Stir in the cherries, orange zest, and vanilla and bake without stirring for another ½ hour.

4. Remove from oven and allow to cool to room temperature.

5. Preheat broiler at highest setting. Rub together brown sugar and the remaining ¼ cup white sugar and scatter evenly over surface of rice pudding.

6. Place casserole under broiler and allow sugars to melt and caramelize, producing a rich brown crust over the entire surface of the pan. Refrigerate. Serve chilled.

Per serving:

fat grams 0.5	protein grams 7
fiber grams 1	carbohydrate grams 59
calories 260	sodium milligrams 91

Fruit Flan

YIELD: 10 SERVINGS

Fresh fruit rests on a base of a sweet polenta made from durum wheat flour.

2 cups skim milk

1/8 teaspoon salt

1/2 cup sugar

2 tablespoons unsalted butter

2 teaspoons grated lemon peel

3 tablespoons semolina flour

1/2 cup cornmeal

1/2 cup raisins

2 tablespoons heavy cream

2 pounds fresh fruit (apples, peaches, apricots, plums, pears, etc.)

1/4 teaspoon cinnamon

2 tablespoons powdered sugar

1/4 cup apple jelly

1. Preheat oven to 325 degrees.

2. Combine the skim milk, salt, sugar, butter, and lemon zest in a small saucepan and bring to a boil. Whisk in the semolina and cornmeal, stirring constantly to prevent lumping. Return to a low simmer and cook for 20 minutes. Remove from heat and add the raisins and heavy cream.

3. Line a 9- to 10-inch cheesecake pan with wax paper and coat lightly with nonstick vegetable spray. Pour in the mixture.

4. Prepare the fruit. Apples or pears should be peeled, cored, and sliced very thin. Peaches, plums, or apricots should be pitted and cut into wedges.

5. Arrange the fruit over the top of the mixture so that it covers the surface. Combine the cinnamon and the powdered sugar and sprinkle over the fruit.

6. Bake for 45 minutes. Remove from the oven and allow to cool to room temperature.

7. Heat the jelly in a small pan or in the microwave until melted. Brush the surface of the fruit until well glazed. Refrigerate the flan before dividing and serving.

Per serving:

fat grams 4

fiber grams 2

calories 206

protein grams 3

carbohydrate grams 42

sodium milligrams 56

Pumpkin Bread Pudding
YIELD: 9 SERVINGS

This makes a nice dessert for holiday entertaining or just for yourself.

Be sure to choose white bread made without shortening (true French bread is good).

You can serve this with raspberry Glacé (see page 353).

2 cups fresh apple cider	*1½ cups canned pumpkin puree*
½ cup raisins	*1 teaspoon ground gingerroot*
1½ cups skim milk	*½ teaspoon cinnamon*
¼ cup brown sugar	*⅛ teaspoon nutmeg*
1 egg	*⅛ teaspoon ground cloves*
2 egg whites	*4 cups 1-inch-cubed white bread*
1 teaspoon vanilla extract	*1 tablespoon powdered sugar*

1. Combine cider and raisins in a small saucepan and place over high heat. Bring to a boil and allow to boil until the liquid coats a spoon, about 10 to 15 minutes. Remove from heat and cool to room temperature.

2. In a medium bowl, combine raisins and cider syrup with milk, sugar, egg, egg whites, vanilla, pumpkin puree, and spices.

3. Toast bread cubes in a 400-degree oven until lightly browned. Remove and reserve. Reduce heat to 325 degrees.

4. Place bread into a 9-inch soufflé dish or a 9-by-9-inch cake pan. Pour liquid mixture over bread and toss carefully, allowing the bread to soak thoroughly. Allow to soak for 20 minutes.

5. Place soufflé dish in a larger pan and pour boiling water into surrounding pan to a depth of 1 inch.

6. Bake for 45 minutes or until a knife inserted in pudding comes out clean.

7. Remove from oven and allow to cool slightly.

8. Dust with powdered sugar and divide into 9 servings.

Per serving:

fat grams 3   protein grams 8

fiber grams 2   carbohydrate grams 47

calories 244   sodium milligrams 179

Pumpkin Crème Caramel

YIELD: 8 SERVINGS

Pumpkin lends a nice flavor as well as fiber to this dessert.

6 tablespoons sugar   *1/2 teaspoon cinnamon*

1 teaspoon lemon juice   *Pinch of nutmeg*

3 cups skim milk   *Pinch of cloves*

3/4 cup brown sugar   *1 tablespoon vanilla extract*

1/2 cup ground gingersnap cookies   *6 egg whites*

1 cup pumpkin puree   *4 egg yolks*

1. Preheat oven to 325 degrees.

2. Lightly coat 6 soup cups or 8-ounce soufflé molds with non-stick vegetable spray. Combine 6 tablespoons of the sugar with the lemon juice in a small saucepan. Heat the sugar over high heat until it melts and cooks to a light caramel. Quickly divide the caramel among the bottoms of the cups.

3. Combine the skim milk and brown sugar in the same small saucepan and bring to a simmer. Remove from the heat and add the ground gingersnaps, pumpkin puree, spices, and vanilla. Mix thoroughly.

4. Add the egg whites and yolks and mix thoroughly again. Divide the mixture between the caramel cups.

5. Place the cups into a large cake pan and add boiling water until the cups rest in 1 inch of water. Bake for 45 minutes or until the custard is set and a knife inserted into the custard comes out clean. Cool and refrigerate overnight.

6. Release the custard from the cups by running a knife around the outside edge of the cups and inverting onto plates. Shake the cup and plate together until the custard falls out onto the plate.

Allow the caramel to drizzle over the custard and create a sauce.

Per serving:

fat grams 5

fiber grams 0.6

calories 240

protein grams 8

carbohydrate grams 43

sodium milligrams 142

Tapioca Pudding with Figs and Basil

YIELD: 4 SERVINGS

This classic comfort food is given a Mediterranean twist with basil, orange peel, and stewed figs. To the basic pudding recipe, you can add your own favorite flavors and fruit.

If you use fresh figs, stew them in a syrup made of 1 cup water and ½ cup sugar for about 15 minutes; cool in syrup before using.

⅓ cup small pearled tapioca

1 cup water

2 cups skim milk

⅛ teaspoon salt

⅓ cup sugar

2 egg yolks

½ teaspoon vanilla extract

2 teaspoons grated orange peel

12 figs stewed in syrup (fresh or canned)

1 tablespoon finely shredded fresh basil

1. Soak tapioca in cold water overnight.

2. Drain the tapioca, place in a saucepan, and add the milk and salt. Bring to a boil and reduce to a simmer. Allow to simmer over a low heat for 45 minutes (if using quick-cook tapioca, cook only 8 to 10 minutes).

3. Combine the sugar and egg yolks in a mixing bowl and whisk until light and lemon colored. Pour some of the hot tapioca mixture over the egg yolk mixture, stirring constantly. Return this mixture to the saucepan and return to a boil, stirring constantly. Cook for about 1 minute and remove from the heat.

4. Add the vanilla and orange peel. Divide among 4 bowls and chill.

5. Before serving, top the puddings with the stewed figs and basil threads.

Per serving:

fat grams 3   protein grams 6

fiber grams 3   carbohydrate grams 54

calories 257   sodium milligrams 135

Warm Apricot Pudding

YIELD: 6 SERVINGS

Rather like a fallen soufflé, this dessert is sure to be a hit.

5 tablespoons sugar   1 cup white wine

4 ounces dried apricots   3 ounces low-fat cream cheese

1 piece lemon peel, ½ inch by   (Neufchâtel)

   2 inches   3 egg whites

1. Lightly coat a 1-quart soufflé mold with nonstick vegetable spray. Lightly dust with 1 tablespoon of the sugar and tap out any excess.

2. Preheat oven to 375 degrees.

3. Combine the apricots, lemon peel, and white wine in a small saucepan and bring to a simmer. Simmer until all the liquid is reduced and the pan is nearly dry. Remove from the heat and discard the lemon peel. Place the cooked apricots in a blender or food processor with the cream cheese and 1 tablespoon of the sugar. Process to a very smooth puree. Transfer to a medium-sized mixing bowl.

4. Place egg whites in a second mixing bowl and beat. When the whites begin to stiffen, slowly add the remaining 3 tablespoons sugar and continue to beat until soft peaks form.

5. Add half of the meringue to the apricot puree and carefully fold together. Add the second half of the meringue and continue to fold being careful not to overmix.

6. Pour the mixture into the sugared soufflé mold and bake until the soufflé has doubled in volume, about 20 minutes.

7. When the soufflé is done, remove from the oven, slice into 6 wedges, and serve immediately.

Per serving:

fat grams 3

protein grams 4

fiber grams 2

carbohydrate grams 23

calories 157

sodium milligrams 87

Yogurt and Berry Parfait Americana

YIELD: 4 SERVINGS

In this nice, light dessert, yogurt is transformed into a mousse.

1 cup fresh blueberries, washed

1 cup fresh strawberries, hulled, washed, and quartered

4 tablespoons sugar

¼ cup white wine

½ tablespoon unflavored gelatin

1½ cups plain nonfat yogurt

1 teaspoon vanilla extract

2 egg whites

1. Prepare blueberries and strawberries and place in 2 separate small bowls. Sprinkle 1 tablespoon of the sugar over the strawberries only and mix. Set aside.

2. Place wine in a soup cup and scatter gelatin over surface. Place in a microwave and heat on high just until wine starts to produce steam, 30 to 45 seconds. Do not boil. Or place in a small saucepan on the stove over high heat and heat to just before boiling, then remove from heat.

3. Place yogurt and vanilla extract in a bowl. Add the wine and gelatin mixture in slow steady stream, stirring constantly.

4. Combine the egg whites and remaining 3 tablespoons sugar in a 1-quart stainless-steel bowl. Beat well. Place the bowl over a lightly simmering pan of water and continue to beat with an electric beater until the meringue is light and thick, about 7 to 10 minutes. Remove the bowl from the simmering water and allow to set at room temperature until cooled.

5. Fold the meringue into the yogurt, being careful not to over-mix.

6. Select 4 tall clear parfait (or pilsner beer) glasses. Place a spoonful of the yogurt mixture in the bottom of each glass. In each

glass, spoon a layer of strawberries, a portion of half the remaining yogurt, the blueberries, and the remaining yogurt mixture. Place in the refrigerator to chill for at least 2 hours before serving.

Per serving:

fat grams 2

fiber grams 2

calories 149

protein grams 6

carbohydrate grams 27

sodium milligrams 64

Caramel Apple Soufflé

YIELD: 4 SERVINGS

Even though this recipe requires a bit more work than the average, I'm sure that you will agree it was worth the extra effort.

Save it for a day when you want to show off how well you're feeling.

1 tablespoon unsalted butter, softened

11 tablespoons sugar

1/2 teaspoon lemon juice

1/2 cup Granny Smith apple, peeled and cut into small thin slices

2 tablespoons water

1 cup skim milk

1 strip orange peel (cut with a vegetable peeler approximately 1/2 by 2 inches)

3 tablespoons cornmeal

2 egg whites

9 ounces cinnamon Glacé (see page 353)

1. Prepare 4 small soufflé molds by rubbing them inside with 1/2 tablespoon of the butter. Add 2 tablespoons of the sugar to the first mold and roll it around until it forms a light coating. Pour the excess into the second mold and repeat until all the molds are coated. Add any extra sugar to step 2.

2. Place 3 tablespoons of the sugar and the lemon juice in a small saucepan and place over high heat until the sugar begins to caramelize. Reduce the heat and continue to heat until all the sugar has melted and the caramel is a rich tan color. Add the apples and the water and cook until the caramel dissolves and coats the apples with

a thick caramel. Remove from the heat and swirl in the remaining ½ tablespoon butter. Divide the apple mixture among the 4 soufflé molds and allow to cool.

3. Place the skim milk and orange peel in a small saucepan and bring to a simmer. Combine 3 tablespoons of the sugar and cornmeal and whisk into the simmering milk, stirring continually to prevent lumping. Return to a boil and reduce the heat to a low simmer. Cook for approximately 20 minutes. Remove from heat and allow to cool to room temperature.

4. One-half hour before you are ready to serve the soufflé, preheat the oven to 350 degrees.

5. Beat together the egg whites and the remaining 3 tablespoons sugar until medium peaks form.

6. Carefully fold ⅓ of the meringue into the cornmeal and milk base. Follow with the remaining ⅔ being careful to fully incorporate but not overmix.

7. Divide the soufflé mix among the 4 prepared soufflé molds and bake for 20 minutes. The soufflés are ready when risen but still creamy at center.

8. Unmold the 4 soufflés onto plates and serve immediately with cinnamon Glacé divided evenly over the tops of each.

Per serving:
fat grams 5   protein grams 7
fiber grams 1   carbohydrate grams 48
calories 252   sodium milligrams 92

Sauces and Accompaniments

Berry and Amaretto Breakfast Syrup

YIELD: 2 CUPS

Heat in the microwave before serving with low-fat waffles, French toast, or hotcakes. Unlike maple syrup, this syrup supplies fiber, vitamins, and minerals.

Make it up in large batches and store in the refrigerator.

3 cups fresh or frozen unsweetened berries (blueberries, strawberries, or raspberries)
1 tablespoon lemon juice
1 teaspoon lemon peel, grated
1/4 cup light corn syrup
1/2 cup sugar
2 tablespoons amaretto liqueur (optional)

1. If using fresh berries, wash and hull if necessary. Place half of the berries in a blender or food processor and puree. Strain the puree into a nonreactive medium saucepan and add the lemon juice, lemon peel, corn syrup, sugar, and remaining berries. Place over a high heat and bring to a boil. Reduce heat to a simmer and cook, stirring frequently, until reduced by half. Remove from heat and allow to cool.

2. If desired, stir in the amaretto.

3. Cover and refrigerate until needed.

Per serving (1/4 cup):
fat grams 0.4
fiber grams 1
calories 115
protein grams 0.3
carbohydrate grams 29
sodium milligrams 5

Black Bean Sauce

YIELD: 1 QUART

Use this deeply flavorful sauce in Southwest cooking. It adds fiber without excess fat and calories, and goes great with a lot of different foods. It can also be turned into chili if garnished with toasted tortillas, grated nonfat cheese, and Yogurt Cheese (see pages 386–87).

Ancho chilis are found dried or canned in specialty food stores and many supermarkets. Other chilis may be substituted but will provide a different heat and character.

⅔ cup dried black beans	*1 bay leaf*
½ strip bacon, finely chopped	*½ teaspoon ground cumin*
½ cup minced onions	*1 teaspoon salt*
1 clove garlic, minced	*¼ cup sun-dried tomatoes*
2 cups chicken broth	*1 dried ancho chili*
1 teaspoon dried oregano	*2 tablespoons red wine vinegar*

1. Rinse the beans. Cover with cold water and allow to soak overnight. Drain.

2. Heat a 2-quart saucepan over medium heat and add the bacon. When the bacon is nearly crisp, add the onions and garlic. Sauté the onions and garlic until they are translucent.

3. Add the broth, beans, oregano, bay leaf, cumin, and salt and bring to a boil. Reduce the heat to low and simmer for 1 hour or until the beans are tender but not falling apart.

4. Place the sun-dried tomatoes and the ancho chili in a small bowl and add 1 cup of the hot bean mixture. Allow the tomatoes and chili to soak for 15 minutes then place in a blender and puree to a smooth paste. Combine the puree with the rest of the bean mixture. Discard the bay leaf and add the red wine vinegar.

5. Refrigerate in a covered container until used.

Per serving (¼ cup):

fat grams 1	protein grams 3
fiber grams 2	carbohydrate grams 7
calories 44	sodium milligrams 176

Blackberry Ketchup

YIELD: 3 CUPS

This is a great sauce for grilled or roasted poultry and meats. Brush it on the meat during cooking to keep it moist, or drizzle it over the cooked meat. This sauce is even good on ice cream.

Don't be afraid to make a good-sized batch since it keeps for many months if covered tightly and refrigerated.

1 pound frozen blackberries
1 cup red wine vinegar
1 cup water
1 1/2 cups brown sugar
1/2 teaspoon ground cloves

1/2 teaspoon ground ginger
1 teaspoon cinnamon
1/2 teaspoon cayenne pepper
1/2 teaspoon salt
1 tablespoon unsalted butter

1. Combine the berries, vinegar, water, brown sugar, and spices in a medium saucepan and place over moderate heat. Bring to a boil, then reduce the heat to a simmer. Allow to cook for 30 minutes or until the juices in the pan appear to thicken slightly.

2. Remove from heat and allow to cool slightly. Puree in a blender. Strain the puree to remove the seeds.

3. Whisk the butter into the sauce. Pour into a glass jar and cool before covering tightly and refrigerating.

Per serving (1/4 cup):
fat grams 1
fiber grams 2
calories 139

protein grams 0.5
carbohydrate grams 34
sodium milligrams 111

Cider Sauce

YIELD: 2 1/2 CUPS

Use as a dessert sauce or a nutritious substitute for maple syrup on breakfast foods. Try it on pumpkin Glacé (see page 353) or Warm Apricot Pudding (see pages 366–67). It can be made in advance and kept for up to a week in the refrigerator.

4 cups fresh apple cider, preferably
  unfiltered (not clear)
1 tablespoon cornstarch
3 tablespoons water

1 Granny Smith apple, peeled and
  cut into matchsticks
⅛ teaspoon cinnamon
Pinch of nutmeg

1. Place cider in a medium saucepan and bring to a boil. Allow cider to boil until reduced to approximately 2 cups.

2. In a small bowl, mix together the cornstarch and water. Whisk the boiling cider while slowly adding the cornstarch mixture. When cider returns to a boil add the apples, cinnamon, and nutmeg.

3. Remove from heat and serve, or refrigerate until used.

Per serving (¼ cup):

fat grams 0.2	protein grams 0.2
fiber grams 0.4	carbohydrate grams 14
calories 54	sodium milligrams 7

Cowboy-style Barbecue Sauce
YIELD: *1* QUART

There are as many barbecue sauce recipes as there are backyards, but this very piquant, Southwestern barbecue sauce is one to turn to when you want to get serious.

When you remove the fat or skin from poultry or meat before pan-grilling it, use a coating or basting sauce so the heat doesn't produce a dry, unpleasant surface (especially noticeable for chicken breasts and pork medallions). This chuckwagon-style barbecue sauce will keep things moist and add a lot of life to the food, too.

This sauce will keep all summer long in the refrigerator.

1 tablespoon safflower oil
1 large onion, finely minced
4 garlic cloves, minced
2 teaspoons seeded and minced
  jalapeño peppers
1 6-ounce can tomato paste

2 tablespoons excellent chili powder
  (like Pecos Valley brand)
1 cup leftover brewed coffee, the
  older the better
¾ cup Worcestershire sauce
¾ cup cider vinegar
¾ cup brown sugar

1. Heat the oil in a medium saucepan over moderate heat and add the onions, garlic, and jalapeño peppers.

2. Sauté over a low heat, stirring occasionally, until the vegetables are tender, about 2 minutes.

3. Add the tomato paste and chili powder and cook over a low heat for 5 minutes, stirring often.

4. Add the remaining ingredients and bring to a simmer.

5. Simmer slowly for 30 minutes, stirring occasionally.

6. Remove pan from heat and transfer to a blender or food processor. Puree.

7. Pour sauce into a glass jar and cool before covering tightly and storing in the refrigerator.

Per serving (1/4 cup):

fat grams 1	protein grams 1
fiber grams 1	carbohydrate grams 15
calories 71	sodium milligrams 198

Creamy Herb Salad Dressing
YIELD: 2 1/2 CUPS

Experiment with other herbs you like, too. A nice addition is to fold capers into the finished dressing (rinse and chop them first).

1/4 cup part-skim ricotta cheese	*1/4 cup basil*
1 tablespoon shallots, peeled	*1 1/2 cups nonfat yogurt*
1 clove garlic, peeled	*1/4 cup red wine vinegar*
1/4 cup chives	*3 tablespoons Dijon mustard*
1/4 cup parsley	

1. Place the ricotta cheese, shallots, garlic, chives, parsley, and basil in a blender or food processor and process to a silky smooth consistency. Stop the machine several times and scrape down the sides of the bowl to ensure that all of the cheese is processed.

2. Add the yogurt, vinegar, and mustard and process to incorporate.

3. Strain the mixture. Cover and refrigerate until used.

Per serving (1 tablespoon):

fat grams 0.4   protein grams 2

fiber grams 0   carbohydrate grams 2

calories 17   sodium milligrams 47

Enlightened White Sauce

YIELD: 2 CUPS

This low-fat version of white sauce (usually made with butter and milk) is a useful base for pasta sauces, meat sauces, and creamed vegetables such as corn or peas. Substitute it for white sauce called for in your other recipes. For a quick sauce with a lot of character without the fat, add herbs or some shredded nonfat cheese.

The sauce will keep in the refrigerator for a week.

2 cups chicken broth (or clam   *½ cup evaporated skim milk*
juice), divided   *½ teaspoon salt*
3 tablespoons cornstarch   *Pinch of white pepper*

1. Place 1½ cups of the broth into a small saucepan and bring to a boil over high heat.

2. Mix the remaining ½ cup cold broth with the cornstarch. Add to the boiling broth while mixing with a wire whisk. As soon as the broth returns to a simmer remove the pan from the heat.

3. Mix in the evaporated skim milk, salt, and pepper.

4. Use in recipe, or place into a container and chill, cover, and refrigerate until used.

Per serving (¼ cup):

fat grams 0.2   protein grams 2

fiber grams 0   carbohydrate grams 4

calories 28   sodium milligrams 202

Raspberry Sauce

YIELD: 2 1/2 CUPS

This is a simple recipe for the most popular dessert sauce around. It is used in other recipes of this book, and also works well as a flavoring for the frozen Glacé (see page 353).

Don't be afraid to use unsweetened frozen berries since they often have as much or even better flavor than fresh.

Make up a large batch and freeze it in small plastic containers.

2 cups fresh or frozen unsweetened raspberries (or other berries)
5 tablespoons honey

1/4 cup white wine
1 tablespoon kirschwasser (cherry brandy, optional)

1. Combine the berries, honey, and white wine in a blender and liquefy.
2. Place in a nonreactive saucepan and just bring to a simmer. Remove from heat and strain through a fine sieve.
3. Add the kirschwasser if desired.
4. Chill. Serve, or keep in refrigerator or freezer until used.

Per serving (1/4 cup):

fat grams 0.1	protein grams 0.3
fiber grams 2	carbohydrate grams 12
calories 52	sodium milligrams 0.8

Red Pepper Sauce

YIELD: 2 CUPS

This colorful puree can be used as a warm sauce with pastas, a cold sauce with seafood, or as a base for salad dressings or marinated salads. Green or yellow peppers may be substituted.

4 red bell peppers, seeded and
  coarsely chopped
¼ cup coarsely chopped onion
2 cloves garlic, minced
1 cup chicken broth

¼ teaspoon salt
¼ teaspoon black pepper
1 tablespoon balsamic vinegar
Fresh herbs such as basil or
  cilantro, chopped (optional)

1. Heat a 2-quart saucepan over low heat. Lightly coat with nonstick vegetable spray. Add peppers, onions, and garlic. Sauté the vegetables for 10 minutes without allowing them to brown.

2. Add the chicken broth and increase heat to high. Bring to a rolling boil and cook until only a small amount of moisture is visible at the bottom of the pan. Remove from the heat and place contents of saucepan into a blender. Blend to a very fine puree.

3. Add salt, pepper, vinegar, and herbs if desired, and mix thoroughly.

4. Place in container, cover, and refrigerate until used (up to 2 weeks).

Per serving (¼ cup):

fat grams 0.2
fiber grams 1
calories 21

protein grams 1
carbohydrate grams 4
sodium milligrams 93

Tartar Sauce

YIELD: 1½ CUPS

This is a lighter version of the all-American favorite fish accompaniment. It will keep for two weeks in the refrigerator.

1 cup Kraft Free mayonnaise
1 teaspoon Dijon mustard
1 tablespoon chopped parsley
2 tablespoons chopped sweet pickles
1 tablespoon chopped capers

1 hard-boiled egg, chopped
1 teaspoon chopped shallot
1 teaspoon fresh lemon juice
Pinch of white pepper

1. Combine all ingredients and blend well. Store refrigerated in a sealed container until needed.

Per serving (1 tablespoon):

fat grams 0.6	protein grams 0.6
fiber grams 1	carbohydrate grams 5
calories 22	sodium milligrams 209

Tomato Sauce

YIELD: 1 QUART

With small containers of this sauce in your freezer, you'll never have to use high-fat, high-sodium jarred spaghetti sauce again. Also use this excellent tomato sauce on pizza or sautéed chicken or fish.

For spaghetti sauce, simply double the oregano and add some fresh or dried basil. Leave the sauce a bit coarse.

1 teaspoon olive oil	*4 cups chicken broth*
1 onion, minced	*1 tablespoon oregano*
4 cloves garlic, minced	*2 sprigs parsley*
6-ounce can tomato paste	*1 teaspoon thyme*
3 pounds plum tomatoes, cored and	*1 teaspoon sage*
chopped (2 32-ounce cans diced	*½ teaspoon salt*
tomatoes, drained)	

1. Heat olive oil in a 4-quart saucepan over low heat. Add the onions and garlic. Cook slowly for 10 to 15 minutes.

2. Add the tomato paste and continue to cook slowly for another 10 to 15 minutes.

3. Add the remaining ingredients, increase heat to high, and bring to a boil. Reduce the heat to a simmer. Cook the sauce for 2 hours.

4. Remove from heat and puree sauce in a food processor or blender until smooth. Strain sauce through a coarse sieve and allow to cool before transferring to a container and refrigerating. (You can omit the straining, but it does perfect the sauce.)

5. To freeze, divide into small containers. Cover tightly. Thaw in microwave or at room temperature as needed.

Per serving (¼ cup):

fat grams 1   protein grams 3
fiber grams 2   carbohydrate grams 7
calories 41   sodium milligrams 132

Mango Relish

YIELD: 2 CUPS

This complex, fragrant relish with the flavor of the Islands is used for specific dishes in this collection, and it is also well suited to accompany baked or pan-grilled fish and poultry. Do not make an oversized batch since the flavor is best the first day.

1 fresh mango, peeled, deseeded,   *1 tablespoon lime juice*
*   and diced*   *2 tablespoons chopped cilantro*
½ cup diced red bell pepper   *¼ teaspoon salt*
¼ cup diced red onion

1. Combine all ingredients and allow to marinate for 1 hour before serving.

Per serving (¼ cup):

fat grams 0   protein grams 0.3
fiber grams 1   carbohydrate grams 5
calories 21   sodium milligrams 68

Mushroom "Bacon"

YIELD: 1 CUP

If you miss bacon, you'll love the smoky, sweet flavor and texture of these chips made by concentrating the flavor of oriental shiitake mushrooms. Sprinkle them on your salad or on top of a baked potato, or make a "bacon" and nonfat egg omelette.

1 pound fresh shiitake mushrooms
1 tablespoon olive oil
¼ teaspoon salt (fine "popcorn
  salt" if available)

1. Preheat oven to 350 degrees.

2. Destem the mushroom and slice the caps very thin. Toss the mushrooms in a mixing bowl with the olive oil until the oil is evenly absorbed.

3. Place the mushrooms in a shallow layer on a cookie tray and bake until they become rich brown and very crisp (somewhere between 12 and 30 minutes). Use a spatula to stir the mushrooms occasionally during the baking process to allow the mushrooms to brown evenly.

4. Transfer mushrooms to absorbent toweling and sprinkle with the salt.

5. Pack in a tightly sealed container and store in a cool dry place until needed (do not refrigerate).

Per serving (2 tablespoons):

fat grams 2	protein grams 1
fiber grams 1	carbohydrate grams 3
calories 29	sodium milligrams 69

Oven-dried Tomatoes

YIELD: 2 CUPS

Slow roasting is one of the great secrets of flavorful cooking, because it concentrates and intensifies flavors. These slow-roasted "tomato raisins" practically holler with flavor. They are much fresher tasting and more "garden-like" in flavor and texture than dried tomatoes you can buy in the store—they're like a concentrated tomato burst on the palette.

Top a pizza with them, chop them and add to a light sauce for pasta, or toss them with a mixed salad.

Make a bunch and store them covered in the refrigerator. They will keep for at least a month (if you can keep yourself from snacking on them!).

12 ripe tomatoes (preferably roma or plum)	*½ cup chopped fresh basil*
	½ teaspoon salt
3 cloves garlic, minced	*1 teaspoon black pepper*

1. Preheat oven to 200 degrees.
2. Cut tomatoes into quarters.
3. Combine garlic, basil, salt, and pepper in a large bowl.
4. Toss tomatoes with seasoning mixture and place skin side down on a cake rack over a sheet tray.
5. Place in a very low oven (or with just a pilot light) for 4 to 8 hours or until tomatoes take on a dried and leathery texture.
6. Remove from rack and store covered in refrigerator until needed.

Per serving (¼ cup):

fat grams 0.6	protein grams 2
fiber grams 3	carbohydrate grams 9
calories 43	sodium milligrams 151

Fresh Salsa

YIELD: 3 CUPS

Salsa has become America's number-one condiment, surpassing even ketchup! But store-bought varieties are often expensive and rather blah. This fresh version shows why salsa has become so popular. It's on the hot side; you can decrease the jalapeño to mellow the "bite."

For a snack, serve this with oven-baked nonfat tortilla chips (made by yourself or purchased). For a breakfast burrito, use it to sauce some nonfat eggs in a flour tortilla.

1 pound ripe tomatoes (about 4—or 2 cups drained, diced, canned tomatoes)	1 small bunch scallions, minced
	2 cloves garlic, minced
	1/4 cup chopped fresh cilantro
1 tablespoon seeded and minced jalapeño pepper	1/2 teaspoon salt
	2 tablespoons cider vinegar

1. Split the tomatoes across and squeeze to remove the seeds. Coarsely chop.

2. Place the tomatoes in a glass or nonreactive metal bowl and add the remaining ingredients. Marinate for at least 1/2 hour before serving.

Per serving (2 tablespoons):

fat grams 0	protein grams 0.3
fiber grams 0.4	carbohydrate grams 1
calories 6	sodium milligrams 52

Savory Mustard

YIELD: 2 CUPS

Use this mustard as a sandwich spread, as a dip for hors d'oeuvres, or as a sauce for warm meats. Its sweet-hot flavor accents a variety of foods.

Covered and refrigerated, this condiment will keep four to six months.

1/2 cup powdered dry mustard	5 tablespoons cider vinegar
1/2 cup water	2 tablespoons all-purpose flour
1 cup brown sugar	1/4 teaspoon salt

1. Combine all ingredients in a small saucepan and whisk until smooth.

2. Place over medium heat and heat until contents of the pan come to a boil.

3. Remove from the heat and cool.

4. Place in a tightly sealed jar and refrigerate.

Per serving (1 tablespoon):

fat grams 0	protein grams 0.2
fiber grams 0	carbohydrate grams 9
calories 34	sodium milligrams 20

Sweet Pepper Marmalade

YIELD: 3 CUPS

This sweet-and-sour condiment makes a great accompaniment to cold lamb or chicken, shrimp, and hearty fish such as salmon or tuna. Properly covered and refrigerated, it will keep two to three months.

2 pounds red bell peppers, stem,
   seeds, and ribs removed
½ cup honey
½ cup red wine vinegar

½ cup red wine
½ teaspoon salt
¼ teaspoon white pepper

1. Grate peppers with a hand grater or with the grating attachment of a food processor.

2. Combine the peppers with all remaining ingredients in a 10-inch sauté pan and place over medium heat.

3. Cook, stirring often, until the liquid in the pan boils down to a syrupy consistency, about 15 to 20 minutes.

4. Chill for at least 1 hour before serving, or store in a sealed container in the refrigerator until needed.

Per serving (2 tablespoons):

fat grams 0	protein grams 0.4
fiber grams 0.6	carbohydrate grams 7
calories 29	sodium milligrams 46

Tomato Chutney

YIELD: 2 CUPS

Instead of fatty mayonnaise, use this perky condiment to add zest to leftover chicken or meat in a sandwich or green salad.

The recipe works well with tomatoes, mangoes, plums, peaches, apples, and other fresh fruits and vegetables—experiment with spices until you find your favorites. Try apple with rosemary or sage, peach with thyme and lavender, plums with sage, or mangoes with the same spices as the tomatoes.

This will keep two to three months in the refrigerator.

1 1/2 cups ripe tomatoes, peeled, seeded, and diced
1 tablespoon cider vinegar
1/3 cup brown sugar
1/2 cup diced onion
2 cloves garlic, minced
1 teaspoon minced fresh gingerroot
1/4 teaspoon ground mace

Pinch of ground cloves
1/2 teaspoon seeded and minced jalapeño pepper
1/2 lemon, juice and zest
1/4 cup chopped raisins
2 tablespoons chopped walnuts or pine nuts
1/4 teaspoon salt

1. Combine all ingredients in a small nonreactive saucepan and bring to a boil. Reduce heat to a simmer and cook until the contents have reduced to a heavy consistency, about 15 to 20 minutes.

2. Cool and store refrigerated in a glass container until needed.

Per serving (2 tablespoons):

fat grams 1

fiber grams 0.6

calories 38

protein grams 0.5

carbohydrate grams 8

sodium milligrams 39

Other Versatile Base Recipes

Brown Stock

YIELD: 2 QUARTS

This stock may seem like a lot of work but it is really quite easy and well worth the effort, as it has a neutral flavor that complements many different ingredients, yet it adds richness and body to main dishes and sauces. It is much healthier than typically high-fat and high-sodium canned brown sauce or gravy. If you keep small containers of this basic stock in your freezer, you'll find that it will come in handy many times, especially when you are in a hurry.

10 pounds veal knuckle bones,
   purchased precut from butcher
2 gallons water
1/4 cup safflower oil
1 cup coarsely chopped celery
1 cup coarsely chopped onions
1 cup coarsely chopped carrots
1 cup coarsely chopped leeks

1/2 cup tomato paste
2 cups red wine
1 clove garlic
2 bay leaves
Pinch of thyme
3 tablespoons cornstarch
1/2 cup cold water

1. Preheat oven to 350 degrees. Spread the bones evenly on a roasting pan and roast for 30 minutes or until golden brown. Place into a large stock or soup pot. Reserve roasting pan and drippings.

2. Add 2 gallons water to bones and place over high heat. Bring to a boil, then reduce the heat to a very low simmer.

3. To roasting pan add the oil, celery, onions, carrots, and leeks. Place roasting pan in oven and bake for 30 to 45 minutes or until vegetables are a rich brown color.

4. Add the tomato paste to the vegetables and reduce the oven temperature to 300 degrees. Bake the tomato paste with the vegetables for 30 minutes, scraping the bottom and sides of the pan occasionally to prevent burning. Remove the roasting pan from the oven and add the wine. Stir. Add the contents of the roasting pan to the simmering bones. Add the garlic, bay leaves, and thyme.

5. Slowly simmer the stockpot for approximately 6 hours, skimming the surface occasionally.

6. Strain the stock using a fine sieve and place in a large saucepan.

7. Simmer over moderate heat until the sauce is reduced to approximately 2 quarts.

8. Mix together cornstarch and the cold water. Add to simmering stock while mixing with a wire whisk. As soon as stock returns to a simmer remove from heat and strain through a fine sieve.

9. Cool and divide into small containers. Freeze until needed.

Per serving (¼ cup):

fat grams 0.3	protein grams 2
fiber grams 0.2	carbohydrate grams 2
calories 15	sodium milligrams 54

Yogurt Cheese
YIELD: ½ CUP

This is one of the mainstays of the low-fat kitchen. This method gives nonfat yogurt the consistency of firm sour cream.

You may want to make a larger batch since it keeps two to three weeks and you will be finding your own ways to use it in the kitchen. Use it to top a baked potato, to garnish Mexican dishes, or in recipes calling for sour cream. Compared to the ersatz sour cream sold in supermarkets, this tastes fresher and has fewer added gum stabilizers, etc.

1 cup nonfat yogurt

1. Place a paper coffee filter in a funnel or coffee filter holder and set over a small canning jar that holds at least ½ cup. Place the

yogurt in the coffee filter and place assembly in the refrigerator overnight or until ½ cup of water has drained from the yogurt. Discard water. Place yogurt in jar and refrigerate until needed.

Per serving (1 tablespoon):

fat grams 0	protein grams 2
fiber grams 0	carbohydrate grams 2
calories 16	sodium milligrams 22

Ricotta Pastry

YIELD: ENOUGH FOR TWO 10-INCH TARTS, 20 SERVINGS

One of the culprits of many pastries is the short dough traditionally used as the crust. This low-fat version is slightly less flaky than you may be used to, but it is still wonderful, and much lower in fat. Be careful not to overmix this dough.

For a quiche or savory pie, omit the vanilla and sugar.

Nonfat canned pie fillings work well in this crust. Even pumpkin pie can be produced with nonfat eggs and skim milk. As a savory dough, it can be used as topping for chicken pot pie, meat turnovers, and little hors d'oeuvres.

When rolling out a pie, use a lightly floured board and rolling pin. Allow the dough to relax before baking, as it does tend to shrink more than normal short dough.

½ cup part-skim ricotta cheese	*⅓ cup sugar*
3 tablespoons skim milk	*⅛ teaspoon salt*
1 egg white	*2 cups all-purpose flour*
1 tablespoon safflower oil	*2 tablespoons baking powder*
2 teaspoons vanilla extract	

1. Puree the ricotta cheese in a blender or food processor until silky smooth.

2. Combine ricotta cheese puree, skim milk, egg white, oil, and vanilla in a large mixing bowl.

3. In a medium bowl, sift together the sugar, salt, flour, and baking powder.

4. Add the dry ingredients to the wet ingredients. Carefully mix just until incorporated. Do not overmix. Divide into 2 pieces.

5. Refrigerate for 30 minutes before rolling.

Per serving (2 tablespoons):

fat grams 1	protein grams 2
fiber grams 0.3	carbohydrate grams 13
calories 74	sodium milligrams 124

Whole Wheat Crêpes
YIELD: 25 6-INCH CRÊPES

Crêpes are a fun and versatile item to have in your freezer. This collection uses them to make breakfast foods. You can also wrap them around salad fillings for lunch, and fill them with sweet fruit fillings for dessert.

Freeze crêpes in small packets of 6 to 8 since they tend to dry out if not used quickly after thawing.

1 egg	*¾ cup whole wheat flour*
¼ teaspoon salt	*(or all-white)*
¾ cup all-purpose flour	*1 tablespoon sugar*
	2 cups skim milk

1. Combine the egg, salt, flours, sugar, and 1 cup of the skim milk in a mixing bowl. Mix with a wire whisk until smooth. Add the remaining milk and whisk. Refrigerate for at least 1 hour before making the crêpes.

2. Lightly coat a 6-inch nonstick skillet with nonstick vegetable spray. Place over medium heat.

3. When the pan begins to show the first sign of smoke, remove it from the heat and add 2 tablespoons of batter. Quickly tilt the pan to roll the batter around the inside of the pan so that the batter evenly coats it up to about ½ inch from the rim.

4. Replace the pan on the heat and cook until the crêpe is dry on the top surface and the bottom begins to brown slightly, about 30 to 45 seconds. Carefully flip the crêpe using a nylon (hard plastic) spatula and slightly brown the second side. Slide the crêpe from the pan onto wax paper to cool.

5. Repeat the process until all the batter is used.

6. Stack the crêpes, placing small squares of waxed paper between them to prevent sticking. Wrap, then refrigerate or freeze until needed.

Per serving (1 crêpe):

fat grams 0.4	protein grams 2
fiber grams 0.5	carbohydrate grams 7
calories 37	sodium milligrams 34

MENUS

಄

ere are a few samples of the many ways that you can put together a day's dining using the recipes in this book and other healthful foods. As you cook the recipes in the collection, and explore new foods from your supermarket, you'll be able to invent many more combinations to enjoy. You know what you like!

It's impossible to create a menu that will fill the nutritional needs of every person with cancer. For one thing, your eating plan will change depending on the kind of cancer you have. Tailor these menus and others you create to reflect the recommendations in Part 2 on specific cancers.

Also, these menus assume that you are an "average-sized person." If you look at the fat-gram chart on page 404, you'll see that taller people can have more fat grams each day and still have 20 percent of their calories from fat; the reason is that they will no doubt eat more each day. A petite woman just plain eats less than a man who's six-foot-two. If you're in the middle of that chart, the nutrient breakdowns will work for you, and if you're at either end, you'll probably be eating more or less food each day and should adjust the fat grams accordingly. Because we aimed at averages, the fat-gram percentages of most of these menus are lower than recommended in the book. We figured that many people will consume fewer calories than the menu totals, and thus their fat percentage will go up. Also, it's not too difficult to up your fat grams by changing the snack or "stealing" french fries at lunch, so it's not a bad idea to start out on the low side anyway!

More than providing nutrient counts, the value in these menus is in helpiong you picture how a day's eating might lay out. They show that when following your cancer recovery eating plan, you'll never go hungry, and can look forward to many delicious meals every day.

DAY ONE

BREAKFAST

Total cereal
with Skim Milk and Strawberries
Half grapefruit

A.M. SNACK

Fruit yogurt

LUNCH

Swiss Chard and White Bean Chowder
Honey Whole Wheat Bread
Skim milk

P.M. SNACK

Apple

DINNER

Sweet Potato Soup
Tossed salad with Creamy Herb Salad Dressing
Broiled Fish with Black Bean
Sauce and Mango Relish
Steamed zucchini
Banana and Caramel Custard Pie

fat: 25 grams
fiber: 35 grams
calories: 1948
protein: 104 grams
carbohydrate: 342
    grams
cholesterol: 174
    milligrams

Calories from protein:
    21%
Calories from
    carbohydrates: 68%
Calories from fats: 11%

Vitamin A: 3586 RE
Vitamin C: 294
    milligrams
Vitamin E: 21
    milligrams
Calcium: 1816
    milligrams
Sodium: 3718
    milligrams

Based on portion sizes given with recipes in this book and on the following
amounts: 2 cups loose-leaf lettuce, 1 cup Total cereal, 2 cups skim milk, ½ cup
strawberries, 1 cup yogurt, ½ cup zucchini

DAY TWO

BREAKFAST
Apple and Raisin Bran Muffin with preserves
Orange
Skim milk

A.M. SNACK
Banana

LUNCH
Curried Chicken Salad Pita Sandwich
Carrot sticks
Skim milk

P.M. SNACK
Popcorn
Fruit Yogurt

DINNER
Tossed Salad with Creamy Herb Salad Dressing
Penne à la Vodka
Skillet Corn Bread
Cherry Rice Pudding Brûlée

fat: 24 grams
fiber: 32 grams
calories: 2212
protein: 90 grams
carbohydrate: 427
　grams
cholesterol: 181
　milligrams

Calories from protein:
　16%
Calories from
　carbohydrates: 75%
Calories from fats: 9%

Vitamin A: 2826 RE
Vitamin C: 168
　milligrams
Vitamin E: 5
　milligrams
Calcium: 1686
　milligrams
Sodium: 2231
　milligrams

Based on portion sizes given with recipes in this book and on the following amounts: 2 cups skim milk, 2 cups air-popped popcorn, 2 tablespoons jam, 2 ounces raw carrots, 2 cups loose-leaf lettuce, 1 cup low-fat yogurt

DAY THREE

BREAKFAST
Apple, Raisin, and Cheese Breakfast Blintzes
Cranberry juice cocktail
Honey Whole Wheat Bread with preserves
Skim milk

A.M. SNACK
Orange

LUNCH
Pasta and Shrimp Salad
Skim milk

P.M. SNACK
Oven-dried tortilla chips
Fresh Salsa
Skim milk

DINNER
Pinto Bean Soup
Blackberry-glazed Pork Tenderloin
Mashed Sweet Potatoes with Ginger
Asparagus Glazed with Orange
Peach Crisp

fat: 25 grams
fiber: 36 grams
calories: 1899
protein: 96 grams
carbohydrate: 335
 grams
cholesterol: 150
 milligrams

Calories from protein:
 20%
Calories from
 carbohydrates: 69%
Calories from fats: 12%

Vitamin A: 3478 RE
Vitamin C: 308
 milligrams
Vitamin E: 13
 milligrams
Calcium: 1559
 milligrams
Sodium: 2747
 milligrams

Based on portion sizes given with recipes in this book and on the following
amounts: ½ cup cranberry juice cocktail, 2 tablespoons jam, 3 cups skim milk

DAY FOUR

BREAKFAST
Peach and Ricotta Pancakes
Orange
Skim milk

A.M. SNACK
Apple and Raisin Bran Muffin

LUNCH
Mexican Tortilla Pie
Skim milk

P.M. SNACK
Plain popcorn
Skim milk

DINNER
Hearty Lentil Soup
Veal and Sun-dried Tomato Meatloaf with Basil Sauce
Mashed Potatoes with Caramelized Onions
Steamed green beans
Tapioca Pudding with Figs and Basil

fat: 26 grams
fiber: 35 grams
calories: 1778
protein: 105 grams
carbohydrate: 299
   grams
cholesterol: 218
   milligrams

Calories from protein:
   23%
Calories from
   carbohydrates: 65%
Calories from fats: 13%

Vitamin A: 1521 RE
Vitamin C: 169
   milligrams
Vitamin E: 6
   milligrams
Calcium: 1585
   milligrams
Sodium: 2412
   milligrams

Based on portion sizes given with recipes in this book and on the following
amounts: 3 cups skim milk, ⅔ cup green beans, 2 cups air-popped popcorn

DAY FIVE

BREAKFAST
French Toast
Half grapefruit
Skim milk

A.M. SNACK
Apple and Raisin Bran Muffin
Banana

LUNCH
Tuna fish sandwich on Honey Whole Wheat Bread
Skim milk

P.M. SNACK
Fruit yogurt
Orange

DINNER
Lettuce salad with Creamy Herb Salad Dressing
Fusilli Pasta with Pan-grilled Chicken and Red Pepper Sauce
Bran Bread (2 slices)
Upside Down Pear Pie with Cinnamon Glacé

fat: 24 grams
fiber: 30 grams
calories: 2018
protein: 108 grams
carbohydrate: 362
 grams
cholesterol: 123
 milligrams

Calories from protein:
 21%
Calories from
 carbohydrates: 69%
Calories from fats: 10%

Vitamin A: 1429 RE
Vitamin C: 275
 milligrams
Vitamin E: 7
 milligrams
Calcium: 1635
 milligrams
Sodium: 2752
 milligrams

Based on portion sizes given with recipes in this book and on the following amounts: 2 cups skim milk, 2 cups loose-leaf lettuce, 1 cup low-fat yogurt, 1 ounce water-packed tuna, drained

DAY SIX

BREAKFAST
Mix of Total and All-Bran cereals with Strawberries and
skim milk
Orange
Toast

A.M. SNACK
Apple

LUNCH
New England Clam Chowder
Honey Whole Wheat Bread
Skim milk

P.M. SNACK
Fruit yogurt

DINNER
Black Bean and Cornmeal Loaf (Appetizer)
Chicken Breast in Tortilla Sauce
Brown Rice Pilaf
Jicama Slaw
Warm Apricot Pudding

fat: 23 grams
fiber: 40 grams
calories: 1878
protein: 104 grams
carbohydrate: 331
    grams
cholesterol: 132
    milligrams

Calories from portein:
    21%
Calories from
    carbohydrates: 68%
Calories from fats: 11%

Vitamin A: 2785 RE
Vitamin C: 241
    milligrams
Vitamin E: 13
    milligrams
Calcium: 1592
    milligrams
Sodium: 2895
    milligrams

Based on portion sizes given with recipes in this book and on the following
amounts: 2 cups skim milk, ½ cup Total cereal, ½ cup All-Bran cereal, ½ cup
strawberries, 1 cup low-fat yogurt

DAY SEVEN

BREAKFAST
Whole Wheat Crêpes with Apricot and Cheese Filling
Apple and Raisin Bran Muffin
Skim milk

A.M. SNACK
Nonfat yogurt
Banana

LUNCH
Grain Burger
Skim milk

P.M. SNACK
Orange

DINNER
Summer Gazpacho
Vegetable Stew with Couscous and Harissa
Warm Berry Stew

fat: 23 grams
fiber: 23 grams
calories: 1695
protein: 67 grams
carbohydrate: 331
  grams
cholesterol: 42
  milligrams

Calories from protein:
  15%
Calories from
  carbohydrates: 73%
Calories from fats: 12%

Vitamin A: 1981 RE
Vitamin C: 262
  milligrams
Vitamin E: 8
  milligrams
Calcium: 1516
  milligrams
Sodium: 2576
  milligrams

Based on portion sizes given with recipes in this book and on the following amounts: 1 cup skim milk, 1 cup nonfat yogurt

FOR THE DOCTOR

❧

C an food actually affect the neoplastic process? Although
much remains to be learned, there is abundant evidence
that the answer is a very emphatic "yes." The application
of exciting new findings in this area is the focus of this book for
persons with cancer.

No one is closer to your patients' individual health needs than
you and your patient, so I have emphasized throughout this book
that undertaking any diet and life-style changes during recovery
from cancer must be done in consultation with the members of the
health-care team—and that the judgment of the physician regard-
ing the needs of each individual should override any general or
specific recommendations in this book. This brief summary of what
those recommendations are, and the scientific findings on which
they are based, is for you.

THE PROGRAM

Basically, the program emphasizes:

- Reducing dietary fat intake
- Increasing dietary fiber intake
- Achieving a balance of nutrients from a variety of foods daily, as described in the Food Pyramid recently developed by the U.S. Department of Agriculture
- Emphasizing foods containing the chemopreventive agents that have been proven to be, or are strongly suspected to be, effective in specific cancers
- Incorporating a gently graded plan of exercise, which has many known health benefits and, according to very recent findings, may play a role in reducing cancer risk

These recommendations are presented in the context of the many nutritional obstacles that arise from cancer and its therapies. Tips on overcoming these obstacles, as well as specific instructions on gradually and successfully integrating the program into the daily routine, are provided in detail, in language that your patient can understand. More than 100 recipes that support the goals of the program, and a number of resources for assistance with specific problems related to cancer, are provided.

You and your staff or consulting nutritionist will very likely be called upon to help set and maintain individual dietary goals for the patient. I have not suggested any specific dietary supplements and suggest that use of supplements should be discussed with you.

CALCULATING DAILY FAT INTAKE GOALS

One area in which your patient may need help is in setting goals for reduced daily fat intake. Because we don't know yet what the ideal level of dietary fat intake is, and because the recommendations may ultimately vary for various cancers, there is no precise way to calculate what an exact fat-gram goal should be. Based on current knowledge, I have recommended that people with breast cancer, colon cancer, and prostate cancer take in *no more than 20 percent* of daily calories as fats, and people with other cancers, *25 percent.* But current clinical trials will refine this level, probably downward.

There are three ways to calculate daily fat gram goals. The first way is to use a table like that on page 404, which gives approximate fat-gram intakes for a 20 percent fat-calorie diet. This table is based on approximate caloric intake levels for given heights and weights, and factors in medium frame size and basal activity levels.

Another method of calculation is to take an arbitrary basal level of 25 calories per kilogram of actual body weight and multiply by weight in kilograms, to get a basal caloric intake level. (To get weight in kilograms, multiply weight in pounds by 0.45.) Thus, a 150-pound person weighs 68 kilograms and has a basal calorie level of 68 × 25 or 1,700 calories per day. Twenty percent of this is 340 fat calories. You then divide by 9 to get 38 fat grams daily. This gives a basal level somewhat lower than the other method.

A third way is to have your nutritionist give the patient a diet diary to record all foods eaten for three or four days. The nutritionist then calculates the average daily calorie intake and derives the fat-gram goal from this.

THE SCIENTIFIC BASIS OF THE PROGRAM

Our understanding of the relationship between cancer and nutrition is expanding rapidly. One of the constant challenges in writing this book was to keep the text abreast of new findings.

It is already known that many substances found in foods, from macronutrients to micronutrients to trace elements to a host of nonnutritive chemicals, can and do modify one or more of the steps in carcinogenesis. Some of these substances can protect normal cells from the effects of carcinogens; others may interfere with replication

APPROXIMATE MAXIMUM DAILY FAT GRAMS
FOR 20 PERCENT CALORIES FROM FAT

HEIGHT (NO SHOES)	FAT GRAMS OVER AGE 50*	FAT GRAMS UNDER AGE 50
MEN		
5'2"	30	34
5'3"	31	35
5'4"	32	36
5'5"	33	37
5'6"	34	38
5'7"	35	39
5'8"	36	40
5'9"	37	41
5'10"	38	42
5'11"	39	43
6'0"	40	44
6'1"	41	45
6'2"	42	46
WOMEN		
5'0"	25	28
5'1"	26	29
5'2"	27	30
5'3"	28	31
5'4"	29	32
5'5"	30	33
5'6"	31	34
5'7"	32	35
5'8"	33	36
5'9"	34	37
5'10"	35	38
5'11"	36	39
6'0"	37	40

* Levels decline after age 50 because of decreased activity.

* These fat gram amounts are calculated on basal levels of calories needed for ideal body weight at a particular height for adults of medium frame. If you are very active and have reached your daily fat gram goal but are still hungry, eat fruits, vegetables, and nonfat snacks, not more fat.

of cells already committed to malignancy; and still others act by mechanisms not fully understood.

Intense research is being conducted in each of these areas. In 1993, over forty cancer and nutrition–related abstracts were submitted to the meeting of the American Association for Cancer Research alone; other professional organizations have experienced similar trends. Here are the major areas of study at this time.

MACRONUTRIENTS

High consumption of animal fat is associated with breast, colon, prostate, endometrial, and other cancers. Even lung cancer has recently been linked to fat intake. Evidence in breast cancer strongly points to a role for fat in stimulation of growth of existing cancer, and this is now being evaluated in clinical trials. Since the typical American consumes 35 to 40 percent of daily calories as fat, these findings have tremendous implications for American health.

Suspected mechanisms for the fat-cancer relationship include the cancer-enhancing effect of the caloric energy in fat, the effect of certain fatty acids, and the hormonal changes associated with a high-fat diet.

High consumption of fiber is inversely correlated with colon cancer, and perhaps breast and prostate cancer. A number of mechanisms for fiber's protective effects have been proposed. Among these are absorption of gut carcinogens, speeding up gut transit time, various effects on gut microflora, and possible changes in hormone metabolism. Of course, a bonus of a high-fiber diet is that it is typically a low-fat diet as well.

High intake of protein has been connected to various cancers in some studies. Since the two major sources of protein in the American diet—meat and cheese—are high in fat, limitation of protein intake would accomplish a concomitant reduction of dietary fat intake. Also, recent evidence indicates that potent carcinogens are produced by high-temperature cooking (over 300 degrees F) of animal proteins.

MICRONUTRIENTS

Fruits and vegetables are high in fiber and low in fat, but also contain a host of micronutrients and other chemicals with no known nutrient function. Increased fruit and vegetable consumption is associated with decreased risk of lung, colon, bladder, upper aerodigestive, and stomach cancers. This effect may be due to the antioxidant vitamins (A, C, and E) contained in fruits and vegetables, or to their content of other anticancer substances. These phytochemicals can alter the carcinogenic process in a variety of ways. Some of these are: blocking carcinogen activation or function, acting as free-radical scavengers, altering membrane structure, suppressing nucleic acid and gene product synthesis, and causing redifferentiation of undifferentiated cells.

The developing field of chemoprevention is devoted to producing and testing drugs that block or reverse cancer development. Many promising chemopreventive agents have been derived from foods, including several vitamins and analogues, minerals such as calcium, certain trace elements, and a number of other phytochemicals. Approximately forty chemoprevention clinical trials are in progress around the world.

Some interesting phytochemicals are:

Monoterpenes—These substances, found in fruits and vegetables, can modulate certain cellular proteins and growth-factor receptors, thereby inhibiting tumor growth. Limonene, found in citrus fruits, is an example.

Isoflavones—Present in soybeans and other plants, these substances appear to have antioxidant, antihormone, and antiangiogenesis actions, and can modulate enzymes involved in signal transduction. Genistein is an example of this class of compounds; in animals, genistein inhibits skin cancer and colon cancer induced by carcinogens.

Various allium sulfides—Garlic and other allium vegetables contain a large number of chemicals that can induce carcinogen-metabolizing enzymes, act as free-radical scavengers, modify immune responses, and inhibit the promotion phases of carcinogens.

Fiber components—Recent investigations have revealed that certain fiber components called lignins have structures similar to estrogens. These are similar to the soy isoflavones. Such "phytoestrogens" may have tamoxifenlike activity, making them potentially useful against established hormone-dependent cancer cells. Some new data indicate that phytic acid, which is found in grains, nuts, and seeds, may have an anti–colon cancer effect. It is not yet clear whether phytic acid has an independent or synergistic effect with fiber.

VARIETY

In order to get the full potential benefit of all these vitamins and phytochemicals, and because the relative importance of individual phytochemicals is not known, a basic concept of the diet program described in this book is to eat a *variety* of fruits and vegetables. Among the drawbacks to a monotonous diet, there is the possibility of excessive intake of some phytochemicals (for example, indoles) that can potentially have cancer-promoting actions. A varied diet ensures that a number of nutrients and phytochemicals are consumed and that none is taken to excess.

A related hypothesis is the "single nutrient bolus" hypothesis. Boluses of fat are known to increase colon cell proliferation. This suggests that repeated fatty meals—and perhaps an occasional binge on fat, even if total fat consumption is acceptable—are potentially harmful.

TIMING

At present, there is no reliable evidence that dietary manipulation significantly benefits patients with advanced metastatic cancer. In fact, several clinical trials have shown no benefit for nonvolitional feeding in such cases, and in some studies, this method has been associated with net harm. The American College of Physicians has published a position paper that states such feeding (hyperalimentation) is appropriate in advanced cancer only in clinical trial settings.

The development of cancer is a multistage process. Based on this fact, and the evidence described above, it is clear that the prime time to interfere with the cancer process is during its earliest stages. Stopping a carcinogen before it damages DNA, or blocking the growth stimulatory or angiogenic effects of damaged genes, is far better than trying to eradicate large numbers of uncontrolled malignant cells. Thus, in theory, increasing fiber or decreasing fat or taking a chemopreventive drug will be more effective than giving chemotherapy for advanced metastatic cancer.

Clearly, if nutritional and chemopreventive manipulation is to have real effects, it must be started as an adjuvant to therapy, early—when lesions are premalignant, such as oral leukoplakia, cervical dysplasia, and adenomatous colon polyps—or when malignant disease burden is minimal (for example, after removal of a breast mass or colon lesions). Some clinical trials are showing that this is both feasible and workable. These advances are stretching the mileage we can get out of a clinical trial. Using this approach, trials of high fiber in colon polyps and low fat in resected breast cancer become both prevention *and* treatment trials. All of this is clearly an argument for early detection of cancer and appropriate therapy— medical, surgical, radiation—for early disease. At this point, manipulation of nutrition is an adjunctive measure, at best. It is also an argument for identifying those at high risk of cancer and starting risk-reduction measures early. These are the people for whom primary prevention strategies are designed, and it is for them that such measures will be developed and refined in the future.

The dietary changes recommended in this book are an important first step, but much more needs to be done. Clinical trials now in progress will provide data supporting additional disease-specific dietary guidelines. Future trials will evaluate and better define appropriate chemopreventive drugs for cancers and for other diseases.

I believe that by the end of the 1990s, truly effective chemopreventive agents will be available. They must be, if we are to meet the needs of those who, through emerging genetic analysis techniques, will prove to be at high risk of cancer, as well as those who have had their lives prolonged by cancer therapy and are at risk for second primaries and recurrent disease.

USING THIS BOOK

As a medical oncologist, I know that questions about nutrition are increasingly frequent and that many patients want to take a stronger role in their care. This book will answer many of your patients' questions about nutrition and give them up-to-date information about the role of diet in cancer treatment and prevention.

The diet program outlined in this book offers many advantages. The recommendations for low-fat, high-fiber eating are in keeping with current recommendations for cardiovascular health. With professional guidance from you and the nutritionist, the program can be adapted to the needs of diabetics and others with special dietary requirements. Needless to say, the family, as well as the individual with cancer, can benefit from the risk-reducing changes recommended in this program as well.

A less tangible, but equally important, benefit of this program is that it restores to the person with cancer a sense of control, in a situation that is otherwise overwhelming. It provides a meaningful way to participate in one's own healing and prognosis. As presented, it fosters a hopeful alliance with the health-care team and the goals of treatment.

I hope the information in this short chapter is interesting to you and that it will help you help the people with cancer who are in your care. Furthermore, I hope it will make you want to keep up with the rapidly developing field of cancer prevention and control.

RESOURCES FOR PEOPLE WITH CANCER

୬

ALL CANCERS

American Cancer Society
Provides information and referrals to numerous support services, including CanSurmount, I Can Cope, International Association of Laryngectomies, Look Good . . . Feel Better, Reach to Recovery. Toll-free hot line provides free information on all aspects of cancer, including locations of comprehensive cancer centers. Check the phone book for your local division office or call the toll-free number listed below.
1599 Clifton Road, NE
Atlanta, GA 30329
(800) ACS-2345

American Association of Sex Educators, Counselors, and Therapists
For assistance with problems in sexual relationships that develop from cancer or cancer therapies—this organization can provide names of therapists in your area.
Suite 1717
435 N. Michigan Avenue
Chicago, IL 60611
(312) 644-0828

The American Dietetic Association
Through the National Center for Nutrition and Dietetics' toll-free Consumer Nutrition Hot Line, you can talk with registered dietitians about your food or nutrition questions, listen to recorded nutrition messages from registered dietitians, or locate registered dietitians in your area for nutrition counseling.
(800) 366-1655

American Medical Record Association
Can assist with matters pertaining to your medical records.

Office of Legislative Affairs
875 N. Michigan Avenue
Chicago, IL 60611
(312) 787-2672

Burger King Cancer Caring Center
Provides support in coping with the emotional impact of cancer.
4117 Liberty Avenue
Pittsburgh, PA 15224
(412) 622-1212

CAN ACT (Cancer Patients Action Alliance)
Works to resolve problems of access to advanced cancer treatments, the FDA drug approval process, and insurance reimbursement issues.
26 College Place
Brooklyn, NY 11201
(718) 522-4607

Cancer Care
Nonprofit social service agency that provides professional social work support and counseling.
1180 Avenue of the Americas
New York, NY 10036
(212) 302-2400

Cancer Conquerors Foundation
Cancer survival training and self-study programs, emphasizing mind/body/spirit integration.
P.O. Box 3444
Fullerton, CA 92634
(800) 238-6479

Cancer Guidance Hotline
A networking service; trained volunteers have experienced cancer themselves or within their families.
1323 Forbes Avenue
Pittsburgh, PA 15219
(412) 261-2211

Cancer Information Service
Toll-free hot line for information about any aspect of cancer; up-to-date information for patients about clinical trials.
National Cancer Institute
(800) 4-CANCER

Cancer Response System of the American Cancer Society
Toll-free hot line for information about any aspect of cancer; information referrals.
American Cancer Society
(800) ACS-2345

Cancer Support Network
Peer support groups, educational programs, community workshops, and social gatherings for cancer patients and their families.
Suite L-10
Essex House
Baum Boulevard at S. Negley
  Avenue
Pittsburgh, PA 15206-3703
(412) 361-8600

Candlelighters Foundation
Information, support, and advocacy for young people with cancer and

their families. Check your phone book for local listings or contact the address below.
Suite 1001
1901 Pennsylvania Avenue, NW
Washington, DC 20006
(202) 659-5136

CANCERVIVE

Offers support, information, and advocacy for cancer survivors; this new group is still forming local chapters.
Suite 500
6500 Wilshire Boulevard
Los Angeles, CA 90048
(310) 203-9232

CanSurmount

One-to-one peer support and visitations. See the listing under American Cancer Society.

ChemoCare

Personal support to persons undergoing chemotherapy or radiation treatments, from trained and certified volunteers who have been through it.
220 St. Paul Street
Westfield, NJ 07090
(800) 55-CHEMO (outside New Jersey)
(908) 233-1103 (inside New Jersey)

The Chemotherapy Foundation

Up-to-date information for the public and patients about chemotherapy.

Suite 403
183 Madison Avenue
New York, NY 10016
(212) 213-9292

Children's Oncology Camps of America

Fun camping experiences for children with cancer and their families.
c/o Dr. Michael S. Trieger
2309 W. White Oaks Drive
Springfield, IL 62704
(217) 793-3949

Choice in Dying

Advocates for death with dignity and protection of individual rights at the end of life.
200 Varick Street
New York, NY 10014
(212) 366-5540

Coping Magazine

Bimonthly consumer magazine for people whose lives have been touched by cancer.
2019 N. Carothers
Franklin, TN 37064
(615) 790-2400

Corporate Angel Network

Networks to obtain space on corporate flights for persons with cancer who must travel for treatments.
Westchester County Airport
Bldg. 1
White Plains, NY 10604
(914) 328-1313

Families Against Cancer
Coalition of cancer patients and their families. Advocates in matters of national policy on cancer.
P.O. Box 588
DeWitt, NY 13214
(315) 446-5326 / 6385

Hereditary Cancer Institute
Studies the genetics of family cancer. Contact in writing.
Creighton University
Omaha, NE 68178

Hospice
See the listing under National Hospice Organization.

I Can Cope
Addresses educational and psychological needs of persons with cancer and their families. See the listing under American Cancer Society.

Make Today Count
Provides emotional support.
c/o Connie Zimmerman
Mid-America Cancer Center
1235 E. Cherokee
Springfield, MO 65804-2263
(800) 432-2273

National Cancer Institute
The government agency charged with research into cancer, its diagnosis, and treatment. See the listing under Cancer Information Service.

National Cancer Survivors Day
A nationwide celebration of life, celebrated on the first Sunday in June.

2019 N. Carothers
Franklin, TN 37064
(615) 790-2400

National Coalition for Cancer Survivorship
Support for cancer survivors and their families.
5th Floor
1010 Wayne Avenue
Silver Springs, MD 20910
(301) 650-9127

National Health Information Center
Assists with finding information on cancer topics.
P.O. Box 1133
Washington, DC 20013-1133
(800) 336-4797
(301) 565-4167 (in Maryland)

National Hospice Organization
Support and care for terminally ill patients, with emphasis on comfort and death with dignity.
Suite 901
1901 N. Moore Street
Arlington, VA 22209
(800) 658-8898

National Insurance Consumer Organization
Assists with consumer problems with insurance.
121 N. Payne Street
Alexandria, VA 22314
(703) 549-8050

National Women's Health Network

Dedicated to advocacy for women in need of health care.
224 7th Street, SE
Washington, DC 20003
(202) 347-1140

Oley Foundation

Information, support, and outreach for persons needing parenteral or enteral nutrition therapy (tube or intravenous feedings).
Albany Medical Center, A-23
214 Hun Memorial
Albany, NY 12208
(800) 776-OLEY

R. A. Bloch Cancer Foundation, Inc.

Information and advocacy for persons with cancer.
The Cancer Hotline
4410 Main Street
Kansas City, MO 64111
(816) 932-8453

Ronald McDonald Houses

Provide housing for children with cancer and their families during treatment. Check the phone book for local listing or contact:
National Coordinator
Golin Communications, Inc.
500 N. Michigan Avenue
Chicago, IL 60611
(312) 836-7384

Vital Options

Provides support for the emotional and psychosocial needs of young persons (ages seventeen to forty) with cancer or other life-threatening disease.
Suite A
4419 Coldwater Canyon Avenue
Studio City, CA 91604
(818) 508-5657

SPECIFIC CANCERS

American Brain Tumor Association

Offers information, support-group lists, referral information, and a pen pal program.
3725 N. Talman Avenue
Chicago, IL 60618
(800) 886-2282

American Foundation for Urologic Disease

Provides information and referrals to support groups, including US TOO (for men with prostate cancer).
Suite 401
300 W. Pratt Street
Baltimore, MD 21201-2463
(800) 828-7866

American Kidney Fund

Provides financial assistance for those with kidney disease.
7315 Wisconsin Avenue
Bethesda, MD 20814-3266
(800) 638-8299
(301) 986-1444 (in Maryland)

American Lung Association
Dedicated to the prevention and control of lung disease. Check your phone book for local listings or write:
1740 Broadway
New York, NY 10019

Bone Marrow Transplant Family Support Network
Helps families to connect through all phases of bone marrow transplantation, from decision making to follow-up care.
P.O. Box 845
Avon, CT 06001
(800) 826-9376

Bone Marrow Transplant Newsletter
Bimonthly newsletter and book on issues of concern to patients. Provides attorney referrals for assistance with insurance reimbursement problems.
1985 Spruce Avenue
Highland Park, IL 60035
(708) 831-1913

Encore
Discussion and exercise program for women who have had breast cancer surgery. Contact your local YWCA or:
Encore—National Board, YWCA
726 Broadway
New York, NY 10003
(212) 614-2827

International Association of Laryngectomies
Support and information for persons in whom the voice box has been removed.
Mr. Keith Fitzgerald
IAL—At the American Cancer Society
1599 Clifton Road, NE
Atlanta, GA 30329-4251
(404) 329-7651

International Myeloma Foundation
Information for patients with this disease, and support groups.
2120 Stanley Hills Drive
Los Angeles, CA 90046
(800) 452-CURE

Leukemia Society of America
Dedicated to finding the causes and cure of leukemia; support for leukemia patients.
600 Third Avenue
New York, NY 10016
(800) 955-4LSA

My Image After Breast Cancer
Twenty-four-hour HOPEline for accurate information on breast cancer.
Suite 203
6000 Stevenson Avenue
Alexandria, VA 22304
(703) 461-9616

National Alliance of Breast Cancer Organizations
A coalition forged to advance the cause of women's breast health. Provides information on breast cancer and on related legislative issues.
Second Floor
1180 Avenue of the Americas
New York, NY 10036
(212) 719-0154

National Brain Tumor Foundation
Support and education for brain tumor patients.
Suite 510
323 Geary Street
San Francisco, CA 94102
(800) 934-CURE

National Lymphedema Network
Information on the prevention and management of lymphedema, a possible side effect of mastectomy.
Suite 404
2211 Post Street
San Francisco, CA 94115
(800) 541-3259

National Marrow Donor Program
Authorized by the U.S. Congress, this is a nationwide computerized data network to match bone marrow donors with patients in need of a bone marrow transplant.
3433 Broadway Street, NE
Minneapolis, MN 55413
(800) MARROW-2

Patient Advocates for Advanced Cancer Treatments
Promotes diagnostic and therapeutic treatments for prostate cancer.
1143 Parmelee, NW
Grand Rapids, MI 49504
(616) 453-1477

The Skin Cancer Foundation
Information on skin cancer and its prevention.
Box 561
New York, NY 10156
(212) 725-5176

Susan G. Komen Breast Cancer Foundation
Promotes research, education, screening, treatment, and prevention of breast cancer.
Suite 370
5005 LBJ Freeway
Dallas, TX 75244
(800) I'M AWARE

United Ostomy Association
Support for returning to normal life after ostomy surgery. Check your phone book for local listings or contact:
Suite 120
36 Executive Park
Irvine, CA 92714
(714) 660-8624

Reach to Recovery
Assistance for physical, emotional, and cosmetic needs of women with breast cancer. See the listing under American Cancer Society.

Women's Breast Advisory Center
Provides information on all aspects of breast disease. Contact in writing:
11426 Rockville Pike
Rockville, MD 20850

Y-ME—National Organization for Breast Cancer Information and Support
Hot-line counseling, educational programs, and self-help meetings.
18220 Harwood Avenue
Homewood, IL 60430-2104
(800) 221-2141

Chartered Divisions of the American Cancer Society, Inc.
The American Cancer Society is the nationwide, community-based, voluntary health organization dedicated to eliminating cancer as a major health problem by preventing cancer, saving lives from cancer, and diminishing suffering from cancer through research, education, and service. For more information call the American Cancer Society: (800) ACS-2345.
National Headquarters: American Cancer Society, Inc., 1599 Clifton Road, NE, Atlanta, GA 30329-4251.

Cancer Centers
The institutions listed have been recognized as Cancer Centers by the National Cancer Institute. These centers have been rigorously reviewed by the National Cancer Advisory Board. They receive financial support from the National Cancer Institute, the American Cancer Society, and many other sources.

Cancer Centers

The institutions listed here have been recognized as Cancer Centers by the National Cancer Institute. These centers have been rigorously reviewed by the National Cancer Advisory Board. They receive financial support from the National Cancer Institute, the American Cancer Society and many other sources.

ALABAMA
University of Alabama at Birmingham*
Comprehensive Cancer Center
(205) 934-5077

ARIZONA
University of Arizona*
Arizona Cancer Center
(602) 626-6372

CALIFORNIA
The Kenneth Norris, Jr. Comprehensive
  Cancer Center*
University of Southern California
(213) 226-2370

Jonsson Comprehensive Cancer Center*
University of California at Los Angeles
1-800-825-2631

La Jolla Cancer Research Foundation
(619) 455-6480

University of California at San Diego Cancer Center
(619) 543-6178

City of Hope Beckman Research Institute
(818) 359-8111

Armand Hammer Center for Cancer Biology
Salk Institute
(619) 453-4100

COLORADO
University of Colorado Cancer Center
University of Colorado Health Sciences Center
(303) 270-3007

CONNECTICUT
Yale University*
Comprehensive Cancer Center
1-800-4-CANCER

DISTRICT OF COLUMBIA
Lombardi Cancer Research Center*
Georgetown University Medical Center
(202) 687-2192

FLORIDA
Sylvester Comprehensive Cancer Center*
University of Miami Medical School
(305) 545-1000

ILLINOIS
University of Chicago
Cancer Research Center
(312) 702-6180

Lurie Cancer Center
Northwestern University
(312) 908-5250

INDIANA
Purdue University Cancer Center
(317) 494-9129

MAINE
The Jackson Laboratory
(207) 288-3371

MARYLAND
The Johns Hopkins Oncology Center*
(410) 955-8800

MASSACHUSETTS
Dana-Farber Cancer Institute*
(617) 632-3000

Worcester Foundation for Experimental Biology
(508) 842-8921

Massachusetts Institute of Technology
Center for Cancer Research
(617) 253-6421

MICHIGAN
Meyer L. Prentis Comprehensive Cancer Center
  of Metropolitan Detroit
(313) 745-4329

University of Michigan Comprehensive Cancer Center*
(313) 936-9583

MINNESOTA
Mayo Comprehensive Cancer Center*
(507) 284-3413

NEBRASKA
Eppley Institute
University of Nebraska Medical Center
1-800-999-5465

NEW HAMPSHIRE
Norris Cotton Cancer Center*
Dartmouth-Hitchcock Medical Center
(603) 650-5000

NEW YORK
Cold Spring Harbor Laboratory
(516) 367-8397

Memorial Sloan-Kettering Cancer Center*
1-800-525-2225

Roswell Park Cancer Institute*
1-800-ROSWELL

Albert Einstein College of Medicine
Cancer Research Center
(718) 920-4826

Columbia University Comprehensive Cancer Center
(212) 305-6921

Kaplan Comprehensive Cancer Center*
New York University Medical Center
(212) 263-6485

University of Rochester Cancer Center
(716) 275-4911

Nelson Institute for Environmental Medicine
New York University Medical Center
(212) 263-5280

American Health Foundation
(212) 953-1900

NORTH CAROLINA
Duke University Comprehensive Cancer Center*
(919) 684-2748

Lineberger Cancer Research Center*
University of North Carolina
(919) 966-3036

Wake Forest University*
Comprehensive Cancer Center
Bowman Gray School of Medicine
(919) 716-4464

OHIO
Ohio State University*
Comprehensive Cancer Center
Arthur G. James Cancer Hospital
1-800-638-6996

Case Western Reserve University
Ireland Cancer Center
(216) 844-5432

PENNSYLVANIA
Fox Chase Cancer Center*
(215) 728-2570

University of Pennsylvania Cancer Center*
(215) 662-6364

Wistar Institute Cancer Center
(215) 898-3926

Fels Research Institute
Temple University School of Medicine
(215) 221-4000

Pittsburgh Cancer Institute*
University of Pittsburgh
1-800-537-4063

RHODE ISLAND
Brown University
Roger Williams Cancer Center
(401) 456-2071

TENNESSEE
Drew-Meharry-Morehouse
Consortium Cancer Center
(615) 327-6927

St. Jude Children's Research Hospital
(901) 522-0306

TEXAS
M.D. Anderson Cancer Center*
University of Texas
(713) 792-3245

San Antonio Cancer Institute
(210) 677-3850

UTAH
Utah Cancer Center
University of Utah School of Medicine
(801) 581-4048

VERMONT
Vermont Cancer Center*
University of Vermont
(802) 656-4414

VIRGINIA
Massey Cancer Center
Medical College of Virginia/VCU
(804) 371-5116

University of Virginia Cancer Center
(804) 924-5811

WASHINGTON
Fred Hutchinson Cancer Research Center*
(206) 667-5000

WISCONSIN
Comprehensive Cancer Center*
University of Wisconsin
(608) 263-8600

McArdle Laboratory for Cancer Research
University of Wisconsin Medical School
(608) 262-2177

*Indicates Comprehensive Cancer Center.

Chartered Divisions of the American Cancer Society, Inc.

Alabama Division, Inc.
504 Brookwood Boulevard
Homewood, Alabama 35209
(205) 879-2242

Alaska Division, Inc.
406 West Fireweed Lane
Anchorage, Alaska 99503
(907) 277-8696

Arizona Division, Inc.
2929 East Thomas Road
Phoenix, Arizona 85016
(602) 224-0524

Arkansas Division, Inc.
901 North University
Little Rock, Arkansas 72203
(501) 664-3480

California Division, Inc.
1710 Webster Street
Oakland, California 94612
(510) 893-7900

Colorado Division, Inc.
2255 South Oneida
Denver, Colorado 80224
(303) 758-2030

Connecticut Division, Inc.
Barnes Park South
14 Village Lane
Wallingford, Connecticut 06492
(203) 265-7161

Delaware Division, Inc.
92 Read's Way
New Castle, Delaware 19720
(302) 324-4227

District of Columbia Division, Inc.
1875 Connecticut Avenue, N.W.
Washington, DC 20009
(202) 483-2600

Florida Division, Inc.
3709 West Jetton Avenue
Tampa, Florida 33629-5146
(813) 253-0541

Georgia Division, Inc.
2200 Lake Blvd.
Atlanta, Georgia 30319
(404) 816-7800

Hawaii Pacific Division, Inc.
Community Services Center Bldg.
200 North Vineyard Boulevard
Honolulu, Hawaii 96817
(808) 531-1662

Idaho Division, Inc.
2676 Vista Avenue
Boise, Idaho 83705-0836
(208) 343-4609

Illinois Division, Inc.
77 East Monroe
Chicago, Illinois 60603-5795
(312) 641-6150

Indiana Division, Inc.
8730 Commerce Park Place
Indianapolis, Indiana 46268
(317) 872-4432

Iowa Division, Inc.
8364 Hickman Road
Des Moines, Iowa 50325
(515) 253-0147

Kansas Division, Inc.
1315 SW Arrowhead Road
Topeka, Kansas 66604
(913) 273-4114

Kentucky Division, Inc.
701 West Muhammad Ali Blvd.
Louisville, Kentucky 40203-1909
(502) 584-6782

Louisiana Division, Inc.
2200 Veteran's Memorial Blvd.
Suite 214
Kenner, Louisiana 70062
(504) 469-0021

Maine Division, Inc.
52 Federal Street
Brunswick, Maine 04011
(207) 729-3339

Maryland Division, Inc.
8219 Town Center Drive
Baltimore, Maryland 21236-0026
(410) 931-6868

Massachusetts Division, Inc.
247 Commonwealth Avenue
Boston, Massachusetts 02116
(617) 267-2650

Michigan Division, Inc.
1205 East Saginaw Street
Lansing, Michigan 48906
(517) 371-2920

Minnesota Division, Inc.
3316 West 66th Street
Minneapolis, Minnesota 55435
(612) 925-2772

Mississippi Division, Inc.
1380 Livingston Lane
Lakeover Office Park
Jackson, Mississippi 39213
(601) 362-8874

Missouri Division, Inc.
3322 American Avenue
Jefferson City, Missouri 65102
(314) 893-4800

Montana Division, Inc.
17 North 26th
Billings, Montana 59101
(406) 252-7111

Nebraska Division, Inc.
8502 West Center Road
Omaha, Nebraska 68124-5255
(402) 393-5800

Nevada Division, Inc.
1325 East Harmon
Las Vegas, Nevada 89119
(702) 798-6857

New Hampshire Division, Inc.
360 Route 101, Unit 501
Bedford, New Hampshire 03110-5032
(603) 472-8899

New Jersey Division, Inc.
2600 US Highway 1
North Brunswick, New Jersey 08902-0803
(908) 297-8000

New Mexico Division, Inc.
5800 Lomas Blvd., NE
Albuquerque, New Mexico 87110
(505) 260-2105

New York State Division, Inc.
6725 Lyons Street
East Syracuse, New York 13057
(315) 437-7025

□ **Long Island Division, Inc.**
75 Davids Drive
Hauppauge, New York 11788
(516) 436-7070

□ **New York City Division, Inc.**
19 West 56th Street
New York, New York 10019
(212) 586-8700

□ **Queens Division, Inc.**
112-25 Queens Boulevard
Forest Hills, New York 11375
(718) 263-2224

□ **Westchester Division, Inc.**
30 Glenn Street
White Plains, New York 10603
(914) 949-4800

North Carolina Division, Inc.
11 South Boylan Avenue
Raleigh, North Carolina 27603
(919) 834-8463

North Dakota Division, Inc.
123 Roberts Street
Fargo, North Dakota 58102
(701) 232-1385

Ohio Division, Inc.
5555 Frantz Road
Dublin, Ohio 43017
(614) 889-9565

Oklahoma Division, Inc.
4323 63d, Suite 110
Oklahoma City, Oklahoma 73116
(405) 843-9888

Oregon Division, Inc.
0330 SW Curry
Portland, Oregon 97201
(503) 295-6422

Pennsylvania Division, Inc.
Route 422 & Sipe Avenue
Hershey, Pennsylvania 17033-0897
(717) 533-6144

□ **Philadelphia Division, Inc.**
1422 Chestnut Street
Philadelphia, Pennsylvania 19102
(215) 665-2900

Puerto Rico Division, Inc.
Calle Alverio #577
Esquina Sargento Medina
Hato Rey, Puerto Rico 00918
(809) 764-2295

Rhode Island Division, Inc.
400 Main Street
Pawtucket, Rhode Island 02860
(401) 722-8480

South Carolina Division, Inc.
128 Stonemark Lane
Columbia, South Carolina 29210-3855
(803) 750-1693

South Dakota Division, Inc.
4101 Carnegie Place
Sioux Falls, South Dakota 57106-2322
(605) 361-8277

Tennessee Division, Inc.
1315 Eighth Avenue, South
Nashville, Tennessee 37203
(615) 255-1227

Texas Division, Inc.
2433 Ridgepoint Drive
Austin, Texas 78754
(512) 928-2262

Utah Division, Inc.
941 East 3300 S.
Salt Lake City, Utah 84106
(801) 483-1500

Vermont Division, Inc.
13 Loomis Street
Montpelier, Vermont 05602
(802) 223-2348

Virginia Division, Inc.
P.O. Box 6359
Glen Allen, Virginia 23058-6359
(804) 527-3700

Washington Division, Inc.
2120 First Avenue North
Seattle, Washington 98109-1140
(206) 283-1152

West Virginia Division, Inc.
2428 Kanawha Boulevard East
Charleston, West Virginia 25311
(304) 344-3611

Wisconsin Division, Inc.
P.O. Box 902
Pewaukee, Wisconsin 53072-0902
(414) 523-5500

Wyoming Division, Inc.
2222 House Avenue
Cheyenne, Wyoming 82001
(307) 638-3331

FOR MORE INFORMATION CALL THE AMERICAN CANCER SOCIETY: 1-800-ACS-2345.

The American Cancer Society is the nationwide, community-based, voluntary health organization dedicated to eliminating cancer as a major health problem by preventing cancer, saving lives from cancer, and diminishing suffering from cancer through research, education, and service.

National Headquarters: American Cancer Society, Inc., 1599 Clifton Road N.E., Atlanta, GA 30329-4251

BIBLIOGRAPHY

❧

Bellerson, K. *The Complete and Up-to-Date Fat Book.* New York: Avery Publishing, 1993.

Boves and Church's Food Values of Portions Commonly Used, 15th edition. Philadelphia: J.B. Lippincott, 1989.

Briggs, M.H. *Recent Vitamin Research.* Boca Raton, Florida: CRC Press, 1984.

Briggs, M.H., ed. *Vitamins in Human Biology and Medicine.* Boca Raton, Florida: CRC Press, 1981.

Brody, J.E. *Jane Brody's Good Food Book.* New York: Bantam Books, 1985.

Brown, M., ed. *Present Knowledge in Nutrition.* Washington, D.C.: International Life Sciences Institute Nutrition Foundation, 1990.

Debahey, M., A. Gotto, L. Scott, and L. Foreyt. *The Living Heart Diet.* New York: Simon & Schuster, 1984.

Foods for Health. DHHS, NIH publication number 85-2036. 1985.

Goodhart, R.S., and M.E. Shils. *Modern Nutrition in Health and Disease,* 6th edition. Philadelphia: Lea and Febiger, 1980.

Jacobs, M., ed. *Vitamins and Minerals in the Prevention and Treatment of Cancer.* Boca Raton, Florida: CRC Press, 1991.

Lipkin, M., H. Newmark, and G. Kellogg, eds. *Calcium, Vitamin D and Prevention of Colon Cancer.* Boca Raton, Florida: CRC Press, 1991.

Moon, T.E., and M.S. Micozzi, eds. *Nutrition and Cancer Prevention: Investigating the Role of Micronutrients.* New York: Marcel Dekker, 1989.

Netzer, C.T. *The Complete Book of Food Counts.* New York: Dell, 1988.

Reddy, B.S., and L.A. Cohen, eds. *Diet, Nutrition, and Cancer: A Critical Evaluation.* Vol. 11: Micronutrients, Non-Nutritive Dietary Factors and Cancer. Boca Raton, Florida: CRC Press, 1986.

Rowland, I., ed. *Nutrition, Toxicity and Cancer.* Boca Raton, Florida: CRC Press, 1991.

Schottenfeld, D., and J. Fraumeni, eds. *Cancer Epidemiology and Prevention.* Philadelphia: W.B. Saunders, 1982.

Schover, L.R.: *Sexuality and Cancer.* American Cancer Society publication 4657-PS, 1991.

Spiller, G.A., ed. *Handbook of Dietary Fiber in Human Nutrition.* Boca Raton, Florida: CRC Press, 1986.

GENERAL INDEX

RECIPE INDEX

ABOUT THE AUTHOR

DANIEL W. NIXON, M.D., is a leading researcher and educator in the area of cancer and nutrition. He is currently at the Medical University of South Carolina in Charleston, where he is director of cancer prevention and control, associate director of the Hollings Cancer Center, Folk Professor of Experimental Oncology, and professor of medicine.

Previously he was the vice president for professional education of the national office of the American Cancer Society.

Dr. Nixon was formerly associate director, Cancer Prevention Research Program, at the National Cancer Institute, and has conducted research into nutritional support for cancer therapy under several NCI grants. He was a professor of medicine at Emory University and head of the Winship Clinic's Medical Oncology Unit. He lectures at numerous medical schools and is editor-in-chief of the journal *Cancer Prevention International.* He is also on the editorial board of the *Journal of Cancer Education* and has published over a hundred articles in medical journals.